Harvard Historical Studies • 166

Published under the auspices
of the Department of History
from the income of the
Paul Revere Frothingham Bequest
Robert Louis Stroock Fund
Henry Warren Torrey Fund

SETTLER SOVEREIGNTY

*Jurisdiction and Indigenous People in
America and Australia, 1788–1836*

LISA FORD

Harvard University Press
Cambridge, Massachusetts, and London, England

First Harvard University Press paperback edition, 2011

Library of Congress Cataloging-in-Publication Data

Ford, Lisa, 1974–
  Settler sovereignty : jurisdiction and indigenous people in America and Australia, 1788–1836 / Lisa Ford.
      p. cm.—(Harvard historical studies; v. 166)
   ISBN 978-0-674-03565-2 (cloth: alk. paper)
   ISBN 978-0-674-06188-0 (pbk.)
   1. Indians of North America—Legal status, laws, etc.—Georgia—History.
2. Aboriginal Australians—Legal status, laws, etc.—Australia—New South
Wales—History. I. Title.
   K3247.F67   2010
   346.01'3—dc22   2009013937

Contents

Maps

A Note on Maps

The maps in this volume were redrawn from contemporary sources by Philip Schwartzberg of Meridian Mapping. They are as accurate as possible, but must, of necessity, incorporate some of the many inaccuracies in the originals. They are drawn from the following sources:

Georgia, 1796: Tanner, Georgia from the Latest Authorities, *American Atlas* (New York: Reid, 1796).

Georgia, 1823: Tanner, Georgia and Alabama, *American Atlas* (Philadelphia: Tanner, 1823).

Georgia, 1831: Young and Delleker, *Georgia: A New Grand Atlas* (Philadelphia: Finlay, 1831).

Australia, 1798: Governor Hunter, Map of New South Wales in 1798, *Historical Records of New South Wales: Volume 3, Hunter* (Sydney: Charles Potter, 1895), 346.

Australia, 1831: The National Archives: Public Records Office, Colonial Office (TNA: PRO CO) 700/AUSTRALIA 9: Map of Australia. Compiled from the Nautical Surveys made by order of the Admiralty, and other authentic documents, by James Wyld, Geographer to the Queen. Published 1838. Inset: Van Diemen's Land.

Australia, 1838: TNA: PRO CO 700/AUSTRALIA 10: The South Eastern portion of Australia. Compiled from the Colonial Surveys and from details furnished by Exploratory Expeditions, by John Arrowsmith. Published London, 2 August 1838.

Settler Sovereignty

Introduction

THE LEGAL TRINITY of nation statehood—sovereignty, jurisdiction, and territory—has a recent history that is yet to be told. It is a history suspended between empire and statehood, between local and global. It is about defining sovereignty as the ordering of indigenous people in space: a project undertaken by Anglophone settler polities around the globe between 1822 and 1847.[1]

In 1822, a criminal court in Upper Canada claimed that violence between indigenous people on the streets of Amherstburg could be punished by British law because territorial jurisdiction flowed from British settlement there.[2] In the same year, when Chief Tommy Jemmy executed a Seneca woman for witchcraft, the New York legislature claimed jurisdiction over all indigenous violence within the borders of New York State.[3] In 1830, a convention of judges declared that George Tassel could be tried and executed for killing another Cherokee on Cherokee land within the territorial boundaries of Georgia.[4]

Just six years later, the New South Wales Supreme Court decided that British Imperial law governed violence among Aboriginal people on the grounds that Aborigines had no law and no land rights that could survive the advent of British settlement.[5] Across the Tasman Sea and within weeks of signing the Treaty of Waitangi (1840), the British government demonstrated the meaning of sovereignty by trying a Māori man for killing a settler in New Zealand.[6] In 1847, Ranitapiripiri (alias Kopitipita) was tried for murdering another Māori by "drowning him . . . in the river Manawatu," because every murder in New Zealand came within the jurisdiction of British courts.[7]

Much more was at stake in these trials than murder; they redefined sovereignty and its relationship to territory and jurisdiction. Sovereignty and jurisdiction have always been intertwined, but they have not always been territorial in nature. Though commonly understood to mean "the final and absolute political authority in the political community,"[8] in its long history, sovereignty has described myriad modes of territorial and personal power.[9] In law, sovereignty is practiced through jurisdiction. To this day, jurisdiction imports authority over territorial units, people, things, *or* bodies of law.[10] Settler courts in the 1820s and 1830s, then, did something quite radical.

By exercising criminal jurisdiction over violence between indigenous people, settler courts asserted that sovereignty was a territorial measure of authority to be performed through the trial and punishment of every person who transgressed settler law in settler territory. Perfect settler sovereignty rested on the conflation of sovereignty, territory, and jurisdiction. Their synthesis was both innovative and uniquely destructive of indigenous rights. After 1820, courts in North America and Australasia redefined indigenous theft and violence as crime, and in the process, they pitted settler sovereignty against the rights of indigenous people.

The stakes were clear in George Tassel's 1830 appeal. Counsel argued that Georgia had no jurisdiction to try Tassel for murder because the Cherokee were a sovereign, self-governing people. The convention of judges responded with the logic of territoriality:

> Indeed it is difficult to conceive how any person who has a definite idea of what constitutes a sovereign state, can have come to the conclusion that the Cherokee Nation is a sovereign and independent state. . . . That a Government should be seized in fee of a territory and yet have no jurisdiction over that country is an anomaly in the science of jurisprudence.[11]

The same tenets were recited in the Supreme Court of New South Wales (1836) by puisne judge William Burton. He declared that the Supreme Court could try Jack Congo Murrell for murdering Jabingee because "the aboriginal natives of New Holland . . . had not attained at the first settlement of the English people amongst them to such a position in point of numbers and civilization, and to such a form of Government and laws, as to be entitled to be recognized as so many sovereign states governed by laws of their own." That privilege could only rest with Great Britain, which had "obtained and exercised for many years the rights of Domain and Empire over the country."[12]

Such was the moment of settler sovereignty: the legal obliteration of indigenous customary law became the litmus test of settler statehood.

This book tells its local and global history through two exemplars: the state of Georgia and the colony of New South Wales from 1783 to 1836. It focuses not on legal treatises, but on the transformation of everyday legal practices that brought George Tassel and Jack Congo Murrell into court. In daily practice lies unexpected trans-Pacific continuity. Daily practice makes it clear that the British arrived in Savannah and Port Jackson understanding that Crown sovereignty was limited in nature. It did not contain clear rights to exercise jurisdiction outside major settlements and seldom extended over indigenous people at all. Before the 1820s, neither indigenous people nor settlers were uniformly tried for their violence. Settler violence against indigenous people, indigenous violence against settlers, and indigenous violence against indigenous people were seldom construed as crime. They constituted justice or the threat of war. Violence drew meaning from a shared blend of legal regimes encompassing natural law retaliation, common law culture, and customary indigenous law. This multiplicity did not equate to confusion, however. On both sides of the Pacific, settlers and indigenous people understood the legal frameworks surrounding their conflicts and manipulated them deftly. All understood the spatial and juridical limits of colonial and state sovereignty in the early decades of the nineteenth century. This study re-creates the parameters of legal pluralisms and the tendrils that bound them together through time and space.[13]

Territorial jurisdiction became a necessary accoutrement of sovereignty later. In doing so it did not fulfill a genocidal promise inherent in settler colonialism since the seventeenth century.[14] This study shows that settler polities extended jurisdiction in the 1820s and 1830s because they imagined for the first time that it was necessary to shore up the legitimacy of settlement.[15] Curiously and slowly, at the same time and in similar ways, indigenous violence came to pose an intolerable ideational challenge to sovereignty in North America and Australia. After 1800, plural legal practices came under pressure. Evolving global discourses of sovereignty combined with new technologies of governance brought new people and new ideas to settler peripheries. In just two decades, settler and indigenous violence became crucibles of sovereignty talk, as the idea of perfect territorial sovereignty clashed with tenacious pluralities. Territorial jurisdiction became a logical necessity of settler sovereignty for the first time after 1820, a cause and effect of changing local jurisdictional practices. All came to center on the trial and incarceration of indigenous people. This is why, since the 1830s, indigenous subordination has been a founding tenet of settler sovereignty in North America and Australia. This is a global and a local story.

It is a global story because settler polities redefined sovereignty at the same time as it was recast in other centers, peripheries, and places in between. Settler sovereignty forms a peculiar chapter in Lauren Benton's story about the global drive of colonial states to control plural regimes of law in Latin America, America, Asia, Australia, and Africa in the second quarter of the nineteenth century.[16] It forms part of legal reform in the British Empire, which set about interposing magisterial power between masters and slaves, settlers and indigenous people from the Cape of Good Hope to the Caribbean from 1800.[17] Territoriality was contracted and spread by men and women circulating throughout the Anglophone world. British settler colonies were reformed or created after the American Revolution by a very mobile and educated network of bureaucrats and businessmen who moved about the Atlantic, Pacific, and Indian Oceans with Vattel and Blackstone under their arms.[18] Settler sovereignty arrived at the same time as post-Napoleonic European states embarked on a campaign to assert jurisdiction over their plural peripheries, a project that was destructive of European indigenous law and self-governance.[19] Settler polities joined polities throughout the world—South America, Asia, and Europe—in declaring territorial statehood.[20] Indeed, as David Armitage has argued, it was the American War of Independence—a settler rebellion—that started the "contagion of sovereignty."[21] Suspended as they were between processes of colonization, aspirations to self-governance, and the cultural and political networks of the British diaspora, settler polities have special explanatory power in this moment of legal ferment.

Their explanatory power, ironically, rests at the level of the local.[22] The story of settler sovereignty can only be told by sifting out the changing legal meanings attached by participants to the daily struggles of indigenous peoples for resources, for dignity, and for survival. It is also part of the quest for local, settler autonomy. Settler sovereignty was created, after all, by courts in Amherstburg, Milledgeville, Sydney, and Towranga, not in Washington or London.[23] In this respect, settler sovereignty is a paradox of federalism: peripheral states and colonies asserted sovereignty in their own, federal and/or imperial right.[24] The real content of their claims, however, was local, territorial control over the process of indigenous dispossession. As such, it rested on even more local histories. To bring settlers and indigenous people to court for their violence required local settlers to recognize violence as crime. Magistrates and constables had to investigate and arrest perpetrators. Perpetrators had then to be tried before a settler jury. In short, exercising jurisdiction over settler and indigenous violence required local investment in the idea of territorial jurisdiction and in the authority of the state to exercise it. It rose through pervasive local complicity. Its most important context is the daily, systemic, and ongoing subordination of indigenous people.

Continuity and Difference

What follows, then, is a local history of ideas and practices in two settler polities: the early national state of Georgia and the colony of New South Wales. It is less a comparison than an exploration of continuity between two very unlike places joined by language, institutions of local government, a history of settlement, and cultures of common law.[25] These places were extraordinarily dissimilar in many respects, yet what little they shared influenced their redefinition of sovereignty in the specific demographic, intellectual, legal, and economic contexts of the early nineteenth century.

I have chosen to focus on Georgia and New South Wales for a number of reasons. The first is because together they exemplify the moment of settler sovereignty. After 1820, Georgia and New South Wales engaged in long debates about the relationship between their sovereignty (state, colonial, or imperial), their jurisdiction, and the legal status of indigenous people. Georgia's debate was fierce and public. In New South Wales, debate was more demure—conducted in courts and councils—but no less transformative. In the process, both created a rich archive of legal argument that culminated in the remarkably similar legal declarations in 1830 and 1836 that indigenous violence must fall within the jurisdiction of settler courts because territorial, settler sovereignty could not tolerate indigenous self-government. Indeed, of all the settler polities that linked territorial sovereignty with jurisdiction over indigenous crime between 1820 and 1850, Georgia and New South Wales did so most proximately. They used the same legal arguments at the same time to articulate the most complete iterations of perfect settler sovereignty produced in the Anglophone world.

One was a state and the other a new colony, yet both were involved in similar processes of colonization within inherently federal structures of governance. Together with New York and Upper Canada, they exemplify the embeddedness of settler statehood in empire and colonization. This is because of the peculiar structural continuities that constituted Anglophone settler colonialism, bound as it was by a combination of economic, demographic, legal, and imperial histories. The most important continuity was the fact that, from the sixteenth century, North America and the Caribbean formed the reference point, the font of experience, law, and practice that defined British settler colonialism thereafter. Next in importance came institutions of local government grounded in "a culture of legality" rooted in "customs in common" and the common law.[26] These caused similar tensions between local legal practice and central policy because they gave local settlers a monopoly over jurisdictional practice. In Anglophone settlements, magistrates and constables defined the practical limits of the state at the local level. The more legally minded among them also shared a common historical preoccupation with the contest and expansion of jurisdiction. Legal pluralism was a fact of life in early modern Britain, and had a long afterlife in settler peripheries.[27]

In addition, settler colonialisms had several broad, structural continuities. Unlike most British colonial projects, settlers in North America and Australia (and in Britain's Caribbean and South African "Cape" colonies) did not seek to govern through indigenous hierarchies in order to extract commodities. Instead they settled. Where the disease environment was favorable, they reproduced and grew crops chiefly for export. They began as or evolved into colonies of settlement where "immigrants intended to establish societies as similar as possible to those they had left behind."[28]

North American and Australian were distinguished from other Anglophone settler projects in several respects, however. They were demographically distinct projects of colonization. These settlements were founded in regions either with low densities of indigenous population, or where indigenous populations were devastated by European and African disease.[29] Unlike indigenous survivors in the Caribbean islands, surviving indigenous communities in North America and Australia occupied arable or pasture land. Therefore, indigenous displacement, removal, or assimilation remained a precondition of settler expansion long after settlement began. Finally, unlike southern and eastern Africa or parts of meso-America where indigenous populations were much larger, farming in North America and Australia did not proceed on the forcible co-option of indigenous labor. Instead in the Anglophone peripheries I discuss here, most indigenous people labored indirectly for the benefit of colonizers. In early Georgia, Indians harvested wildlife for trade pelts, and in early New South Wales, Aborigines aided in the policing of convicts by killing them when they escaped into the bush.[30] Settler farms were chiefly run by imported free, indentured, or slave labor. Accordingly, these peculiar settler polities were imagined and to some extent organized as places of indigenous exclusion.[31] They had special potential to fold colonization into modern statehood when the global ferment of the nineteenth century changed ideas and practices of law and governance.

Structural continuity does not diminish difference, however. Of this small cluster of polities, Georgia and New South Wales are in many respects the least alike. I have chosen them partly because they form two poles of settler experience, casting light on the gradations between. Georgia was formed as a colony in 1733 on land squabbled over by Spain and Britain for half a century, though it was wholly controlled and peopled by the powerful Creek and Cherokee Confederacies. By 1800, Georgia claimed land from the east coast of North America to the Mississippi, though it was in negotiations with the new federal government to cede most of this land, a move that would soon turn its indigenous frontier into an indigenous bubble in the middle of settled cotton lands. Its borderlands in 1800 were international. Spain controlled Florida to its South, France and Spain took turns claiming Louisiana, and the British had traders and emissaries operating in both. All courted and treated with the well-armed, diplomatically savvy, and culturally interconnected Indian nations that inhabited Georgia's peripheries. In 1800, Georgia was also a colonizing state rather than a British colony—a status it struggled fiercely to control and define against the new federal government and indigenous people.

Yet, of all the differences between Georgia and New South Wales, slavery is the most important. Georgia by 1800 was a society deeply immersed in the ideologies and economics of race slavery. Moreover, race slavery held important ramifications for frontier conflict. Though violence and land were perhaps the most important causes of conflict between Georgia and surrounding Indians,[32] conflict had deeper roots in South Carolina's disastrous attempt to enslave indigenous people in the early eighteenth century, and was exacerbated daily by the escape of slaves into Indian Country. The incorporation of African slaves and of slave labor into Indian agricultural economies, meanwhile, helped to precipitate legal crisis in Georgia.[33]

New South Wales could scarcely differ more in 1800. It was a nascent convict colony, formed as an open-air prison in 1788 and just beginning to reimagine itself as a self-sustaining agricultural community premised on forced convict labor. It was an uncontested zone of British imperialism. Though Britain recognized the priority of Dutch claims to the western half of the continent, only the visits of a few French and Russian explorers attested to any European interest in Australia. Indigenous people there had neither the curse nor the benefit of long experience with European colonization. So in 1800 Aborigines were unarmed, had no European allies and few intercultural brokers, and suffered terribly from smallpox. Accordingly, though Governor

Phillip arrived in 1788 with instructions to "conciliate" with Aborigines, he signed no treaties recognizing their rights to land and self-government. No document shows that this was official policy, though it may have been.[34] The absence of a treaty may also be explained by the fact that, at first, local Aborigines refused to talk, let alone trade, with colonists. Colonists took to kidnapping Aboriginal men to create intermediaries. Thereafter, the modest goals of early convict settlement, very different indigenous customs, and the enormous tactical and epidemiological disadvantage of Australian Aborigines made written treaties unnecessary to ensure the survival of settlement in New South Wales. Indigenous-settler conflict in New South Wales, then, was much less grounded in local networks of exchange and was uncomplicated by the institution of slavery. For indigenous people, conflict revolved around life-or-death access to resources, access hampered by settlers' occupation of land, their monopolization of water, and their relentless destruction of animal habitats.[35]

Despite their manifest difference, Georgia and New South Wales shared practices of legal pluralism that they abandoned at the same time. This historical congruence is so unlikely that it requires investigation. Much of what follows focuses on common pluralities stemming from shared history, shared assumptions, and shared institutions. The transformation of settler sovereignty, however, was also precipitated by what these different settler peripheries exchanged. In the 1820s they exchanged some news. The movement of bureaucrats, commodities, and newspapers between British settler colonies and of whalers crossing the Pacific facilitated the spread of news about indigenous-settler conflict among Anglophone peripheries. New York and Amherstburg, after all, were separated by more than 200 miles but connected by geographically mobile indigenous communities and settler troublemakers in the 1820s.[36] American local papers show that relevant players knew of key legal and political controversies over indigenous legal status throughout the early United States. Georgia certainly knew about New York's claims to territorial sovereignty in the 1820s.[37] New South Wales papers carried news of the removal of Indians from the southeastern United States in the 1820s and 1830s, though there is little evidence that *Tassel* or the Cherokee cases were reported there.[38]

Georgia and New South Wales also shared tentative networks of people. Chief Justice Francis Forbes, who led the first Supreme Court of New South Wales to extend jurisdiction over some indigenous-settler violence in the 1820s, was the grandchild of a southern loyalist, raised in a slaveholding family with property and trade interests in

Georgia. He was deemed thoroughly North American and dangerously republican in some spheres of politics and legal decision-making.[39] More broadly, from the 1810s, New South Wales was staffed by men of the world. Governor Lachlan Macquarie rambled from North America, through Russia and India, before coming to New South Wales in 1810. Governor Ralph Darling served in the Caribbean and Mauritius before arriving in the 1820s. Judge William Burton, who declared that indigenous people in New South Wales had no sovereignty or jurisdiction in 1836, came to New South Wales via the Cape Colony, fresh from claiming extensive powers over African slaves and apprentices for the Crown.[40] Migration and circumnavigation broke homeland communities into immigrant communities in different Anglophone settler polities—communities linked, as the centuries wore on, by ever improving networks of communication.

Georgia and New South Wales shared a unique historical moment. Settler sovereignty was precipitated by transnational economic and demographic events that had special impact on settler peripheries. Britain's victory over France in 1763 secured its dominance as a global imperial power, a dominance that disempowered indigenous North Americans by removing long-standing European allies, and radically disadvantaged Australian Aborigines by forestalling imperial rivals who could ply them with guns.[41] After 1815, both industrialization and post-Napoleonic mass migration fed astounding demographic and economic growth in Anglophone settler peripheries.[42] The American southwest and every New South Wales frontier were suddenly and extensively populated by people, sheep, and cotton fields.[43] The Cherokee Nation, though situated on poor cotton country, was overrun with prospectors when gold was discovered there in 1828.[44] Digging minerals and producing fibers for British and American mills created unprecedented pressure to dispossess, destroy, or subordinate indigenous people.

Finally, in this unique historical moment, Georgia and New South Wales shared books. Among them, Emer de Vattel's *Law of Nations* stands out as a book for the times, peddling a powerful synthesis of neo-Lockean legal and racist thought about indigenous people in North America and Australasia.[45] It underpinned both George Tassel's execution in Georgia in 1830 and Jack Congo Murrell's trial in New South Wales in 1836. Vattel's dismissal of indigenous property rights and indigenous sovereignty joined territory with sovereignty with new clarity—a new clarity that Anglophone settler courts read, after 1820, as an injunction to exercise jurisdiction over indigenous crime in colonial peripheries.

National Histories, Settler History

Tracing similarity through difference also asks new questions of two relatively insular histories. Though a number of distinguished scholars have compared settler colonialism generally, and United States and Australian frontier history in particular,[46] they have tended not to focus on legal relationships between settlers and indigenous peoples in North America and Australasia before the late nineteenth century.[47] American frontier histories are rarely comparative, though their several trajectories aid enormously in framing this study. Backcountry scholarship shows the importance of local networks to the politics of race, slavery, and expansion in the southeast.[48] Histories of the intersection between the institution of slavery, nineteenth-century westward expansion, and indigenous-settler relations point to the exceptional nature of Georgia's frontier by showing the degree to which slave property became an item of contest, an impetus to expansion, and a site of cultural adaptation.[49] Even so, these particular histories illustrate a shared settler problem: reckoning with the legal ramifications of multifaceted indigenous resistance to settler expansion.

The important work done by ethnohistorians on settler-indigenous relations in North America has provided a rich account of frontier conflict, indigenous custom, and diplomacy.[50] Richard White and Daniel Richter, in particular, have shown the degree to which indigenous people in colonial North America could dictate the terms of settler colonialism by playing off imperial rivals, by negotiating with colonists, and by appropriating European objects and practices to their own use.[51] However, their focus on diplomacy has largely neglected the interface between indigenous and settler legal practice.[52] Legal histories of southeastern North America, in contrast, focus almost exclusively on the Cherokee cases with little attention to the matrix of frontier exchange that created, maintained, and eventually eroded legal pluralism in the southeast.[53] Some recent histories take a more synthetic view of indigenous and settler history in the South in the context of the expansion of cotton agriculture and slavery.[54] Other recent works stress the importance of indigenous borderlands to the construction of British colonies and American states.[55]

This project draws from all of these important stories to do different work. It focuses on the myriad ways that indigenous people and settlers in the southeast made and limited sovereignty by controlling jurisdiction. In doing so, it shows how the local and cultural specificities prized by ethnohistorical and backcountry scholarship constituted and transformed settler law. The law stories presented herein recover the rich history of the transition from treaty-based diplomacy to the forcible removal of indigenous people from southeastern North America. They do so by showing how everyday local practice was gradually and haltingly subordinated to jurisdiction, even as it mired all levels of the state in the negotiation of sovereignty. They show how discussions about and exercises of jurisdiction worked through older practices of diplomacy and exchange to change sovereignty.

The history of indigenous-settler conflict in early New South Wales has stressed Australian exceptionalism because the British Empire signed no treaties with indigenous people in New South Wales. Indigenous legal history has focused on a narrow archive in order to effect legal change. Both lawyers and historians have focused on constitutive colonial documents and the prevarications of the first Supreme Court of New South Wales over its jurisdiction to try crimes between indigenous people because both sources have precedential value before courts.[56] Pioneering frontier histories from the 1970s onward pursued a related advocacy, by emphasizing warfare between settlers and indigenous people. Most famously, Henry Reynolds argued that Australian frontiers were in a sustained state of war from settlement into the twentieth century.[57] In contrast, recent histories of early Australian frontiers stress accommodation rather than conflict, and only a few of these investigate how settlers understood British sovereignty and jurisdiction in early New South Wales. This trend follows from the recent politicization of frontier history, but it also rests on important intellectual history.[58] Recent analyses of eighteenth- and nineteenth-century British political philosophy in particular suggest that British political philosophy, colonial *mentalité,* and the logic of settler colonialism left little space for indigenous juridical independence in Australia.[59]

By placing New South Wales in a North American perspective, and by telling a social legal history of frontier conflict, this study challenges the terms of legal and historical accounts of indigenous-settler relations in early New South Wales.[60] I argue that there was nothing radical about the project of colonization in New South Wales. Its construction on broad claims of territory, sovereignty, and jurisdiction varied only slightly from the British charters written between 1607 and 1732 for North America. Indeed, despite the new facility of late eighteenth-century metropolitan ideology and the fact that settlers signed no treaties with Aborigines, colonial officials fostered a remarkable degree of legal pluralism in early Australian settlements.[61] Aborigines were even called Indians by some early commentators.[62] In New South Wales, North American notions were coupled with North American practices—commonalities that become obvious in everyday jurisdictional practice.

So it was that shared everyday jurisdictional practice shaped, bounded, and produced sovereignty in early national Georgia and colonial New South Wales. Their shared history led settlers and indigenous people in both places to participate in the global recasting of discourses of statehood in the nineteenth century. After 1800, they redefined everyday violence in towns and on their farthest frontiers. In Georgia and New South Wales, conflicts about sovereignty came to center on quotidian disputes about whether, when, and where indigenous-settler conflict could be read as crime. Indigenous violence had always defined the nature and limits of settler state power. Between 1820 and 1850, however, controlling indigenous violence became the measure of legitimacy—a legitimacy guarded not just by governors and courts, but by farmers and local constables. This book tells the story of what was lost and found in these very local instantiations of global change. In these small contests lies the secret history of modern settler sovereignty.

CHAPTER ONE

Jurisdiction, Territory, and Sovereignty in Empire

PERFECT SETTLER SOVEREIGNTY had its immediate origins in everyday indigenous-settler conflict in the early decades of the nineteenth century, but it was rooted in the peculiar history of Anglophone settler colonialism from 1607. Its global context lies, moreover, in the changing relationships of sovereignty, territory, jurisdiction, and empire between the sixteenth and the twentieth centuries. Sovereignty, jurisdiction, and territory were embroiled in settler colonialism as it unfolded in North America and then in Australasia between 1607 and 1802.

Though the story of sovereignty is most often told as a history of statehood, recent scholarship suggests that its most important context is empire.[1] Empire changed sovereignty because it altered the relationship of people with space.[2] In the process, it created the conditions for the redefinition of sovereignty through the legal subordination of people in defined territorial units. In particular, imperial legal discourse defined what it meant to be a community under a sovereign by identifying what was not. Between the sixteenth and the twentieth centuries, it set the conditions for conquest, defined what land was empty, what land was as good as empty, and which sorts of political communities could exercise rights over land and people and under what conditions. It did so as the first definitions of modern sovereignty were being penned.[3] Thus, empire and sovereignty grew at the same time and in dialogue.[4] European expansion, in short, necessitated the testing of sovereign authority at its fragile margins.

North America proved a fragile margin indeed for the European powers that clustered there from the sixteenth century.[5] In particular, its in-

digenous peoples, their semi-sedentary agriculture, their unfamiliar political configurations, and their rapid mastery of inter-imperial diplomacy
challenged everything Europeans knew about claiming authority over
territory and people. This does not mean, however, that they did not try.[6]

Christianity laden with Roman law was duly applied to the appropriation of North America, where it proved a boon and a burden. Papal claims
to imperium over all Christians combined with canon law justifications
for anti-Islamic crusades provided a rich archive for the earliest adventurer princes. They were mobilized, in effect, to declare the new world
full of infidels but empty of sovereigns. Pope Alexander VI set the tenor
of Christian arrogance by dividing the non-Christian world between its
first discoverers, Spain and Portugal, in 1493.[7] Spain added novel rules of
conquest to their Christian monopoly on sovereignty. Spanish conquista-
dors read a proclamation demanding submission and threatening war to
uncomprehending meso-Americans and assumed, for legal purposes, that
all subsequent relations between them, amicable or otherwise, were of
conqueror and subject.[8]

In 1608, Sir Edward Coke argued for the application of similar rules to
Britain's scarce imperial peripheries.[9] In Calvin's Case he declared in obiter dictum that "[a]ll Infidels are in Law *perpetui inimici,* perpetual enemies" and, upon conquest, infidel laws were null and void: "if a Christian
King should conquer a kingdom of an Infidel, and bring them under his
subjection, there *ipso facto* the Laws of the Infidel are abrogated, for that
they be not only against Christianity, but against the Law of God and
Nature."[10] By 1760, his formula of 1608 was translated by many to
mean that North America was held by fictive conquest under English and
later British law. Yet, importantly, insofar as it purported to determine
indigenous legal status, Coke's maxim was never put into legal practice
and was comprehensively rejected by Lord Mansfield in Campbell v. Hall
(1774).[11]

This was in part because Christian legal theory was not uniformly dis-
missive of indigenous rights.[12] Early modern Christian theorists of empire were schooled in pagan philosophy and natural law as well as the
church-made law of crusade. These were not in agreement over the legal
rights of indigenous people to land and political community. In his dis-
quisition on meso-American Indian rights for Charles V of Spain, Fran-
cisco de Vitoria argued that at least some indigenous people possessed all
of the significant rights of European princes and should be treated accordingly.[13] Protestant natural lawyers were likewise unwilling to assume
that indigenous people could not own property or form recognizable political communities.[14] In England, this unwillingness was likely bolstered

by the local legal context: early modern English jurists were creatures of pluralism, schooled more in jurisdictional controversy than juridical neatness.[15]

So, even as he said it in 1608, Coke's arguments for the extension of English law to North American colonies rang hollow. In any case, as Christian legal doctrine gave Spain much better title than England to the Caribbean Islands and North America, England needed a much more worldly law to displace Spanish claims. Elizabethan diplomats and pamphleteers mobilized Roman law's affinity for possession to limit Spanish claims to those parts of the globe that they had actually conquered or settled. One chapter of Justinian's *Digest* contained "the only legal precedent of international standing from which to draw." It stated that title could be derived by possession of empty land, by long and uninterrupted possession of someone else's land, by cession, by treaty, or by conquest.[16] Possession could be fairly easily established and maintained on an island like Barbados, where the indigenous Caribs had long since been devastated by disease, murder, and exile. However, possession was a problematic notion when applied to the expanses of North America. It was deployed to mean physical settlement or the domination of indigenous people.[17] From the outset there, possession was in tension with indigenous rights.

John Locke, who was secretary to the proprietors of the Carolina Colony, provided justification and impetus to English expansion like no other.[18] Between 1680 and 1690, he combined the North American empire and the Hobbesian state with the new English ideology of improvement to create a uniquely Protestant and English synthesis, independent of the legal archive of Crusade. He did so by defining indigenous North Americans as creatures of nature. Natural men, in no social contract, could neither own property nor exercise sovereignty over people or land. They shared the earth in common.[19] As Indians harvested the products of nature, they could own nothing more than the carcasses of wild beasts. Property in land came only from improvement.[20] North America, then, was truly vacant land—and under ancient Roman law it was free for the taking—absent farmers therefore absent sovereigns and absent laws.[21]

Lockean theory would become a powerful legal and ideological tool, but again it was no panacea for early British colonists carving out claims against jealous Europeans and hoping against hope that indigenous people would happily move aside. Locke's moment came much later. In the meantime, adventurers had to be more eclectic in their legal methods of acquisition. As Benton has argued, adventurers from the British Isles

(with their competitors) engaged in "symbolic overkill of legal enactments" in the New World. They trotted out Arthurian legend, buried coins,
placed markers, drew maps, planned fortifications, and had indigenous
people participate in rituals of submission that they could not possibly
have understood.[22]

Seventeenth- and eighteenth-century English Atlantic charters gathered
together Catholic, natural law, and proto-Lockean theory into spectacu-
larly broad and untenable claims to sovereignty, jurisdiction, and property over North America. They took figurative possession of huge swathes
of the New World in the name of the English King by vesting property
and jurisdiction over demarcated territory not in the possession of other
Christian princes to corporations of adventurers in perpetuity. They mobilized feudal models of "territorial lordship, and a distinct approach to
the definition and exercise of jurisdiction," an approach grounded in "the
control of expanse."[23] The Charter of Virginia of 1606 vested in a council
of thirteen men the right to grant land and manage and direct "all Matters
that shall or may concern the Government, as well of the said several
Colonies, as of and for any other Part or Place, within" a territory from
the east to the undiscovered west coast of America.[24] The Charter of Massachusetts in 1629 gave property and jurisdiction to the company over a
strip of land from the east to the west coast of America on the condition
that the colony was not planted on land "actuallie possessed or inhabited
by any other Christian Prince or State."[25] Georgia's 1732 charter vested in
a board of proprietors property from coast to coast on the southern borders of Carolina (largely on Spanish land) and jurisdiction over "all and
every person and persons who shall at any time hereafter Inhabit or reside
within" those extensive boundaries.[26]

Some have argued that charters heralded a peculiarly Anglophone settler drive to impose constitutional uniformity on colonial peripheries—a
drive that led inexorably to the extinguishment of indigenous rights to
land and to self-governance in the 1830s.[27] Patrick Wolfe has described
the legal accoutrements of early settlement as a "theoretical expropriation asserted at discovery" that already contained within it the assertion
that "natives" were mere occupiers with no "dominion," or real ownership of their lands. In this context, any persisting rights to indigenous
self-government were illusory, a ruse designed by agents of empire to
exclude indigenous people, placing them both outside and beneath the
category of subjecthood.[28] This straight line of intention between the diffuse legal project of settlement in seventeenth-century North America
and the Marshall cases of the 1820s and 1830s has all of the benefits of
neatness but comes at a cost to history.

Figurative possession through tenuous claims of sovereignty and jurisdiction was of fundamental importance to English expansion for a number of less totalizing and apocalyptic reasons. First, charters attempted to displace competing European claims based on what Protestant theorists deemed to be flimsier premises, like Papal donation, discovery, or the placement of markers. Colonial charters functioned as supporting documents in the emerging field of the European law of nations. They also established constitutional claims to crown authority over the companies who organized and the subjects who undertook settlement.[29] What they clearly did not do is extend any meaningful jurisdiction over indigenous people. The messy work of settlement itself required a much messier array of legal practices: and herein lies the real history of sovereignty and possession in the New World.

English Settler Sovereignty in the New World

In practice, the contest between empires defied paper treaties signed by European nations, let alone paper charters granted by aspiring imperial monarchs to their subjects. In this respect, the colony of Georgia was exemplary. In 1733, Georgia was founded squarely on a tract of land claimed by Spain. This tract had been declared by treaty between Britain and Spain to be a "neutral zone" dividing Spanish Florida from the Carolina colony.[30] In its western reaches, French traders dominated commerce with independent Indian tribes on both sides of the Mississippi. Thus, the legal language of territorial right contained in Georgia's charter masked a far more complicated reality of diplomatic intrigue, treaty breaking, and cynicism among European competitors.

European competition was not the only factor limiting Crown sovereignty in English colonies. Regulating settler communities and the process of settlement itself required constant juridical innovation between the seventeenth and eighteenth centuries because the relationship of diasporic communities to the Crown was both novel and unsettled. North America was not England's first empire, but it was very different from the various conquests, cessions, and inheritances that had bound Wales, the Channel Islands, Ireland, and a goodly portion of France to the Crown in centuries before.[31] North America's jurisdictional status as a territory depended on the force of analogy. Early modern Englishmen and a steady stream of increasingly independent-minded colonists spent two centuries debating whether American colonies were like "crown lands" within England or like one of the external "dominions," each of which had its own long-mooted jurisdictional relationship with the King and Parliament.[32] This unstable legal situation was further complicated by metropolitan upheaval as the British Isles were themselves transformed by revolution, enclosure, unification, and modernization between 1600 and 1800. After the Civil War and the Glorious Revolution, to whom were settlers answerable? What rights did these extraordinary charters leave to the Crown? What relationship did settlers and their political communities have to Parliament? Who owned title to the soil? The King? Indians? Settler corporations?

Finally, English claims to sovereignty and possession bore no relationship whatever to the complex legal and quasi-legal rules that governed settler-indigenous relations in North America or on any other seventeenth-century or eighteenth-century periphery. These relationships clustered instead around the fluid raison d'être for settlement. When the English set down in a fetid swamp that they called Jamestown, they did so as much to take part in global trade and local plunder as to claim land for the English Crown.[33] Indeed, piracy, pelt trading, and the production of cash crops for a global market lay at the heart of the English colonial effort from the mid-sixteenth century. The pelt trade relied on diplomacy with indigenous people, not on their subordination. Those settlers who grew cash crops used mostly imported labor: poor Englishmen, convicts, and eventually African slaves worked their farms. Carolina's colonists flirted with a trade in Native American people from 1680, selling them off-shore because they lacked a viable cash crop. But that venture ended badly—with the establishment of Georgia as a buffer zone between Carolinians and well-armed, angry indigenous people.[34] As indigenous people were integrated only marginally into local economies of production, settlers had no reason to imagine that American Indians should fall within the jurisdiction of settler courts.

Early colonial North America, therefore, was not a zone of conquest or even of large-scale settlement. The legal pluralisms of the trading ports of the Near and Far East, rather than the forced labor regimes implemented by the Spanish in meso-America or the doctrine of title by improvement advocated by Protestant theorists, guided most early settlement in North American colonies.[35] Their pluralisms fed on and into the diplomatic compromises and alliances forged by British sailors with hybrid Carib and escaped slave communities on the less populated islands of the Caribbean.[36] So North America began and remained a field of cooperation, inter-imperial competition, and increasingly, gradual dispossession. This process might have been unequal, but as the chapters that follow will demonstrate, only in the nineteenth century did it come to rely on sweeping legal claims about the absence of indigenous rights.

Accordingly, despite claims to sovereignty and jurisdiction in colonial charters, English colonists exercised jurisdiction over indigenous people in very few cases—and then chiefly in the colonial American northeast where God's work rather than money-making preoccupied settlers for a while.[37] After their devastating victories in the Pequot War of 1637 and Metacomb's War in 1675, Connecticut and Massachusetts both overlaid their charter claims with bold new territorial claims to sovereignty over settled portions of their colonies.[38] Even then, the practice of jurisdiction was extended slowly and steadily, often in dialogue with indigenous people. It was not imposed, ipso facto, as a result of conquest.[39]

The power of treaty diplomacy and legal pluralism even in the eighteenth-century northeast is nowhere more apparent than in the famous Mohegan controversy. The Mohegan tribe in Connecticut had allied itself with the colonists in the Pequot War in 1637 in return for the protection of the colony. By the eighteenth century, Connecticut construed "protection" to mean a unilateral right in the colony to sell Mohegan land. The tribe appealed to the King and the Privy Council in England (not an uncommon strategy in the region by the end of the eighteenth century).[40] Though its decision was ultimately overturned, the first commission of inquiry staffed by prominent officials under Governor Dudley of Massachusetts reminded Connecticut that treaty and pluralism defined indigenous-settler relations in North America. It declared that Owaneco was the "true Sachem of the Mohegan Indians" and that "the Government of Conecticut have by several treaties acknowledged them to have lands of their own etc."[41] The Appellate Committee of the Privy Council went on to confirm that the Mohegans appeared to be "a Nation with whom frequent Treatys have been made."[42]

In contrast to the exceptional northeast, the colony of Georgia exemplifies the centrality of diplomacy and legal pluralism elsewhere in Anglophone North American colonies. Established as a borderland colony on Creek Indian land claimed by Spain, and surrounded by some of the best armed and diplomatically well-connected indigenous peoples of the continent, colonial Georgia, like New York, was a center of colonial diplomacy.[43] Here, despite the vast claims to property and territorial jurisdiction contained in Georgia's charter, every treaty signed with the Creeks, with the partial exception of the first in 1733, recognized the plurality of jurisdiction in the region. In the Treaty of Augusta (1763), for example, Creeks were enjoined to punish members of their nation who committed crimes against settlers and to hand over settlers who committed crimes against Creeks. Settler jurisdiction was explicitly defined by British subjecthood rather than territory. It did not comprehend indigenous people.

The far reaches of Georgia were not deemed to be empty or even emptiable; they were filled with "savages" and overlaid with competing and largely alien legal regimes.[44]

Sovereignty, Territory, Revolution

If Georgia exemplifies the importance of indigenous diplomacy and of legal plurality in the British-American order of things, then the American Revolution shows the degree to which sovereignty, territory, indigenous rights, and indigenous property were bound together in North American settler projects by the end of the eighteenth century. Indigenous legal status lay near the heart of the American Revolution. After the French and Indian wars, the British Government openly supported indigenous rights to land and to jurisdiction in the Proclamation of 1763 and in a series of treaties signed in the southeast and northwest with powerful indigenous tribes. They did so at a time when indigenous-settler trade was in steep decline, immigration burgeoned, and indigenous land became the most important commodity in North America. Settler speculators mobilized indigenous rights to property and sovereignty to argue that Crown title was illusory and that indigenous people could sell land to speculators without imperial intermediaries.[45] Poor frontiersmen mobilized indigenous sovereignty in more visceral ways. Imperial law left indigenous violence unpunished, so settlers used "indigenous justice" (which they equated to retaliation) to depopulate their regions of indigenous people.[46] Others denied indigenous rights completely, either to justify squatting on Indian land illegally or to bolster the claims of landed colonies to the vast expanses of land on their peripheries.[47]

The endemic legal ambiguity of British territorial right and jurisdiction in North America took main stage in Revolutionary rhetoric. The Glorious Revolution and the Act of Union (1707) had established the King in Parliament at Westminster as the sovereign of Britain and all within it. When Parliament turned its attention to America, however, it confronted political and juridical chaos. The King had little clear authority in America. Royal prerogative underlay early modern theories of discovery, conquest, and imperial expansion, and the Privy Council had established itself as the final court of appeal for colonial litigants, but colonial charters and loose practice left colonial legislatures as virtual sovereigns over an ill-defined set of people and places in North America. If the King had limited authority, then Parliament was in a worse position. Its authority was founded on the novel jurisprudence of the seventeenth century, and American colonists were remarkably conservative.[48] In both theaters of contest—indigenous rights and Parliamentary sovereignty—the questions of sovereignty, territory, and jurisdiction were deeply intertwined.

Anglophone settler colonies in North America, from the seventeenth century to the American Revolution, helped to define sovereignty globally by claiming jurisdiction and territory on the farthest peripheries of empire. They did so before sovereignty as we understand it now became a hegemonic notion. In and against settler colonies, different discourses of sovereignty, mastery, and possession were deployed, tested, and discarded by metropolitan theorists, by politicians, by imperial agents, and by settlers. The colonies were also places of contest and plurality—of people, of claims, and of laws—a plurality that Georgia exemplified. From the eighteenth century onward, imperial administrators tried and failed to create a notion of imperial sovereignty that could both countenance and control plurality. They succeeded only in ensuring that territory, sovereignty, and jurisdiction became the central concerns of Anglophone settler polities everywhere in the first decades of the nineteenth century.

Early National Georgia and the New Settler Sovereignty

So it was that Britain's most ambitious colonial project became one of the first diasporic states. The problems of territorial right, sovereignty, and jurisdiction over its peripheries preoccupied the early national United States even more than they had the British Empire. In their eagerness to gather to themselves all the disparate and evolving attributes of sovereignty, the United States led the world in the articulation of modern sovereignty against indigenous rights. And of the new states that comprised the nascent union, none did so more forcefully or completely than the state of Georgia.

Georgia was a landed state. Its colonial charter granted it land from the east to the west coast—claims curtailed by the treaties of Paris of 1763 and 1783 to the eastern bank of the Mississippi River. Conflicts between landed and unlanded states over who could dispose of western peripheries, who could govern independent-minded frontier inhabitants, and who could expropriate or purchase Indian lands threatened to dissolve the early confederacy and plunge it into civil war. Only the surrender of western land claims to the new federal government saved the nascent union.[49] Georgia was the last landed state to do so. It maintained its claims to western lands stretching to the Mississippi until 1802, despite the fact that only Native Americans, nominally Spanish traders, and the British trading company of Panton had any sway at all in the region.[50]

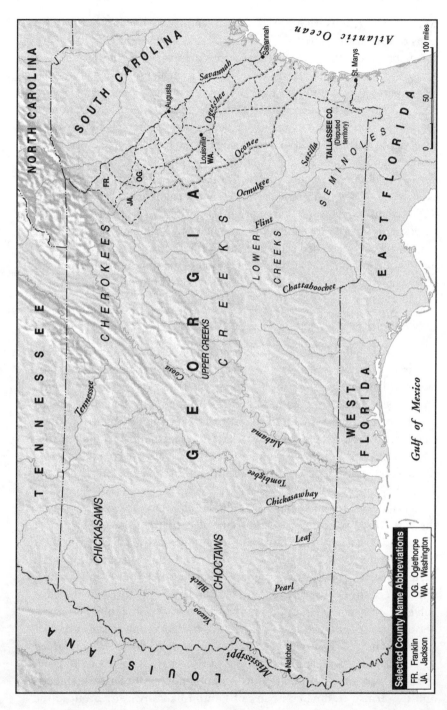

Georgia, 1796

Selected County Name Abbreviations

FR. Franklin	OG. Oglethorpe
JA. Jackson	WA. Washington

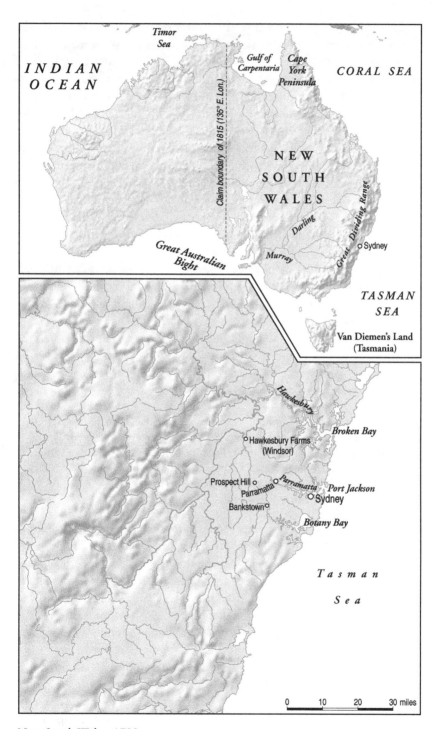

New South Wales, 1798

Georgia fought, as no other settler colony or state did, to maintain the rights to treat and to war with its indigenous neighbors—especially those who resided within its extensive territorial claims. Indeed, indigenous people rather than African slaves placed the first serious strain on Georgia's relationship with the union.[51] Section 9 of the Articles of Confederation provided the confederate government with "the sole and exclusive rights and power of ... regulating the trade and managing all affairs with the Indians, not members of any of the States, provided that the legislative right of any State within its own limits be not infringed or violated."[52] The clause contemplated the continuation of state control over partly assimilated or praying Indians in Connecticut, Massachusetts, Maryland, and Virginia, and may have been intended to extend state jurisdiction over citizens living in Indian Country lying within the chartered boundaries of the states.[53]

Georgia did its best to interpret the section otherwise, as an affirmation of its right to conduct its own Indian affairs in its extensive borderlands. The close link between indigenous rights and Georgia's sovereignty is manifest in its vociferous protestations against federal treaty making. When, in 1785, the new Confederate government negotiated the Treaty of Hopewell with the Cherokee Nation whose territory traversed Georgia's northwestern boundaries, commissioners from Georgia and North Carolina protested that

> [this] pretended treaty, and all other proceedings that have yet transpired, are a manifest and direct attempt to violate the retained sovereignty and legislative right of this State, and repugnant to the principles and harmony of the Federal Union; inasmuch as the aforesaid commissioners did attempt to exercise powers that are not delegated by the respective States to the United States in Congress assembled.[54]

Yet, when federal agents cancelled negotiations with the Creek Nation at Galphinton in 1785, Georgia's commissioners negotiated a different (and illegal) treaty that showed the degree to which Georgia's sovereign-treaty-making pretensions were predicated on legal pluralism. In the treaty of Galphinton, a small faction of the Creek Nation agreed that they were "members" of the state of Georgia and so fell outside Article 9 of the Articles of Confederation and within the purview of the state. However, the same treaty acknowledged that the Creek tribe had absolute jurisdiction over Creek crime against settlers in Indian Country.[55]

This arrangement signals another significant feature of early national Georgia. Despite its loud claims to sovereignty and jurisdiction vis-à-vis the federal government, early national Georgia was beset by plurality.

Until 1814, the vast majority of the territory that Georgia claimed lay under control of very powerful indigenous tribes whose diplomatic allegiance to the United States was the object of many treaties, but was never assumed. The Creek Nation in particular, which occupied most of Georgia's modern boundaries, kept diplomatic ties with Britain and Spain in the early national period. Indeed, Alexander McGillivray led the southern towns of the Creek Nation into allegiance with Spanish Florida in the 1780s. In 1785, McGillivray informed William Clark of Georgia that

> as a free Nation we had a right to choose & enter into alliance & friendship with any power that would be most agreeable to us. We have done this with the Spanish Nation, they stand engaged to protect our territories entire to us.[56]

In the period between the American Revolution and the Constitution of 1787, territorial sovereignty was a notion parlayed between American states and their nascent federal government. In Georgia and elsewhere, indigenous legal status and western lands lay at the heart of disputes over state and federal sovereignties even as they illustrated the fictive, aspirational quality of their sovereignty talk.

The Compact of 1802 signed by Georgia and the federal government exemplifies both the fiction and the aspiration bound up in state and federal negotiations. In this agreement, in return for the surrender of Georgia's extensive western land claims, the federal government undertook to extinguish indigenous title within Georgia's boundaries as soon as it was peaceably possible.[57] The Compact of 1802 marks the culmination and the beginning of two things: the triumph of the United States federal government's struggle to create itself as a territorial and juridical entity after the Revolutionary War; and the beginning of the teleology of Indian Removal, which ended with the forcible expatriation of Indian tribes from the eastern seaboard of the United States to lands west of the Mississippi in the 1830s.

For the purposes of this chapter, however, the Compact of 1802 had much more immediate and global import. It announced Georgia's intention to become a modern state and a settler society by purging itself of Indian lands and Indian polities. It was the first settler polity to recognize the need to recraft itself explicitly as a defined, territorial space emptied of indigenous people and their laws: a perfect territorial sovereignty. Thus, it was Georgia, not New South Wales as many scholars presume, that announced the first explicit, modern effort to pin settler sovereignty to the eradication of indigenous rights.

The Imperial Century and Its Settler Exceptions

This is one of many reasons why the United States in general, and Georgia in particular, belong in a story bridging settler colonialism and settler statehood. More important reasons lie in the fact that British North America, New South Wales, and eventually New Zealand had much more in common with the United States than they did with the many other imperial peripheries of the nineteenth-century British Empire.

The British Empire changed markedly after the American Revolution. British policy makers focused on building an empire of trade grounded on the extraction of valuable commodities from populous colonies by instituting decentralized but carefully structured imperial governance through indigenous elites. To this end, in India and parts of Africa, the second British Empire mobilized existing structures of indigenous governance into empire, including courts exercising customary jurisdiction. In China, it negotiated for control of small territorial units in which its jurisdiction extended over British subjects and their interlocutors.[58] Plurality remained the norm—though it was a legal pluralism controlled by the imperial metropolis as never before.[59] In this context, the colonies of Australia, Canada, and eventually, New Zealand were anachronisms in the new nineteenth-century British imperial order.[60]

As settler colonies, the British Cape and Caribbean colonies also broke the mold of the second British Empire. Their histories intersect, vitally, with North America and Australasia. All were involved in the production of cash crops for export. The demise of slavery and its replacement with systems of sharecropping or indenture link the Cape and Caribbean colonies to the United States still more intimately in the nineteenth century.[61] At the same time, Cape frontiers were embroiled in controversies over expansion, law, and order that spanned between second-empire plurality and the legal struggles of North American and Australasian settlements.[62]

Yet indigenous displacement and intensive settlement preoccupied North American and Australasian settler peripheries to a unique degree.[63] By setting up imperfect "neo-Britains" overseas with imported labor, moreover, settlers in Canada, New South Wales, and New Zealand forged institutional continuities with the United States.[64] Settlement in New Zealand, unsupervised and unauthorized before 1840, became a field of low-scale, largely unofficial European competition.[65] British settlement in Canada and New South Wales, meanwhile, was in important respects the direct result of Britain's constitutional crisis in North America. Upper Canada was the loyalists' reward for exile and continued in the mold of the British-indigenous relations forged before and after 1763. Claimed for Britain by James Cook in 1770 and settled in 1788, New South Wales was, first and foremost, conceived of as an open-air prison to replace Virginia and Maryland, where convicts had been sent in their thousands.[66] In the aftermath of the American Revolution the British government reconceived its solution to the convict problem entirely. It sought a place of reform and redemption in the wilderness. In New South Wales, they hoped, convicts could serve their time then live productively as degenerate but regenerated farmers, far away from the metropolis.[67]

Indigenous people figured no more in plans for New South Wales than they had in plans for seventeenth-century North American colonies. James Cook's traveling botanist, the celebrated Joseph Banks, convinced colonial officials in London that Australia was relatively fertile and thinly inhabited by extremely uncivilized and timid indigenous people who would recede before European settlement without treaty, cost, or violence.[68] In 1787, the Colonial Office issued governors instructions and a Charter of Justice for New South Wales that, like North American charters before it, assumed sovereignty over half of the continent and vested jurisdiction over it in the governor of New South Wales and his courts. The Colonial Office sent Admiral and Governor Arthur Philip to New South Wales with instructions to "conciliate" the Aborigines but to otherwise leave them to their own devices.[69] He arrived with the expectation that they would be few in number and scattered, a practical and juridical nonissue. This proved not to be so.

It is a curiosity that the New South Wales experiment was so poorly designed given that, by the end of the eighteenth century, Britain had much better ideological tools at its disposal with which to carve up the globe.[70] Lockean principles, created to legitimize existing plural empire in North America, were hegemonic by 1788. Sovereignty itself—having been reformulated through the Glorious Revolution, two centuries of European political theory, and the contests of British North America from 1750 onward—had a far more central place in the discourse of empire.[71] The publication and propagation of Vattel's *Law of Nations* (1758) had joined Lockean improvement with sovereignty in empire. This Swiss theorist globalized the notion of territorial sovereignty and synthesized two centuries of thought about its relationship with European expansion. He argued that sovereignty and dominion arose when wandering tribes appropriated land through cultivation and formed political communities.[72] Settlement, a legal doctrine rarely invoked in North America, seemed a viable mode of territorial acquisition after the rise of

Vattel and the demise of Coke's doctrine of conquest in Campbell v. Hall.[73] However, no document proves that Colonial Office officials intended its application in 1788 to the colony of New South Wales.[74] Twentieth-century Australian courts assume that the Colonial Office intended to settle Australia as *terra nullius* (often rendered as "the land belonging to no one"). However, this term did not come into wide currency until the late nineteenth century.[75]

In addition, the British enjoyed unique strategic advantages over indigenous peoples in New South Wales. There, epidemiology, late-eighteenth-century military technology, the relative absence of European competition, and the scarcity of sought-after, tradable commodities in presettlement Australia all gave British settlers more power over Australian Aborigines than they had enjoyed in seventeenth- and eighteenth-century North America. The fact that British administrators did not sign treaties with Australian Aborigines was the most important upshot of these new technologies of empire. This departure distinguishes New South Wales from every other settler project. The only treaty signed there in the nineteenth century was negotiated by private adventurers on the southeastern tip of the continent in 1835. In one of the clearest expressions of territoriality before 1836, Governor Richard Bourke denounced John Batman's treaty as a threat to the rights of the Crown and of every property-holding settler besides. [76]

Despite this fundamental difference—a difference that has had lasting ramifications for indigenous people in Australia—early New South Wales, like late colonial and early national Georgia, was beset with plurality. Indeed, in unexpected ways, Britain's assumption that Aborigines would fade away from the perimeters of its modest penal settlement bound its venture in New South Wales into a very North American problematic of sovereignty, territory, and jurisdiction. When its colonists met Aborigines—who, despite disease and a host of other material disadvantages, refused to recede or disappear—Britain's assumptions about its sovereignty over and its rights to territory in the continent proved simply inadequate to the task of dealing with the geopolitical realities of colonial life in New South Wales.

No colonist in New South Wales tipped tea into Sydney Harbour to protest the British Parliament's right to legislate for the colony, though they did overthrow a government bent on controlling the importation, production, and sale of rum. Yet New South Wales followed the pattern of disjuncture that characterized colonial North America and the early national United States. As in Georgia, Britain might have claimed the right to settle, to govern, and to own absolutely land stretching from the east coast of the continent over a vast and unexplored interior, but from settlement until the 1820s it made no pretence whatever to govern New South Wales territorially. Instead a hybrid system of personal jurisdiction overlaid with very flexible territorial claims over modest areas—what Lauren Benton has described as "enclaves" and "corridors" of power—governed the settlement of New South Wales.[77]

Sovereignty, territory, and jurisdiction were crucial to all early modern projects of empire, yet their relationship remained fluid and uncertain. Their fluidity and uncertainty took particularly troubling forms on settler peripheries, where settlement itself was predicated on indigenous dispossession, and indigenous peoples organized their lives in ways that were largely illegible to European law. Here the precise constellation of sovereignty, territory, and jurisdiction depended on historical context. Legal claims to empire mounted against other Europeans underpinned expansive claims to sovereignty, territory, and jurisdiction. In contrast, these claims had little or no impact on indigenous people until a very different moment in history. In British North America pluralism and negotiation ruled on the ground. Pluralism and negotiation persisted through revolution, state building, and the nineteenth-century recasting of British Empire. Pluralism and negotiation were so axiomatic that they bound the imagination of Anglophone settlers into the nineteenth century.

CHAPTER TWO

Pluralism as Policy

S ettler sovereignty was a fluid and contested notion in the early nineteenth century—much more fluid and contested than most historians of Georgia and of New South Wales acknowledge. The fluidity of sovereignty is nowhere more apparent than in jurisdictional practice—the responses of governors, law officers, and courts to indigenous violence against settlers. In the early decades of the nineteenth century, the state of Georgia and the colonial executive of New South Wales rarely defined indigenous violence as crime. Instead, they pursued pluralism as policy.

The banishment of an Aboriginal man named Duall and the controversy surrounding two Cherokee Indians accused of murder show the degree to which government jurisdictional practice in Georgia and New South Wales was infused with reciprocity and retaliation, notions shared by indigenous people in the nineteenth century.[1] In 1812, two Cherokees, Buffington and Daniel, were accused of stabbing Jacob Witworth in a street brawl in Jackson County, Georgia. Then they escaped from Georgia's settled counties into a part of the Cherokee Nation located in Georgia. In the process, Buffington and Daniel exposed the deficiencies of Georgia's sovereignty: territorial boundaries and federal Indian treaties conspired with older, shared norms of reciprocity and retaliation to thwart Georgia's efforts to maintain any semblance of territorial order in its frontier towns.

In New South Wales, the arrest and transportation of an Aboriginal man named Duall (or Dewall) in 1816 reveals the extent to which the colonial government fostered legal pluralism on its peripheries. In early

New South Wales, even more consistently than in early national Georgia, indigenous theft and violence fell outside the purview of criminal courts. With a very few notable exceptions, the New South Wales executive used negotiation, state-sponsored violence, and decentralized violence—not trial and imprisonment—to resolve indigenous-settler disputes before 1822. It assumed that British sovereignty did not establish British jurisdiction over territory and everyone in it in New South Wales. These assumptions were so strong that, when Governor Lachlan Macquarie tried to define indigenous violence as crime in 1816, he subverted his own pageant of jurisdiction into an act of diplomacy.

The jurisdictional conflicts centering on Buffington, Daniel, and Duall show that sovereignty was an unstable and increasingly contested notion in these two very different common-law settler states in the early nineteenth century. Indigenous legal status lay at the heart of this contest. Tensions between diplomacy and jurisdiction in both Georgia and New South Wales produced legal and quasi-legal conflict of increasing urgency as the first quarter of the nineteenth century progressed—conflict that culminated in the redefinition of sovereignty in the 1830s. In short, the jurisdictional history that Georgia and New South Wales share invites us to read the legal history of divided sovereignty in the United States and of *terra nullius* in New South Wales as two iterations of a settler story about jurisdictional practice, indigenous legal status, and evolving international definitions of sovereignty.

The Case of Ellis Buffington

Reports of the stabbing of Jacob Witworth vary. Georgian participants swore that Ellis Buffington and Robert Daniel (both of whom Meigs described as "half-blood" Cherokees) were implicated in Witworth's "atrocious murder."[2] Cherokee reports, in contrast, suggested that both Daniel and Witworth had been bystanders, and that Witworth's death was accidental.[3] Daniel was taken into custody, Buffington escaped into Cherokee Country, yet neither man stood trial in Georgia. Daniel escaped or was released from a Georgia lockup, and he and Buffington remained at large despite the fact that Georgia's governors spent the next two years demanding their surrender to the state.[4]

Buffington's brawl illustrates the palpable limits of state and federal jurisdiction as a matter of law, of ideology, and of practice on the borders of Indian Country. In 1812, the geographical limits of Georgia were defined by an assembly of legal documents including Georgia's colonial charter, the Treaties of Paris in 1763 (Great Britain, France, and Spain) and 1783 (Great Britain and the United States), Pinckney's Treaty (United States and Spain), and the Compact of 1802 (Georgia and the United States). Together these documents set the boundaries of Georgia much as they are today.

The geographical limits of Georgia's jurisdiction, however, were constructed on a different set of legal documents which defined more than half of Georgia's charted territory as Indian Country—jurisdictional enclaves within Georgia's boundaries but outside its jurisdiction. This was so primarily because the federal Constitution of 1787 (and arguably the Articles of Confederation that preceded it) granted the federal government power to treat and to regulate trade with the indigenous peoples living in Georgia's peripheries. The boundaries of Georgia were defined by federal treaties with indigenous people—many of which were conducted without Georgia's input and were contrary to Georgia's interests. Under Georgia's 1797 and 1799 Judiciary Acts, the boundaries of Georgia's settled counties marked the boundaries of what Georgia called its "ordinary jurisdiction"—a space in which its officers could police the populace, serve process, and levy taxes, and in which its courts could try cases.[5] There and only there did Georgia enjoy the promise of perfect territorial sovereignty and, with it, jurisdiction over citizens and sojourners. Though it lay within Georgia's borders, Indian Country constituted a separate jurisdictional space.[6]

In this frame, Indian Country constituted more than a bordered zone of jurisdictional exemption. Its formal plurality allowed both federal and indigenous law to chip away at the "ordinary jurisdiction" of the state of Georgia. In the Trade and Intercourse Acts of 1791–1802, the federal government mobilized its constitutional right to draw all settler-indigenous interactions within the purview of federal courts. This meant, in theory, that Georgia citizens trading with Indians in frontier counties fell under federal rather than state law. Their contracts, their crimes, and their cooperations, though they occurred within the "ordinary jurisdiction" of the state, fell largely under federal jurisdiction. In addition, before 1812, some frontier citizens preferred to use liminal, extrajudicial forums, set up by federal officers in Indian Country with Indian consent, to resolve their disputes with indigenous people, including some that might have been dealt with in Georgia's courts.

To understand the threat posed by this process to Georgia, one must bear in mind the fact that federalism itself was in the process of becoming in 1812. It constituted a series of hard-fought compromises between self-styled states that warily gave up (or had wrested from them) an ever-growing list of powers. Federal government was an ill-defined and con-

troversial legal construct in the first decades after the American Revolution.[7] In this context, the uncertain status of Indian Country made it a
specifically federal threat to Georgia's statehood. Accordingly, federal
jurisdiction over Georgia's citizens in and around Indian Country was a
matter of deep federal-state conflict. In the state's view, the federal government used Indian Country illegitimately to erode state sovereignty.
Georgia's executive watched jealously as federal jurisdiction crept into
the borders of the state.[8]

Buffington's brawl occurred in Jackson County in Georgia's "limits" or
"ordinary jurisdiction." Accordingly, it was "supposed that" it was governed by Georgia's law.[9] However, once Buffington and Daniel made it
into Cherokee Country, they were out of Georgia's reach. Federal treaties
and the state judiciary act meant that Georgia could not send so much as
a constable over the county border to arrest them, though they took refuge within the charted boundaries of the state.

They could not be extradited from Indian Country. No settled procedure allowed for the seizure or handing over of wrongdoers from this
complicated juridical space—whether settler or indigenous. In part this
was because Georgia had latent jurisdictional claims there: Georgia's
legislature termed Indian Country "unlocated" state territory overlaid
with state rights, which in their view were truncated by federal and indigenous collusion.[10] Under the federal and Indian treaty law, it was almost
impossible to obtain indigenous offenders for trial. Article 10 of the
Treaty of Holston (1791) (like Article 8 of the Treaty of New York
[1790] with the Creeks) required the Cherokees to surrender indigenous
offenders against citizens or their property to United States' jurisdiction.[11] Only the Trade and Intercourse Acts of 1791–1802 made any attempt to provide mechanisms of treaty enforcement, and these purported
chiefly to regulate settlers, not indigenous people.

Section 14 of the 1802 Act dealt with indigenous-settler violence and
theft. Section 14 recognized the right of a state to arrest and try an indigenous person for theft or violence against citizens within the ordinary
jurisdiction of the state if, and only if, they were captured there. However, it did not provide for the arrest or trial of indigenous offenders taking refuge in Indian Country for any wrongs against citizens, whether
they were committed in Indian Country or within the ordinary jurisdiction of the state. Instead, Section 14 stipulated a procedure whereby an
aggrieved citizen or his or her lawyer could obtain individual compensation. In this way, it enshrined premodern remedies, which saw most theft
and violence as compensable wrongs rather than crimes against the state.
However, compensation also indicated the partial nature of federal

claims to sovereignty in Indian Country. For example, Section 14 made no provision at all for the compensation of theft and violence committed by Indians against settlers in Indian Country. Redress rested solely on diplomatic negotiation under the treaties.[12] In addition, though it regulated citizen trade and crime against indigenous people, the 1802 Act made no provision for citizen-citizen crime in Indian Country.[13]

The federal Trade and Intercourse Law, then, did not set up an alternative juridical order to defend the rights of citizens and the jurisdictional boundaries of the state. Instead, it presupposed the continuation of a robust indigenous jurisdiction—an alternative order of indigenous customary law that had ill-defined reach over indigenous people, indigenous land, and settlers. This was so in part because the Trade and Intercourse Acts themselves were an exercise in federal self-imagination: an early experiment in federal jurisdiction making. Accordingly, they were riddled with lacunae—some occasioned by politics, some simply unplanned, and others proceeding from the conceptual limits of early nineteenth-century settler sovereignty. At the same time, the early United States lacked both the will and the legal imagination required to formalize and control indigenous jurisdiction. Despite the efforts of the state and federation, then, pluralism in early nineteenth-century southeastern borderlands left much more room for diplomacy than it did for jurisdiction.

Once Buffington and Daniel were ensconced in Indian Country, negotiation, not criminal prosecution, followed. The state had to rely on federal diplomacy to secure their surrender, and practice governed this process. Practice dictated that Georgia's executive petition the federal agent to the Cherokees, Return J. Meigs, to demand Buffington and Daniel from the tribe.[14] Meigs then had to deliver the demand to the Cherokee Nation and negotiate for its execution. On 12 March 1812, James Blair delivered to Meigs a "solemn demand of you as the United States Agent for the Cherokee Nation of Indians, that you have Ellis Buffington and Robert Daniel two quarteroons of Said Nation apprehended and delivered up to us."[15] The state could do no more.

Between 1789 and 1820, only a handful of the Creeks and Cherokees demanded by Georgia ever made it into court. Before the War of 1812, it seems that very few indigenous people made it into custody in Georgia for crimes committed within the ordinary jurisdiction of the state.[16] Of those Indians arrested, I have found only one unambiguous mention in the Indian Agency records of a conviction in Georgia. An Indian named Tites, "regularly sentenced to the penitentiary" in Georgia, resisted arrest in 1808 and was shot and killed by Georgia's constabulary.[17] The real numbers of incarcerated, tried, and convicted indigenous people may have been much higher than this source indicates, and they almost certainly increased over time.[18]

Reciprocity and Retaliation

Georgia tried very few indigenous people before 1820 not only because the federal treaty system made it difficult to do so, but also because principles of reciprocity and retaliation inhered in and subverted Georgia's resort to jurisdiction. Reciprocity and retaliation both had deep normative roots in North American indigenous societies and in Anglophone legal culture. Since first settlement there, they had grown into a set of unwieldy, syncretic rules that bound much settler-indigenous interaction.

Reciprocity was an important principle in southeastern indigenous societies. Well into the period of settler-indigenous encounter, social cachet in both Creek and Cherokee communities was garnered not through the accumulation of wealth but through its distribution to the community.[19] From the outset, the southeastern Indian encounter with settler trade goods, and their adoption of settler-traders and settler agricultural practices, placed strain on the reciprocal bonds that framed town life.[20] Yet, at least until the turn of the nineteenth century, indigenous treaty making itself was driven by their desire to establish sacred bonds of obligation to create fictive kinship with attendant obligations of reciprocity.[21]

Retaliation, meanwhile, underpinned crucial aspects of southeastern indigenous social discipline. In the Creek and Cherokee Nations, colonial and precontact indigenous laws regulating murder required that the kin of the deceased kill either the murderer or one of the murderer's kin in retaliation for the crime—a rule they abstracted to govern murders by settlers. If the colony or state failed to "do justice" to its indigenous neighbors by executing settler murderers, the kin of the deceased Creek or Cherokee "took satisfaction" by killing a settler (the fictive kin of the guilty party). Though retaliatory killing was outlawed by the Creeks by 1799 and by the Cherokee in 1810, the decentralized nature of governance, particularly in the Creek nation, ensured that blood revenge underpinned much indigenous-settler violence throughout the early national period—often with the tacit consent of the federation and the state.[22]

Reciprocity and retaliation also had deep resonance in Anglophone legal culture. English common law, its criminal law, and European civil law were all infused with norms of reciprocity (evident in the persistence of compensation rather than punishment for violent crime, and in expansive notions of provocation and self-defense).[23] Indeed, in early national

Georgia, the moral and legal power of retaliation was evident in the prevalence of assault and battery charges before frontier courts. Though the state brought assault and battery charges against offenders, settler juries ordered that batterers give minimal compensation to their victims and did not imprison repeat offenders.[24] The notion of blood debt, meanwhile, resonated with European natural law assumptions that violent retaliation, the punishment of death by death, was a fundamental rule of human society.[25] Between first contact and the early nineteenth century, settlers and indigenous people developed their historically distinct affinities with reciprocity and retaliation into a body of syncretic, uneven, and at times mutually misunderstood practices.[26] The resulting syncretic normativity of reciprocity and retaliation tended to push indigenous-settler theft and violence outside the purview of federal and state courts. This was so because it set constraints on how local, state, and federal governments understood indigenous theft and violence, and more importantly, shaped the rhetoric and the process of government responses.

Those constraints came under pressure in incidents like Witworth's demise not least because of the ambiguity of racial and therefore of legal identity in early national Georgia. As noted, Buffington and Daniel were described variously as "halfbloods" (by the federal agent) and as "quarteroons" (by Georgia's emissaries), which most likely indicated that they were "racially" Indian with half or one-quarter European lineage on the male side.[27] Specifying race may simply have been habit in a slave state, wherein people of mixed indigenous or African heritage were subject to a range of legal disabilities, including having no right to testify in court. It might also have signaled their culpability: perhaps their half-whiteness made Buffington and Daniel more morally responsible in the eyes of Meigs, and their quarter-whiteness, more savage in the eyes of Georgia's emissaries.

Race had the potential to unsteady their indigenous legal standing also, because if Buffington or Daniel had a European mother, then matrilineal custom meant they could be Cherokee only by adoption.[28] In addition, some children of Indians and Europeans had the option of passing as American citizens, a process that became particularly common after the 1830s.[29] Conversely, if "half-blood" or "quarteroon" indicated African heritage, the situation became more tenuous in both Cherokee and state legal orders. Cherokees with African forebears were particularly susceptible to illegal enslavement: free Cherokees, like free African Americans, could be passed off as slaves. As the nineteenth century progressed, African heritage became a bar to Cherokee citizenship. Race came to define Cherokee sovereignty almost as closely as it did Georgian sovereignty. By mid-century, Cherokee statutes regulated interracial marriages, and African-Indian offspring were excluded from tribal membership.[30]

In this case, as it happened, the conflicting racial classification of Buffington and Daniel was legally superfluous. All accepted that the accused were Cherokees; as such their legal status was defined. Their status committed the Cherokee and their accusers to a conversation about fault, punishment, and compensation instead of jurisdiction, parameters that all participants understood well. All were bound within the lexicon of reciprocity and retaliation.

The Logic of Diplomacy

If the federal treaty system conditioned jurisdiction on successful negotiation (a request for the surrender of offenders), then shared norms of reciprocity and retaliation ensured that the most notorious incidents of indigenous arrest in Georgia and its surrounds ended in diplomacy rather than jurisdiction. In 1798, Tuskeegee Tustunnagau was accused of raping a white woman in Oglethorpe County Georgia, then released after a local inferior court used a writ of habeas corpus as a vehicle for a peace talk (much to the dismay of the governor). In 1801, Stone (a Cherokee) was abducted from the Cherokee Nation for trial in Tennessee on what was likely a trumped-up charge of horse theft. After much correspondence, his release before trial was brokered by the federal agent, Meigs, and two high-ranking soldiers who posted his bail.[31]

Diplomacy, based on norms shared by indigenous people and settlers, also undermined what may be the only time that federal troops arrested an Indian in Cherokee Country for crimes against settlers before 1830. In 1808, after Cherokee Chief James Vann rounded off a year of escalating animosity against American travelers, traders, and agents in the Cherokee Nation by wounding two citizens of Georgia and Tennessee, Meigs marshaled the "military" to arrest Vann in the Cherokee Nation for trial in Tennessee.[32] Meigs planned Vann's arrest as a show of state and federal power rather than as an exercise of state and federal jurisdiction.

> Vann ought to be taken & tried by the laws of the United States and altho' I suppose nothing more than pecuniary damages is expected, it would have a good effect & would Strengthen the hands of the friends of Government who ought by every reasonable means be supported. . . . [A] small party composed partly of the militia ought to be sent to take Vann, for even if he should make his escape, it will have a very valuable effect on the nation & will shew that the United States will not suffer their citizens to be Shot, & Stabbed, or insulted by a Savage, & their laws trampled on with impunity.[33]

His efforts failed, however, because Indians and others defended the protocols of diplomacy and exploited loopholes in federal criminal jurisdiction. First, two Tennessee lawyers, Tremble and Dardis, informed Meigs that Vann could not be tried according to law. As Meigs noted, "It would appear that if the opinion of Messieurs Tremble and Dardis is correct that the law as it now Stands will not reach the case of Vann or Similar ones." The details of their opinion are not included in agency records, but it is clear that neither treaty nor statute gave federal troops the right to arrest an Indian in Indian Country for any crime, notwithstanding the fact that the tribe was obliged by treaty to surrender Vann for trial in an adjoining state.[34] Second, Vann himself acted to subvert law with diplomacy. He undertook to desist from harassing citizens passing through the nation and offered to pay one of his victims $1,000.[35]

This collapse of jurisdiction into diplomacy matters because it reveals practical and conceptual limits of state sovereignty that are difficult to see from a modern legal vantage point. Diplomacy and jurisdiction are both acts of law. Diplomacy conducted between states by properly constituted authorities is, after all, legal. Criminal jurisdiction, in contrast, is an exercise of sovereignty over the actions of a person—whether a subject, a citizen, or a sojourner-in-situ. The cases of Tuskeegee Tustunnagau, Stone, and Vann all show that formal pluralism was not the only fetter on jurisdiction in Georgia's early nineteenth-century borderlands. Rather, diplomacy inhered in state and federal exercises of jurisdiction, disrupting jurisdiction from within.

Buffington's case gives rare insight into the power of reciprocity as a principle of diplomacy in the early national period. This is so because it shows the degree to which indigenous people defended reciprocity in its most syncretic and shared iteration. In 1812, the Cherokee preempted Georgia's demand for Buffington's and Daniel's surrenders by appealing to shared notions of reciprocity, in contradistinction both to blood revenge and to settler jurisdiction. In a long letter to Governor Mitchell, the Cherokee chiefs abjured retaliation against the innocent. They "respectfully request that you will restrain any; if there are such, who may attempt to resort to the vile principle of retaliation on innocent persons," appealing instead to "justice and impartiality."[36]

Justice and impartiality, in this case, would not be served by criminal trial or state jurisdiction. Reciprocity and equality of exchange constituted justice. The chiefs reminded Mitchell that two white men, taken before a magistrate for murdering a Cherokee in front of his wife and children earlier in 1812, were liberated "without Bail" for want of legal (i.e., white) testimony.[37] They argued that if Buffington and Daniel remained at large, in both cases "justice is evaded" and reciprocity is preserved. The letter asserted parity: two escapes from justice and two murders meant that retaliation was superfluous and jurisdiction unnecessary. According to syncretic notions of reciprocity, Buffington's crime and his escape restored balance between the Cherokee Nation and the state.[38]

In 1812, Return J. Meigs, federal agent to the Cherokees, explicitly defended the Cherokee's logic of reciprocity, though he did so by appealing to the deficits of settler legal process. Meigs argued that discriminatory testimony rules ensured that Buffington and Daniel could not receive fair trial in Georgia because "their testimony on oath is not admissible."[39] Again, despite their mixed racial heritage, they were defined as Indians by Georgia's courts. In this case, Cherokee accounts "var[ied] materially" from the depositions enclosed with Georgia's demand for the surrender of both men. So, until testimony laws changed, they could not receive a fair hearing in the state.[40]

Meigs also acknowledged that racist testimony laws ensured that the states of Georgia and Tennessee owed the Cherokee a debt of blood. On the verso of his "Reflections on Cherokee Concerns," Meigs listed seven cases since 1801 in which settlers had been acquitted of murdering Cherokees for want of legal testimony. According to Meigs, Buffington and his relatives reasoned "that, even if it is a murder it ought to be set off against the murder of the Cherokee above mentioned, that in a political light they say this would be but just. They complain & say that before the case mentioned they have Eight lives standing against us . . . their language is that we owe them eight lives . . . this I have no doubt is true." Law, in this case, necessitated diplomacy because the latter, alone, could do justice between the Cherokee and the state.[41]

Meigs's defense of reciprocity here shows its normative power in the federal agencies in Georgia's Indian Country, not least because Meigs was at best an ambivalent friend to Cherokee law-ways. His usual practice was to set up commissions in Cherokee Country to adjudicate civil disputes between settlers and Indians. However, as he staffed these commissions with settlers and ran them remarkably like common law courts, they constituted an oddly imperialist endorsement of Cherokee jurisdiction. At the same time, Meigs advocated the extension of state jurisdiction over the Cherokee Nation—well before these arguments were mobilized by Georgia to attack indigenous rights. In 1811, he told the secretary of war that Cherokees had surrendered all right to legislate for themselves in the Treaty of Hopewell of 1785. He insisted, as a matter of legal principle, that the Cherokees were a dependent people, and as such had no innate right to maintain their tribal integrity or independent governance.[42] In

Buffington's case, however, Meigs acknowledged that the manifest failure of settler law to do justice to the Cherokees removed its normative advantage over syncretic reciprocity. Middle-ground exchange here displaced Georgia's law—morally and practically.

Syncretic reciprocity had even more power in early national Creek Country. Throughout his tenure as federal agent to the Creeks, Benjamin Hawkins almost always refused to demand the surrender of Creek wrongdoers for trial in Georgia—a policy that became increasingly controversial on the eve of the 1812 war.[43] He deemed even fairly half-hearted attempts at tribal punishment sufficient fulfillment of Creek treaty obligations.[44] This, in part, reflected the conflicting goals of Indian civilization.[45] Hawkins fought to centralize Creek political institutions and to create an effective police force there. But his efforts at cultural imperialism were cast in terms he felt the Creeks could understand. As a result, new institutions of law embodied syncretic understandings of reciprocity and retaliation. The importance of retaliation as a frame for federal-Creek relations during Hawkins's tenure is also apparent from the fact that "debts of blood" formed part of diplomatic discourse "at every Creek/American treaty negotiation."[46]

The Role of the State

Indians and federal agents were not the only parties involved in the subordination of jurisdiction to diplomacy in Indian Country. Georgia's legal evisceration could not have been so complete without the participation of the state. The logic of reciprocity, retaliation, and diplomacy also infected state practice. Settlers, local militiamen, local judges, and magistrates all embraced them at different times and for different reasons. Buffington's case shows the extent to which the state's executive itself participated in the logic of reciprocity, even as it demanded the exercise of jurisdiction and law.

On several occasions in the early national period, various governors of Georgia acknowledged that state jurisdiction was bound by shared notions of justice. At times, they acknowledged that any offense against indigenous people not amounting to murder was beneath the notice of the state. When Mr. Oates was rumored to have shot a Creek Indian in March 1798 in retaliation for the killing of a Mr. Allen several days before, Governor James Jackson suggested that no state action was necessary against Oates until the death of the Creek was confirmed.[47] In doing so he invoked notions of criminal responsibility in a number of southeastern nations, where "Homicide was the exception. . . . No other event of which we know brought into action legal forces beyond the individuals involved."[48] Jackson acknowledged the economies of retaliation on Georgia's frontier even more explicitly when, at the request of Oates, he later informed the Creeks that Reuben Lawson (not Oates) was responsible for wounding their countryman, lest indigenous vengeance be directed against the wrong man.[49]

Lawson's violence in 1798 was particularly irksome to the governor of Georgia, less because of its illegality than because it displaced any normative claim the state could make to exercise jurisdiction over Creek killers. In the calculations of the Creek Nation and the state of Georgia, jurisdiction and retaliation had equal weight. Allen's killer had not been disciplined by the Creek Nation or surrendered to Georgia for trial. So, Lawson's act of retaliation obviated state jurisdiction because it paid the Creeks' debt of blood.[50]

In addition, reciprocity, retaliation, and war were central metaphors in state-indigenous (as well as federal-indigenous) negotiations throughout the early national period. When a boy was killed in 1790, after the signing of the Treaty of New York, no one demanded the killer's surrender. Creek chiefs from Coweta and settlers counseled Georgia's Governor Edward Telfair that the killing was not an act of war, but retaliation for several unatoned murders by "*white* people" the year before. Joseph Savage assured Telfair that the boy's death avenged a death "last summer," and, even so, he reported that the chiefs promised to kill the perpetrator as soon as his name and location could be discovered.[51]

Retribution bolstered Buckner Harris's claims for the surrender of James Vann in 1808. He threatened the Cherokee that militiamen and settlers would eagerly enter the nation to take Vann, and satisfy their grievances with swords and guns.[52] Georgia's demands for Buffington were more subdued in 1812 and 1813, but Hugh Montgomery threatened to inflict "exemplary punishment" on the tribe if Buffington and Daniel were not surrendered to Georgia's jurisdiction—illustrating the fast bond between the two.[53] As Georgia's southern and western frontiers devolved into endemic indigenous-settler violence and war in 1812, retaliation, not jurisdiction, occupied the minds of Georgia's executive. Mitchell assured Brigadier General John Floyd that the state would soon act "not only to protect our frontier but to take satisfaction for past injuries."[54] Thus, the state collaborated in its own prostration—it belied its most strident appeals to jurisdiction and law by practicing or acquiescing in the logics of reciprocity and retaliation.

The bitter complicity of Georgia's executive in frontier pluralism suggests that the ideological underpinnings of settler-indigenous relations

are more complex than some early national histories allow. Many historians of early national Georgia argue that both state and federal governments bent their energies toward the dispossession of indigenous people
from the American Revolution onward. Some advocated indigenous removal, others indigenous assimilation, but all sought to rid the federation of Indian Country. In this frame, early national diplomacy between
the United States and Indians was nothing more than a temporary expedient to preserve peace, to avoid expensive Indian wars, and to aid Indian civilization. The federal treaty system that established a degree of
formal legal pluralism in Georgia, then, merely facilitated the orderly
dispossession or the corporate dissolution of indigenous peoples.[55]

The furor over Jacob Witworth's murder, however, suggests that legal
pluralism in Georgia's indigenous borderlands was propped up by much
more than convenience and necessity. Indigenous people and Indian Country set crucial limits on the imagination and the articulation of settler sovereignty in Georgia in the early national period. This is why, in the 1820s,
both figured so centrally in the debate about states' rights. The system of
formal pluralism embodied by Indian treaties and the Trade and Intercourse Acts left much indigenous and settler violence unregulated. Yet, this
formal pluralism merely gave structural expression to the plurality of settler sovereignty in and around Georgia's Indian Country. Jurisdictional
practice—whether through institutions fostered by federal agents in Indian
Country, or through informal accommodations reached by settlers, state
officials, and their indigenous neighbors—showed that there were no clear-
cut territorial divisions among state, federal, and indigenous jurisdiction.

Georgia, the first common-law settler state to marry expansion with
modern notions of state sovereignty in the Compact of 1802, spoke too
soon. Between 1789 and 1812, both state and federation lacked the authority or the legal tools to perfect jurisdiction—to imagine a state without Indians. Consequently, other rules of law, war, and diplomacy governed indigenous people and settlers in and around the state of Georgia.

The Banishment of Duall

In 1816, an Aboriginal leader, was transported from New South Wales to
Norfolk Island for his role in the widespread destruction of property and
a number of killings in the western reaches of the colony.[56] In accordance
with unusually specific instructions from Sydney, Duall (or Dewall) was
captured by local settlers and placed in a local jail, where he was recovered by troops, marched to Sydney, and held in custody until his solemn
transportation for seven years from the colony.

Duall's arrest and transportation sound like textbook exercises of British colonial jurisdiction over indigenous people on the New South Wales frontier. His incarceration and transportation followed a carefully constructed pageant of law. Between 1814 and 1816 Governor Lachlan Macquarie, soldier, man of enlightenment, and self-proclaimed friend to Australian Aborigines, responded to sustained Aboriginal violence in the western borderlands of the colony in a manner that led, inexorably, to Duall's transportation. He enjoined settlers to abstain from retaliation, asserted repeatedly that Aborigines were amenable to British law for their violence, and told soldiers and settlers to capture rather than kill as many Aborigines as possible and to bring them to Sydney, where they might be "dealt with according to Justice."[57] When these measures failed to bring peace, he "outlawed" ten named Aboriginal men deemed to be instigators of and principals in the violence. For the first time in the history of the colony, in short, Macquarie clothed state violence in the language of law. It was a pageant of law, however, that lacked the substance of jurisdiction. Though he was transported from the colony, Duall was not tried for his crimes.

Duall's case marks both the high point of colonial jurisdictional abstinence and a turning point in legal history of New South Wales. Macquarie's legal ambitions notwithstanding, before 1824 it seems that very few Aborigines were tried for crimes against settlers in the colony of New South Wales. Their exemption from colonial jurisdiction, moreover, was not limited to the frontiers of the colony. It operated within and outside the geographical limits of British settlement.

This is especially significant given the fact that Britain had never signed a treaty with Australian Aborigines that formally acknowledged Aboriginal rights to territory and self-governance. The absence of a treaty has led historians of all political persuasions to argue that, whether because of the doctrine of *terra nullius* or because of eighteenth-century racial and political philosophy, the British Empire claimed, and in law held, territorial sovereignty throughout the colony of New South Wales from 1788, and with it jurisdiction to control indigenous and settler crime.[58] Legal pluralism, in this frame, is no more than an anomaly: frontier violence, a deficit of colonial state power rather than a deficit of right. I argue instead that though the British Empire hoped that New South Wales would prove to be a place without proprietors, sovereignty, or law, New South Wales officials acknowledged indigenous jurisdiction and their juridical separateness consistently in their early jurisdictional practice in the colony. Being outside British law, of course, was no panacea in New South Wales: it could make Aborigines objects as well as perpetrators of unrestrained intercultural violence.[59] It does, however, hold important ramifications for our understanding of the historical underpinnings of law and policy in Australia.

Like his counterparts in Georgia, Macquarie was caught in a paradigm of diplomacy. Aboriginal exemption from settler jurisdiction was so axiomatic that Macquarie could not break the mold in 1816. His attempt to impose jurisdiction became, instead, an abiding symbol of the disjunctures between sovereignty, land rights, and practices of jurisdiction in the early colony of New South Wales.

Aboriginal Resistance to Settlement

Though no treaties were signed between Aborigines and the colonial state, diplomacy, gift-giving, and negotiation formed the substance of their nonviolent interactions well into the nineteenth century.[60] In 1801, Governor King had assured indigenous Australians that, "as it is a practice strictly observed among the natives that murder should be atoned by the life of the murderer or some one belonging to him . . . when Pemulwye [a hostile Aboriginal leader] was given up they should be re-admitted to our friendship."[61] Negotiation by the governor preceded and concluded state-sponsored violence in 1805. In that year, magistrate Samuel Marsden met with a number of tribes to negotiate an end to hostilities and to ascertain the names of principal depredators. After interviewing disgruntled "branch natives" himself, Governor King assured them that no more settlers would occupy the southern branch of the Hawkesbury River.[62] The *Sydney Gazette* in May of 1805 deplored the predilection of Aborigines for violence before, and diplomacy after, settlers harvested their annual crop of corn.[63]

Governor Macquarie himself used diplomacy as a basis of state-indigenous relations. From 1814, he held yearly feasts and occasional fêtes for local chiefs and visiting tribes, chiefly to enjoin Aborigines to settle on farms or to send their children to the native school, but also to communicate government policy and to accept tribes and individuals into his protection.[64] In 1814, the *Sydney Gazette* celebrated the governor's success in "reaching an understanding" with Aborigines on the western frontiers of the colony. Macquarie's diaries, meanwhile, note several meetings with Aboriginal chiefs from 1814 to 1816 that centered on peacemaking.[65] Nor did these practices disappear when the colony started to modernize its jurisdictional practice after 1824. In 1824, Governor Brisbane recommended sending to Aboriginal "Chiefs" "gaudy Articles, such as those presented to the Chiefs of the North American Tribes" including "fowling Pieces and Tomahawks" to attach "these Chiefs to His Majesty's Government."[66] As late as 1831, soldiers were sent to negotiate with Mountain Tribes or Gundungurra people near Goulburn Plains. They discovered that violence there was caused primarily by the failure of the colonial state to give gifts (whether of tribute, peace, or compensation) to local Aborigines.[67]

When negotiation and conciliation failed, the colony made war. Military posses were sent out to kill or capture Aborigines in 1790, 1795, 1799, 1801, 1804, 1805, and 1816.[68] None of these campaigns was accompanied by a declaration of martial law. This is significant because martial law contains within it an assertion of sovereign authority over subjects or citizens—it authorizes the suspension of civilian justice.[69] Moreover, each of these military actions was accompanied by a general or partial delegation of state violence to settlers.

In 1795, Administrator Paterson made it a crime for settlers to shelter or encourage Natives to "lurk about their farms"; to "withdraw or keep back their assistance from those who may be threatened or in danger of being attacked" by Aborigines; and to "wantonly fire at" or kill "Natives."[70] How settlers were to interpret this jumble of injunctions without running afoul of colonial law is a mystery. The instructions did, however, implicitly authorize settlers to kill Aborigines on the least suspicion of aggression and to drive them off their farms. Indeed, four years later, a group of settlers were pardoned for murdering Aborigines on the Hawkesbury in part because of the ambiguous wording and even more ambiguous duration of these instructions.

In 1801, after Dharug Aborigines killed one settler and some sheep, Governor King ordered settlers around Parramatta, George's River, and Prospect Hill to drive Aborigines "back from the settlers' habitations by firing at them."[71] In 1805, in response to a murder, King required that "no Natives be suffered to approach the Grounds or Dwellings of any Settler until the [Aboriginal] Murderers" were "given up" to what he described elsewhere in the proclamation as "Justice."[72] "Justice" for King approximated a confused notion of indigenous, not settler, law, as we shall see.[73]

When violence intensified on New South Wales's frontier between 1813 and 1816, Governor Macquarie followed more tenets of local practices than he broke. Like virtually every Governor before him, he responded to sustained Aboriginal violence with a combination of negotiation and state-sponsored retaliation. However, he qualified each step with new appeals to jurisdiction. His first proclamation addressing indigenous violence in June of 1814 enjoined settlers to refrain "from taking the law into their *own hands* . . . against the Natives who are in like

Manner with themselves under and entitled to the Protection of the British Laws so long as they conduct themselves conformably to them."[74] Other early efforts at resolving Aboriginal unrest in 1814 included sending a posse of friendly Aborigines and settler intermediaries to the frontiers of the colony under the direction of John Warby and John Jackson. Their task was to bring five named "wild mountain natives" suspected of murder to Sydney "in order that they may suffer the Punishment due their crimes." Macquarie's instructions explicitly forbade the party from "making terms" with the accused men, or "of holding out to them any promise of Pardon or indemnity for the various crimes they have committed."[75]

In May of 1816, Macquarie directed three detachments of soldiers to Liverpool Plains, the Cow Pastures, and Windsor with instructions to incarcerate but not to kill Aborigines. They were to ask hostile groups to surrender and to shoot only those Aborigines who resisted or who ran away. If violence was necessary, he ordered his soldiers, where possible, to punish the guilty and spare the innocent, especially women and children. At the governor's express request, however, slain Aboriginal men (guilty or innocent) were to be "hanged up on trees."[76] In addition, his proclamation of May 4th gave settlers far more insidious power by declaring Aborigines who bore arms within one mile of a British settlement to be enemies of the colony.[77] In July of 1816, settlers, magistrates, and friendly Aborigines were instructed, where possible, to "seize upon and secure" ten Aboriginal men, though they could kill them with impunity if seizure proved inconvenient.[78] Throughout, Macquarie's instructions show that he had his heart set on exercising settler sovereignty through jurisdiction.[79] However, his instructions all explicitly countenanced a different exercise: of the power and wrath of the colonial state.

Incarceration in Early New South Wales

The history of indigenous incarceration in New South Wales forms part of the same story of jurisdictional exemption. Duall was not the only indigenous person incarcerated in New South Wales before 1816. Colonial records suggest that at least seventeen indigenous people were detained by the colonial state before Duall's arrest. Their arrests and detention, however, were usually means to the end of indigenous-settler diplomacy, and all but one was resolved without recourse to imperial jurisdiction. The most significant of these incarcerations illustrates both these points. In June of 1805, eleven Aborigines were captured after starting a fire in Parramatta. A number were liberated after promising to bring in "Mosquito and Jack."[80] Tedbury, the son of the notorious Bidjigal leader Pemulwye, remained in custody until August, but his relatives negotiated his release, pledging themselves as surety for his future good conduct.[81] State and indigenous violence ceased when Mosquito and a man named Bulldog were surrendered to the colonial state. The two men were not arrested or captured. They were surrendered as objects of negotiation and diplomacy.

The surrender of Mosquito and Bulldog presented the colonial administration with a dilemma—a dilemma that prompted the writing of the first and most ambiguous opinion about the legal status of Australian Aborigines. Governor King asked Judge Advocate Atkins in 1805 whether Mosquito and Bulldog could be tried for their crimes under imperial law. In a very roundabout fashion, Atkins said no. He suggested that though Aborigines were "within the Pale of H.M. protection" they could not legally be tried because they were "totally ignorant" of the "meaning and tendency" of British legal proceedings. Moreover, the colony's Court of Criminal Jurisdiction could not legally hear Aboriginal cases because it was empowered by law "to give a true Verdict according to the *Evidence.*" Indigenous evidence could not be heard in court, so no verdict could be reached.[82] Instead, he counseled the governor to meet Aboriginal depredations with decentralized violence through the formation and deployment of local militia. Meanwhile, he argued, settlers were excused in law from charges of murder for shooting and wounding Aborigines who stole their corn since the latter were "as common depredators."[83] Settlers could also kill Aborigines in retaliation for killing settlers. Their actions were justified by policy, by natural law, and by "self-defense." In short, Atkins solemnized a rather crude marriage between imperial protection and natural law.

"Protection" itself was a vague legal term used to describe either the status of individual foreigners residing in Britain or the status of a weak sovereign under the thrall of a stronger one. Neither status necessarily implied the loss of individual liberties or of corporate sovereignty, though individual sojourners under "protection" usually fell within the jurisdiction of their host sovereign.[84] If imperial "protection" of Aborigines in New South Wales did not equate to jurisdiction over them, retaliation might be a legitimate response to Aboriginal violence under European principles of natural law.[85] Perhaps this is what Atkins meant when he argued that Aborigines were "within the Pale of British Protection" but bore none of the burdens or benefits of British Law.

If Atkins's opinion presents somewhat of a puzzle, then Governor King's interpretation of it amounts to an explicit embrace of diplomacy

and retaliation over jurisdiction in New South Wales circa 1805. In a letter to the Earl of Camden enclosing Atkins's opinion, King noted that

> Your Lordship will observe the existing Objections and inconvenience of try-
> ing the Natives whose Natural inclination for taking the most sanguinary
> Revenge for trifling supposed ill treatment scarcely makes it a Crime with
> them—Their customs admitting the Murderer of another and his Friends to
> defend himself against the Relations or Tribe of the deceased. The Settlers
> etc. killed by the Natives were four, viz. Two Settlers and Two Stockmen—
> From the necessity of coercive Measures being taken, Six of the Natives and
> those the most Guilty were Shot in a pursuit by the Settlers—I have therefore
> impressed on the Natives that altho' the Delinquents now in custody ought
> to suffer, Yet as Two Black Men more than Settlers have been shot, I shall
> forego any further retaliation, but as they were so desirous of shewing their
> Sorrow for what had passed by giving up the Delinquents and requiring they
> might be punished, I should try the expedient of sending them to another
> Settlement to labour which has been much approved of by the rest.[86]

As far as Governor King was concerned, Mosquito's and Bulldog's surrender, even their eventual transportation to Norfolk Island without
trial or sentence, was part of a discourse of diplomacy between indigenous people and the colonial state—a discourse founded in (albeit
crudely construed) indigenous notions of justice rather than the common law.[87]

Retaliation and reciprocity were very important tenets of Aboriginal
society—as they were in indigenous North American cultures. However,
it seems that King knew more about North American practices of blood
revenge than he did about Aboriginal law and custom. Retaliatory killing
was just one of several social punishments in southeastern Aboriginal
societies. Settler accounts suggest that retaliatory killing could follow the
death of an Aborigine by violence.[88] Early accounts suggest that, in the
vicinity of early British settlements at least, Aboriginal social discipline
centered on corporate punishment of indigenous offenders or their kin.
When indigenous people committed wrongs for which they could not
make restitution (especially murder and abducting or raping married
women), they or their kin were forced to fend off spears thrown by aggrieved relatives after a process of corporate conciliation. This punishment was usually final. If the wrongdoer avoided injury, they were still
absolved of their crimes.[89] There is some evidence of less structured retaliatory violence.[90] It is also possible that when Aborigines killed settlers to
protest invasions of land, abuse of women, murder of their kin, or failure
to abide by other fundamental rules of reciprocity, they acted according
to a different lexicon of violence, one grounded in new syncretic prac-

tices of retaliation forged after their experience of European settlement and European arms.[91] Whatever the complexities of indigenous jurisdiction, Atkins read indigenous violence and theft against settlers as random acts of savage retaliation.[92] King, meanwhile, used cultural knowledge from North American indigenous-settler conflict to interpret practices of reciprocal violence shared by settlers and indigenous people in New South Wales.

It seems that the legal synthesis of 1805 marked the absolute limit of colonial jurisdiction until 1816. Criminal court records, the newspaper, and the colonial secretary's correspondence do not record the transportation of any other indigenous person in the interim, despite periodic outbreaks of sustained violence and a number of killings and thefts by known Aborigines during this period.[93] Ironically, it seems that early governors of New South Wales were far less invested in creating pockets of perfect jurisdiction than were their Georgia counterparts, who tried episodically and in vain to assert jurisdiction over indigenous people within the ordinary jurisdiction of the state. Early New South Wales governors drew no distinction between Aborigines enmeshed in the local economy or urban communities and those committing depredations on the increasingly far-flung borders of settlement. All were exempted from colonial jurisdiction.

Sometime after 1795, a Branch Aborigine named Charley was sent from the Hawkesbury to Sydney to answer to the governor for killing a settler. Governor John Hunter set him free, declaring "that he could not take upon himself to punish the native in cool blood."[94] In 1799, John Randall (an Aborigine) was accused by a servant and a constable of attempting twice to take plates and glasses from the governor's house.[95] After hearing evidence, the Bench of Magistrates did not sentence Randall; rather they submitted "to His Excellency the Propriety of ordering the Offender such exemplary Punishment" as he saw fit. Governor Hunter liberated Randall when the latter expressed contrition for the crime.[96] Similar treatment was given to an Aboriginal man who stole property from a traveler on the Parramatta Road in 1815. Though settler-highwaymen were routinely sentenced to death by hanging, the *Sydney Gazette* reported that this indigenous highwayman was incarcerated solely to induce him to return the money stolen. When it became apparent that he had spent the money, he was confined for two weeks and released on his solemn promise never to hold up traffic again—all without the intervention of a court.[97]

Charley, Randall, and the unnamed indigenous highwayman were unusual insofar as they were imprisoned for their misdeeds, then released from custody. A number of colonial inquests into settler murders deferred more explicitly to subsisting Aboriginal jurisdictional independence. In November of 1811, the coroner declared that Richard Luttril had been killed by Mulgowie Aborigines in the Hawkesbury region in just retaliation for his habit of consorting with Aboriginal women and stealing the weaponry of Aboriginal men.[98] This verdict was welcomed by local Aborigines, who seemed to fear state-sponsored retaliation rather than incarceration for his murder.[99] And when the coroner announced that Branch Aborigines Mary Ann, Dick-Coohairy, Guttermatong, Munnijoy, Yaring, and another were guilty of murdering Richard Evans at Portland Head in 1813, no warrants were issued for their arrest. Rather, the coroner requested that local Aborigines bring the perpetrators in dead or alive.[100] The first case participates in shared expectations of reciprocity and retaliation: the coroner excused Luttril's murderers because Luttril had committed crimes punishable in both settler and indigenous society, namely wife-stealing or adultery. The second, perhaps as a matter of convenience rather than principle, defers to Aboriginal rights to arrest their kin or foes. Even if the state intended to try Mary and her accomplices, they could do so only with the cooperation of local Aborigines.

Scholars uniformly acknowledge that violence between Aborigines fell outside the jurisdiction of the colonial state before 1836. However, they also uniformly underplay the fact that colonial officials did not exercise jurisdiction over indigenous theft and violence against settlers, except to note in passing that state-sponsored violence was the usual response to sustained Aboriginal warfare in the peripheries.[101] In the process, they underestimate the plurality of settler sovereignty in early nineteenth-century New South Wales. Whether or not Britain should have or could have recognized Aboriginal sovereignty from within their Enlightenment legal *mentalité,* jurisdictional practice in New South Wales reveals a lost plural understanding of British sovereignty in New South Wales. As in early Georgia, the government of New South Wales did not equate settler sovereignty with territorial jurisdiction. Indigenous people marked the juridical boundaries of the colony.

The power and importance of this distinction is apparent in what is likely the only full trial of an Aborigine by a superior court in the first three decades of settlement: the trial and conviction of Mow-watty for raping a settler girl in "the vicinity of Parramatta" in September of 1816.[102] This case represents part of the Macquarie regime's aspiration to erode indigenous legal independence, yet it also shows the continuing and palpable limits of settler jurisdiction in New South Wales. First, the crime was a rape on a farm near the center of settlement—which, as the case of Tuskeegee Tustunnagau had shown in Georgia in 1798, always constituted a fundamental rupture in settler-indigenous relations. Second, court officers and witnesses went to great lengths to explain the legal exceptionality of the defendant. Witnesses testified that Mow-watty "was brought up in the families of Europeans" and had traveled in England "in the Service of Mr Kerry" before 1811. He had been known to Parramatta settlers for periods ranging from twelve to twenty years. Though Mow-watty was naked and lived in "the bush," in 1816 he worked on a Pennant Hills farm for his living. Robert Lowe Esq. attested that Mow-watty was "a sensible man; very intelligent, and ... much pleased with the manners and customs of Europeans." Most importantly, however, Mr. Blaxland deposed that Mow-watty knew of and abided by European laws as a matter of choice, not as a necessary accoutrement of British sovereignty:

> he had a clear conception between ... good and evil acts. ... [F]rom his constant habits he must be aware of any act that would give offence to our laws and usages; and upon those occasions where it had been found necessary to proscribe certain natives for their atrocities against the settlers, he had always shielded himself under the protection of the law by adhering to the habits in which he had been reared; he knew that crimes were punished by the law, and could not if he committed a crime be ignorant that he was doing wrong.[103]

In this reckoning, Mow-watty was tried and convicted in 1816 not because the British were sovereign in New South Wales, but because Mow-watty had personally accepted the legal protection of British law. Mow-watty's interpretation of this relationship is lost to history, but settlers themselves drew careful distinctions in his case between British sovereignty and the exercise of jurisdiction over indigenous crime. Just a few months later, the transportation of Duall for murder reaffirmed legal plurality even as it signaled change in the colony of New South Wales.

Shifting Boundaries

When Governor Lachlan Macquarie responded to sustained Aboriginal violence in the western borderlands of the colony in 1816, he responded with state-sponsored violence clothed, for the first time, in the language of law. Under his instructions, twenty-two Aborigines found their way into the jails of Sydney in 1816.[104] Never before had the colonial state incarcerated so many indigenous people. Yet even this mass-incarceration subordinated jurisdiction to diplomacy. Fifteen of those incarcerated were women and children held purely as hostages both to control information about the movement of troops and to encourage the surrender of Aborigines directly involved in depredations.[105] These prisoners fitted into a longer tradition of hostage taking and negotiation in New South Wales.

Times were changing, however. Macquarie did not release his hostages in return for the surrender of suspected murderers or the cessation of hostilities. Instead, he released most in honor of the King's Birthday—a celebration on which pardons were given and fêtes held for British prisoners of the Crown. Macquarie's diary entry about the incident is significant: he noted that he had "released all [but one of] the Black Native Prisoners who were some time since taken and confined in Jail on suspicion of being concerned in the recent Hostilities." A month in jail had transformed Macquarie's hostages into suspects. By extending the King's mercy to these Aborigines, along with convicts and criminals, Macquarie applied to them the words, but not the substance, of subjecthood and law.[106]

When his military regiments failed to capture many Aboriginal depredators, Macquarie, by outlawing ten named Aborigines, made his most radical appeal to settler jurisdiction.[107] Never before had a governor or law officer suggested unequivocally that Aborigines had been "in-lawed." For example, in May 1801, Governor King had specifically refrained from outlawing Aborigines for violence against settlers. Instead, King outlawed two convicts at the same time as he ordered retaliatory violence against the Aborigines with whom they were in league.[108]

In December of 1816, Macquarie ended hostilities by inviting outlawed Aborigines not already killed or apprehended to "surrender and give themselves up" so they could be "forgiven and pardoned for their past Offences, and taken under the Protection of the British Government in the colony."[109] His offer is a jumble of diplomacy and jurisdiction. He suggests here and elsewhere that Aborigines (whether outlawed or not) had yet to submit themselves to His Majesty's protection, and perhaps more importantly, that they had some corporate or individual choice in the matter. The King's pardon was offered here not as an exercise of jurisdiction, but as a reward for submitting to the King's law.[110]

Macquarie rounded off his awesome exhibition of ambivalence by transporting Duall from the colony without trial. According to his own accounts, Macquarie used the power "vested in" him to "remit the Punishment of Death, which his repeated Crimes and Offences had justly merited. . . . And commute the same into Banishment from this part of His Majesty's Territory of New South Wales to Port Dalrymple, in Van Diemen's Land, for the full Term of Seven years."[111] His sentence mimicked a term of transportation: convicts were, at least in popular parlance, "banished" from Britain for a term of years.[112] Duall was sentenced for his crimes, but not as the result of a recognizable exercise of criminal jurisdiction.

Macquarie's incoherence was not the result of error or inconsistency. It is an expression of his lost, historical moment. Macquarie was trapped in a paradigm of settler sovereignty that required the exemption of all but the most acculturated and willing Aborigines from settler law. Neither "sentence" nor "pardon" here were acts of territorial jurisdiction. Like his counterparts in Georgia, Macquarie stumbled toward a new, more perfect settler sovereignty. In 1816, however, he lacked the conceptual tools.

Nevertheless, Macquarie's efforts foreshadowed a change in jurisdictional practice. Proliferating discourses of perfect sovereignty filtered into jurisdictional practice for the first time in New South Wales in December 1822, when Hatherly and Jackie were tried before the Court of Criminal Jurisdiction for killing a stockman at Newcastle. All indications suggest that this was the first full trial of Aborigines for murder before a settler court. It seems also to be the first trial of an Aborigine not residing near and in some way bound to the center of the colony. All were sensible of its novelty. Judge Advocate Wylde even asked the new Governor Brisbane if the trial should be abandoned; apparently, Governor Brisbane thought not.[113]

The case itself devolved into a jurisdictional comedy because only indigenous evidence could prove that Hatherly and Jackie committed the murder. Hatherly and Jackie admitted to their involvement, each accusing the other of principal responsibility for the crime, but their testimony was inadmissible. The colonial state was thus caught in the noose of common-law testimony rules. Just as Judge Atkins had suggested in 1805, the Court of Criminal Jurisdiction could not convict, because it was enjoined to do so only on the basis of sworn evidence—evidence that no indigenous witness could provide. No pleas survive disputing the legality of this novel exercise of colonial jurisdiction over indigenous people. Perhaps in the very different legal environment of the 1820s, twenty-five years of diplomacy disappeared into law without demurrer. Legal contest over indigenous status in New South Wales would follow later.

Vast distance and difference separated early national Georgia from colonial New South Wales. Yet indigenous people in both places enjoyed practical jurisdictional exemption from state, federal, and colonial law before the 1820s. Despite the expansive claims to sovereignty and jurisdiction over territory enshrined in colonial charters and legislation, in the early nineteenth century the highest levels of settler government all tempered settler jurisdiction with plural logics of reciprocity, retaliation, and diplomacy.[114]

Before the War of 1812, long practice and gap-ridden formal pluralism in Georgia bound the state's executive, its courts, and federal agents into a discourse of retaliation and reciprocity with indigenous people even as the new state (and, to a lesser degree, the new federation) tried to mark out its sovereignty through meticulously defined jurisdictional boundaries. In the colony of New South Wales, officials in London and Sydney did not treat with local Aborigines, but this failure did not translate into the extension of jurisdiction over Aboriginal violence. Instead, officials at every level of the colonial state resolved conflict by applying the same older and shared logics as their counterparts in Georgia.

Georgia and New South Wales, in short, show the flexibility of nineteenth-century understandings of sovereignty. When dealing with indigenous-settler violence, their practice was suspended between jurisdiction and diplomacy. This was no mere convenience: it indicated more than ignorance of law. It stemmed from a passing moment in the history of settler sovereignty that spanned the Pacific Ocean. Neither policy makers nor settlers understood settler sovereignty to imply unfettered territorial jurisdiction in the early nineteenth century. Instead, together with indigenous people, they crafted and practiced plural jurisdiction, the boundaries of which were policed by governments, settlers, and indigenous people in the centers and peripheries of settlement.

CHAPTER THREE

Indigenous Jurisdiction and Spatial Order

NDIGENOUS PEOPLE PLAYED a central role in the articulation of sovereignty as a territorial measure of authority in Georgia and New South Wales. This was so in part because they insisted that plural legal orders governed British and American settlements of the early nineteenth century. They traversed settler boundaries, governed settlers in ungovernable places, and exercised jurisdiction over indigenous transgressions in the towns, the highways, and the byways of Anglophone settlements. Indigenous jurisdiction (the binding authority of indigenous customary law), overlaid, supplemented, and undermined the early stirrings of territoriality in Georgia and New South Wales.

Two very different stories exemplify the contested reach of indigenous customary law in Georgia and New South Wales. The first is the case of Cormick and Olive v. the Cherokee Nation, which involved none other than Ellis Buffington, the same Cherokee who killed Jacob Witworth in Jackson County in 1812. Buffington intervened in a dispute between two Georgians—a creditor and a debtor—traveling through the Cherokee Nation on the Federal Road. The ensuing quasi-legal proceedings generated some of the richest settler insights into the nature and limits of indigenous jurisdiction in Indian Country in the early national period. In New South Wales, the pervasive reach of indigenous jurisdiction can be traced in Governor Macquarie's Proclamation of 1816—a document that acknowledged the fact of legal pluralism in early New South Wales even as it wished it away from settler towns.

In this period, most scholars argue that indigenous jurisdictions experienced inevitable decline in the American southeast, and existed only as a logical anomaly in Australia. However, a closer look at jurisdictional practice in Georgia and New South Wales reveals something much more complex. In these places, indigenous jurisdiction had an important if contingent place within and outside settler legal orders. In New South Wales, indigenous people met and fought in the most intimate of settler spaces—early Sydney. In Georgia, contest centered instead on who had the right to adjudicate settler misdeeds in Indian Country and in its liminal places—frontier counties and the federal roads.

In both places, indigenous jurisdiction governed people and/or places in amorphous, poorly understood but necessary ways—ways at odds with emerging nineteenth-century understandings of settler sovereignty premised on exercises of territorial jurisdiction. Indeed, at remarkably similar junctures, settler administrators and judges in North America and Australasia began to understand indigenous jurisdiction as a threat to settler sovereignty. They started to see indigenous jurisdiction as a breach in the increasingly inflexible banks of territorial right. Though one was a colony, both Georgia and New South Wales began to adhere to a modern notion of statehood that required the displacement or extinction of indigenous jurisdiction. The stories told here hold the promise and the threat of indigenous jurisdiction in the same breath. They illustrate the modernity of territorial sovereignty.

The Case of Olive, Wheeler, and Cormick

In late 1810, Charles Wheeler set off from Georgia with eleven slaves, five or six horses, and two saddlebags full of money: a pretty cache of property to be driving through the woods.[1] He followed a road through the Cherokee Nation stretching from Jackson County, Georgia, to Knoxville, Tennessee—one of several carved out by the Cherokee in accordance with treaties and informal agreements spanning 1791 to 1805.[2] Wheeler left behind him secured and unsecured debts that exceeded $30,000.[3] United States embargos on British trade to the American South had a devastating impact on the southern economy, ruining Wheeler and eroding the value of the land he had mortgaged. So he packed up his worldly possessions—cash, horses, humans—and set off for a new life in the Mississippi territory, beyond the ken, if not the reach, of Georgia law.[4]

Naturally, Wheeler's creditors followed. James Olive and John Strother sped after him down the path. Olive carried with him some documents proving his mortgage over Wheeler's slaves. Strother carried no power of attorney, and had only copies of notes proving Wheeler's extremely large debt to a well-connected businessman named John Cormick. On their way, Olive and Strother convinced some Cherokees to join the chase—persuading them that the Cherokee Nation would be liable to compensate Wheeler's creditors if it suffered such a vast amount of property to be smuggled out of Georgia through its territory. With their help, Olive and Strother overtook Wheeler. Wheeler, his property, and his pursuers then returned to Buffington's Inn, where they planned to spend the night before returning to Georgia.

While the party was lodged at Buffington's Inn, it gave Wheeler's property to Buffington for safekeeping, or Buffington took it. The next morning, Buffington demanded that Olive and Strother prove their claim on Wheeler's debts. Olive showed his mortgage, and Strother departed the nation to obtain better proof and a power of attorney from Cormick. Olive and Wheeler agreed to remain with the property at Buffington's Inn until Strother's return. In the meantime, however, Buffington returned the disputed property to Wheeler and sped him on his way to the Mississippi Territory. These events have three possible explanations: (1) Dissatisfied both with Olive's proofs and Strother's delay, and increasingly suspicious of all parties involved in the transaction, Buffington regretted his interference and sent Wheeler on to Mississippi. (2) Olive and Wheeler "drank together" and negotiated. Wheeler gave Olive better proof of his debts, and in return, Olive agreed to let Wheeler go.[5] They announced to Buffington that they had reached an agreement and that Wheeler had Olive's express consent to continue on his journey. This way, they hoped, Wheeler could keep his property and Olive and Cormick could fraudulently seek redress from the Cherokee Nation. Wheeler's property, after all, could not meet his debts, but with a bit of creative testimony, the Cherokee annuity might. (3) Alternatively, according to Olive's testimony, Wheeler bribed Buffington and others to take his property from Olive and to prevent Olive from following Wheeler down the road.

Olive and Cormick tried to recover all of Wheeler's debts from the Cherokee. They tested their claims before two arbitration committees assembled by the federal agent in the Cherokee Nation. The first, in 1811, commanded the Cherokee to pay James Olive $2,200 for his lost slaves but denied Cormick any remedy (scenario 3). The second, in 1812, again refused to grant Cormick any of the money he claimed on the grounds either that Buffington had not taken the property forcibly, or that Olive, Wheeler, and possibly Cormick had conspired to defraud the Cherokee (scenario 1 or 2). In the process of reaching these wildly inconsistent decisions, these arbitration commissions were forced to grapple with the relationship of settler sovereignty and indigenous jurisdiction.

Had Buffington stopped Wheeler or divested Olive of possession of his property on a highway in the ordinary jurisdiction of Georgia, he would have been a highwayman or a tortfeasor, no matter how pure his intentions to act as judge and arbiter of Wheeler's, Olive's, and Cormick's claim. Context and content, however, changed the nature of Buffington's act entirely. In Indian Country, Buffington's act barely registered as a wrong. Unless Buffington had stolen the property, no treaty required his surrender for trial in Georgia, and even if it had, no statute provided a procedure by which Olive and Cormick could recover. The Cherokee agreed to compensate Olive if he was "a good man."[6] So Cormick and Olive had to convince the Cherokee and a commission of settlers constituted with Cherokee consent that Buffington had acted unjustly. Justice depended in part on Cherokee construction, not least because the wrong in question was committed by a Cherokee on Cherokee land. This was the case unless Cormick and Olive could show that the Federal Road was a place of jurisdictional exception in Indian Country.

Cherokee and Creek customary laws were fluid.[7] They were comprised of broadly related but distinct customary legal regimes. First and foremost, they were rapidly evolving systems. Both the Cherokee and Creek Nations were "shatter zone" societies, emerging from the rapid decline of Mississippian mound-building cultures in the face of European diseases introduced by the Spanish and French from the sixteenth century.[8] By the early nineteenth century, 150 years of trade and intermarriage had wrought significant changes in Cherokee and, to a lesser extent, Creek society. Most importantly, they gave rise to a new culturally hybrid elite that sought to recast legal and social order in Indian Country.[9]

Cherokee jurisdiction changed enormously between the early eighteenth and early nineteenth centuries. Until 1810, clans regulated all interpersonal relationships, ranging from property disputes to homicide. The latter was dealt with by blood revenge—the death or injury of the perpetrator or their kin. Community issues like diplomacy, war, and peace were dealt with by town councils, though their decisions were not binding. These forums dispensed some public punishments for individual transgressions, including shaming, ostracism, and scratching.[10] Personal grievances short of murder were renounced and absolved every year at a Green Corn ceremony.[11]

By the early national period, in direct response to colonialism—and with it the rise of mixed-race elites in the Cherokee Nation—the town council of Chota became a National Council with considerable influence. With centralization came innovation: the creation of a constabulary (light-horse brigade) and magistracy (1799), the abolition of blood revenge (1810), the publication and promulgation of laws (1816), and the institution of a territorial judicial system (1820).[12] Evidence suggests, however, that despite these reforms, most Cherokees continued to resolve interpersonal disputes and wrongs according to kin-based customary law.[13]

Creek jurisdiction changed according to a different meter. Despite colonization and intermarriage, clan and town remained the coordinates of Creek juridical identity throughout the first decades of the nineteenth century, so exile was the ultimate punishment. Though matrilineal clans managed most interpersonal disputes, town councils administered "punishments such as scratching and whipping . . . for bad behavior and as correctives to the young."[14] The Creek National Council met once a year during Benjamin Hawkins's tenure as federal agent at Tuckabatchee or Coweta.[15] Under Hawkins's tutelage, the National Council attempted to establish jurisdiction over interpersonal disputes in the nation: it revoked blood revenge, devised punishments for theft and murder, and created a "warrior police" under the supervision of a "warrior magistrate." Its decrees, however, had little impact and were nonbinding.[16]

By and large, fundamental principles of retribution and reciprocity underlay customary law in and between the Cherokee and Creek Nations in the pre-Removal period—as they did much of settler criminal law.[17] And, of course, these principles also underpinned state-federal-indigenous discussions about diplomacy and jurisdiction, at least until the War of 1812. For Georgia, then, indigenous jurisdiction was not merely savage and alien; to some degree it was also intimate and inherent.

However, the reach of indigenous jurisdiction is most apparent in the very paucity of settler law in and around Indian Country. Before the 1820s, indigenous jurisdiction in Georgia's borderlands was both personal and territorial in nature. All indigenous transgressions against indigenous people fell within indigenous jurisdiction, wherever they were committed. Neither Georgia's imagination of settler sovereignty nor the patchy fabric of federal statute and treaty law comprehended control over indigenous conflict in settler space.

Inside the Indian boundaries—in Indian Country—indigenous torts, breaches of contract, or anything short of capital crime fell entirely outside the purview of treaty or federal law. Article 6 of the Treaty of Hopewell (Cherokee 1785),[18] Article 10 of the Treaty of Holston (Cherokee 1791),[19] and Article 8 of the Treaty of New York (Creek 1790)[20] required the Cherokee and Creek Nations only to "deliver up" indigenous people who "shall steal a horse from, or commit a robbery or murder, or other capital crime" on "citizens or inhabitants of the United States" for trial. Federal legislation, however, did not provide a procedure by which indigenous wrongs against settlers in Indian Country could be compensated, let alone tried in a settler court.[21]

Nevertheless compensation became the normal remedy for wrongs committed by Indians in Indian Country. This was so in part because the federal government simply withheld funds to meet claims from annuities owed by treaty. Compensation also fit neatly into the normative framework of Creek and Cherokee law.[22] As in Olive's case, Indian nations agreed to compensate injured settlers. In 1811, however, it was far from clear that Buffington had committed a compensable wrong. According to most accounts, he had done his best to do justice between the parties to preserve himself and the tribe from harm.

Indeed, in one frame, Buffington's was a legitimate act of jurisdiction over settler-sojourners in Indian Country. Buffington might not have had any authority to adjudicate settler disputes in the Cherokee Nation as a matter of Cherokee National, town, or clan law, but some testimony suggested that the parties had invited him to adjudicate their claims, by giving him their property for safekeeping while they stayed at his inn on the Federal Road. At the very least they had acquiesced to his judgment: when prompted, Olive offered proof of his charge over Wheeler's property, and Strother left the nation to fetch proof of Cormick's claim.

The status of settler-sojourners under law and treaty confirms that Indian Country was both a place of territorial exception and a place of overlapping jurisdictions. Article 7 of the Treaty of Hopewell, Article 11 of the Treaty of Holston, Article 9 of the Treaty of New York, and Section 4 of the Trade and Intercourse Act of 1802 purported to govern settler crimes and settler trade in Indian Country. The treaties required that settlers committing crimes against indigenous people should be given up for trial in a state or federal court. They assumed, in short, that Indian nations had jurisdiction enough to arrest and hand over wrongdoers. The Act gave jurisdiction to federal courts to punish and to compensate for settler crimes against indigenous people in Indian country.[23] Within this scheme, settler torts and breaches of contract as well as their crimes against other settlers had no statutory remedy whatever.

Their status was further complicated by Article 8 of the Treaty of Holston and by Article 6 of the Treaty of New York, which provided that "If any citizen of the United States, or other person not being an Indian, shall settle on any of the [Cherokee or Creek] lands, such person shall forfeit the protection of the United States, and the Cherokees [or Creeks] may punish him or not, as they please." These articles created a whole and growing category of settlers who might fall outside federal law.[24]

Finally, long-held convention suggested that long-term residents of Indian Country were subject to indigenous jurisdiction. The persistence of settler "residence" and "membership" in the Cherokee Nation is evident in the Removal era, when it became important to ascertain who was entitled to benefit under the Removal treaties.[25]

Practice made settler status even more uncertain. When the Creek Nation agreed in 1799 to give agent Benjamin Hawkins control over settlers in the nation, Hawkins understood that he exercised delegated Creek jurisdiction, not federal authority.[26] In a letter to Thomas Jefferson, he noted:

> As the Creeks are an independent nation I shall go in to dispense justice among white and black people according to the authority vested in me . . . until I am otherwise directed by our Government or that Congress can legislate on the subject.[27]

Even after 1799, the tribe continued to assert that a variety of settler activities were governed by Creek law. White traders marrying Creek women continued in the early national period to live and work within the matrilineal clans.[28] Hawkins noted that they suffered many of the burdens and few of the benefits of membership in Creek society.[29]

Hawkins supervised the trials of a number of settlers by the Creek National Council. In 1799, Hawkins reported that the Council ordered the whipping of a "white man . . . for negro stealing."[30] In 1806, the National Council tried a slave owned by a settler for killing an Indian woman. The same "court" tried two "white men, part of a banditti forming in this quarter to live by theft, charged with stealing a valuable mare from a traveler"—a procedure hailed by Hawkins as the first fair trial in the nation.[31] Though Green and Ethridge both argue that the Creek National Council was a creature of federal imperialism, it nevertheless dispensed, and was understood by settlers to dispense, Creek jurisdiction over settlers. Creek Country, in Hawkins's view, was an entirely separate jurisdictional space:

> Altho' the United States have legislated on certain characters within the Indian Country, I cannot suppose they have on native Indians for transactions within the Indian Country . . . they can only be bound in a national capacity for Offences against the law of Nations.[32]

Cherokee jurisdiction lacked a champion like Hawkins.[33] Under Meigs's jealous eye, it was exercised over settlers more apologetically, if more endemically, before 1812.[34] In 1801, the tribe claimed the right, under Section 14 of the Trade and Intercourse Laws, to retaliate against a settler who had killed a Cherokee woman if he was not tried promptly by Tennessee courts. Here, they asserted that their jurisdiction over settlers was defined not by territory but by the failure of the federal or state government to do justice. Curiously, Meigs noted, the nation offered to "wait Eighteen months [for satisfaction], having reference to the language of the 14th Section of the Intercourse Law, which they seemed to think would apply to them in such cases."[35]

In 1808, the Cherokee chief John Lowry beat Jessey Huddlestone for trying to convince Lowry's slave to go with him "to the Spanerds and he wold set hur free." After confronting, confining and releasing Huddlestone, Lowry concealed himself with Cherokee witnesses to gather "plain proof" of Huddlestone's transgressions. He then "tide them both up and Whuped them." In this account, charges were laid, evidence gathered, and justice done. Lowry defended his violence as a legitimate exercise of indigenous jurisdiction over United States citizens residing in the Cherokee Nation on two legal grounds. He claimed that "when a man lives in the nation" it is necessary "for him to abide By the laws of the nation." In whipping Huddlestone, Lowry protested, "we only giv him the Law of the nation." Alternatively Lowry argued that Huddlestone's crime was punishable under the law of nations. Huddlestone, he argued, "is a grand Villen" and "I think that all Villens aut to bee Punished let them be in what Cuntery thay may."[36] These acts of jurisdiction over settler transgressions suggest that the Cherokee themselves were unclear about the reach of their jurisdiction over settler crime. In 1801, the tribe used the procedure of the Trade and Intercourse law to justify blood revenge. In 1808, Lowry used due process (gathering evidence), Cherokee law, and the law of nations to justify whipping Huddlestone for attempted slave theft.

The Cherokee Council was more self-assured in 1810 when, in one of its more explicit acts of jurisdiction, it pardoned William Reed for killing U.S. citizen Henry McGhee in a part of the Cherokee Nation falling within the charted boundaries of Georgia.[37] The Council informed Meigs that "the several clans composed in the Cherokee people have passed an act of oblivion for lives amongst us and we have thought proper to include William Reed resident in our country for the Crime which he has been charged with." "Pardon" was Meigs's term.[38] It was apt, nevertheless, because William Reed was never charged in state or federal court for his crime, though some vigilantes in South Carolina gave him trouble in 1811.[39] Similarly, when a settler called Owen beat John Tally in the Cherokee Nation in 1813, the nation determined that Owen was a "white man amenable to the laws of the nation" and offered compensation to his victim "as a peace offering" for his injuries.[40]

In this frame, Ellis Buffington's intervention into the affairs of Charles Wheeler, James Olive, and John Cormick at his inn on the Federal Road might also be read as an uncertain act of Cherokee jurisdiction over settlers in the nation. This, indeed, was the understanding of the first board of commissioners assembled in the nation to decide whether the Cherokee should indemnify Olive and Cormick. The first board accepted evidence that Buffington had wrongfully divested Olive of Wheeler's property. However, it determined Cherokee liability on the basis that Buffington should and could have weighed and judged the settlers' claims. The Commission found that Buffington "assisted" Wheeler "to violate "his promise . . . well established to $2200" and to other monies "not yet fully proven" by wrongfully taking Olive's property and assisting Wheeler's escape. In contrast, Cormick's claim could not be supported in evidence:

> The said Strother had nothing but copies of the Notes without a power of attorney, and had to leave the property to return to Georgia, for better evidence, and was not in possession of the property when it was rescued and as we have nothing before us but copies of the Notes and the affidavit of Cobb that is doubtful whether the Nation ought to indemnify Cormick, as it is not probable that the Indians or Nation had much of the means to investigate Cormicks Claim, and as the vouchers Strother had . . . would not have authorized in a Court of equity, or Court of Law.[41]

Although the Commission hesitated to apply formal rules of evidence to Strother and Cormick, it decided that they had some obligation to prove Cormick's claim to Buffington and the Cherokee.[42] The first commission assumed, in short, that even if Buffington neglected to do so, as a Cherokee in Cherokee Country, he could and should have weighed the evidence of Olive and Strother's debt and made a just (and legal) adjudication of the parties' rights.

The second court was less certain about Cherokee jurisdiction, focusing instead on whether Buffington took the property forcibly from Olive, and whether he had been defrauded into doing so by Olive and Wheeler. The commission's focus on whether Buffington took property forcibly may have been an attempt to construe his acts as a capital crime for the purposes of the Treaty of Holston or merely as a compensable wrong in the Cherokee's normative frame.[43] In his notes on the second case, Meigs highlights jurisdictional uncertainty, citing Cherokee credulity and their insecurity about the reach of their own authority as the cause of their unfortunate predicament.[44]

In the plural universe of Georgia's indigenous borderlands before 1812, an unstable form of indigenous jurisdiction followed settlers in the

Indian nations, on their highways, and sometimes beyond. It was an indeterminately personal and territorial order that shows the flexibility of early nineteenth-century settler sovereignty. Settlers could disappear from the purview of the state of Georgia without leaving its charted boundaries. Even on a public highway, settlers might be stopped by Creek or Cherokee brigands or even be subjected to Cherokee justice without remedy under treaty or statute. Just as indigenous jurisdiction over indigenous crime spilled out of Indian Country into Georgia's ordinary jurisdiction, so settler contracts forged and broken in Georgia might be adjudicated by Indians under indigenous jurisdiction in the state of Georgia. In this moment, before the articulation of perfect settler sovereignty, the juridical boundaries of the state of Georgia were marked by the crimes and contracts of indigenous people. These marked the jurisdictional limits of the state.

Commissions of Arbitration

At the same time, indigenous jurisdiction was a field of intense imperialism. This is nowhere more apparent than in the two commissions of inquiry that sat in the Cherokee Nation in 1811 and 1812 to determine Olive's and Cormick's claims. The first commission was convened in 1811, and was staffed by Meigs, his assistant William Lovely, Enoch Parsons (later attorney general of Tennessee), Nicholas Byars, and Azariah David JP. The fact that the commission heard Cherokee evidence and was presided over by Return J. Meigs suggests that the hearing was held in the nation, likely with Cherokee consent.[45] As such its most likely character was that of a contractual arbitration, though it might also have been conceived of as a delegated exercise of Cherokee jurisdiction.

According to the Secretary of War, William Eustis, its determinations were final.[46] By 1812, however, Cormick was claiming $33,032 from the Cherokee and Eustis's resolve wavered.[47] This enormous sum included interest, the $6,100 worth of horses and cash that Wheeler reputedly carried through the nation, and the depreciation of the assets Wheeler had mortgaged to Cormick in Georgia. In short, as Meigs noted, though Wheeler's whereabouts were well known in Mississippi, Cormick sought to indemnify both his secured and his unsecured loans against Cherokee annuity. Cormick sought to make the Cherokees

> reinstate the value of property in Georgia which had been depreciated by the Attrocious injustice of the British Government. . . . This whole pursuit is founded in fiction or a perversion of the real facts by vicious construction

on such grounds they have calculated to take many thousand dollars from the Cherokees who have few friends & no ability to defend themselves.[48]

It is even less clear by what authority the second board sat. It was comprised of Michael Hays, John Cosby, James Cosby, W. D. Francis, and Meigs—a less illustrious and legally minded crew, but nevertheless men of consequence, including a medical doctor and at least one militia officer. This commission called a much longer list of witnesses before dismissing Cormick's claim by a very slim margin. The board was divided. Some found that there was no remedy because Buffington had done no wrong. Others decided that though Buffington had "forcibly taken" property from Olive, Cormick could not recover because Olive had conspired with Wheeler to defraud the Cherokee Nation.

Inquiries like these were hosted by the federal agents in both the Creek and Cherokee Nations often before the War of 1812 and at key moments after it.[49] As Section 14 of the Trade and Intercourse Act only authorized the agent to investigate indigenous-settler crime in the ordinary jurisdiction of the state, in these cases the agent acted as a diplomat, investigating claims not governed by statute or treaty. Their primary role was to investigate claims arising between settlers and indigenous people about the theft of property or broken promises.[50]

Much of the business settled by federal agents pertained to disputes arising in Indian Country itself. However, some also pertained to violence and theft in frontier counties,[51] or to torts or breaches of contract in Georgia, the Mississippi territory, or Tennessee.[52] Slave property was particularly contentious because indigenous adoption rules and later their own slaveholding created serious disincentives to return escapees to Georgia.[53] The federal agents drew disputes out of federal and state courts into Indian Country to fill gaps in common law process—to supplement settler law. In these alternative and hybrid forums, indigenous people had full rights to defend themselves, to seek remedies against settlers (less often), and perhaps most importantly, to testify. In 1805, Hawkins rebuffed attempts by the attorney general to formalize investigations in Indian Country under Sections 4 and 14 of the Trade and Intercourse Act on the grounds that formal rules of evidence would exclude indigenous testimony.[54] Return J. Meigs made the same point to the secretary of war in 1812, when he protested Georgia's demand to have Buffington and Daniel surrendered to Georgia for trial for the murder of Jacob Witworth in Jackson County.[55]

The very process of garnering evidence, passing judgment, and awarding compensation constituted a radical act of legal imperialism—the imposition of modified common-law process in Indian Country. Common-law process was itself imbued with hybrid notions of reciprocity and retaliation. However, in Creek and Cherokee Country, it combined with the rise of mixed-race elites to subtly transform the way that indigenous people understood property and the rights that attached to property, as well as crime and punishment.[56] So in 1802, when a Creek Indian killed a Georgian constable named Moreland and then escaped into Creek Country, the nation offered to put a relative of the killer to death to sate the blood debt owed by the Creeks to the state. The killer himself was being concealed by a powerful chief, so they offered instead "according to Indian rule . . . a bad man" who was "somewhat instrumental in . . . [the killer's] escape. . . . This man is now here and can be executed immediately, or delivered up as Col. Hawkins will direct." The offer, however, was made "with some apprehensions from the doctrine of Col. Hawkins on guilt and innocence." Hawkins responded with his own syncretism: he rejected the life of the "worthless" "Succuh Haujo" and demanded instead the life of the "three great Chiefs" who failed to arrest the killer himself.[57]

Also in 1802, on Meigs's request, James Vann took "depositions" from two Cherokees "being solemnly called on . . . to speak the truth in the presence of the Great Spirit," to attest to the innocence of Stone, a Cherokee held in a Nashville jail.[58] In an effort to reassert their own jurisdiction over indigenous theft in Cherokee Country, the chiefs also promised to try Stone "according to the Law of this Country."[59] The impact of legal imperialism in Cherokee Country is even more evident in the 1812 controversy over Buffington's brawl in Jackson County. Though Buffington's family argued that Witworth's death satisfied a blood debt owed by the state to the Cherokee, the Cherokee National Council argued that Buffington and Daniel's crime should be met with settler-style justice instead of shared notions of retaliation:

> These barbarous acts were committed by *Individuals,* of our, & your people; and it is our desire that the perpetrators should be brought to fair trial; & that the *individuals* only should be punished; and that these unhappy events shall not be chargeable on your people at large; or on our people; who are innocent.[60]

Olive and Cormick v. Cherokee Nation illustrates a legal imperialism both more subtle and more pervasive. All parties retained counsel. Cormick and Olive were represented by Mr. Cobb, while the Cherokee or Return J. Meigs employed Edward Scott and William Kelly to represent the Cherokee for the 1812 hearings.[61] The commission formally called witnesses to attend the trial (adopting the form of a subpoena).[62] More importantly, the commissioners themselves used common law and equity as primary determinants in their evaluation of evidence. The first commission argued that Cormick could not recover because the proofs of debt presented to Buffington by Strother on his behalf "could not have authorised in a Court of equity, or Court of law," though they acknowledged that "all the technical formality adhered to in Courts of Justice" should not be required to prove a debt outside a court because "equity forbids and Common Law and common sense revolts at the idea." Formal standards of proof and informal exceptions to them both, here, used settler law as their compass.

In this case, however, legal imperialism cut both ways. In the end, investigation, sworn testimony, adversarial disputation, and written judgments all vindicated Cherokee rights. The first commission endorsed the Cherokees' right to inquire into the affairs of settlers in the nation. The second embraced Cherokee evidence of a monstrous fraud against a people "whose only crime is the want of ability to judge the respective rights of" Cormick, Olive, and Wheeler.[63] Legal imperialism here gave indigenous words power over settlers in Indian Country. It also constituted a partial vindication of indigenous jurisdiction, even as it subordinated indigenous law to common law procedure.

Federal Roads in Indian Country

At the heart of the dispute in Olive and Cormick v. Cherokee Nation, however, lay a deeper conundrum: how to characterize Cherokee Country and the federal roads that bisected it. Cherokee Country covered parts of Tennessee, North Carolina, and Georgia in 1811. Indian Country was a juridically disorderly space that unsteadied settler jurisdiction on both sides of its boundaries. As noted, settlers could not be taxed, mustered, arrested, or sued in Indian Country before 1814. Most importantly, perhaps, Creek and Cherokee Country together cut Georgia off from its hinterlands, preventing the transportation of valuable commodities from farms in the southwest through Georgia's ports and back.[64]

This context explains the fierce contest over federal roads. Federal roads provided access through Indian Country. These were truly liminal places: hard-won paths of free passage linking Georgia with Tennessee and the Mississippi Territory.[65] Under some of the agreements signed with the Cherokee and Creek between 1791 and 1806, the Indian nations undertook to maintain and to provide services for travelers on federal roads.[66] More roads were opened through a mixture of bullying and compensation as war approached in 1811 and 1812.[67] These paths formed arteries of settlement and expansion—facilitating, perhaps more than any other factor, the demographic explosion of the old southwest.[68]

Contest over who could order the roads was physical and legal. Disgruntled Creeks stopped settlers on the road, allowing only trade goods and traders through the nation.[69] Disgruntled Cherokees stopped miners on the road, protesting the sale or lease of national assets to settler entrepreneurs.[70] Disgruntled settlers sought the orderly transit of goods and people.[71] To this end, travelers themselves became advocates of jurisdictional imperialism in this hybrid and contentious space—a role that, as we shall see, settlers did not always embrace.[72] On the roads, more than anywhere else in Indian Country, Creeks and Cherokees had to define and defend their jurisdiction over indigenous theft and violence.[73]

The jurisdictional problem of the roads is evident in their name, their legal classification, as well as their vital economic function. By 1811, the sheer bulk of goods and people who traversed the roads made them sites of special jeopardy. The designation "federal" indicates their part in a project of nationalization undertaken by Presidents Washington, Adams, and Jefferson between 1789 and 1809 and continued on a grander scale with the aid of federal money from the War of 1812 to 1837.[74] Federal authority to make roads in states was fiercely contested. Most recent accounts focus on Jacksonian debates over who would pay for roads.[75] However, anti-federalists in the first quarter of the nineteenth century also feared that federal military and post roads in states would "increase the jurisdiction of congress over the territory of the state."[76] Their fears were well founded. In May of 1822, Congress passed a bill to levy tolls on the Cumberland Road—a bill vetoed by James Monroe on the grounds that "Congress lacked constitutional authority to exercise jurisdiction over internal improvements."[77] By 1894 the attorney general of the United States acknowledged the right of the federal army to "keep [military roads] unobstructed and available for military purposes," including railroads traversing states.[78] Roads threatened to be arteries of jurisdiction as well as commerce, war, and communication, eroding the sovereignty of the states.

The primary threat to state sovereignty in 1811 came not from the presence but the absence of federal jurisdiction over Indian roads. First, federal treaties guaranteeing "free and unmolested use" provided no clear right of redress for minor crimes and torts and no procedure to obtain compensation for major crimes committed on the roads, not least because it was unclear whose law governed them. Second, before 1811 it was unclear whether "free and unmolested use" even allowed settlers to use the roads without first obtaining a passport—documents issued by a governor or the Indian agent, giving a right of passage through Indian land.[79] One informal agreement between the Cherokee and the federal agent stipulated that

> Article 3rd . . . The United States shall make such regulations as may be found proper to prevent persons from evading the payment of ferriage, or toll, and shall fix the rates of ferriage & toll according to custom in such cases.
>
> Article 4th In order to prevent disorders from being communicated to the Cherokee live Stock, no Neat Cattle from the Southern States shall be driven through the said Nation, and in order to prevent the Stealing of Horses, or purchasing them without license, or other impositions affecting the Horses and Cattle of the Cherokees, a description of Horses and Cattle, and their number shall be inserted in the passports of those persons who may be taking them through the said nation, and the Cherokees shall not be answerable for estrays [strays] from the citizens of the United States on said road.[80]

This agreement in 1803 implies that free passage on the Federal Road through the Cherokee Nation was fettered both by tolls and by passports. In contrast, Section 19 of the Trade and Intercourse Act (1802) stipulated that unless "the Indians object," even paths through Indian Country established by custom, rather than treaty, could be traveled without a passport.[81] If federal roads were construed as zones of free passage without passports, then in some senses they were less constrained by state and federal law than the rest of Indian Country. They were places where anyone and anything could go.

In contrast, the very limits placed on Cherokee liability for "estrays" in the agreement of 1803 indicate that roads were also places of jurisdictional aspiration where settler-travelers sought order and redress at the expense of the Cherokee. As the Cormick and Olive case shows, settlers sought corporate redress from the Cherokee Nation, not from individual Indian wrongdoers. This was an artifact of federal-Indian treaties through which the Cherokee Nation pledged to pay compensation for the wrongs of its members. However, it also suggests that federal roads fell within the sphere of Indian jurisdiction—a conclusion supported by an 1811 federal court case that held that Georgia settlers could not be prosecuted under federal or state law for killing other settlers on federal roads in Indian Country.[82] In this place of qualified free passage, federal and state control over entry was uncertain, federal jurisdiction was severely limited, and the corporate responsibility of the Cherokee for the actions of individual Indians was tentatively presumed.

The Cormick and Olive case reflected this uncertainty. Before it could determine Cherokee liability, the first commission had to determine the jurisdictional status of the road. It found that "in cases of this kind no passport was necessary in order to travel the Federal or public road through the Nation, nor was the Intercourse Law violated by Olive and Strother to follow Wheeler along said road."[83]

Yet it went on to find that Buffington had the right, according to the standards of common law and equity, to judge the claims of Olive and Cormick to Wheeler's property. On the basis of this finding, Olive instructed Cormick to look into "Indian Laws." He counseled Cormick to investigate "their relation to, or connexion with, our Government, and particularly our rights on the Federal road."[84]

Cormick demanded that the secretary of war meet his claim by stopping the Cherokee annuity on the grounds that federal roads formed a special spatial category of federal jurisdiction and of corporate indigenous liability in Indian Country. If, as the commission found, Olive and Strother needed no passport on the Federal Road, and their detention of Wheeler's property was not lawful under state or federal law, "then it must have been unlawful for the Indians to rescue it." He also contested Buffington's jurisdiction to weigh evidence of Wheeler's debts: "surely the Indians were not to be the judges."[85] According to Cormick, in this place of exception, federal or state laws applied.[86] Under Section 14 of the Trade and Intercourse Act (governing indigenous wrongs in state jurisdiction) Buffington's intervention was a crime or a tort compensable under settler law.

The refusal of the War Office to pay Cormick from the Cherokee annuity suggests that it was unwilling to assert that the Federal Road was a zone of exclusive federal jurisdiction. On the eve of the 1812 war, the War Department needed the cooperation of indigenous people and states in the construction of federal roads, cooperation likely to be withheld if federal roads carried the promise of exclusive federal jurisdiction over Indians and settlers. Meantime, it is unclear whether the second commission held in the Cherokee Nation in December 1812 agreed or disagreed with Cormick's jurisdictional arguments. Its focus on whether Buffington took Wheeler's property forcibly from Olive did not rest on the jurisdictional categorization of the road as federal, state, or Indian space. Federal roads remained a jurisdictional conundrum at the end of 1812.[87]

In the early nineteenth century, indigenous jurisdiction overlaid and undermined territorial order in Georgia, spilling over its boundaries with Indian traders and carousers and drawing Georgians into Indian Country to attend hybrid arbitrations. In this context, federal roads were a space of jurisdictional aspiration and jurisdictional liminality—an unsightly reminder of the incompleteness of this Anglophone settler sovereignty. They are contested to this day. A number of recent cases in the United States have defined federal roads as arteries not only of commerce but of state jurisdiction in modern-day Indian Country.[88] Cormick and Olive's dispute shows what was at stake, then and now. Federal roads promised and failed to temper the insistent plurality of Indian Country. They were more fiercely contested than any other space in the early nineteenth-century South.

In this way, the encounter of Buffington, Olive, and Wheeler on the Federal Road binds the formal pluralism of Georgia's Indian Country into a settler story about the rise of territoriality—a story that includes the very different colony of New South Wales. Both places, at very similar times, began to grapple with the disjunct between their growing territorial aspirations and the fact of legal pluralism. Cormick and Olive waged their jurisdictional assault on the Federal Road through Cherokee Country in 1811 and 1812. In 1816, Lachlan Macquarie battled for some semblance of spatial order in the center of Sydney.

Aboriginal Jurisdiction in the Empty Continent

In his Proclamation of May 1816, Governor Macquarie did a number of notable things.[89] He declared war on the frontiers of New South Wales after three years of escalating indigenous-settler violence and invited Aboriginal families to give up their wandering ways and to settle under the protection of the Crown. Most importantly, Macquarie's 1816 Proclamation set up a series of unprecedented and unstable boundaries of spatial authority that at once recognized and tried to control legal pluralism in the colony of New South Wales.

The Proclamation declared first, that "no Black Native, or Body of Black Natives shall ever appear at or within one Mile of any Town, Village, or Farm, occupied by, or belonging to any British subject, armed." Second, it declared that "no Number of Natives, exceeding in the Whole Six Persons, being entirely unarmed, shall ever come to lurk or loiter about any Farm in the Interior." Violation of either provision would result in the offending Natives "Being considered enemies" of the colony and "treated accordingly." The most interesting clause by far, however, provided

> That the Practice hitherto observed amongst the Native Tribes, of assembling in large Bodies or Parties armed, and of fighting and attacking each other on the Plea of inflicting Punishments on Transgressors of their own Customs and Manners, at or near Sydney, and other principal Towns and Settlements in the Colony, shall be henceforth wholly abolished, as a barbarous Custom repugnant to the British Laws. . . . Any armed Body of Na-

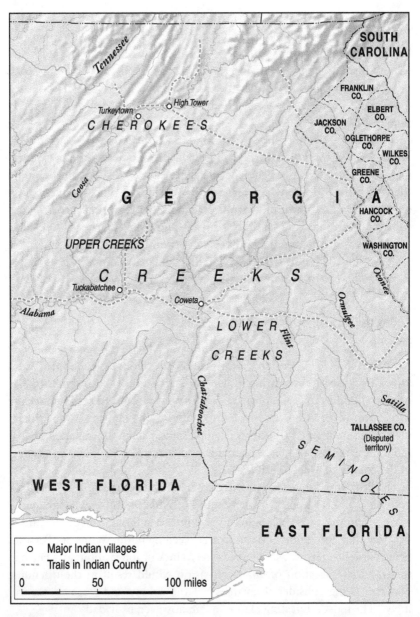

Roads and Trails in Georgia, 1796

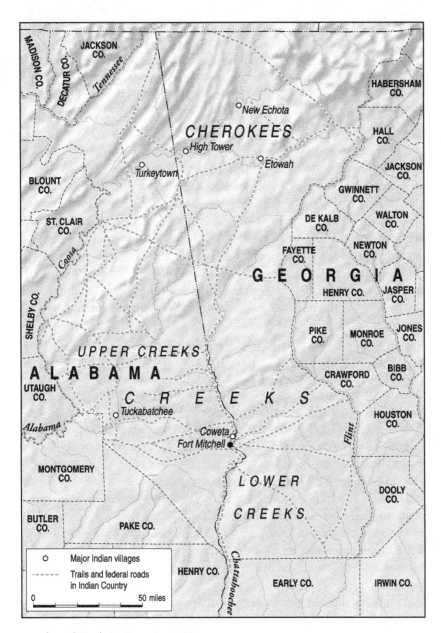

Roads and Trails in Georgia, 1823

tives, therefore, who shall assemble for the foregoing Purposes, either at Sydney or any other Settlements of this Colony after the said Fourth Day of June next, shall be considered as Disturbers of the Public Peace, and shall be apprehended and punished in a summary manner accordingly. The Black Natives are therefore hereby enjoined and commanded to discontinue this barbarous Custom not at or near the British Settlements, but also in their own Wild and remote places of resort.[90]

This proclamation divided New South Wales into a variety of juridical spaces that had little to do with the claims to imperium and *dominium* collected in various governors' instructions and the 1787 Charter of Justice. Armed Aborigines could not come to any British settlement, village, or farm. Unarmed Aborigines could not even assemble in family groups without being considered enemies. Aborigines visiting major settlements armed with a view to exercising indigenous jurisdiction over indigenous offenders, however, would not be considered enemies. Rather, Aborigines bent on effecting tribal law in the few urban centers of the colony—even if it resulted in the death of Aboriginal people—would be treated merely as disturbers of the Public Peace.

Ironically, this last provision contained a far more radical claim to sovereign authority than the threat to treat Aborigines visiting the fringes of the colony as enemies of the state. Colonial administrators had treated Aboriginal violence as enmity since 1788.[91] By substituting the Public Peace for a state of war in the very few populous regions of the colony, however, Macquarie made new claims to territorial jurisdiction in New South Wales. He asserted, first, that Aboriginal jurisdiction could be displaced (geographically rather than juridically) by a new, spatial category— the Public Peace—that did not spread beyond the major clusters of British settlement. Second, he asserted that in this place barbarous Aboriginal customs might be displaced by British law.

Macquarie's second argument invoked a particularly liberal (and by 1816, anomalous) iteration of the ancient laws of conquest. The case of Tanistry in 1608 held that in a conquered country like Ireland, local law subsisted until displaced by the King. However, British conquest automatically invalidated any local customary laws that were of their nature "barbarous" or against natural law. In Calvin's Case, in contrast, Coke had argued that none of the laws of infidels could survive English conquest.[92] This notion of (largely fictive) conquest held sway in metropolitan and peripheral ruminations about Britain's North American colonies before the American Revolution. However, by the end of the eighteenth century, Enlightenment philosophy had created a new ideological universe—a universe in which Australian Aborigines were a people so savage that they were unable to claim property or to constitute political society.[93] Though this radical philosophy would one day effect the judicial abnegation of indigenous jurisdiction, it was far less complete in its instantiation in 1816.[94] Macquarie did not propose to try and to convict Aborigines for killing each other on the streets of Sydney, merely to treat their violence as a disturbance of spatial order. This is an important distinction. In Macquarie's imagination, the Public Peace was an incompletely territorial order. It could geographically exclude but not criminalize Aboriginal violence.

The Plurality of Sydney Town

Macquarie acted in 1816 to displace physically indigenous jurisdictional practices that were, most likely, very ancient indeed.[95] Indigenous jurisdiction in early New South Wales, like indigenous jurisdiction in Georgia, was a notion suspended somewhere between Aboriginal customary practices and European misunderstanding.[96] Tribal governance, according to contemporary accounts and modern anthropologists, was predicated on deference for seniority and perhaps for strength.[97] Mid-nineteenth-century observers suggested that social rules were enforced by education, fear of supernatural punishment, and "ritualized combat and collective punishment."[98] Aborigines accused of procuring death by magic were killed by an armed party in retaliation.[99] Minor interpersonal wrongs were resolved privately either by words or by retaliatory violence.[100] The most visible response to crime, however, was the throwing of spears at wrongdoers by aggrieved relatives for serious intratribal wrongs.[101] Meanwhile, intertribal disputes were resolved through ritualized "tournaments," beginning with "the hurling of insults by senior women," followed by the sequential throwing of spears by individual warriors on both sides.[102]

Both ritual corporal punishment and intertribal contests defined Aboriginal jurisdiction for early settlers because both were staged in Sydney. Settler memoirs and the *Sydney Gazette* reported dozens of instances of Aboriginal warfare, Aboriginal jurisdiction, and Aboriginal drunken violence in New South Wales's major population centers and the highways that joined them in the years between settlement and the 1820s.[103] In 1803, a large number of indigenous people gathered in Pitt Street in the middle of Sydney town. They came to punish Mosquito and another Aboriginal man for killing two local Aborigines. In the very center (in 1803 the only center) of British settlement, they surrounded Mosquito and threw sixty-five spears at him. They threw only nine at his codefendant.[104]

This death and violence on the streets of Sydney fell outside settler law. Aboriginal jurisdiction in Sydney did not draw the ire of the colonial constabulary even when, in 1805, a soldier-bystander was wounded while cheering on an indigenous trial.[105] They were treated as legitimate and separate exercises of jurisdiction, not only by the *Sydney Herald,* but by the colonial state.[106] Instead, these acts of indigenous jurisdiction suggested an alternative spatial order. Indigenous people met repeatedly in "a clear spot between the town and the brickfield"—repetition that suggests ritual. However, a number of incidents occurred near landmarks of settlement itself, on roads, outside the military barracks. Aborigines selected accoutrements of settlement as sites of jurisdiction, perhaps as a matter of convenience, perhaps as a defiant reminder of the legal plurality of settler space.[107]

This was a plurality accepted frankly by settler society. As Samuel Smith noted in 1802, "It is not allowed to meddle with their affairs as they settle their own affairs in a Very Severe Manner by Spears."[108] Even as the *Sydney Gazette* disparaged tribal exercises of jurisdiction in British settlements, it acknowledged the binding character of indigenous jurisdiction over indigenous crime. In the first years of its publication, the *Sydney Gazette* described them ironically as great battles:

> Last week we were favored by a group of natives with a *warlike* spectacle. The opponent warriors had made choice of the new bridge for the celebration of the *games,* and the threatening spear whittled responsively to the uncouth jargon of a hundred tongues. Changing the scene of action to *Bennelong's Point.* The obstinate *fracas* had originated in a cruel adherence to custom. . . . The *lady* of the celebrated *Wilhamanan* had experienced the fate of a *fair Sabine;* and after enduring the brutal rigours consequent upon resistance, was forcibly borne off in savage triumph. . . . Her death being reported gave rise to the above conflict.[109]

In 1809, when an Aborigine died of natural causes and his well-liked elderly brother was punished for his death, the *Gazette* had more to say. It lamented that such a kind, old man "must now submit to an unjust peril which barbarous custom imposes on the male relatives of the deceased, whether by consanguinity or adoption." Such an unjust regime, the writer thought, could only bind a savage: it reflected "a bigotted adherence to prejudices which superstition invests with uncontrolled dominion in the unlightened mind." On this occasion, the *Gazette* warned settler-spectators that if Aborigines were civilized (or, it intimated, if they were more human), Aboriginal contests might be construed as murder, and spectators themselves might be accessories to the crime.[110] Here, the very savagery that obviated treaties and negated Aboriginal property rights sustained a separate legal regime. According to this settler newspaper, civilization, not savagery, would extinguish Aboriginal jurisdiction.

Savagery, however, was a jurisdictional category untempered by Aboriginal acquaintance with urban life. Most of the incidents reported by the *Gazette* involved Aborigines well known in and around the town: participants were often named, the *Gazette* always knew the nature of the transgression. Indigenous prosecutors and defendants, here, were deemed savage by cultural affiliation or by race, not by the location of their residence. The intimacy of local Aborigines with settler society shows the personal rather than territorial nature of settler jurisdiction in New South Wales. Only an Aborigine like Mow-watty, raised and schooled in settler ways, could be inducted into British law, and then only because he raped a nonindigenous woman near the colony's second largest settlement.[111] Settler jurisdiction followed British subjects most places, and indigenous people not at all.

Try as he might, Governor Macquarie could not displace indigenous jurisdiction from intimate settler space in 1816. He had much more success in straightening than in ordering Sydney's streets.[112] His radical Proclamation changed very little about jurisdictional practice in the urban settlements of New South Wales in the following two decades. Within eighteen months of the 1816 Proclamation, an Eora man known as Mirout was killed by another Aborigine, called Dulmike, in Sydney. His reputedly drunken Aboriginal killer was arrested, and though the *Gazette* called Dulmike a "criminal," it seems he was taken into custody merely to protect him from retaliation. He was certainly not tried for murder.[113] In 1818, the *Sydney Gazette* lamented a fortnight of "many irregularities among the natives" in George Street. Here, the *Sydney Gazette* pontificated about the inconvenience of Aboriginal violence in the settler towns, invoked the 1816 Proclamation, and even suggested that settler onlookers should be culpable for the death of Aborigines "as much under the protection of the Crown Law as [themselves]." Despite the Proclamation, it seems that Aborigines continued to bring their weapons into Sydney and use them in inter- and intratribal disputes. The *Sydney Gazette* might use the language of law to decry their violence, but neither the newspaper—nor, it seems, Sydney's constabulary or courts—thought it necessary or plausible to charge or incarcerate indigenous people for their breaches of the peace.[114]

Indigenous people continued to meet, fight, and die on the streets of British settlements outside the purview of British law until 1836. In 1829 the attorney-general of New South Wales asked the relatively new Supreme Court whether an Aboriginal man called Ballard (or Barrett) could be tried for murdering Dirty Dick (an Aborigine from another tribe) near the Governor's Domain in the middle of Sydney. In an extraordinary endorsement of Aboriginal legal independence, the Supreme Court said no.[115]

Before 1816, discourse and practice show that the British colony of New South Wales was at best a community of the King's subjects, not a regime of territorial governance covering half the continent, or even that portion of territory settled by British farmers. In it, indigenous people shared space with settlers, and were bound by their own laws. This intimate pluralism is remarkable when placed in the context of Britain's peculiar claims to sovereignty and jurisdiction in New South Wales—much more so, indeed, than the insistent plurality of Georgia's borderlands. Whereas early national Georgia was divided into formal jurisdictional enclaves, the borders of which were muddied by indigenous jurisdiction, early New South Wales was, at least in theory, a single jurisdictional space. In practice, however, the very heart of the colony was shared space, overlaid by parallel systems of adjudication.

Early records of indigenous jurisdictional practice remind us that British colonial jurisdiction was never defined by charters or legislation— these were purely aspirational in nature in New South Wales, as they had been in every North American colony.[116] As in Georgia, settler practice in New South Wales amounted to no less than a recognition of indigenous cultural and legal independence. To be sure, it was an independence that was mobilized at times to effect great violence against indigenous people. However, it was an independence that shows the fluidity of imperial sovereignty and jurisdiction in the decades before the advent of the modern settler state.

In this context, Macquarie's Proclamation of 1816 marks a turning point in the history of New South Wales. It might not have changed practice, but it articulated a new drive to territoriality. It acknowledged the depth and breadth of pluralism even as it wished it away from colonial centers to unsettled peripheries. Macquarie acknowledged the independence of indigenous people from the Crown by inviting them to surrender as families to His Majesty's protection. His attempt to drive Aboriginal jurisdiction from urban space, in contrast, acknowledged Aboriginal independence from normal, criminal jurisdiction (killing, wounding, or battery inter se) even as it asserted that indigenous jurisdiction could be construed as a punishable breach of the peace. In Macquarie's unfamiliar legal universe, indigenous jurisdiction was both a fact of life and a growing threat to the territorial aspirations of the colony.[117] His concerns were not so different from those of settlers in Georgia who called for order on the Federal Road, except that his goals were in every way more modest.

Cormick, Olive, and dozens of others defended the road as an artery of expansion. Macquarie defended town limits to mark out just a few square miles of British order in a wilderness of jurisdictional plurality.

Aborigines, Convicts, and Workers

As Macquarie noted in his Proclamation of 1816, rural districts and wilderness were both legitimate sites of plurality. In neither place did indigenous people fall under the King's protection or the King's law. Nevertheless, Macquarie drew a juridical line between farms (sites of settler and convict labor) and wilderness (uncharted and unsettled land). Near farms, indigenous people were potential enemies to be fought and killed. From May 1816, they could not bring arms near farms nor congregate in family groups without risking summary execution. Near farms, indigenous violence was an act of war. Beyond, they lived, quite literally, in a world of their own. Away from all settlement, indigenous violence constituted the order of things—a separate and in some ways complimentary jurisdictional order. In neither case, however, did Macquarie assert criminal jurisdiction over indigenous people's violence against settlers. Instead, he marked a geographical boundary, outside which indigenous people could exercise some manner of jurisdiction over Aborigines and settlers alike.

In doing so, he drew on precedents that understood indigenous violence as legitimate retaliation—a framework constructed in North America and applied in New South Wales from 1788. From the outset, the colony's executive had read Aboriginal violence against convicts as retaliation grounded in principles of indigenous law.[118] Watkin Tench decided after a few years in the colony that "the unprovoked outrages committed upon them, by unprincipled individuals among us, caused" indigenous people to kill or wound "unarmed stragglers."[119] Judge Atkins, the second judge advocate of the colony, thought indigenous retaliation was justifiable in natural law, but took issue with the fact that indigenous people killed "the first white man" they found for the crimes of others. When a convict was found dead in May of 1792, pierced by dozens of spears, Atkins assumed the death was an exercise of indigenous jurisdiction:

> This Evng a Convict was found murdered by the Natives about 3 miles from this place on the road to Prospect Hill; He had received 25 or 30 wounds by spears. . . . I mentioned about that on the 18th a man was fired at and supposed to have been wounded, it is probable the Man is since dead, and it is an invariable rule with them to Kill the first white man they can in revenge.

He went on to note, "Blood for Blood is justifiable. . . . But to shed the Blood of an innocent man for the crimes of another shews a savageness of disposition not compatible with civilized state."[120] Like Benjamin Hawkins and Return J. Meigs in Georgia's indigenous borderlands, Atkins accepted the validity of retaliation. In the wilderness, killings by indigenous people looked more like law than war. Like Hawkins in Creek Country, however, Atkins imposed limits on just retaliation. In his view, for retaliation to be legitimate, only the guilty could be punished.[121]

In 1790, Arthur Philip tried to demonstrate the proper bounds of retaliatory violence to Aborigines. When he organized the public flogging of some convicts for stealing Aboriginal fishing tackle, he invited local Eora Aborigines to attend. Local Aborigines, however, responded with horror and hostility to the spectacle of violence. One Eora woman tried to halt the flogging. British jurisdiction, as far as she was concerned, had a monopoly on barbarity.[122] Governor Philip, it seems, misunderstood the character and the bounds of indigenous retaliatory violence.[123]

Throughout the first decades of settlement, indeed, governors, magistrates, and judge-advocates as frequently explained Aboriginal violence as acts of retaliation grounded in notions of justice or indigenous custom as they described them as ungrateful and inexplicable treachery.[124] In 1800, Governor Hunter told the Duke of Portland:

> Much of that hostile disposition which has occasionally appear'd in those people has been but too often provoked by the treatment which many of them have received from the white inhabitants. . . . Their violence against the military proceeded from a soldier having in a most shamefull and wanton manner kill'd a native woman and child.[125]

In 1805, Governor King assumed that Aboriginal violence in the Hawkesbury had legitimate cause. When he met with local Aborigines, he discovered that they made war because settlers obstructed their access to food and water.[126]

From 1810 to the 1830s, Aboriginal violence was attributed largely to the misdeeds of convict laborers and unrespectable settlers on the peripheries. In 1811, a coroner thought Mulgowie Aborigines' execution of Richard Luttril was just retaliation for his habit of consorting with Aboriginal women and stealing the weaponry of Aboriginal men.[127] In 1826, Governor Darling blamed Wonnarua and Awabakal violence in the Hunter region on the theft, murder, and rape by convict stockmen. He had gone so far as to encourage local Aborigines to arrest convict workers who mistreated them, a policy questioned by Lord Bathurst. Though he sent troops to the region, Darling told settlers that they should fend for themselves, as "Vigorous measures amongst yourselves would more effectually establish Your ascendancy than the utmost power of the Military." He also urged absentee owners to return to their properties to prevent "irregularities on the part of your own people, which I apprehend is in many instances the cause of the disorders committed by the Natives." In this frame, Aboriginal reprisal was a warranted if not legitimate response to settler violence.[128]

In the early years of settlement, Aboriginal violence against settlers was not only understood as a legitimate or illegitimate resort to indigenous jurisdiction tolerated by the colony; as in the early national United States, it filled gaps in the net of settler governance. Aboriginal jurisdiction over settlers was more contingent than its counterparts in Georgia, but it still had a role in governing convict escapees in the early decades of settlement. New South Wales began as a penal colony—an enlightened social experiment in punishment, forced labor, and reform.[129] From the outset, Aborigines inhabiting the peripheries of the colony, whether the immediate environs of Port Phillip in 1790 or the territory separating Port Macquarie from Sydney in the 1820s, served as de facto jail keepers for the colonial state. Government sources and newspapers reported (with a certain amount of satisfaction) the frequent return of escaped convicts from "the bush" wounded, stripped, and much abused by Aboriginal tribes. In 1790, Governor Philip reported that, not only were Aboriginal attacks on "straglers . . . natural," but that "the punishments they sometimes meet with . . . have had a good effect."[130] These attacks seldom provoked state intervention. Rather, Aboriginal hostility against escapees was an accepted mode of control.

As the colony grew, penal centers were pushed further and further into the peripheries: first to the Hunter Valley and then to Moreton Bay. The colonial government sought to separate hardened criminals from the centers of settlement. It was, therefore, a matter of some convenience that "independent" Aboriginal tribes cut off penal colonies from farms and towns.[131] Where convicts were workers, however, the equation changed. Their injury and death was not justice, it was a disruption of settlement itself.[132] This is the very distinction that Macquarie sought to make in spatial terms in 1816 when he drew clear lines between sites of convict labor (farms) and sites of convict escape and trespass (the wilderness).

The continuing importance of Aborigines to the policing of illegitimate convict activity is apparent in the fact that some Aborigines living closer to settlements were incorporated directly into colonial governance, turning their skills as hunters and trackers into a lively trade in convict bodies, hostile Aborigines, and stolen property.[133] By the 1820s some indigenous people had been appointed as constables on the peripheries of the colony.[134]

In 1816 Macquarie deployed a feeble territoriality indeed to displace indigenous jurisdiction and control plurality. He sought to establish spatial jurisdictional boundaries in New South Wales by controlling indigenous jurisdiction in British towns, by defining the spatial field of Aboriginal jurisdiction over settlers, and by inviting indigenous families to accept formally the protection of the Crown.[135] He and his officers had long been formalizing another more effective strategy: incorporating indigenous people into the colonial state as law-keepers to harness their unique capacity to control convicts in the bush.[136] At some level both strategies simultaneously acknowledged and controlled indigenous juridical independence in early New South Wales—a role that would be taken over by legal discourse in the courts from 1824.

Georgia and New South Wales differed nowhere more than in the nature and degree of indigenous jurisdiction exercised over indigenous people and settlers in their centers and peripheries. The treaty system begun by the British and continued by the United States bound Georgia to accept indigenous jurisdiction within circumscribed areas within the state, whereas no treaty acknowledged indigenous land rights or independence in New South Wales. Nevertheless, these very different iterations of indigenous jurisdiction are two parts of a related history of Anglophone legal pluralism.

Indigenous jurisdiction could not be geographically contained in either North America or the Antipodes. No border or treaty, however carefully drawn or negotiated, could keep indigenous jurisdiction out of Georgia's counties or keep Georgia's settlers out of the purview of Indian justice. In New South Wales, no edict could change the view shared by settlers and indigenous people that the latter were bound by separate laws—laws that followed them into the centers of settlements and onto the roads that facilitated the business of expansion.

Macquarie's 1816 Proclamation reminds us of another history shared by Anglophone settler states in the early nineteenth century. In both Georgia and New South Wales, spatial plurality was maintained, first and foremost, by indigenous people themselves. In Sydney, diverse Aboriginal communities continued old ways even as they forged new ways to deal with social conflict, despite the growth of a British urban settlement on their land. They met in places where they had most probably always met, in places of continuing significance despite the erection of barracks, of roads, and of the governor's residence. In Georgia, the Creek and Cherokee aggressively defended their right to govern indigenous crime wherever it was committed. They did so, however, in defiance of Georgia's carefully drawn jurisdictional boundaries and its vociferous jurisdictional aspirations. Meanwhile, they asserted an unexpected degree of control over settlers in their nations and on the roads that bisected them, despite gap-ridden treaties and federal laws investing jurisdiction over settler crime in the federal government.

Indigenous jurisdiction flourished not only because of the persistence and insistence of indigenous people. In both places, indigenous jurisdictions were a necessary tool of governance at the same time as they transgressed increasingly important notions of spatial order. Business in Georgia's Indian Country could not work without indigenous testimony and syncretic forums of adjudication. These could only be provided out of the reach of discriminatory common law courts, made even more forbidding by the legal accoutrements of race slavery. Centuries of trade diplomacy in southeastern North America meant that the Creek and particularly the Cherokee tribes articulated and practiced jurisdiction in ways that were recognizable to their common-law equivalents in the states. In their own ways, settlers and indigenous people all understood the logic of reciprocity, retaliation, and compensation. In New South Wales, indigenous jurisdiction flourished because of its very illegibility, even in Sydney town. Convict horror of the wilderness and the savages it contained, meanwhile, provided a welcome supplementary check on early escapees—a check that would become a threat only when convicts became the worker-agents of imperial expansion.

Indigenous jurisdiction flourished because settler statehood itself was in flux in the early nineteenth century, its geographical and juridical bounds yet to be articulated. However, indigenous jurisdiction challenged the fundaments of settler sovereignty, even as it filled the gaps left by settler law. Olive, Wheeler, and Cormick's machinations show how poorly indigenous jurisdiction was understood, and how contested was its spatial reach in Georgia. The Proclamation of 1816 shows the deep anxiety indigenous jurisdiction caused to imperial officers bent on asserting the rudiments of spatial order in the centers of settlement in New South Wales. Most importantly, then, these two very different instances show how indigenous status and spatial order became more contested over time, as settlers in these very different places sought to puzzle out the nature and the geographical limits of indigenous and settler jurisdiction.

It is not a matter of chance, then, that jurisdiction over indigenous people became a primary focus of sovereignty discourse in the nineteenth century. During this period, indigenous people confounded attempts to demarcate sovereignty as a spatial order in North America and Australasia. In the 1820s, indigenous people became the testing sites of sovereignty in court cases centering on the nature and the extent of "territorial" authority and the "Public Peace."

CHAPTER FOUR

Legality and Lawlessness

FRONTIER SETTLERS IN AUSTRALIA and America were seldom merely lawless. Many settlers were savvy masters of the discourses and the politics of settler jurisdiction. They were eager for its bounties and wary of its gaze, crafting their contests and cooperations with indigenous people to fit the shifting parameters of colonial, state, and indigenous jurisdictional practice.

Provocation, self-defense, and justifiable homicide lay at the heart of settlers' engagement with state jurisdiction—notions grounded as much in shared notions of reciprocity and retaliation as in common law.[1] Though settlers, particularly in Georgia, were a disparate bunch, the localism and the openness of common-law institutions gave constables, magistrates, and juries a controlling stake in the administration of criminal law.[2] Meanwhile, their neighbors had a monopoly on evidence, as indigenous oaths were not accepted by Anglophone courts. Settler stories of fear, danger, and retaliation, therefore, had legal force in courts and communities.

Settler violence, then, was clothed in law—a law which, in important respects, settlers constituted and controlled. Recent comparative legal histories have emphasized how settler communities and their legislatures manipulated laws of property and civil law better to fit the project of indigenous dispossession and of property development.[3] Some very recent frontier histories have suggested that lawlessness in late eighteenth- and early nineteenth-century North America contained within it a metanarrative about indigenous sovereignty. As Cumfer and Dowd have shown, when they systematically ignored indigenous rights and murdered indigenous people, Tennessee and Pennsylvania frontiersmen contributed to the discourse and practice of settler sovereignty over indigenous people and their land.[4]

Settlers in Georgia and New South Wales did something more complicated still. In the first decade of the nineteenth century, some of them used law stories to both inhabit and curtail state jurisdiction. So, on the Georgia-Creek boundary in 1802, Benjamin Harrison, one of the most notorious Indian-killers in the state of Georgia, collaborated with notable local men to conceal the murder of a Creek Indian in an elaborate pageant of law. The Creek was arrested, bound, then shot "while trying to escape," according to the oaths of participants. In the Hawkesbury region in 1799, a group of respectable settlers murdered two Aboriginal boys, aged 12 and 15, to avenge the murder of two settlers and to forestall imminent Aboriginal attack. These cases show the power of retaliation and of justifiable homicide in settler communities and settler courts at the beginning of the nineteenth century.

In these efforts to conform to and to control the limits of jurisdiction lies another instability in early nineteenth-century sovereignty. Settler frontiers were neither lawless nor lawful.[5] Rather, settlers used their control of legal discourse, legal evidence, and juries to ensure that common law served the interests of plurality in early Georgia and New South Wales. By making their lawlessness law-like, Abraham Blackshear and the Hawkesbury settlers brought plurality into the legal process itself. In doing so, they subjoined common law in ways that limited the nature and reach of settler sovereignty.

Abraham Blackshear's Humble Oath

In Washington County, Georgia, in 1802, a local justice of the peace, his family, a constable, and an Indian-killer claimed to have arrested a Chehaw Indian of the Creek Nation after he sold stolen horses to Captain Benjamin Harrison.[6] They took the Chehaw into custody while he was drunk and tied him to a post at magistrate David Blackshear's Mill. The Indian's accomplices, it was alleged, had crossed back peacefully into Creek Country before they could be arrested. Abraham Blackshear swore that constable Daniel Hill shot the Chehaw prisoner while the latter was trying to escape from custody. In short, he swore that justice would have been done according to law if the Chehaw had not tried to escape.[7]

Rumors circulating in the community, however, told a different story. James Bush Junior related a tale quite at odds with the deposition of Abraham Blackshear. He had heard that the Chehaw was seized before

Blackshear's party knew that he had sold them stolen horses. He also heard that the Indian was not killed while trying to escape: he was bound and shot with a bullet recovered from the body of a settler. The settler had been shot accidentally by his companions in the course of the Chehaw's arrest.[8] Legally inadmissible rumors from Indian Country confirmed Bush's testimony. Creeks told Benjamin Hawkins (the federal Indian agent resident in the nation) that, though the dead Chehaw and his friends were probably horse thieves, the conspirators had tried to kill them all, and the dead man's "arrest" and "escape" were staged to give the imprimatur of law to vigilantism, murder, and perjury.[9]

The governor, the federal agents, and the Creeks all called for the punishment of the offenders. This homicide was likely to place the fragile Indian peace in jeopardy. It was committed with the aid of one of the state's most violent men (Benjamin Harrison), who remained at large despite having killed more than a dozen Creeks seven years earlier.[10] It avenged no settler death, so did not conform to Creek rules of blood revenge, and was disproportionate to the crimes of horse theft or conversion of stolen property (punishable by corporal punishment or restitution in the nation).[11]

The killing at David Blackshear's mill happened in a particularly violent corner of Georgia's Creek frontier, but its principal actors and the oaths they swore tell a great deal about the ways in which frontier settlers shaped state jurisdiction in Georgia's early national peripheries. Respectable men worked with known murderers to stage a death that fitted into legal narratives of self-defense and the defense of property. Their conspiracy did more than subvert law, however. In important ways, these settlers forced state jurisdiction into their service to legitimize—more still, to legalize—their actions. The crimes and corruptions of Blackshear and his cronies show how common-law discourse and common-law rules of evidence tethered state jurisdiction to plurality.

The most fascinating aspect of this case lies in the Herculean efforts of the Washington County conspirators to fit their violence into law. If Bush's testimony was correct, the killers at Blackshear's Mill displayed acute awareness of the ambiguities of law when they captured and shot their Chehaw victim in 1802. If the unnamed Chehaw had indeed stolen horses from Georgia and then resold them to the conspirators (a fact that Benjamin Hawkins doubted sincerely), he was in breach of Georgia's criminal laws. In theory, then, he was liable to citizen-arrest in Georgia and to trial in Georgia courts.[12] Therefore, under Georgia's peculiarly broad defense of "justifiable" or "excusable" homicide, Harrison and company were justified in shooting him as he tried to escape arrest.

Early national Georgia made it fairly easy to get away with murder. It seems that public peace in Georgia required settlers to kill each other, their slaves, and Indians more often than their English or New South Wales counterparts.[13] No doubt this state of affairs stemmed in part from the institution of race slavery. Slaves outnumbered settlers in many counties of Georgia, and white control of state-sponsored and private violence formed a cornerstone of Georgia's criminal and civil law. In other respects, however, Georgia's criminal law was merely old-fashioned, importing premodern flexibility into newer state-directed criminal proceedings. According to Clayton's *Georgia Justice,* homicide was "justifiable" if committed by an officer or a member of the public in the interests of "public justice"—a category that included killing a person who resisted arrest. Homicide was "excusable" if it occurred by accident—an accidental shooting or accidental excessive punishment of a criminal or a child. Killing was "excusable" if committed in self-defense or in a chance medley (a cognate of provocation in English law that excused killing during a fight but fell into disuse in the eighteenth century).[14] Clayton went to some effort to distinguish self-defense from planned retaliation or preemptory killing. Significantly, he noted that retaliation or preemptory killing was unlawful because "men need only have recourse to the proper tribunals." As indigenous people could rarely be brought before "the proper tribunals," Clayton's formulation of homicide suggests that different rules might be applied to settlers who killed Indians. State and federal jurors certainly tended to think so. As a matter of practice, juries read legal excuses broadly—and they had a great deal of power to do so in Georgia.[15] However, on the narrowest construction of "justifiable" homicide alone, Blackshear's story could excuse the Washington County conspirators of crime in 1802.[16]

Why did they go to all of this trouble? I think that the efforts of the conspirators to emulate legal process in order to get away with murder shows the normative importance of common law on the most lawless of Georgia's frontiers. This is not to say that the rule of law governed Georgia's indigenous borderlands. Rather, it suggests that settlers used the forms of common law procedure to garner popular acceptance of their violence against indigenous people.

Settler law, however, had no monopoly on normativity. Shared settler and indigenous norms of retaliation gave this killing an alternative, quasi-legal legitimacy.[17] The killers at Blackshear's Mill embraced syncretic norms of retaliation even as they nodded to protocols and procedures of the common law. Indeed, by buying a horse from a Creek Indian, Blackshear and company broke the federal Trade and Intercourse Law—they were liable to prosecution under federal law themselves, even if a state jury accepted their tall tale of citizen-arrest and justifiable homicide.[18] They clearly banked on the fact that the whole community stood behind the summary punishment of Indian horse thieves, whereas no one but the federal agent and a few federal troops stationed in Creek and Cherokee Country cared for the enforcement of the Trade and Intercourse Law.[19]

The power of retaliation as an excuse for settler crime is also apparent in a petition sent by Jackson County jurors to Governor Jackson in April 1799. Though they convicted William Hodge of stealing horses from an Indian, the jurors begged for mercy on his behalf. They reminded Governor Jackson that Hodge had been

> unfortunately prosecuted by an Indian in the above case. Consider the novelty of the case, and reflect how often the . . . crual murderors has Stained their hands with the blood of Our Feabler Sexes.[20]

Retaliation trumped law in 1804 in Clarke County. When a settler called Milligan Patrick (or Killpatrick) shot a Creek Indian who he claimed was a horse thief, Patrick's community mobilized to ensure that he would not go to trial. A frustrated official noted that "a number of the Citizens of Clark County was determined that at the risk of their lives he should not be taken out of their county" for trial. Using shared rules of retaliation, they reasoned that Patrick had avenged the death of a popular constable, Moreland, several years before. Besides, the dead Creek was a horse thief and Patrick had been his victim.[21] This was also the excuse made in 1808 by a settler-regulator who claimed that his beating of a Cherokee horse thief (who later drowned) in the Cherokee Nation was a legitimate application of indigenous jurisdiction.[22] Nor was the government of Georgia above justifying settler violence in these terms. In 1798, Governor Jackson wrote to the secretary of war asserting that the Creek Nation's "delay of punishment of the Indian Offenders" who had killed a settler named Brown "may . . . have also led to retaliation," though he conceded the unlawfulness of the latter.[23]

In 1802, then, by constructing a pageant of (almost) law through their actions and their oaths, Benjamin Harrison, the Blackshears, Daniel Hill, and their accomplices embraced a plural vision of state law that held sway in Georgia before 1812. Common law norms and shared settler-indigenous norms provided language and an audience to allow the Washington County conspirators to avoid prosecution for murder.

The Federal Courts

Normativity—or perhaps the mere fact that the perpetrators were settlers and their quarry Indians—virtually ensured that the conspirators would not be convicted or even prosecuted for the killing. Georgian magistrates, judges, and juries were very sympathetic to settlers who used force to protect themselves, their neighbors, or their property against marauding Indians. Accordingly very few incidents of violence made it before the courts, even if they prompted investigations at the county or state level.[24]

In theory, settler violence committed within the boundaries of Georgia could be prosecuted in state courts. Militiamen committing crimes in Georgia's ordinary jurisdiction or over the Indian boundary might also be tried by courts-martial.[25] Settlers of any description could be tried before federal courts for a limited number of offenses, ranging from trespass to murder in the Creek or Cherokee Nation under the federal Trade and Intercourse Law. Finally, settlers resident in, trading in, or sometimes just passing through Indian Country might be subject to indigenous jurisdiction. The result was a confusion of overlapping forums for settler crime—so much so that when militia officers Henry Gaster and James Ford lured Creeks over the Indian boundary to trade and drink in Georgia, Governor Jackson pointed out that they risked prosecution under military, state, and federal jurisdiction.[26]

Federal courts had special jurisdiction over breaches of trade regulations and over settler wrongs against Indians in Indian Country, almost all of which were misdemeanors. The Trade and Intercourse Act provided that settler-criminals were entitled to be tried in their state of residence, in most cases by a jury and certainly by a federal judge of the local circuit who was resident in the region if not the state—circumstances highly favorable to their acquittal.[27]

It is very difficult to ascertain the number of settlers tried before federal courts for crimes in Indian Country because court minutes very rarely record the location of offenses. The federal district and circuit courts in Georgia tried most shipping, customs, counterfeiting, and mail offenses, as well as crimes and misdemeanors in Indian Country. Of fifty prosecutions for a range of offenses before the circuit court between 1793 and 1814, only six homicides and sixteen lesser offenses were at all likely to have occurred in Indian Country.[28] There is no way to be sure, as the first explicit mention of Indian Country in a prosecution occurred in 1824, when three men were charged on "Indictment for making settlement in Indian Country."[29]

The district court's records are a little more informative, though its criminal jurisdiction was extremely limited. There, two groups of men were charged with misdemeanors in Indian Country before 1814. Of these, the first, in 1797, occurred in Creek Country. William Yarborough, Mial Moak, Ephraim Morr, and Obadiah Morse were charged with crossing the Oconnee River to hunt on Creek lands, an act they admitted, but argued that they had no idea of its illegality. Their charges were dismissed.[30] These were probably the same men who provoked a minor crisis between Georgia's Governor Jackson and the federal war department. In early 1798, Governor Jackson protested the arrest of citizens of Georgia for trespass on Creek lands—arrests he saw as unprecedented intrusions on Georgia's sovereignty and jurisdiction.[31]

We know that more than one group of settlers was tried in Georgia for committing misdemeanors in Indian Country, however. In December 1810, Hawkins reported that a number of Georgian squatters had been prosecuted "at the last term of the Federal Court . . . at Milledgeville on the 14th for a misdemeanor":

> Two of them, Colonel Roderick Easley and Mr. Hammot, both men of property and standing in the State, have been taken and traversed the Indictment which will be tried in May term at Savannah.[32]

Curiously, the charge against Roderick Easley was not minuted in the circuit court records. Moreover, of the twelve men charged with misdemeanors in December 1810, two were excused, six were indicted on lesser charges, and none, it seems, were brought to trial.[33] Indeed, of sixteen misdemeanor charges brought before the court between 1789 and 1814, only one appears to have ended in conviction.[34]

Meanwhile, Benjamin Hawkins's correspondence with the secretary of war suggests that prosecution was a last resort in the agency—at least for squatting on Indian land. In the same letter in 1810, he notes that, "This is the third time we have moved the Intruders by a military force and the first that they have been delivered over to the civil authority." Trial in court for squatting, for Hawkins, was exemplary punishment rather than an act of jurisdiction:

> Col. Roderick Easley, being a man of property and standing in the Country, one who was personally warned for year past by me . . . and who promised me to conform to the Law . . . is a fit and proper person to make an example of.[35]

Meigs's practice in Cherokee Country was similar. Meigs was very sympathetic to settler-squatters.[36] He ordered troops to remove intruders from the nation only after extensive negotiation or provocation.[37] Here again, prosecution was a last resort. Part of the problem was process. As far as Meigs was concerned, only federal troops were able to arrest settlers in Indian Country, and even then he referred to their authority to do so in speculative terms:

> the duty of the military force is pointed out in aid of that authority by which it appears that without the aid of military force there was no power competent for apprehending & punishing offenders against that act. The military force then contemplated was probably the regular troops of the United States: but it may be a question whether a District Judge of any of the federal courts cannot issue process & send the marshal or his deputies to apprehend persons in all criminal cases where the offender has made an asylum of the Indian Country. I think it can be done as I conceive the militia to be effective military force, and such is the Posse comitatus under the direction of the marshal, but at present I presume there is no law making civil process legal within the limits of the Indian boundary and as the regular troops are not in this quarter there is no power here competent to remove or bring out Citizens who have taken refuge in the Indian boundary for either civil or criminal offences.[38]

Squatters defied federal and treaty law by setting up farms on Indian land, but they played on federal sympathy to stay and harvest their crops year after year until a cession could be arranged. In short, they breached federal law, but anticipated the extension of state law, which they hoped would reward their illegitimate possession with legitimate title.[39]

The federal minutes suggest that hardly any settlers came before federal courts for serious crimes in Indian Country. It seems that state officials and federal troops tried and failed to bring a number of offenders to court, especially in the 1790s. Adam Carson was arrested for occupying a fort in Indian Country in defiance of federal authority in 1794. He escaped from custody.[40] Benjamin Hawkins oversaw the arrest of two settler-soldiers for horse stealing in Creek Country in 1802.[41] Daniel Currie and Robert Mitchell were arrested and bound over in Montgomery County in 1798 for trial in the federal tribunal.[42]

Before 1815, the federal circuit court laid six indictments for murder not specified to have been committed on the high seas.[43] Presuming for the sake of argument that these murders occurred in Indian Country, an interesting pattern emerges. John Depriest and company, accused of murder in April 1800, took bond to appear for trial in November 1800, but were not tried for their crimes.[44] John and Sarah Stewart were bonded to appear for a murder trial in December 1801. John Stewart escaped from custody, but Sarah, a slave, was surrendered to her owner without trial.[45]

George Peoples objected to the jurisdiction of the court. Though he was bound over to face charges for murder in 1803, there is no record of his trial.[46] The indictment of Robert Fluker and James Morgan was quashed in 1810 because they had killed a settler in Indian Country—a crime not governed by federal or state law.[47] Prior Crittendon was charged with murder in 1812, but was convicted of manslaughter, fined $1.00, and imprisoned for only six months.[48] Finally, the grand jury refused to indict Robert Hand for murder in 1814.[49] This is hardly a long list given the number of murders and thefts reputedly committed by settlers in and around Indian Country, and it shows, uniformly, that settler-murderers walked away from murder charges before the federal court with or without the blessing of jurors.

Another reason for the scarcity of successful federal prosecutions is the fact that federal jurisdiction over settlers anywhere was fiercely contested by both settler-defendants and the state.[50] Federal troops exercising federal jurisdiction were sometimes subjected to civil suits within the state.[51] In U.S. v. Watkins in 1794, the state solicitor general himself argued before the federal court that Watkins should be tried for an unspecified crime under state not federal law.[52] In 1810, John Macpherson Berrien argued before the court that Fluker and Morgan could not be tried in federal court for killing a citizen in Indian Country.[53] Federal minutes record that the court quashed the indictment "for want of legal provision for punishing offences committed without the temporary jurisdiction of the state of Georgia, by citizen against citizen."[54] Georgia acted to stem this legal gap in 1814.[55] In 1815, a similar case in Tennessee would prompt federal Congress to pass the General Crimes Act 1817, which purported to govern settler and Indian crime in Indian Country.[56]

The State Courts

Meanwhile, state jurisdiction in Georgia was entrenched in the local. Suspects were bound over by local inferior court judges and tried by local juries before a superior court comprised of judges from their local district.[57] The patchy nature of early Georgian court records makes it very difficult to trace state responses to settler crimes.

Based on a survey of Franklin County—a county lodged on the boundaries of the Cherokee Nation for most of the early national period—it seems that settler-crime against settlers or indigenous people in and around Indian Country hardly ever made it into court. In the first place, it seems no murder trials in Franklin's superior court arose from settler-indigenous violence. Occasionally settlers in Indian Country got embroiled in civil matters in the county. Nathaniel Wofford of Wofford's illegal settlement in the Cherokee Nation was party to an action for debt in October 1805.[58] In 1816, a justice of the peace despaired of executing a judgment obtained by Elisha Simmonds against Reuben Daniel because the latter had moved to the Cherokee Nation, beyond the jurisdictional limits of the state.[59] After 1816, however, a number of cases appeared on the Franklin County docket involving crimes and civil wrongs by settlers and Indians in Cherokee Country, attesting to a change in jurisdictional practice.

Those few cases that did come before a court or a state-based commission of inquiry were heavily influenced by the prejudice of judges and juries. In 1793, a militia unit at the fort of Colerain, near the St. Mary's River, took to shooting Creek Indians on a regular basis. Their efforts culminated in the assassination of a Creek commissioner who, according to one militiaman, was clearly on a mission of peace. They then refused to surrender the post.[60] A board of militia officers reported that Colerain was in the possession of a "banditti" who

> refuse to obey or adhere to the orders of the Commanding Officer of the County or any other commissioned Officer sent to Command the same (who could be called to account for misconduct or disobedience of order) we therefore consider them as mutineers disobeying the laws of this state and endangering the liberties and happiness of the inhabitants of this country.[61]

The court of inquiry appointed to investigate the death of Cornel felt differently, however. According to the court:

> The Indians, were to blame for sending so desperate & obnoxious a Character on any embassy to the agent for Indian affairs, and that they should put up with the loss of Cornel & the other Indian without asking further satisfaction, as it appears to the Court that those who were at the killing of Cornel & the other Indian are justly to be applauded as they did nothing but in discharge of their duty according to orders.[62]

In addition, a number of notorious incidents suggest that local courts and constables seldom punished even the most egregious violence against indigenous people. It is clear that a number of settler-criminals ended up in Georgian jails for their transgressions in Indian Country: "one Tarvin" was jailed in Wilkes County in 1795 for murdering a Creek and a Cherokee at the "High Shoals of the Apalatchee."[63] His fate, however, is unclear. William Hodge, as we have seen, was tried and convicted in Jackson County for stealing horses from Indians in April 1799, but his jurors begged for mercy.[64] Benjamin Harrison, braggart and erstwhile Captain in Georgia's militia, was arrested two years after killing as many as sev-

enteen Creeks at Carr's Bluff in 1795—and then only after law officers
had formally confirmed their jurisdiction to try him for killing friendly
Indians within the limits of the state.[65] That it all came to naught is apparent from the fact that Harrison lived to brag of further killing at
Blackshear's Mill in 1802. When Governor Matthews decided that the
safety of the state required that Daniel Currie and Robert Mitchell should
be arrested and handed over to federal troops for stealing horses in the
Creek Nation in 1798, he seemed sure that the justices of Montgomery
County would intervene to thwart federal jurisdiction. He warned them
that "if Montgomery does not do justice the County must expect other
steps will be adopted."[66] Judge Clay and others of the federal circuit
seemed equally unwilling to exercise federal jurisdiction in the southeast.
Meigs reported that eight settler-murderers from 1802 to 1812 were acquitted or avoided trial in Tennessee and Georgia state and federal
courts.[67]

Georgia governors themselves acted to discourage the exercise of federal law in particular over setter-indigenous crime. In 1811, when Creeks
reported "the plundering of Indian goods from a camp opposite . . . Col
Jos Philips' Mill," Governor Mitchell counseled local judges not to arrest
or prosecute the perpetrators, but to request that "white people involved . . . deliver up the Articles rather than be prosecuted for the fact
before the Federal Court."[68] Finally, jurisdictional boundaries themselves
thwarted the exercise of state law. Agency records are replete with stories
of settler-fugitives who manipulated the pluralism of Georgia's borderlands by settling in Indian Country beyond the reach of Georgia and
Tennessee sheriffs.[69]

In 1802, our Washington County conspirators knew that they had little to fear from state or federal courts in Georgia. They had the sympathy
of government and the ear of the neighbor judges, neighbor magistrates,
and neighbor juries, so long as they could fit their lawlessness within the
normative parameters of settler law.

The Limits of State Jurisdiction

At another level, the killers at Blackshear's Mill recognized, exploited,
and protested the abrogation of Georgia's territorial jurisdiction by indigenous people. Their pageant of law diverted state jurisdiction from
their violence in part because the state and its citizens all understood the
real limits of jurisdiction over indigenous people in Georgia's peripheries.
The limited nature of state power was a source of frustration for settlers,
even as it authorized the pursuit of folk justice on the frontier.

The incident fits into a discourse of protest that echoed about the state before 1812 as settlers, militia officers, and even local magistrates threatened to take the law into their own hands if the state failed to respond to indigenous theft and violence. In 1793, a Colonel Stewart declared that he was "determined to follow" ten slaves stolen from his farm "to the lower [Creek] towns" if they were not promptly returned by the agent.[70] In 1796, Militia Captain William Melton reported thefts by the Creeks and warned, "Those repeated & aggrevating Savage insults on our frontier will inevitably end in the Effusion of blood, without the interposition of Government."[71] In 1807, a number of leading residents of Tattnal County warned that "Men are apt when injured to lift the hand to swing themselves on their enemies," and enjoined Governor Irwin to intervene in Creek pilfering in their neighborhood.[72] On the eve of hostilities against the Creeks in 1812, the citizens of Pulaski County reminded Governor Mitchell that the social contract itself might rest on the state's capacity to restrain indigenous aggression: "it is well Known that Obedience in the support of Government & protection are duties in their nature reciprocal—that the one can't be exacted without the [unclear: guarantee] of the other."[73] In 1798, Governor Jackson himself threatened that federal neglect of state rights would likewise result in unrestrained extralegal violence, revolution, or war.[74]

Though most of these settlers sought state-sponsored violence, not the exercise of jurisdiction, against Indians in the borderlands of Georgia, their protests contain nascent aspirations to territorial sovereignty over Indian Country. They objected to indigenous lawlessness, to indigenous jurisdiction, and to the erosion of state order effected by the jurisdictional pluralism.

Most importantly, however, the killing at Blackshear's Mill attests to the enormous power wielded by settlers to control state jurisdiction by working in, through, and around the common law. More than any other factor, common-law rules of evidence prevented state and federal courts from punishing settler crimes. This meant, first and foremost, that most settler-indigenous crime could not be proved before federal or state courts. When Benjamin Harrison had remained at large for two years after killing seventeen Creeks in 1795, Governor Matthews ordered that a bench warrant be issued against him, notwithstanding the dearth of legal evidence. His purpose was as much to restrain other acts of militia lawlessness, to quiet federal protests, and to prevent a war with the Creeks as it was to do justice.[75] When Governor Mitchell had Daniel Currie and Robert Mitchell arrested for horse theft in Indian Country, he noted that "the proof not being positive I could only procure him to be bound over to Montgomery Court to answer the charge where the Theft was committed."[76] According to Return J. Meigs in 1812, testimony rules had, more than any single factor, resulted in the inability of federal courts to discipline settler crime. He reported that settlers planned their violence to avoid white witnesses who could give evidence in court against the perpetrators.[77]

Settler use and abuse of the laws of evidence attest to more than a reign of silence on Georgia's frontier. It shows the normative reach of syncretic settler law. Far from being silent, settlers everywhere talked constantly about their misdeeds. They told stories that legitimized violence. Legitimization had a functional and a normative role. By convincing their neighbors that their actions were just, settler thieves and murderers ensured that local judges and jurors would not convict them in court. So, when Benjamin Harrison and his cohorts killed seventeen Creeks at Carr's Bluff in 1795, his accusers had to go to some effort to assure the governor of Georgia that Harrison had not acted to defend himself against a hostile attack.[78] Here and elsewhere, the humble deposition effected a preemptive manipulation of common law, carefully casting settler violence as an act of legitimate defense of self or of property—defenses that had a life of their own in Georgia's judicial system.

In 1802, when Blackshear and his neighbors killed their Chehaw victim at Blackshear's Mill, they knew that no indigenous witnesses could attest to their crimes. They anticipated and subverted state and federal jurisdiction by making sure that there were no (legal) witnesses and crafted their story to fit broad narratives of self-defense, provocation, and retaliation.[79] As it turned out, loose talking in town ensured that alternative narratives of the crime found their way to the state's capital. However, this was the hearsay of outsiders. Words spoken boastfully to a neighbor bore little weight against the carefully constructed narrative of white eyewitnesses. Like most of Georgia's lawless frontiersmen, then, the killers at Blackshear's Mill did not set themselves in defiance of the law and even less so in defiance of justice (popularly conceived). Instead, they were savvy manipulators of its pluralities and its incapacities in early national Georgia.

Tales of Peril on the Hawkesbury

On September 18, 1799, at the Hawkesbury River on the western frontier of the colony of New South Wales, a local constable, Edward Powell, and local farmers Simon Freebody, James Metcalfe, William Timms, and William Butler killed two Aboriginal boys (likely of the Branch tribe) and attempted to kill a third. Reports of the circumstances vary. Some accounts suggest that the boys were living with Powell and had been sent to find a gun lost in the woods when a local settler named Hodgkinson and his settler guide were killed by Aborigines in the woods. Others merely note that the boys, who were known in the local community, had visited Isabella Ramsay to return Hodgkinson's gun. According to witnesses, the boys were armed and Ramsay feared for her life and the life of her children until a local settler named Freebody arrived.[80]

Freebody questioned the two Aborigines about Hodgkinson's death. They told him that they had spent an evening in the company of Hodgkinson before his death but did not admit to killing him. Freebody fetched the constable and some other men. Together they debated whether they should let the Aborigines go free. Powell threatened them, saying that they were murderers who "would not live long." Butler brought his sword and asked, "What Sentence shall we pass upon these black Fellows—I will pass sentence myself—they should be hanged." Metcalfe promised not to kill them. He insisted, instead, that they help to discover Hodgkinson's killers. At their trial, the Hawkesbury settlers alleged that they consulted Hodgkinson's widow about what should be done to avenge her husband's death. The victims were then led off into the bush. One escaped. The others were exhumed a day or so later. They had been bound, one was shot and the other stabbed to death. Both had sustained injuries from a cutlass; they had probably been tortured before their demise.[81]

In their defense, the Hawkesbury settlers argued not that they were innocent, but that their actions were justified. First, they argued that they had merely acted in accordance with a government proclamation authorizing the killing of Aborigines wherever they could be found. This proclamation made it an offense for settlers to "withdraw or keep back their assistance from those who may be threatened or in danger of being attacked" by Aborigines.[82] This directive might, they argued, be construed to require Powell and his companions to kill their Aboriginal victims in Isabella Ramsay's defense.

They also argued that the killings were both simple and justifiable acts of lawful retaliation and a warning to other Aborigines—according to the usual practice in the neighborhood, with or without government sanction. Rumor had it that Branch Aborigines were planning to attack outlying Hawkesbury farms. The two dead Aboriginal children were implicated in recent depredations: one had previously stolen corn, and the other was thought to have been involved in the killing of a settler several years before.

In terms of syncretic revenge, witnesses suggested that the Aboriginal victims could justly and legally be killed. According to a very expanded notion of provocation and of self-defense, popular with juries in the metropolis and on settler peripheries, the Hawkesbury settlers could also argue that they acted to protect their community against imminent violence. They acted in response to specific acts of violence, for which the colony and its courts could provide no remedy.

The court found Powell and company guilty of killing two Aborigines but refused to sentence them to death for murder without express instructions from "His Majesty's Ministers at home." Governor Hunter referred the case to the Colonial Office and, in the interim, allowed the convicted men to return to their farms.[83] In 1802, the Colonial Office requested that the men be pardoned, lamenting all the while that the colony had made such a hash of Aboriginal affairs. They enjoined the new Governor King to make "clearly understood that on future occasions, any instance of injustice or wanton cruelty towards the natives will be punished with the utmost severity of the law."[84] How he proposed to do this while letting confessed killers go free is patently unclear.

The trial of Powell and his neighbors, reproduced with all testimony in the *Historical Records of Australia,* gives remarkable insight into settler engagements with jurisdiction and their attitudes to the legal status of indigenous people. Like the killing at Blackshear's Mill in Georgia three years later, it shows the ways in which settlers constructed their lawlessness to fit within the permissive parameters of legitimate violence—parameters set simultaneously by legal pluralism and by common law. Judges, witnesses, and cross-examiners all adhered to the view that killing Aborigines was a necessary part of frontier life in the colonies of New South Wales, a necessity that was morally and legally justified. Accordingly, the perpetrators had no reason to deny their violence. They merely had to craft it into the normative framework of settler law. Butler "tried" and "sentenced" the men, but everyone else admitted openly that, as Aborigines were not bound by law, they were subject to retribution.

Colonial courts in New South Wales, like state and federal courts in Georgia, thus became sites of pluralism wherein stories of retaliation inhered in exercises of jurisdiction over settler crime. However, this pluralism ill fit emerging notions of territorial sovereignty—notions that required a purer settler law to govern every inch of the colony. Thus, by 1818, settler-murderers were more circumspect. By the early 1830s, settler violence was systematically hushed up, as courts tried and failed to confront settler-driven pluralism head on.[85]

The Doctrines of Provocation and Self-Defense

Settler stories about frontier violence adhered to populist and syncretic notions of common law self-defense and provocation. In theory, these were not as broad in New South Wales as they had become in the rough-and-tumble democracy of early national Georgia. In 1835, the first magistrate's guide produced in New South Wales (written by one of the most important agents of territorial jurisdiction in the colony, Solicitor-General John Plunkett) defined murder and its mitigating factors in very modern terms. In Plunkett's view, self-defense justified murder, so long as the killer took every opportunity to retreat from harm.[86] Provocation, was a partial defense that reduced a charge of murder to "voluntary manslaughter."[87] Like Clayton before him, Plunkett stressed that an unavenged wrong, however egregious, could turn murder into manslaughter only if no time for reflection intervened between the wrong and the act of revenge, even where Aborigines were involved.[88] Defense of property could turn murder into manslaughter, but defense of a house justified homicide entirely.[89]

Yet in practice, the flexibility of provocation and self-defense operated at numerous levels in the first decades of settlement. As in Georgia, most assumed that "whites, as a group, were acting in self-defense when they attacked blacks who, they perceived, posed a threat to their lives or property."[90] Mostly, the mere allegation that settlers killed Aborigines in self-defense or to protect property prevented state inquiry into the matter. So much is clear from the numerous and unembarrassed reports of Aboriginal deaths in the pages of the early *Sydney Gazette,* none of which resulted in arrest, prosecution, or investigation. In July 1804, the *Gazette* reported the shooting of some Aborigines who had stolen a backpack from some soldiers camped among them. Here the Aborigines' "taking to their spears and other offensive weapons, rendered it necessary to fire upon them—one was killed."[91] In September 1805, the *Gazette* reported that a boat on the Hawkesbury was attacked by Branch Aborigines, and the attack was repelled. In the process, Woglomigh was shot through the head, and it was thought that Branch Jack shared a like fate.[92] In 1806, William Witticomb, a convict worker in Port Dalrymple, Tasmania, reported firing at natives only after he was surrounded and attacked by them. His narrative may well have been true, but it followed an oft-repeated narrative of spears, then guns.[93] In January 1809, the *Gazette* reported that "a number of natives assembled about the farm of Mr Bond at Gages river . . . manifested an inclination to plunder." It seems that they threw spears after they were fired at by Bond. After the battle, the settler defenders "had to abandon the place."[94]

Key actors in the early colonial executive also accepted the natural law underpinnings of settler-indigenous violence. When Judge Atkins heard that six Aborigines had been shot near the Hawkesbury in 1794, he wondered, "how far this is justifiable I cannot say."[95] In 1804, Governor King seemed to accept that the defense of property absolved Hawkesbury settlers from any sort of criminal responsibility for shooting at Aborigines crossing farms to access water.[96] Military men also assumed that self-defense provided a broad excuse for killing in 1825. While reporting on the actions of a posse sent out after the murder of Randall Carr in Windsor, John Rolfe noted that the military "fell in with the Natives about 24 or 25 of them on . . . 29th November" and only opened fire on the group after one of their number "exclaimed, fair play and was attempting to throw his spear." Thereafter "3 or 4 of the Blacks" were wounded.[97]

By assuring law officers that indigenous wrongs provoked settler violence, killers asserted effectively that their actions were both legal and justifiable. As in Georgia, tales of peril—carefully crafted and oft-repeated narratives—simultaneously repelled and invoked colonial power. Tales of peril repelled colonial jurisdiction by preemptively justifying violence in law. However, by reporting the death in the first place, participants documented Aboriginal aggression in a manner calculated to invite a military response in defense of settlers.

When this strategy did not suffice to turn the attention of magistrates, governors, and prosecutors away from frontier violence, tales of peril were equally effective before colonial courts and military and civilian juries. The trial of Powell and company in 1799 shows how judges, soldiers, and other community leaders were invested in discourses of self-defense at this very early moment of settlement. Personal peril, indigenous culpability, and provocation infused every aspect of the inquiry. Questions from the bench to witness Thomas Rickerby focused on the history of Aboriginal misdeeds in the region, their ongoing menace to the community, and the colonial practice of retribution. The magistrates asked:

> Have you not known that after such outrages parties have been sent in pursuit of them? . . .
> Have not the parties so sent out often killed some of the Natives they were ordered in pursuit of? . . .
> Did you ever hear of the two deceased Natives having been troublesome, committing in parties Depredations or Murders? . . .
> Do you know that after that Natives have committed depredations and even Murders, that they have been received into the houses of the Settlers?[98]

Cross-examination of witnesses by the accused dwelt likewise on the culpability of the deceased as Aborigines and as individuals. Metcalf asked Isabella Ramsay if she had heard that the deceased "had acknowledged sleeping with Hodgkinson in the woods the night before he was killed."[99] Powell asked instead:

> When I came in and found you alone with the Natives in your house, did you not tell me you was glad to see me for you was in fear of your life? . . .
>   Why did you stand so much in fear of the Natives . . . have you ever sustained any loss or injury by them?[100]

David Brown swore that "the Natives are a very dangerous set of people and not to be trusted for after a man has given them all he has, they would not scruple to kill him."[101] William Goodall professed to have no idea what he was to do if an Aborigine made a threat on his life (as they had done before and would do again) if he might be tried for shooting Aborigines. He made particular note of the fact that one of his Aboriginal attackers had been taken prisoner, only to be liberated without punishment by the governor.[102] Only one witness, a gentleman named Robert Braithewaite, expressed profound distaste at the manner of the killings, though he was more sanguine when questioned about the safety of settlers away from the populous regions of the Hawkesbury.[103] In popular settler parlance, killing indigenous people was integral to survival in the Hawkesbury region in 1799. It was acceptable when it accorded to settler notions of self-defense, provocation, and retaliation.

These normative exceptions continued to function throughout the nineteenth century in colonial Australia. In 1822, when overseer Seth Hawker was tried for shooting an Aboriginal woman in an Illawarra cornfield, a military jury thought his homicide justifiable because Hawker feared for his life. This line of questioning was led by the court itself. The court asked witnesses, first, if local Tharawal Aborigines had been "troublesome" and if they had been warned about the consequences of thieving.[104] Second, the court asked if witnesses believed that Seth Hawker had fired into the dark cornfield in fear for his life. Most answered yes to the first question and gave very illuminating answers to the second. Thomas Poole attested Hawker was in fear of his life because of the "treachery of those people" and because the barking of their dogs suggested that more than one Aborigine was in the corn. A neighboring freeholder also attested to the habitual thievery of Tharawal Aborigines and argued that they "have frequently threatened to kill me to burn the Wheat and fire the house." Despite some contradictory evidence, Seth Hawker was acquitted of murder.[105]

He was not the last settler in Australia to rely on broad constructions of self-defense. The continuing salience of peril as a defense for murder on more distant Australian peripheries is also clear in a case in Western Australia in the 1870s. There, Lockier Clere Burges expressed surprise and outrage when he was indicted for shooting an Aborigine on his farm in 1872—an Aborigine who, he claimed, had merely tried to unseat him from his horse.[106]

In New South Wales, as in Georgia, narratives of peril held the day in the early years of settlement when the colony could not or would not exercise jurisdiction over indigenous people on their frontiers. In 1799, Powell and his co-conspirators walked free with the blessing of the court, the governor, and eventually, the Colonial Office because they told a story about community peril. They had nothing to fear from the boys they killed that evening, but as they told the court, their community had much to fear from the Aborigines that surrounded their settlement.

Settler Stories and the Limits of Legal Lawlessness

At the same time, Powell's case shows that the indulgence of the colony had its limits. Powell and company were tried, after all, for their misdeeds. It comes as no surprise that Powell and company tested the boundaries of community norms when they tried to justify killing two children for a murder they almost certainly did not commit. Even so, their local community stood behind them, arguing that they thought they had the governor's permission to kill any Aborigines, and that the victims had earned their fate anyway, despite their tender age. So, eventually, did the court—but not before the men had come to trial.

Despite the fact that it was constituted absolutely differently from its counterpart in Georgia, the early New South Wales judicial system dealt with settler-indigenous crime in much the same way. Before 1824, magistrates and the judge-advocate in New South Wales constituted the only courts in the colony. Very few of these men had any sort of legal training before 1810.[107] Only military juries were convened in the colony until after 1829.[108] Nevertheless, popular norms infiltrated the practice of the courts from the outset.

Though New South Wales was a penal colony in which convicts were tethered closely by colonial authority, settlers and convicts committing crimes against Aborigines had little to fear from colonial courts. I have located only seven separate incidents of settler-indigenous violence tried before the Court of Criminal Jurisdiction before the 1820s.[109] Of these, only three cases ended in guilty verdicts and only one in execution; the other defendants were reprimanded or pardoned.[110] At least two of these prosecutions involved diplomatic considerations. In 1810, Edward Luttril was charged (and later acquitted) of the crime of shooting and killing Tedbury, a Bidjigal Aborigine reputedly involved in repeated acts of violence.[111] Tedbury had been the object of diplomatic negotiations in the period; his release from custody had been brokered by his tribe in return for a promise of peace in 1805.[112] The colony may have feared that this unprovoked shooting could lead to further violence. In 1820, John Thompson and John Kirby were tried for killing Bunagan, chief of the friendly Awabakal tribe at the penal establishment at Newcastle—a crime that was bound to go badly for convicts and soldiers in the region.[113]

A goodly number of minor infractions were punished summarily by the magistracy, which had quite startlingly broad power over convict crime until the 1820s.[114] It seems, however, that killing—especially when committed by respectable men, soldiers, or free settlers of any description—seldom made it past magisterial inquiry. Magisterial inquiries, meantime, focused only on controversial incidents or incidents close to the heart of settlement. Depositions found their way into the colonial secretary's office or before the Bench of Magistrates on a number of occasions.[115] Yet the records are littered with hundreds of reports and allegations of settler-indigenous violence.[116] Depending on whose evidence one reads, Powell's case itself in 1799 attests to the killing of at least five Aborigines in the Hawkesbury region in the preceding twelve months.[117]

By crafting settler violence into narratives of imminent attack, provocation, and self-defense, settlers set the limits of settler jurisdiction in New South Wales. First, they assumed correctly that the colonial administration could not and would not control Aboriginal violence. Before the 1820s, it either delegated the task of frontier defense to settlers entirely or expected them to aid soldiers in tracking down and killing Aborigines. When William Goodall wondered how he could "act in the future" if settlers could be tried for killing Aborigines on New South Wales's frontiers, he articulated a tenet of faith in his community. Though soldiers were posted in the region, Hawkesbury settlers believed that retaliation and self-defense alone stood between them and mortal peril.[118]

Oaths and Whispers

At the same time, narratives of self-defense in Powell's case exemplify a more important phenomenon. In New South Wales, as in Georgia, settlers had a monopoly on legal evidence. In New South Wales, Powell and his co conspirators could get away with murder because legal practice privileged the words of "respectable" men and relegated Aboriginal testimony to rumor.

No Aborigines appeared before the Court of Criminal Jurisdiction to testify to the events in the Hawkesbury in 1799, though a formal ruling on the admissibility of Aboriginal evidence does not appear on the record until 1805.[119] Aboriginal deponents still turned up in New South Wales from time to time. In 1818, William Richards, alias Charcoal Will, an Aborigine, deposed that his settler employers did not murder Tharawal Aborigines in the Illawarra region[120]—testimony that probably led the Bench of Magistrates to exonerate a local farmer and his servants from the charge of murder.[121] In 1824, an Aboriginal informant named Bulwaddy gave evidence before the governor about the killing of one settler by Fitzpatrick and Colville. Bulwaddy's evidence was not admissible in court, but his testimony before the governor resulted in the execution of the prisoners.[122] These examples, however, merely punctuate Aboriginal silence.

Settler silence about violence on the frontiers of New South Wales followed only later, as new and insistent discourses of territoriality started to erode the plurality inherent in common-law practice. The growing power of silence became apparent when in 1818 the Bench of Magistrates hosted an inquest into what may have been the death of an entire band of Tharawal people in the Illawarra region south of Sydney. The Bench of Magistrates considered depositions sworn by a number of participants in what they all described as an abortive mission to recover two muskets "lent" by O'Brien (an Illawarra settler) to local Aborigines.[123] The inquiry was occasioned by a letter to the governor from Charles Throsby, Magistrate at Illawarra. Throsby alleged that O'Brien, his overseer McLease, and a number of convict servants had gone out in an armed posse and killed at least one local Aborigine.

No one but the participants knew what really happened. Most locals seemed to think that a child received a head wound. Charcoal Will deposed (though this was technically impossible) that that wound was caused by "Phillip," the Aboriginal chief in possession of the guns.[124] In local Aboriginal communities, other rumors abounded. An Aborigine called Bundle reported a rumor that "the Native Men and Women at the River were all killed," but his confidant, Joseph Wild, had heard from other Aborigines that this was untrue. An Aboriginal woman told the local constable that McLease had "fired at the Blacks." In contrast, John McArthy explained gunshots as "parrot" shooting.[125]

The most important evidence came indirectly from McLease. He boasted to the local constable that "he had Shot One" Aborigine who

"Howled like a Native Dog, and that he would Shoot all before him even if the Governor stood by, if they Slip'd a Spear at him."[126] His statement invoked the same broad discourse of peril that had absolved Powell twenty years before. First, McLease substituted corporate for individual aggression (he would shoot all Aborigines, though only one might throw a spear). Second, even as he boasted of his violence, McLease took care with the order of events. As his violence was occasioned by the throwing of a spear, he acted in self-defense.

McLease told this story of fear and violence not to the Bench of Magistrates but to his local constable. In doing so, he incriminated himself when all of his cohorts were happy to swear to his innocence. Like many before him, he sought not to evade conviction before a court but to forestall criminal investigation entirely. Though he could have chosen his words more carefully, the fact that he spoke at all shows great confidence in the power of self-defense to deter the local administration of justice in New South Wales.

Local constables and magistrates oversaw the investigation of alleged crimes and usually instigated state prosecutions. The local constable Mr. Wild should have been a more receptive audience. He had refused to lend guns or aid to O'Brien's posse because "the Aborigines had done no harm"—a statement that intimates that he would have aided a retaliatory raid occasioned by real acts of depredation or hostility. By telling Wild his story, then, McLease gambled on the sympathy of local government and lost. In repeating McLease's boasts, Wild gave the only incriminating evidence against McLease and O'Brien before the court. Significantly, Wild also testified that his own investigations suggested that "no Person else was hurt, nor have I seen the Boy that was wounded." A more sympathetic officer, like David Blackshear of Washington County, Georgia, might have quelled the inquiry entirely.

Mr. O'Brien was more circumspect. He did not testify before the Bench of Magistrates. He told absent employees that he had shot at parrots. When Constable Wild asked O'Brien "why he went after the Natives with Muskets and Cutlasses and Bayonets struck on long Sticks, he said he went to get his Muskets back." He claimed that "he saw no Blacks then only Women." He strove, in short, to keep the colony out of the local business of indigenous-settler relations. He did so in the face of hostile local officials. When told by local Aborigines and by Wild about O'Brien's posse, magistrate Charles Throsby wrote to beg the governor to inquire into the case. Throsby was already wary of local settler violence. He had reported the brutal murder and scalping of a woman and her children several years before—an atrocity that suggests that more than plural practices of imperial law crossed the Pacific.[127] Throsby had no sympathy for O'Brien or his class of settler.

The Sydney bench concluded that Throsby's allegations were not proved, to Governor Macquarie's voluble disgust.[128] The Magistrates conceded that O'Brien was unwise to go searching for natives armed. Though they accepted that McLease had fired at Aborigines in self-defense, they decided no harm was done.[129] At base, only Aboriginal rumors suggested either that a whole community of Aborigines had been murdered or that McLease had shot and wounded at least one Aboriginal child.

Here, as elsewhere, settlers and their convict-servants had a monopoly on evidence, which they deployed to protect their corporate and individual interests. However, this case also shows us something new. First, the case hints at the skewed nature of colonial intervention in early instances of settler violence. Only convicts and employees appeared before the Bench of Magistrates to attest to the alleged crimes of O'Brien and his men, and only the overseer, McLease, was seriously implicated by anyone in the crime. Mr. O'Brien, a free man and landholder, stood above the fray. Second, the case showed the instability of peril as a defense against colonial jurisdiction by 1818. Had McLease stayed silent, there would have been no evidence at all in the matter. O'Brien proved the superiority of silence over tales of peril for all to see. His lesson would be learned again by Nathaniel Lowe and John Jamieson before the new Supreme Court of New South Wales in 1827.

The efforts settlers took to render their lawlessness lawful show how Anglophone common-law culture operated to skew the contents and limit the reach of early nineteenth-century settler jurisdiction. Settlers did not spurn the law, they used it. For this reason, explaining frontier violence as a disjuncture between sovereign authority and colonial/state power misses important attributes of at least some brutal encounters between settlers and indigenous people. Authority itself was enmeshed in and compromised by settler violence. Settler oaths constituted the raw matter of jurisdiction. Settler-magistrates and constables were the foot-soldiers of the state. The alliance of common-law oath-takers, juries, judges with local government, and local settlers limited settler jurisdiction both geographically and substantively. Together, they fought the logic of territoriality and defended older and shared norms of retaliation, self-defense, and justifiable murder.

CHAPTER FIVE

The Local Limits of Jurisdiction

S ETTLERS and their office-holding neighbors monopolized the practice of jurisdiction on the frontiers of common-law settler polities. Frontiersmen and women did not often talk about sovereignty or jurisdiction, but they controlled both through institutions of local government. Peripheral soldiers, magistrates, and constables used their control over offices of local government to defend settler expansion and frontier exchange against jurisdiction. At other times, they marshaled law and government in the service of their interests. Here again, common institutions manipulated by savvy settlers bound the very different indigenous borderlands of Georgia and New South Wales into an Anglophone settler story despite distance, revolution, and the very different modes of indigenous resistance in both places. In the early nineteenth century, that story was suffused with conflicts about sovereignty, as center and periphery fought over the reach and character of settler jurisdiction over frontier violence.

Two notorious jurisdictional controversies in Georgia and New South Wales exemplify the capacity of local government to define the reach of settler jurisdiction. On February 6, 1798, a settler named John Hilton arrived before the Superintendent of Indian Affairs for the Southern Region to report a sensational crime. That morning, he entered his home in Oglethorpe County, Georgia, to find a principal chief of the Creek Nation raping his wife. Now, interracial sex was enough to get Georgia's gentlemen exercised at the best of times. In the jurisdictional vortex of Georgia's borderlands, it was grounds for a crisis of state. Within days, Mrs. Hilton's rape escalated into a metaphor for Georgia's juridical feminization: the governor of Georgia clamored for war, for the repeal of the Trade and Intercourse Acts, and most importantly, for the trial of Tuskee-gee Tustunnagau under state law. In an almost unique act of submission, the Creek tribe surrendered the chief to Georgian officials for trial. How-ever, no trial took place despite the high hopes of the state for a symbolic show of power and sovereignty through jurisdiction. First, a posse of set-tlers made an attempt on Oglethorpe Jail. Then, the inferior court of Oglethorpe County sent the chief back to Creek Country with words of peace and goodwill.

Mrs. Hilton, it seems, was at the root of both embarrassments. After receiving $250 from the Creek tribe by way of compensation, rumor had it that she mobilized her relatives to storm the jail, to release, not to lynch, her violator.[1] Then Mrs. Hilton refused to testify for the prosecution—a move that prompted the inferior court to set Tuskeegee Tustunnagau free. She said she was inspired by philanthropy and "a due sense of the natural consequences that will result from the prosecu-tion" on the frontier.[2] Whatever her motives, Mrs. Hilton's relationship with the chief—whether one of sex, commerce, or fear—exemplified a web of local connections spanning the Indian boundary that, in the end, proved more potent than the executive organs of the state. Using the very institutions of jurisdiction (Oglethorpe's inferior court), Mrs. Hilton and her neighbors subverted the theater of state justice into a theater of nonstate diplomacy.

Half a world away, the trial of mounted policeman Lieutenant Lowe in New South Wales in 1827 promised a different display of colonial juris-diction: the subordination of local institutions of governance on the col-ony's frontiers to a newly conceived imperial rule of law. After a series of killings on the northern frontier of the colony, Lieutenant Nathaniel Lowe arrested and summarily executed Jackey Jackey, a Wonnarua Ab-origine suspected of participating in a number of violent attacks against settlers and their property. To everyone's surprise, the governor had Lieu-tenant Lowe charged with murder. Never before had a soldier sent to protect citizens against Aboriginal violence been tried for such a crime.

Lowe's trial tested colonial power in the peripheries at a number of levels. Northern frontiersmen, including the local magistrate, defended local understandings of colonial jurisdiction by collaborating to thwart the investigation of Lowe's crime: witnesses disappeared, lied under oath, or refused outright to give evidence. Lowe's counsel, meanwhile, translated local resistance into a legal argument that challenged the foundations of British Empire in New South Wales. They argued that, as Britain had never treated with Australian Aborigines and as Aborigines were largely exempted from British law, they could be shot by settlers and soldiers for their crimes. The new Supreme Court of New South Wales rejected this plea on the basis of a British statute granting it jurisdiction over the territory of New South Wales, but a jury of military officers had the last say. After five minutes' deliberation, they acquitted Lieutenant Lowe of the charge.[3] Like Mrs. Hilton and her neighbors, New South Wales settlers defended local autonomy in indigenous affairs against the unwelcome—and, here, unprecedented—intrusions of the colonial state.

In their different ways, both cases show the link between indigenous-settler violence and evolving discourses about sovereignty and jurisdiction in early nineteenth-century common-law settler polities. Mrs. Hilton and her office-holding neighbors insisted that Tuskeegee Tustunnagau was an object of diplomacy, not of state jurisdiction, and they perverted state law to secure his release. Lieutenant Lowe and the Hunter Valley settlers insisted that Aborigines had been exempted in practice and in law from colonial jurisdiction, so their violence should be met with violence. In both places, local communities and local governments defended long-held assumptions that colonial/state jurisdiction was not territorial in nature on the frontiers of Georgia and New South Wales. In doing so, however, they laid bare the threat posed by jurisdictional pluralism to colonial/state sovereignty at the very moment that Georgia and New South Wales asserted new degrees of jurisdictional control. When in Georgia (1798) and New South Wales (1827) settlers deployed local governmental power to defend the anomalous legal status of indigenous people, they confronted the colony/state with its own plurality and, in the process, beckoned the judicial resolutions of the 1830s.

The Case of Mrs. Hilton

The importance of Mrs. Hilton's rape as a contest over jurisdiction cannot be overstated. If Governor James Jackson is to be believed, Mrs. Hilton (and the state of Georgia) was the victim of a crime against *both* sovereignty and womanhood. As James Jackson explained to the secretary of war, the real horror of Mrs. Hilton's rape did not lie in "the fatal stab to Mrs. Hilton's own & what no doubt she must conceive a thousand times worse her husband's peace for life." Jackson pointed out that white women imprisoned in the Creek Nation had had consensual or forced sex with Indians before, to general indifference. It lay, rather, in the fact that Mrs. Hilton was raped "within the ordinary jurisdiction & under the protection of the Laws of the State."[4]

Georgia's ordinary jurisdiction, as we have seen, was itself an artifact of the state's prostration before both the federal government and southeastern Indians. The Creek and Cherokee boundaries were lines settled by Indians and federal agents, and defined most of Georgia's territory to be outside Georgia's jurisdiction. Within its settled counties, however, Georgia aspired to exercise perfect territorial jurisdiction, an aspiration confounded by local networks of exchange that drew Indians over the boundary to trade, to steal, and in this case, to fornicate, but failed to bind them under Georgia's law. When, like most Creek malefactors, Tuskeegee Tustunnagau left Georgia's jurisdiction for Creek Country after committing his "barbarous act," he removed himself from the jurisdictional reach of the state.

Though Tuskeegee Tustunnagau raped Mrs. Hilton within the ordinary jurisdiction of Georgia, the state had no remedy against him that did not rest on the good graces of either the federal government or the Creek Nation. In law, retaliation, compensation, and even the exercise of state jurisdiction required federal or Creek acquiescence. Indeed, it was only through a judicious act of sovereign diplomacy that the Creeks surrendered Tuskeegee Tustunnagau to Georgia for trial. This was a very unusual event in the history of Creek-Georgia relations despite the Treaty of New York in 1790, which required the Creeks to hand over perpetrators of crime for trial in Georgia. Jurisdiction became the linchpin of state "satisfaction" in 1798 only through the diplomatic largesse of the Creeks.[5]

This chafed the state in 1798 more than ever before. First, the new federal constitution lodged Indian diplomacy and Indian land rights at the center of contests over state's rights. Georgia was under acute pressure in the late 1790s to cede its extensive western land claims to the federal government, which was poised to organize the Mississippi territory there.[6] Meanwhile, recent changes in federal policy made indigenous legal status a direct threat to Georgia's jurisdiction and to its sovereignty in the eyes of its jealous executive. Though they were passed by Congress in 1791, the Trade and Intercourse Acts were systematically enforced only after 1796. These Acts sought to control, indeed largely to abolish, frontier exchange economies by licensing all traders in Indian Country, outlawing the purchase of horses from Indians, and regulating the sale and distribution of all commodities within and without the Indian boundary. Under the Acts, settlers trading with Indians or traveling through Indian Country were subjected to federal jurisdiction.[7] Indigenous people, by and large, remained outside Georgia's purview. In Governor Jackson's view, the Act fostered Indian "arrogance" and lawlessness, hampered the state's power to respond, and was therefore directly responsible for Mrs. Hilton's violation.[8]

After 1796, federal usurpation of power in Georgia's peripheries was given new force by the institution of new, improved federal agencies. Federal Indian Agents Benjamin Hawkins, resident in the Creek Nation from 1796, and Return J. Meigs, resident in the Cherokee Nation from 1802, wrested all vestiges of diplomatic and jurisdictional power over Indian Country from the hands of the state.

Thus, when Tuskeegee Tustunnagau crossed into Oglethorpe County to rape Mrs. Hilton, he effected a three-fold penetration, as it were: he violated the state's intimate territorial boundaries, its jurisdictional aspirations, and the unfortunate Mrs. Hilton. According to James Jackson, only "the operation of Law" could redeem the state. By preventing settler retaliation and by reasserting Georgia's territorial jurisdiction over its peripheries through the punishment of indigenous crime, he hoped to convince the whole nation that Georgia's virtue (its sovereignty) must be rescued from marauding Indians:

> Reason & Justice due the Crime, the unfortunate Lady & moreover to the State at large, call aloud let him be a victim to the law & not the victim of individual vengeance. . . . At present all the continent must be with us, they must sympathise with the unfortunate innocent, abhor the brutal act & fix ideas of the injuries we receive from these barbarous hordes.[9]

Mrs. Hilton's rape thus laid bare the threat posed both by Indians and by federal Indian policy to Georgia's juridical integrity, and jurisdiction alone contained the remedy.

Other forces were at play in Oglethorpe County, however. There, settlers were much more invested in the safety of their farms and families and the amicable flow of goods and people across the boundary than they were in the symbolic importance of territorial jurisdiction. Colonel Philips, a local militiaman, ferried urgent promises of peace and compensation from the Creek Nation to their receptive frontier neighbors. Mrs. Hilton's family responded by marshaling a posse to storm the jail, while Mrs. Hilton withdrew her testimony against the incarcerated chief.[10] Then, Oglethorpe's inferior court released Tuskeegee Tustunnagau to the ubiquitous Colonel Philips with words of peace and good will—usurping as they went the power of the federal government to treat and of the state executive to prosecute.[11]

Settler actions in this matter were calculated: they constituted a remarkably sophisticated articulation of the juridical boundaries of the State. Creeks and settlers alike asserted, first and foremost, that violence was a local matter that could and should be settled according to established local protocols of exchange. Creek emissaries did not contact Governor Jackson or the federal agent to beg for Tuskeegee Tustunnagau's release; they contacted Colonel Philips, a respectable settler and militia officer of Oglethorpe County.[12] Speaking for the nation, Tustunnuggee Haujo begged Colonel Philips to "see and judge what is good for both nations" and, by doing so, to preserve the local community against the intrusion of state jurisdiction.

> I and the chiefs with me know you and your friends have always been the friends of justice and of the red people. . . . I wish to inform you and your father, that we have confidence in you and your neighbours, You all know that when accidents happen we must assist one another, that from misunderstandings, bickerings, and war trouble and ruin comes to many, and we should always try to avoid it.[13]

In short, Haujo asserted that diplomacy and reciprocity conducted at the local level was both the just and the customary theater for the resolution of disputes. Colonel Philips was enjoined to do local justice based in syncretic reciprocity—not in jurisdiction—to preserve the peace.

Philips and his neighbors responded to the appeal with diplomacy. He "received and read to his neighbours the address of the Creek Commissioners," and his neighbors "very generally and Immediately agreed" to act as diplomats rather than agents of jurisdiction. Through Philips, the citizens of Oglethorpe acknowledged that Georgia owed the Creeks a debt of blood: the shooting of a Creek Commissioner by a Georgian in December 1797 remained unavenged. They also acknowledged that Tuskeegee Tustunnagau was "friendly in the Extreme to the People of the frontier." With Philips, magistrates, sheriffs, and the hardy Mrs. Hilton undertook the "friendly exchange of Good offices" invoking the long practiced conventions of Indian-state diplomacy.[14]

In this frame, Tuskeegee Tustunnagau himself became a diplomatic offering, readily exchanged by both Creeks and settlers for goodwill. As the inferior court of Oglethorpe County put it:

> The prosecutors or persons injusted do apparently view the situation of the Frontier settlements of the State and having a due sense of the natural consequences that would result from the prosecution do therefore from a Philanthropic disposition drop the prosecution.
>
> While after duly weighing the matter and safety of the frontiers Together with the promises of the nation to smite in oblivion all past negatives [unclear] and will indeavour to brighten the chain of Friendship and peace between the two nations, as appears in their letter to Colo Philips.

In consideration of which we have to promote and preserve peace with mankind. WE therefore liberate the said Indian Chief.[15]

Their invocation of diplomacy was not radical. In many respects it confirmed state and federal practice. Diplomacy underpinned the vast majority of federal and state interactions with southeastern indigenous tribes, despite the fact that early national treaties called on indigenous people to surrender malefactors for trial by the United States. Plural practice was supplemented by Federal Indian Agency policy. The federal agent to the Creeks, Benjamin Hawkins, supported the exemption of indigenous people from state jurisdiction. Hawkins uniformly ignored state demands for the surrender of indigenous criminals. He argued that, so long as the Creek Nation punished Creek offenders for crimes against settlers, they honored the spirit, if not the letter, of Creek–United States treaties. Indeed, when the militiamen and judges of Oglethorpe County brokered the release of Tuskeegee Tustunnagau in 1798, Hawkins explicitly sanctioned their actions. When Governor Jackson enjoined Hawkins to broker Tuskeegee Tustunnagau's second surrender to the state, Hawkins refused. He reasoned that, as the chief was liberated by Georgia magistrates, and the matter had been investigated by the local attorney-general, it would be improper for the governor to "intervene extrajudicially" since "it is a new case and important in its consequences."[16] Hawkins, like the tribe and the good citizens of Oglethorpe County, was satisfied at the deft balance struck by the court between the forms of jurisdiction and the substance of diplomacy.

Nor did Oglethorpe County's diplomacy amount to an uncomplicated rebuttal of state power. Their actions might have usurped executive state power and the exclusive power of the federal government to sign treaties (secured by Section 8 of the Constitution) but they were hardly lawless. In the late eighteenth and early nineteenth centuries, men like Colonel Philips and the judges of the inferior court participated routinely in Indian diplomacy, though they did so in the early national period as state-appointed observers rather than as principals in negotiations. Philips and the judges made peace, as they had done before. In 1798, however, they made peace without executive authority.

By making peace in defiance of the Constitution, and therefore the federal government, the citizens of Oglethorpe County in some respects even reasserted Georgia's power in Indian affairs. They mimicked the protocols and recited the words of Indian diplomacy in the interests of the state, or at least of the state's frontier residents. In doing so they asserted that diplomacy-making was not a federal but a local concern—a position the state itself embraced on other occasions. Tuskeegee Tustunnagau, they acknowledged, was a friend to Georgia's interests. He had hunted down Creek thieves and murderers, returned stolen property to settlers, and bolstered the mission of the new federal agency in Creek Country. It served no long-term state interests to have him tried and executed, especially in the dangerous days of the 1790s, when frontier violence was rampant and war always imminent.[17]

At the same time, Oglethorpe County's diplomacy acknowledged the reach of federal systems of dispute resolution and therefore of the new extent of federal power on its frontier. More than words were exchanged in negotiations between the Creeks and their neighbors. Rumor had it that Mrs. Hilton received $250 and Colonel Philips may have received as much as $3,000 for their pains. This rumor attests to the power of new protocols of compensation and arbitration established by early national treaties, the Trade and Intercourse Acts, and the new federal agencies. These rules and institutions together established monetary compensation as the first and final remedy for most wrongs on Georgia's frontier—a remedy that suited poor frontiersmen's interests. The Hiltons could buy at least four horses with their $250, a far more palpable benefit to them than a hanged chief. With his bounty, Colonel Philips could people a considerable farm with slaves.[18]

Militiamen

More importantly, however, the release of Tuskeegee Tustunnagau was not a simple act of antistate defiance. It was itself a carefully constructed and (almost) legitimate exercise of state power effected by officers of the state entrusted with the exercise of jurisdiction. Militiamen and soldiers were instruments of both violence and jurisdiction in Anglophone settler societies. This conjunction had ancient origins: in England, "Constables were originally petty officers of the local militia and every township had one."[19] Every free man living within the ordinary jurisdiction of Georgia was enrolled in a local militia unit responsible for law-keeping and defense. They were led by locally elected commissioned officers, usually respectable men and sometimes magistrates in their communities.[20] The importance of militiamen as Indian fighters is clear from the fact that many of Georgia's early governors rose to office on the back of militia service on Georgia's indigenous frontiers.[21] Keeping the peace against slaves and Indians was the quotidian work of Georgia's militiamen—and militiamen did this as often to protect their local communities as they did to protect the state.[22]

Militiamen like Colonel Philips both upheld and defied Georgia's jurisdiction to preserve local people and local property. Justice, rather than law, was their primary concern. Militia officers wrote to Georgia's government in the early decades of the nineteenth century threatening rough justice against indigenous thieves and murderers.[23] On other occasions, militiamen and their neighbors rebuffed Georgia's attempts to exercise jurisdiction by defending settler violence against state prosecution. Such was the case in 1804 when local militiamen joined their neighbors to prevent the arrest of Mr. Patrick of Clarke County for shooting a Creek horse thief in retaliation for his theft and an unatoned murder.[24]

Militia officers sought to control indigenous violence by leading illegal retaliatory raids (and sometimes even waging war)[25] outside the jurisdictional limits of the state. However, even these were not uncomplicated rejections of Georgia's jurisdiction. Though the Constitution and the Trade and Intercourse Acts worked together to forbid them from passing the Indian boundary in pursuit of indigenous offenders, militiamen pursued Indians across Georgia's jurisdictional and geographical boundaries so routinely in the first decades after the Revolution that they reported it to the governor without a trace of embarrassment. Exceptionally few reports survive of militia officers disciplined for crossing the Indian boundary.[26] Periphery and center both seemed to accept the expediency (and perhaps the legitimacy) of illegality here. As Captain John Floyd of Camden County pointed out in 1811, indigenous murderers crossed freely beyond Georgia's "jurisdictional limits" over Spanish and Creek boundaries. Unless militiamen pursued them across the border to "their towns, there can be but little prospect of arresting the offenders."[27]

In most cases, Georgia's central government either ignored or was powerless to punish militia violence, thus lending ambiguous legitimacy to their plural notions of justice. In 1795, 150 Georgia militiamen attacked a camp of Creeks gathered in Georgia across the Oconee from Fort Fidius. Their ostensible purpose was to effect jurisdiction—they demanded the surrender or the death of Indians implicated in the death of a Lieutenant Hay, but quickly turned to looting and violence.[28] Significantly, their superiors were far more careful to distance themselves from these thefts than they were from the attempted arrest or killing; the latter was justice (if not jurisdiction), the former, crime.[29] David Blackshear led his militia company across the Indian boundary in pursuit of stolen property on a number of occasions. On the first, in 1796, he deposed that he pursued Indians who had stolen a horse and plundered a settlement, firing on them repeatedly as he did so.[30] On the second, in 1799, reports from Indian Country suggested that his party killed five Creeks caught in the act of roasting Washington County beef.[31] Georgia's governor demanded an investigation into the killings, but not into the illegal boundary crossing bent on recovering stolen property. All of these actions contravened state, federal, and treaty law, and none of them was punished by courts. Militia officers' pursuit of justice, founded in some inchoate notion of Georgia's jurisdiction, had some weight with Georgia's executive and with the federal agents residing in the Creek and Cherokee Nations. Militiamen were mindful, though careless, of the law.

By traipsing across the Indian boundary to make peace, Colonel Philips varied the usual formula, but not the localism, of most militia officers. First, Colonel Philips's role in the liberation of Tuskeegee Tustunnagau shows all the liminality of a militia officer and frontiersman: his rank and his imbrication in frontier exchange singled him out as an ideal diplomat and intermediary for Indians and settlers alike. Significantly, however, the state's executive was much more affronted by Philips's diplomacy than it was by the violence and illegal border crossings of other militiamen. Governor Jackson protested Philips's usurpation of executive powers, suspected him of corruption of his office, sought evidence to punish him for taking bribes, and even accused him of overseeing the attempted jail-break.[32] His offense here was not illegal activity per se; it was the fact that his actions negated state jurisdiction at a moment when the state sought, for the first time, to demonstrate its splendid sovereignty to the world.

Local Magistrates

If Philips's diplomacy affronted the jurisdictional aspirations of the state, then the actions of the inferior court were far more insidious. Its diplomatic statement to the Creeks took the form of a judgment. It called on the sheriff to bring Tuskeegee Tustunnagau to court via a writ of habeas corpus—an action to prevent illegal detention of prisoners by the state.[33] Its fundamental reason for releasing the chief, meanwhile, was Mrs. Hilton's refusal to testify. Here they demonstrated (perhaps willful) ignorance of the law. In late eighteenth-century Georgia, rape was a crime against the state.[34] As Attorney General Van Allen pointed out, Mrs. Hilton was the state's witness, not a prosecutrix. She could be compelled by law to testify.[35] The inferior court judges, then, exercised jurisdiction in the service of diplomacy. Their judgment even used the words of early national diplomacy, putting all bad deeds behind them, and looking forward to peaceful relations with the Creek Nation in the future.

Magistrates and judges in Georgia had special power to determine the jurisdictional reach of settler states.[36] Magistrates lived and worked in the local communities that they ordered, and few, if any, had legal training. As such, they had little incentive to exercise their power in the interests of the state—though this potential had inhered in the office since its creation in the Middle Ages in England, and its mobilization had been essential to English modernization.[37] Georgia's magistrates oversaw militia musters and road building, tried civil cases and petty crime, investigated crime, and had often acted as intermediaries between their communities and their indigenous neighbors at the behest of the state. In short, Georgia's magistrates controlled state jurisdiction (governmental and judicial) at the local level. Magisterial power and its potential either to undermine or to bolster state law were recognized by the state of Georgia when, in 1819, the state circulated five hundred copies of Clayton's *Georgia Justice* on its peripheries.[38]

In Georgia, magistrates constituted local inferior courts that had original jurisdiction to hear civil matters and the usual run of magisterial powers to hear the early phases of criminal matters. Even superior courts charged with hearing capital cases in Georgia were local to a degree. Under the 1797 Judiciary Act, each district had its own superior court staffed by local judges and served by local juries. The state did not have a supreme court with appellate jurisdiction until 1835.[39] Governor Jackson acknowledged their power to thwart justice and jurisdiction in 1798 when he enjoined the superior court justices of Jackson County to try Tuskeegee Tustunnagau fairly: so the Creeks "might witness the fairness of the same which under your Honors direction I am certain [the case] will be conducted with solemnity and candour and every proper indulgence to the unfortunate wretch."[40] He simply did not anticipate that Oglethorpe's inferior court would act to prevent the trial entirely.

For all of this, both Colonel Philips and the judges of the inferior court did their duty, defined as it was by custom, practice, and common law. As community leaders, neighbors, and state officials, they had duties to maintain a balance between local and metropolitan interests that no rule book could define. In Governor Jackson's view, they got the balance wrong in 1798. In the process, they undermined Georgia's already circumscribed territorial jurisdiction. Though they acted for the state, the judges acted out of order: "Laws and Justice must be obeyed and besides those political motives of brightening the Chain of Friendship . . . belong not to any power in the state—Executive, Legislature or Judicial and much less the latter," but to the United States. Worse still, Tuskeegee Tustunnagau's release did not even conform to basic shared notions of retaliation, let alone satisfy Jackson's taste for jurisdiction. The decision, he lamented, "makes the crime of Rape Ridiculous in the eyes of the Indians, who finding they can get off from our Gaols after even confinement will . . . attack & ravish every Woman they came up with."[41]

Mrs. Hilton's rape marked a moment when the state's center and periphery parted ways in their definition of the nature and extent of state jurisdiction. They did not always do so. Networks of interest, friendship, and experience bound periphery to center in the common pursuit of diplomacy, retribution, and increasingly of [illegal] jurisdiction. As the 1810s approached, a growing number of constables, sheriffs, militiamen, and magistrates entered Indian Country illegally, not to kill or pillage, but to effect state jurisdiction in a much more direct fashion. Most of these incidents related to civil, not criminal, matters. Their efforts contravened federal and constitutional law, to be sure, but the federal agents seldom seemed to object. From 1808, creditors demanded the surrender of dozens of white debtors residing in the Cherokee Nation.[42] An Alabama creditor, in 1810, served process on the Creek Indian David Tate for the recovery of slaves mortgaged by his uncle, Alexander McGillivray. Benjamin Hawkins advised Tate to hire a lawyer and plead to jurisdiction. If that failed, he advised Tate to plead the statute of limitations, as the debt was an old one, long unpaid and unclaimed.[43] In 1811, Meigs recorded the attempts of a Georgian to seize Cherokee property and Cherokee slaves to satisfy debts.[44] In the same year, a Georgia sheriff and a creditor chased and arrested an absconding debtor through the Cherokee Nation down the Federal Road, to the jurisdictional bewilderment of all.

Indigenous violence was not exempted from this trend. By the 1810s, militia officers demanded the surrender to jurisdiction of indigenous offenders almost as often as they bayed for blood. Buckner Harris of Jackson County took to doing both at once in his demands for the surrender of Cherokees James Vann (in 1808) and Buffington and Daniel (from 1811 to 1813).[45] Militia officers and their companies turned increasingly from retaliation over the Indian boundary to illegal abduction for trial.[46] By 1821, Cherokee chief Path Killer complained that Cherokee deaths went unpunished, while when "any axdent happens of that kind they meattately apprehend us wether it is just or not."[47] Officers of the superior court of Dooly County, meanwhile, took to demanding the surrender of indigenous wrongdoers by 1823.[48] Jurisdiction here radiated inward from the periphery.

In the early national period, Georgia experienced indigenous-settler violence both as a crisis of jurisdiction over indigenous people and settlers on their frontier, and as a crisis of pluralism within the state. Yet

Mrs. Hilton and her office-holding neighbors showed the limits of territorial jurisdiction in the state of Georgia when the state itself was enmeshed in the business, pain, and pleasure of frontier exchange. Almost every step in Georgia's arrest and trial of Tuskeegee Tustunnagau depended on the fractious local agencies of government in Georgia, all of which had differing ideas about the nature of state authority on Georgia's frontiers. In Georgia, militiamen, magistrates, and judges all lived on the frontiers they ordered. Localism, then, did not dissent from state jurisdiction: it constituted its form and its substance. The business of governance, of diplomacy, of law, and of war on the frontiers of Georgia all focused on the minutiae of frontier life. Using the magistracy and the militia as intermediaries, settlers subjoined state jurisdiction to defend their interests—whether those interests lay in jurisdictional expansion or amicable exchange with their indigenous neighbors. In the process, they show the fluidity of early nineteenth-century sovereignty, and they participated in a settler story that stretched from the Atlantic across the Pacific.

The Case of Lieutenant Lowe

If Mrs. Hilton's ravishment marked an early high point in the manipulation of state jurisdiction by Anglophone institutions of local governance, then the demise of Jackey Jackey in 1826 marks its persistence in the late days of pluralism on the northern frontiers of New South Wales. In 1826, after a series of attacks by the Wonnarua people on the northern frontier of the colony, mounted policeman Lieutenant Nathaniel Lowe arrested and executed an Aboriginal man called Jackey Jackey. Jackey Jackey was handed to Lowe by a local constable, then bound and shot in plain sight of a number of British subjects from the neighborhood. Other rumors also abounded: that Lieutenant Lowe or his men had shot at least three Aboriginal men, and that members of the Hunter Valley settler community had participated in atrocities against indigenous people in their neighborhood.[49]

When rumors reached Sydney of the crime, the governor set out to investigate and eventually had Lieutenant Lowe charged with murder. Charging a soldier for murder when he had been sent to protect a frontier community against Aboriginal depredations was an unprecedented exercise of colonial jurisdiction.[50] The frontier community responded accordingly. Almost everyone, from the magistrates down to convict workers, rebuffed the scrutiny of the colonial state by refusing to cooperate with state-appointed investigators. In court, Nathaniel Lowe's lawyers mounted one of the most explicit and remarkable exegeses of the limited nature of British jurisdiction and sovereignty on the frontiers of New South Wales. Jurors from the New South Wales Corps, meanwhile, acquitted Lieutenant Lowe of the charge.[51] Settlers, their office-holding neighbors, and a Sydney jury comprised of His Majesty's officers again subverted jurisdiction to protect local, plural notions of British sovereignty and of justice.

Like Mrs. Hilton, Lieutenant Lowe's supporters reasserted local conceptions of jurisdiction at a time of intense jurisdictional change. Jackey Jackey's murder caught the attention of the colony and the metropolis three years after the first Supreme Court was established in New South Wales. It is a well-known incident in frontier history, used by some to illustrate settler lawlessness and by others to show the doctrinal development of *terra nullius* by the first Supreme Court.[52]

It is because Lowe's case marks a turning point in jurisdictional practice in New South Wales—a turning point curbed so effectively by settlers, soldiers, magistrates, and jurors—that it constitutes such an important example of indigenous-settler violence in New South Wales. Despite—or perhaps because of—the colonial state's attempts to bring New South Wales's frontiers under its control in 1826, this frontier community used Anglophone institutions of local government and common-law rules of evidence to devastating effect to defend its plural understanding of jurisdiction and of sovereignty. Settlers, at least, understood that the central conflict in the case was not between imperial jurisdiction and settler lawlessness, but between different modes of law-keeping governed by different conceptions of jurisdiction.

In Lieutenant Lowe's New South Wales, as in Mrs. Hilton's Georgia, Anglophone traditions of local governance in important respects constituted the jurisdiction of the colony. This was so despite the fact that the colony of New South Wales circa 1826 differed so much in its constitution and government from the state of Georgia circa 1798.[53] For the purposes of this chapter, the most important differences between Georgia and New South Wales lay in the mechanics of government themselves. Georgia's constitution guaranteed free, white citizens a direct role in state government, the state militia, and the state's juries if they resided within the ordinary jurisdiction of the state. Inferior and superior courts were local institutions, staffed by local judges and local juries. Local militia officers were elected by local militia companies, cementing their position as leading men who supported local before provincial interests. The executive and legislature of the state were embroiled enthusiastically in the business of expansion, though at times they were less enamored of the poor and fractious settlers who crowded Georgia's indigenous frontiers.[54]

In contrast, because New South Wales was established as a penal colony in the wake of the troubles in North America, it was, first and foremost, a police state. The governor of New South Wales was invested with extraordinarily broad powers. He was commander in chief of the armed forces, chief magistrate, and civil authority within the colony, until the introduction of an appointed legislative council after 1823 and the overhaul of the judicial system in 1824.[55] No one was elected there, to any office. Accordingly democracy and localism simply lacked the institutional hegemony they enjoyed in early national Georgia. Moreover, in the early decades of the colony of New South Wales, governors tried to give their authority geographical expression by keeping settlement close to Sydney.[56] Yet in Lowe's case, as in the rape of Mrs. Hilton, the jurisdictional ambitions of the colony fell victim to the power of settler-officers to control jurisdictional practice in the first quarter of the nineteenth century. Though the governor of New South Wales may have been omnipotent in theory, like his counterparts in Georgia, he presided over an uneasy and geographically diffuse government hierarchy.

Lieutenant Lowe himself marks both continuity and difference between Georgia and New South Wales. Unlike Georgia, New South Wales had no militia—not least because, by 1826, most of the people in the colony were convicts or emancipists (freed convicts) and, as such, very uncertain allies of the colonial state. Instead, Lieutenant Lowe *was* the government's agent of peace, war, and jurisdiction in the peripheries. He was an officer in the mounted police, a "specialist [military] police force" designed in 1825 specifically to maintain order on New South Wales's frontiers.[57] This institution existed not only to curb Aboriginal resistance but also to capture escaped convicts-turned-bushrangers and to control proliferating illegal settlements.

The mounted police, however, could no more conjure jurisdiction on the frontiers of New South Wales than they could tie periphery to center. Perennially understaffed and underequipped, Lieutenant Lowe and his men could do little to secure administrative and judicial jurisdiction in the peripheries. Far-flung, *officially* settled areas lay beyond the reach of district magistrates—and often of mounted police. Illegal settlements lay outside the organized jurisdiction of government altogether.[58] At least until the introduction of pastoral leases in 1836, the colonial state suffered a double disadvantage in these places, because illegal frontier settlers were chiefly male, poor, and interested in the extension of Empire only insofar as it did not jeopardize their interests.[59]

Deficits of colonial power were augmented by fissures in colonial authority, some of which only worsened with the advent of the new Supreme Court. In 1827, the new chief justice ruled that convict labor on distant pastoral stations could not be controlled by the colony's government. According to Chief Justice Forbes, only masters could govern convict workers in New South Wales.[60] Meanwhile, some convict workers and illegal settlers cooperated to shield escapees and highwaymen from the colonial administration. The problems of law, order, and distance converged in the appointment of convicts as special constables on the fringes of the colony, where they were simultaneously protagonists and antagonists of the colonial state.[61]

Lieutenant Lowe's role in the Hunter Valley in 1826 reflected confusion over the nature of government power in New South Wales. The mounted police was a liminal institution, neither properly civil nor properly military.[62] Like their counterparts in Georgia, soldiers, and later the mounted policemen, acted as both soldiers and law-keepers.[63] Though they were commanded by the center to visit and control various frontiers, they dispensed state violence in and for the peripheries with minimal state supervision.[64] As Lowe showed the grateful Hunter Valley community, he could dispense violence unflinchingly with, or without, the authorization of the government in Sydney.

Forty years of practice in the colony of New South Wales led settlers to expect nothing less. The nascent colonial state had routinely delegated state violence to frontier settlers before 1824. It had used not jurisdiction, but negotiation and violence (including authorized settler self-defense and military campaigns) to quell Aboriginal resistance before 1822. Prosecutions for settler violence against Aborigines, meanwhile, were exceedingly rare and usually acted to curb convict workers rather than their employers or soldiers. So Lieutenant Lowe's prosecution came as a great surprise. The provincial government, pressured by the metropolis, sought not only to govern New South Wales's frontiers but also to make sure that frontier government conformed to law.

Local Magistrates

Settler resistance to the investigation and trial of Lieutenant Lowe was orchestrated and aided by the local magistrate. As in Georgia, local magistrates' loyalties tended toward their local communities rather than provincial government. In general, "Tensions between the centre and the periphery were characteristic of the magistracy in the second quarter of the nineteenth century."[65] The magistracy was a vital tool of governance in New South Wales, especially when settlement spread rapidly from the late 1810s. Often "the magistrate was the only agent of civil government" on the peripheries of New South Wales. Before 1824, moreover, magistrates were unsupervised by superior courts:[66]

> In addition he was in control of the police in his district, was responsible for the assignment of convicts as servants, organized musters of convicts and other inhabitants, drew up jury lists (after the introduction of trial by jury), organized and presided at public meetings, presented petitions on behalf of the inhabitants . . . was responsible for taking the local census and carried out many other non-judicial functions.[67]

Most magistrates were unpaid, though the proliferation of stipendary posts in the late 1820s introduced a class of persons who depended as much on the state for their subsistence as they did on their farms and local communities. However, even stipendary magistrates were farmers and neighbors in addition to being officers of the state.[68]

New South Wales magistrates did not always defend settler violence against state regulation. A number acted as intermediaries between Aborigines and the colonial state. In 1816 and 1818, Charles Throsby, settler, explorer, and magistrate, deployed his personal rather than official power to protect peaceable Aborigines in the neighborhood of Illawarra, some of whom seemed to view him as a protector and confidant. He informed Sydney officials of rumored local atrocities and gave them information to ensure that soldiers deployed to quell Aboriginal violence did not hurt friendly local tribes.[69] In 1838, seven men were tried for murdering dozens of Aboriginal men, women, and children at Myall Creek only because a local overseer spoke out against them, and a local stipendary magistrate tracked down and arrested his neighbors.[70]

In 1826, however, the Hunter Valley magistrate Mr. Close deployed his considerable authority in the service of concealment. Governor Darling ordered three separate inquiries into the murder of Jackey Jackey. The second, to be conducted by the chairman of the Quarter Sessions, was aborted by shipwreck—a telling reminder that remoteness itself operated to limit the reach of colonial jurisdiction. Mr. Close reminded Sydney more subtly of the "tyranny of distance" and of its social and legal results.[71] He ensured that the first inquiry brought little incriminating evidence to light. Close again sabotaged the third, conducted by Acting Attorney-General Moore. Moore accused him of actively conspiring to obscure the true circumstances of Jackey Jackey's demise.[72] Close refused to force witnesses to answer incriminating questions, thus preserving his place in the local community and preempting any evidence that he had failed in his duty to investigate the matter himself.[73]

Close may have obstructed state inquiries into the incident, but he did not merely defend lawlessness. Instead, he helped his neighbors to defend a plural understanding of colonial jurisdiction. Like their counterparts on the frontiers of Georgia, Hunter Valley settlers wanted state interference on their frontier, but they wanted it on their own terms. It seems that they had sent petitions reporting Aboriginal depredations to Sydney earlier in the year, beckoning both the force and the gaze of the colonial state.[74] Governor Darling was suspicious of their claims, in part because he suspected that Aboriginal depredations there were caused by lawless stockmen. He urged landholders to protect themselves and restrain their employees.[75] Darling here, and elsewhere, preferred to let locals sort out their own problems—with a fair degree of support from London, which was constantly concerned with the cost of expanding law enforcement capacities in the colony.[76] When Darling did send Lieutenant Lowe's regiment to quiet local Aborigines, long practice led local settlers to expect troops to be purveyors of legitimate violence, not of jurisdiction. So, Lieutenant Lowe's conviction was prevented by something much more complicated than lawlessness—though, no doubt, there was a good bit of lawlessness involved. It was prevented by local understandings of colonial jurisdiction and of "justice" on the northern frontiers of New South Wales.

That understanding was translated into a remarkable rebuttal of imperial power by Lieutenant Lowe's counsel, the liberal publishers-*cum*-lawyers, W. C. Wentworth and Robert Wardell. Invoking the full canon of natural and nascent international law, Lieutenant Lowe's counsel argued that there was no written treaty submitting Aboriginal land and people to the jurisdiction and sovereignty of the Crown. Jackey Jackey did not belong to a conquered people, he had not voluntarily submitted to the protection of the British Crown, and he had been afforded none of the rights and privileges of a subject; for example, he had no standing to give evidence and no right to trial by a jury of peers. Therefore, in fact and in theory, he was not "protected" by British law. More significantly, Lowe's counsel argued, in the absence of agreement with the Aborigines, the boundaries of New South Wales (and therefore the court's jurisdiction) could only extend to the settled areas of the colony. Echoing Judge Advocate Atkins's opinion twenty years before, they argued that no authority prevailed on the frontiers and beyond, and that Aborigines as cultural outsiders without civil rights could not be subjected to jurisdiction. If Jackey Jackey could not be justly punished by British law for killing settlers, then natural law rather than British law governed his crimes. Natural law sanctioned the killing of a murderer. So Lieutenant Lowe acted lawfully when he shot Jackey Jackey.[77]

This brief has received much more scholarly attention than the circumstances that gave rise to it. Some argue that Wentworth and Wardell's defense is bound into emancipist politics in the colony; that their discussion of indigenous rights provided a foil for their struggle for settler civil rights.[78] Others argue that it is wrong in international law.[79] Regardless of its status as legal argument, however, this case gave voice to the prevailing logic of diplomacy in everyday practice in New South Wales. Before 1822, almost everyone from the governor to the lowliest settler assumed that violence, not British jurisdiction, was the appropriate response to Aboriginal violence against settlers. Instead, they assumed— whether on natural law or inchoate syncretic principles of justice—that every murderer should be punished with death, and that British subjects alone were governed by British law.[80] In short, sovereignty was not territorial in nature, and Aborigines could be killed because they could not be tried.

This logic was shared by center and periphery before the 1820s. However, the advent of the Supreme Court in 1824, and the increasingly dense networks of ideas, of power, and of legality that bound periphery to center within the British Empire, pitted settlers against their government. Like Mrs. Hilton's Georgia, New South Wales circa 1827 had jurisdictional aspirations. Its new court and its increasingly professionalized government together imagined a new colonial state. In this place, borders, not status, race, or culture, determined the limits of government power. Accordingly, the new court acknowledged the strength of counsel's arguments in the "law of nations," but found itself bound by an act of Parliament.

The court held that, at least as far as Lieutenant Lowe was concerned, New South Wales's municipal law was the *lex loci* of the northern frontier (and indeed of half of the continent), and therefore his crime fell within British jurisdiction. The court argued, alternatively, that as an officer and subject of the Crown, Lowe was "personally within the jurisdiction of this Court." Jackey Jackey's status was less certain. For the purposes of this case, at least, the "native . . . must be considered, whatever be his denomination, a British subject. If not to be an alien friend, or an *alien ami,* in any case he is entitled to *lex loci,* and it is only under peculiar circumstances he can be excluded from that right."[81] The logics of territorial and personal jurisdiction combined here to ensure that Lieutenant Lowe as a subject was susceptible to British law for the murder of

Jackey Jackey, though Jackey Jackey's relationship with the Crown stemmed merely from the location of his demise. Whereas Jackey Jackey's status remained uncertain, settlers and the institutions of local government were all subject to British imperial law.

However, military jurors, two-time agents of government, had the final say. The efficacy of the settlers' conspiracy to silence, combined with the force of colonial practice and the logic of legal pluralism, culminated in the acquittal of Lieutenant Lowe. The decision was greeted with applause from the considerable crowd that had gathered in the courtroom and on the streets outside.

Like Mrs. Hilton and her neighbors in Georgia, low-ranking imperial judicial and military officers cooperated with community leaders to protect Lieutenant Lowe from jurisdiction in 1826. Acting Attorney-General Henry Moore noted "the unwillingness, I saw, as well among the lower class of persons, as the higher, to afford me any intelligence."[82] Governor Darling imputed local noncooperation to "the inhabitants of every class being at least indifferent to the fate of the Natives, and unwilling that any one . . . should be made answerable for his conduct."[83] When the imperial hierarchy stepped in to discipline Lieutenant Lowe, the community closed ranks. In the end, only unfree laborers eager for pardons would testify against Lowe in court, arguing as they did so that they feared for their lives.[84] Whether its actions are best understood as a bid for autonomy, a class-based consensus about Aboriginal policy, or a defense of an empire premised on military action rather than civilian justice, this community successfully disrupted metropolitan efforts to assert a new kind of jurisdiction. In the process it defended not lawlessness, but its own version of plural, imperial law.

The travails of Mrs. Hilton and Nathaniel Lowe suggest important commonalities in the experience of common-law settler states in the early nineteenth century. First and foremost, they show that we cannot distinguish clearly between settler interests and state interests. In common-law settler polities, ancient and shared institutions (the militia and the magistracy) determined the reach of state jurisdiction because they monopolized state power in the peripheries. The state itself was plural, divided by interests and by geographical distance. Settler interests in unfettered geographical expansion or in the maintenance of amicable economies of exchange with their indigenous neighbors did not always accord with central interests in effecting orderly settlement in the peripheries.

It comes as no surprise that divergent interests in these cases ripened into jurisdictional conflict over indigenous-settler violence. Indigenous legal status always carried within it the potential to challenge state authority because, as these cases show, there were deep disjunctures between claims of sovereignty and jurisdictional practice. Settlers, moreover, often crafted their violence to fit within discourses of law or fissures in jurisdiction. Settlers could act with or against the state (as officeholders or as dissenters) to defeat or expand the reach of state jurisdiction, through and against the law.

In 1798 and in 1827, this conflict mattered. The executive of the state of Georgia sought to defend its sovereignty by exercising jurisdiction over indigenous people and others within its newly circumscribed jurisdictional boundaries in 1798. In 1826 and 1827, the metropolitan and provincial government of New South Wales sought to defend its right to control indigenous-settler violence on its peripheries through the rule of law. In both places, settlers and peripheral institutions of the state defended their interests by exploiting the gap between common law and plurality.

CHAPTER SIX

Farmbrough's Fathoming and Transitions in Georgia

B EFORE THE WAR of 1812, legal pluralism in Georgia's borderlands was maintained and contested by settlers, by every level of state and federal government, and most importantly, by indigenous people themselves. Any attempt to define state sovereignty as a territorial measure effected through the exercise of jurisdiction foundered on the plurality of indigenous legal status. Jurisdictional practice followed an older logic, premised on the contingencies of early modern empire rather than modern notions of statehood, rooted in middle-ground conventions of indigenous-settler reciprocity, and in every way inconsistent in its conception and its execution. This fraught arrangement precipitated a crisis when the United States ended the war with the defeat of the Creeks at Horseshoe Bend in 1814.

The controversy over Creek and Cherokee legal status in the years preceding their forcible removal from southeastern North America is a story that scarcely needs retelling. After the War of 1812, Georgia insisted that indigenous people be removed by treaty or coercion from its borders in fulfillment of the Compact of 1802. Once Tennessee war hero Andrew Jackson took office as President in 1829, Georgia's desires became national policy. Indigenous people were driven over the Mississippi by a series of fraudulent treaties, backed by the withholding of indigenous treaty money, widespread lawlessness, and state and federal coercion. Jurisdiction was also of fundamental importance to indigenous dispossession. Foremost among Georgia's efforts to effect indigenous removal was its extension of jurisdiction over Indian Country from June 1830.

Historians have explained Indian Removal from 1815 to 1838 variously as the culmination of settler land hunger in the cotton age, as the result of the sudden explosion of both population and the franchise after the War of 1812, or as an aggressive drive toward economic modernization.[1] Others argue that Removal was the result of a sincere attempt to save indigenous people from eradication,[2] as an aggregation of racist ideologies that displaced enlightenment ambivalence about indigenous people's rights,[3] or most importantly as another dramatic product of the struggle over states' rights.[4] Population explosion, economics, and state's rights converged when the discovery of gold prompted a regional gold rush accompanied by chaos and competition in Georgia's Cherokee Country in 1828.[5] All were necessary conditions for indigenous removal from Georgia, yet none alone or combined explains the role of territorial jurisdiction in the saga.

Told as a story about jurisdiction, Removal forms a crucial episode in the rise of territorial sovereignty in common-law settler societies in the early nineteenth century. Sovereignty talk and jurisdictional practice changed in Georgia between 1815 and 1830. Before 1812, Georgia's aspirations to territorial sovereignty and jurisdiction were partial and contingent. After the war, however, the state bent all of its efforts toward ending a century of (increasingly contentious) plural practice in Georgia's Indian Country. Georgia sought perfect settler sovereignty.

The state of Georgia was only the most extreme interlocutor in the ascendant discourse of territoriality. At key moments in 1818, 1823, and 1826, federal, state, and indigenous sovereignty talk ceased to focus on whether sovereignty imported territorial jurisdiction over all people traversing a given unit of territory and instead came to focus on who wielded this power and where. State representatives mobilized old common-law doctrines of discovery and conquest not only to divest indigenous people of land but also to defend a thoroughly new understanding of settler statehood. Different voices in the federal government began to insist that someone had territorial jurisdiction in Indian Country, whether it be indigenous people or the federal government. Most importantly, the Cherokee, much more so than the Creeks, insisted as never before that Indian Country was a geographical space governed by Indian law. Federal, state, and indigenous governments vied for control of Georgia's borderlands after 1815, and crisis resulted.

The discourse of territoriality had limits, however. In the margins of the state, jurisdictional practice moved much more slowly toward territoriality between 1815 and 1830. An incident of frontier violence in February 1830 shows both the geographical reach and the practical limits of territoriality in the state of Georgia and the Cherokee Nation on the cusp of Georgia's legislative extension of jurisdiction over the nation. On February 21, 1830, Alan Farmbrough, a magistrate in Carroll County, sent a letter to Governor Gilmer of Georgia. He wrote in defense of his neighbors, a community of Georgian squatters who "arrested" four Cherokees on Cherokee land and beat one of them to death. Their victim, Chuwoyee, died from injuries and exposure. One of his companions was imprisoned in Carroll County and later released, and two others escaped, one after receiving a serious chest wound.[6] In defense of these actions, Farmbrough articulated a popular understanding of territorial sovereignty that synthesized fifteen years of ferment in the centers and peripheries of Georgia. Though Chuwoyee and his companions had burned the houses of squatters on Cherokee land, Farmbrough claimed that he had been arrested in Georgia in accordance with Georgia's laws. Farmbrough argued that, as a matter of law, Georgia's sovereignty gave it jurisdiction over Cherokee crimes against settler property in Georgia on both sides of the Indian boundary.

The problem was that Chuwoyee, with a band of Cherokee warriors, had burned the houses as an act of Cherokee territorial jurisdiction. A high-ranking Cherokee chief, John Ross, had ordered Chuwoyee and his companions to burn Cherokee houses inhabited by squatters to harry them from the borders of the nation. By treaty, the federal government was obliged to remove squatters from Cherokee land. However, the federal government had refused this office in the 1820s, telling the nation to fend for itself (even though, in other matters, it claimed increasing jurisdiction over Cherokee affairs). The Cherokee, meanwhile, had announced their arrival as a territorial state through their Constitution of 1827—a document that stood at the apex of a decade of increasingly territorial articulations of power in this increasingly market-driven, agricultural, and politically syncretic society. House burning, it transpires, was not an act of lawlessness at all.

Chuwoyee's death was a grave loss for the Cherokee, but as a matter of principle, they won the day. The secretary of war defended the Cherokees right to expel squatters from their land. The state executive also abandoned the cause of the settler-squatters, despite a decade of vociferous claims about territorial jurisdiction and its demands that these particular Cherokee improvements be given over for the use of Georgia settlers. This being said, there is no evidence that Farmbrough's neighbors were brought to trial for their violence.

Postwar Transformations in State Discourse

Farmbrough's first argument for the lawfulness of Chuwoyee's murder was based on a widespread and perhaps willful misunderstanding of law: "It had been my opinion that the original laws of the state were in full force over the Indians residing within our chartered limits, this opinion is founded upon the act of 1827." In December 1827, in response to the Cherokee Constitution, Georgia legislated to extend jurisdiction over the Cherokee Nation. However, this clause was not due to come into effect until June 1830—a subtlety missed by many at the time. Chuwoyee and his companions burned farms on Cherokee Country in early February 1830, several months before Georgia's jurisdiction was formally extended. Farmbrough discovered his error only when Carroll County's inferior court dismissed Rattling Gourd, Chuwoyee's accomplice, "upon the ground that the criminal law was not yet in operation over them."[7]

His second argument in support of his neighbors' violence was much more important. It contained a very astute summation of a new logic of territorial sovereignty implicit *both* in the discourse of Removal and, to a remarkable degree, in federal and Cherokee dissents from it. Farmbrough argued:

> The U.S. ceded to Georgia their right to the jurisdiction of that country in their boundary of cession to Georgia and why are our laws to be limited in their nation or suspended in operation, are we as the people of a Sovereign State to be thus treated, is our property to be distroyed and the law afford us no security are we as free citizens to have our rights Jeoperdized our persons attacked assaulted and abused and will the State say we are remedeless, If so we who reside in frontier counties must retreat from the vindictive oath of savage vengeance.[8]

He asserted, in short, that Georgia was a sovereign state, and that sovereignty contained within it an unqualified right to exercise jurisdiction. It left no place for indigenous rights or federal law.

At key moments between 1815 and 1830, actors on all sides of the Creek and Cherokee Removal controversy embraced the logic of territoriality.[9] By 1830, even Farmbrough, a citizen of Georgia living on the border of Cherokee Country, had mastered it. It is clear, then, that sovereignty discourse and jurisdictional practice—state, federal, and indigenous—underwent a radical and rapid transformation in the aftermath of the War of 1812.

Farmbrough responded to the rapid evolution of territorial jurisdiction as an idea and a local practice between 1815 and 1830. This story begins with the war waged among the United States, Great Britain, and a number of Indian nations including the Creeks from 1812 to 1814. If the period before the War of 1812 was characterized by inconsistency in the theory and the practice of state, indigenous, and federal jurisdiction, then the War of 1812 constituted a radical turning point in Georgia's attitudes toward its borderlands. The war hastened a decline in indigenous economic and military power that had begun well before, as European interest in America was diverted by the Napoleonic wars, game in the southeast disappeared, and trade of deerskins and other forest commodities dwindled.[10] Indigenous people in both the Creek and Cherokee Nations were increasingly involved in commercial agriculture, and the wealthiest among them had large plantations run by slave labor.[11] However, Georgia saw indigenous farmers as impediments to state expansion—impediments that, in 1814, retained possession of more than half of the territory of the state. This state of affairs became especially irksome after peace with Britain resulted in an explosion in British demand for American cotton—a crop that thrived on Creek land in particular.[12] In this respect, Georgia's Removal crisis was part of an Atlantic and a global story. As Georgia and the Old Southwest turned toward Britain for their livelihood, their indigenous neighbors suffered the fate of indigenous people in all settler jurisdictions providing fibers for the British Midlands mills.

The defeat of the Creek Red-Sticks in 1814 had filled Georgia with hope. Though only one faction of the Creek Nation fought with the British, all southeastern Indians were victims of the war and even more so of the peace. Creek civil war and the defeat of the Red-Sticks by Andrew Jackson portended the final extinction of indigenous military power in Georgia. The peace with Britain in 1814 and the cession of Florida by Spain in 1821 cut southeastern Indians off from European trade and diplomacy.[13] Though the Cherokee fought with the United States, they suffered serious looting and violence at the hands of settlers and militiamen during the war, and emerged with nothing but grievances against the federal government.[14] In these circumstances, Georgia's executive, its legislature, and a goodly portion of its citizens set their hopes on indigenous removal and with it perfect settler sovereignty.[15]

They were disappointed. The huge cessions of Creek land negotiated by General Jackson at the Treaty of Fort Jackson in 1814 comprised land bordering East and West Florida.[16] Jackson was determined to isolate the Creeks from European intrigue. A further treaty in 1818 gave Georgia two additional pockets of land to smooth its frontier line, one of which probably belonged to the Cherokee. Georgia's share of the cession amounted to little more than swampland, hardly the stuff that won the hearts of land-hungry voters.

Georgia's first act of protest was a symbolic act of jurisdiction. In 1814 it passed legislation purporting to incorporate "that part of our unlocated territory which is, for the present, assigned to the Indians for their hunting ground" into the jurisdiction of the state. The symbolic nature of the act became apparent when Franklin County's superior court tried to apply it to indigenous people in 1818. Just a few months later, the act was amended to make clear that it applied to "citizens of this State, or of the United States" and not to indigenous people.[17]

Georgia's second act of protest was discursive. Though, in 1816, the state Senate protested Georgia's paltry gains under Jackson's first treaty,[18] it was not until 1819 that the state regaled Congress with an assertion of its sovereign, jurisdictional, and territorial rights to Indian Country in a manner uncompromised by the syncretic language of retribution:

> It has been the unfortunate lot of our state, to be embroiled in the question of "territorial right," almost from the commencement of her existence.... It has long been the desire of Georgia, that her settlements should be extended to her ultimate limits—that the soil within her boundaries should be subjected to her control, and that her police, organization and government should be fixed and permanent.... The state of Georgia claims a right to the jurisdiction and soil of the territory within her limits. She admits however that the right is *inchoate*, remaining to be perfected by the United States in the extinction of the Indian title.[19]

There was nothing inherently novel about this claim. The logic of territoriality was immanent in the very process of federation in the United States after 1783 and in the dual projects of expropriation and assimilation instituted by the Washington administration in the 1790s.[20] Georgia itself had acted as though it held its land (at that point stretching to the Mississippi) in fee simple in the 1790s, and territoriality figured centrally in the Compact of 1802.[21]

The logic mobilized by Georgia's Senate in 1819, in important respects, had emanated from the center to the periphery. In the lead-up to the 1812 war, Return J. Meigs, federal agent to the Cherokee from 1802 to 1824, had contended that the Treaty of Hopewell (1785) gave the United States Congress the right to legislate for the Cherokee—an argument used by the special federal agent for Removal, Joseph McMinn, in 1818 when he tried to bully the Cherokee into leaving the southeast.[22]

In 1811, Meigs had also advocated the extension of state jurisdiction over Indian Country to quell indigenous and settler lawlessness and to remove the threat of erecting *imperium in imperio* (a sovereign state within a sovereign state).[23] Tennessean Andrew Jackson probably synthesized both strands of argument when he suggested to President Monroe in 1817 that the treaty system should be abolished because it was "absurd for the sovereign to negotiate by treaty with the subject":

> I ask can it be contended with any propriety that [Indian] rights are better secured than our Citizens, and that Congress cannot pass law for their regulation, when it is acknowledged, that they live within the Territory of the United States and are subject to its sovereignty and would it not be absurd to say that they were not subject to its laws.[24]

Meigs's reasoning was also mirrored by the War Office under South Carolinian John C. Calhoun in 1824. He warned the Cherokee that it was "incompatible" with the American form of Government "for you to remain . . . as a distinct society or nation, within the limits of Georgia."[25]

Both arguments underpinned Georgia's legislative protest in 1819. But Georgia's House of Representatives subjoined federal discourse to state's rights. It spoke with new force and authority of the federal government's failure to respect Georgia's indisputable jurisdiction by failing to perfect Georgia's title to Indian land in the treaties of 1814 and 1818. It contended that the federal government had power and authority to extinguish Indian title and, moreover, that it was obliged to do so. This was so because the state of Georgia already held "inchoate" title, sovereignty, and jurisdiction in Indian Country. And in the explosive political environment of 1820s Georgia, these rights became less inchoate by the day.

The Departures of 1823 and 1825

No other federal institution did more to transform Georgia's sovereignty talk into a theory and practice of territorial jurisdiction than the U.S. Supreme Court. It began in 1810. In Fletcher v. Peck (1810),[26] the Supreme Court held that Georgia had the right to sell and grant Indian land in the Yazoo region (bordering the Mississippi) before it ceded that land to the federal government in 1802. Georgia's rights to sell land in the Yazoo region existed despite Indian land rights there—a situation that could only pertain if Georgia had paramount title, sovereignty, and jurisdiction over the region. As a result, claimants under contracts of sale granted and later revoked by the state of Georgia were entitled to compensation from the state or federal government.

This tentative aid and comfort became a mantra in Johnson v. McIntosh in 1823. In this case, two citizens claimed the same piece of land in Indiana. One claimed under a deed of sale from an Indian tribe, the other under a speculative grant made by the colony of Virginia. The court recognized the right of the colonial grantee. After contrasting the harsh practices of Spanish and French imperialism with the benevolence of the British Empire, the court declared:

> The power now possessed by the government of the United States to grant lands, resided, while we were colonies, in the crown, or its grantees. . . . An absolute title to lands cannot exist, at the same time, in different persons, or in different governments. An absolute, must be an exclusive title, or at least a title which excludes all others not compatible with it. All our institutions recognise the absolute title of the crown, subject only to the Indian right of occupancy, and recognise the absolute title of the crown to extinguish that right. . . .
>
> However extravagant the pretension of converting the discovery of an inhabited country into conquest might appear; if the principle has been asserted . . . and afterwards sustained . . . if the property of the great mass of the community originates in it, it becomes the law of the land, and cannot be questioned. So too . . . Indian inhabitants are to be considered merely as occupants. . . . However this restriction may be opposed to natural right, to the usages of civilized nations, yet, if it be indispensable to that system under which the country has been settled . . . it may, perhaps, be supported by reason, and certainly cannot be rejected by Courts of justice.[27]

The Supreme Court, here, created a new judicial philosophy of indigenous subordination. The court need not have read the doctrine of preemption (by which settlers could only take title in land from the Crown) as an indigenous legal disability. It might simply have read preemption as a fetter on settler rights.[28] The court also retold history as a univocal myth of indigenous expropriation. It recast the doctrine of discovery as a fictive right of conquest.[29] In the process, the court provided Georgia with all the legal tools it needed to assert its sovereignty and jurisdiction in Indian Country, and to extinguish Indian land title at will. Though the court crafted its decision in Johnson v. McIntosh to defend federal rather than state sovereignty and jurisdiction, the decision clearly acknowledged that colonies (if not states) had held both rights in their indigenous borderlands. This strain of reasoning had enormous power in the evolution of Georgia's radical discourse of territorial sovereignty: it provided a bridge between long-standing tensions over the nature of state sovereignty in Indian Country and Georgia's pressing desire for Indian land.

The court then recrafted the "extravagant pretension" of empire into a nonjusticiable act of state. The court posited discovery as a foundational moment of settler sovereignty that abrogated indigenous rights against principle, right, or reason. Marshall argued, moreover, that this founding abrogation of indigenous rights underpinned all property, law, and order in the British Empire and the United States. As such, it lay beyond the scrutiny of the courts.[30] Just three years later, the son of an American loyalist would use the same reasoning to justify the extension of British law over the peripheries of New South Wales.[31] Meanwhile, Marshall was clearly enamored of some of the Lockean legal arguments beginning to cluster around the colony of New South Wales. The notion that America might conveniently be deemed vacant land, "desert and uninhabited," certainly figured in Johnson v. McIntosh: "In Virginia . . . as elsewhere in the British dominions, the complete title of the crown to vacant lands was acknowledged. So far as respected the authority of the Crown, no distinction was taken between vacant lands and lands occupied by Indians."[32]

The impact of Johnson v. McIntosh was immediately apparent in the second escalation of sovereignty talk in Georgia in 1823. After 1819, the Cherokee refused to meet with United States treaty commissioners, having famously resolved "not to cede another foot of land." When the Cherokee finally acceded to a meeting with Campbell and Meriwether in 1823, the commissioners used the doctrine of discovery laid out in Johnson v. McIntosh to assert that the Cherokee were mere occupants of Georgia's lands and Georgia must, "sooner or later, pervade the whole."[33] They argued that the Cherokee had no right to refuse their request for a cession, because indigenous rights all derived from the state government alone.

When the secretary of war informed Georgia's Governor George Troup that the Cherokee would not negotiate with Campbell and Meriwether and that, therefore, the federal government had done all it could to extinguish Cherokee title "peaceably" under the Compact of 1802, Governor Troup made the connection between Cherokee rights and the deficit in Georgia's territorial jurisdiction even more explicit. Troup declared that the Compact of 1802 had vested fee simple in all Indian lands in the state and that the Cherokee were mere "tenants in possession."[34] He complained that Georgia alone of the original states "is incomplete; her civil polity is deranged . . . and all, because Georgia is not in the possession of her vacant territory—a territory, waste and profitless to the Indians."[35] Here indigenous possession was waste in the Lockean sense—a place void of property and stateless. Georgia's sovereignty and title was absolute and inviolate throughout its charted limits. Federal tolerance for indigenous rights in this frame was little more than an aggression against the state because it encouraged the Cherokee in arrogations of jurisdiction and sovereignty that were fundamentally at odds with Georgia's territorial sovereignty.[36]

The extent to which Georgia's claims to Indian land comprised territorial claims to legislative and judicial jurisdiction became even clearer two years later, during the federal crisis over Creek Removal. In 1821, the Creeks sought to quiet Georgia's land lust by ceding half of their remaining land in Georgia. They then joined with the Cherokee, declaring that they would not sell more land. A coalition of powerful chiefs declared that any Creek who did so would be put to death. Nevertheless, in 1825 a pro-treaty faction including the chief and speaker of the Creek Nation, William McIntosh, signed over the rest of Creek land in Georgia in the infamous Treaty of Indian Springs. McIntosh was subsequently killed for breaching Creek law. The Treaty was disavowed and replaced with a new treaty in 1826. In the meantime, however, Georgia nearly seceded from the Union, and in the resulting furor, Georgia's arguments about territorial jurisdiction and sovereignty were perfected.[37]

The controversy over the Treaty of Indian Springs and the murder of Creek chief William McIntosh contributed several strands to Georgia's sovereignty talk. The first strand related to the validity of indigenous law and the reach of federal jurisdiction in the nation. Second, the state asserted that the federal government had territorial jurisdiction in Indian Country and demanded, for the first time in history, that federal troops or the federal judiciary should punish the Creek Indians responsible for killing Creek Indians on Creek land. Third, the state argued that it had unilateral power to expel the Creeks with or without a treaty. All of the above rested in part or in whole on the contention that Creek Indians had no law, no sovereignty, and no land title.

Creek jurisdiction became the object of debate because the validity of the Treaty of Indian Springs hinged on whether McIntosh signed the treaty in contravention of tribal law. A valid Creek law forbidding the sale of Creek land to the United States would invalidate McIntosh's treaty ab initio, regardless of his status in the nation. It also jeopardized the fiscal and physical interests of McIntosh's survivors. The taint of illegality threatened the capacity of the Creek treaty party to receive compensation promised them under the treaty. Even if these objections could be overcome, McIntosh's execution itself jeopardized the treaty because the document guaranteed the safety of every chief who signed it. By failing to protect McIntosh from Creek law, the federal government and the state had already violated one of the treaty's terms—rendering its rickety edifice even more liable to legal collapse. Indeed, in July 1825, the survivors of the McIntosh party withdrew their support for the treaty on the grounds that the federal government had failed to protect them and had not compensated them for their losses at the hands of their Creek compatriots.[38] The situation was rendered even more complex by the fact that the principal chiefs of the Creek Nation had promised Georgia (and McIntosh) that McIntosh and his allies would not be punished for selling Creek land.[39]

For these reasons, the state and McIntosh's party focused first on the status of the Creek law forbidding land sales. The chiefs who signed the treaty with McIntosh disputed this law in order to defend a complex form of Creek sovereignty. In a long public address on the subject, the McIntosh party declared that the Creek law forbidding land sales was nonbinding because it was not passed at the Council Ground at Broken Arrow, though propagated by a significant group of chiefs at the urging of the Cherokee.[40] This declaration contains a novel conception of sovereignty in the Creek Nation, because it posits both a single, effective Creek sovereignty and a national legislative procedure that bore a tenuous relationship to the fluid nature of early national Creek politics.[41] Their claims were compromised by rumors suggesting that McIntosh himself had promulgated the law he broke. Missionary Isaac Smith stated before a Georgia inquiry into the treaty that McIntosh had threatened to murder any Creek who sold Creek land to the Americans.[42]

Georgia also attacked the validity of the law in ways that both supported and undermined Creek claims to be a juridically independent state. However, they used different reasoning to assert its invalidity. In 1826, Georgia Senator John Macpherson Berrien declared to the U.S. Senate, not that the law was invalid, but that it had been executed improperly. McIntosh's death "was naked murder. The shallow pretence of a law, and the judgment of a council, was got up ex post facto."[43] Around the same time, state historian Joseph Vallence Bevan declared on historical grounds that the nation was divided in practice, and so not governed by overarching laws or by paramount chiefs. McIntosh's authority to sign treaties instead stemmed from the authority given him as an intermediary. Either as a self-appointed "demagogue" or "through the favor of his white friends," McIntosh had power to sign away Creek land regardless of "national laws."[44]

Georgia's claims became more radical when it argued that the federal government should punish McIntosh's murderers under federal law. This claim rested on the assertion that the Creek law mandating McIntosh's death was invalid, not because it was improperly promulgated, but because Creek law could not withstand federal jurisdiction. The state of Georgia declared that the federal government's failure to protect McIntosh was, simultaneously, a derogation of federal jurisdiction in Indian Country and an abrogation of Georgia's rights to property and jurisdiction over Creek soil. A Milledgeville grand jury reminded the federal court of "recent occurrences within the circle of its criminal jurisdiction" and "deem[ed] it necessary to the character of the Government . . . that the authors, perpetrators, aiders, and abettors of the crimes lately committed should be sought for, and, when ascertained, prosecuted and severely punished."[45]

Governor Troup's criticisms were more explicit about the status of federal jurisdiction in Creek Country after the Treaty of Indian Springs:

> The United States were bound, in honor, under the eighth article [of the Treaty of Indian Springs], to bring to punishment his murderers; to restore to his friends their rank, power, and property, lost in the same cause; and to have coerced the execution of the treaty: all [of] which could easily have been accomplished. But the agents of the United States, indulging more of sympathy for the hostile than for the friendly Indians . . . the hostile party are to be received into the bond of communion and fellowship, with a forgiveness of sins, as if these native of the wilderness, at once the noble and fallen of their species, should, in the darkness of heathenism, do more than the philosophy of the heathen or the fortitude of the Christian ever did.[46]

This was a novel claim indeed. Neither the British Empire nor the federal government had ever asserted jurisdiction over a peacetime intratribal murder. However, Georgia's citizens and their governor here claimed jurisdiction over McIntosh's murder for the federal government. Their claim shows just how far notions about the territoriality of jurisdiction had come since 1812. They had not come far enough, however, to prevent Troup from assuring his Creek allies that old, syncretic laws would rule the day: "my revenge I will have. It will be such as we have reason to believe the Great Spirit would require."[47]

The second strand of sovereignty talk perfected in the Creek controversy was both contradictory to and more radical than the first. It declared the primacy of state jurisdiction in Indian Country—denying the federal government rights to do aught but treat for the extinguishment of Indian title. In the very same address in which he demanded the federal government exercise its criminal jurisdiction over intra-Indian affairs, Governor Troup declared that

> The State of Georgia contends that the jurisdiction over the country in question is absolute in herself; she proves, by all the titles through which she derived her claim from the beginning; by the charters and proclamations of the mother country; by the repeated acknowledgements of the United States themselves; and by their solemnly expressed recognition in the first and second articles of the agreement and cession of 1802. It was shown that, if Georgia had the jurisdiction, Georgia had never parted with it; and that, if she had it not, she can never have it in virtue of any authority, of any power, known to her.[48]

This contention in particular spread like wildfire throughout the state. Not only did Georgia's newspapers print every word said about Creek Removal in Congress, townships everywhere joined in the chorus of territoriality, pledging to defend Georgia's jurisdiction to the death. In one of dozens of public resolutions published by the *Savannah Georgian* in 1826, the citizens of Jackson County declared that Georgia was "free, sovereign, and independent," and that

> [by] the Treaty of cession of 1802, between Georgia and the United States, Georgia surrendered none of her rights of jurisdiction or soil within her then ... chartered limits, but only granted the General Government the privilege of treating with the Indian occupants for her vacant lands, and for her benefit.... Resolved: That the protection guaranteed by the United States to the Nations of Indians within the limits of the State, is unconstitutional and a trespass on State sovereignty.[49]

In this reckoning, the whole edifice of the agency system, the Trade and Intercourse Acts, and federal court jurisdiction over traders in the charted boundaries of Georgia was an invalid intrusion upon Georgia territorial sovereignty.[50]

The third strain of sovereignty talk created in 1825 declared Georgia's aspirations as a sovereign settler-polity by denying Indian title and Indian sovereignty itself. In this formulation, which closely follows the structure of Marshall's judgment in Johnson v. McIntosh, Governor Troup declared that indigenous people could do nothing more than hunt on Georgia's land, and then only at the pleasure of the state:

> The Indian right of occupancy is the only one acknowledged by the European Powers, from the beginning; the only one acknowledged by all the public instruments through which Georgia derived her title; the only one conceded to the Indians by Georgia, in all her treaties with them. ...
>
> The Spaniards and the French, without respecting even this right, have forcibly appropriated to themselves entire countries, when and where it suited them. The English and Americans have so far respected it, as to make compensation for the relinquishment of claim or abandonment of use. It is true that, with regard to this right of use, the United States, in their own territory, might have given it any latitude which pleased them, because the soil and jurisdiction belonged to them; but, with regard to the territory of Georgia, where the soil and jurisdiction are indisputably hers, this right of use can only be construed to mean what in all the treaties it did mean—the right of use for hunting. When, therefore, the United States, by changing the mode of life of the aboriginal upon the soil of Georgia, changed essentially this right, and cause her lands to be separately appropriated for the purpose of tillage ... they violated the treaties in their letter and spirit, and did wrong to Georgia.[51]

Georgia's sovereignty here incorporated absolute rights to soil and juris-diction, subject only to the Indian rights to hunt and wander—a very weak legal right. Even federal attempts to civilize indigenous people con-stituted a violation of Georgia's rights to soil and to jurisdiction because indigenous farming founded much stronger claims to land title and, in Lockean terms, to political independence.[52] Indian civilization, in short, threatened Georgia's statehood directly. This was no idle fancy, despite Troup's penchant for drama. British colonial officers in 1840 expressed very similar concerns about civilizing Aborigines in New South Wales—lest civilization give Aborigines there a better claim than the Crown to public lands.[53]

In 1826, the state senate requested Georgia's congressional members to convince the federal Congress to use its jurisdiction to dissolve indig-enous polities altogether:

> Procure the passage of a law, which shall treat these tribes as dependents, as they in fact are, which shall point the way to their own preservation, and command them to pursue it—That is a doubtful benevolence which in-dulges its object in a violation or a caprice which tends to its own extermination—That benevolence is still more doubtful, which surrenders its subjects to be the victims of misrule and prolificacy.[54]

Here, finally, was the logic of modern settler sovereignty. In this third formulation, the plural history of British practice and Anglophone insti-tutions gave way to a new sense of sovereign entitlement. Georgia's sta-tus as the heir of a European, imperial conqueror, and its aspirations to become a modern sovereign state combined to make indigenous jurisdic-tion an intolerable burden. All rights to soil and jurisdiction in Georgia rested in the state as empire, sovereign, and settlement. These rights could be delegated to indigenous people as a matter of expedience or humanity, but indigenous sovereignty was an illusion. Indian land rights and jurisdiction derived wholly from the state.

1830 Watersheds

Georgia conflated the meaning of sovereignty, jurisdiction, and land title between 1818 and 1826. This explains why, when the Cherokee crafted a constitution declaring their sovereignty and independence from the state in 1827, Georgia responded with legislation extending its jurisdiction over Cherokee Country from June 1830. The federal government fol-lowed not far behind. In February 1830, a U.S. House committee em-braced the notion that state sovereignty comprised both land title and jurisdiction though it was ambivalent about Georgia's rights vis-à-vis the federal government to act autonomously in Indian Affairs.[55]

Just one month later, Jackson's attorney general, Georgian John Macpherson Berrien, showed just how far Georgia's logic had infiltrated into the cloisters of the federal government. When asked about the status of land abandoned by Cherokee emigrants and occupied by Georgian squatters after the Treaty of 1817, he responded with a comprehensive rebuttal of indigenous property rights. On the basis of the Treaty of Paris, Fletcher v. Peck, and Johnson v. McIntosh, he declared the United States had title to Cherokee soil, "subject only to the Indian right of occupancy." Indian treaty law amounted to no more than an expression of indigenous subordination, growing "out of the relations between a civilized community, and the savage tribes which roved within the limits of [without derogating from] its jurisdiction and sovereignty."

Cherokee rights in Georgia were even weaker. By the Treaty of Hopewell, Berrien argued, the Cherokee divested themselves of all residual rights of property, sovereignty, and jurisdiction; the treaty merely granted them "a base and determinable interest" in "hunting grounds . . . without conferring on them any permanent interest in them, the fee in which remained in the State, within whose jurisdictional limits it was— and *these hunting grounds were acknowledged to be within the sovereign limits of the United States.*" Therefore, when the United States signed the treaty of 1817, it extinguished Cherokee title to land abandoned by emigrants. Under the Compact of 1802, this title reverted to Georgia.[56] Perfect territoriality, as conceived by Georgia, then, permeated the executive, a goodly portion of the Congress, and the state by 1830.

Meanwhile, the fact that this new discourse of territoriality was extolled in town meetings throughout Georgia explains why it was that a straggling band of squatters near Carroll County Georgia invoked jurisdiction and sovereignty to get away with murder in February 1830. In the context of this new and pervasive logic of territoriality, Farmbrough's defense of the arrest, wounding, and murder of Indians in the Cherokee Nation in 1830 makes perfect sense.

State Practice in Transition

As it happened, Farmbrough's fathoming unwittingly exposed the practical limits of Georgia's new rhetoric of territoriality in the months before it actually extended jurisdiction over Georgia's Indian Country. When Farmbrough's neighbors arrested four Cherokee men for burning settler houses in the Cherokee Nation, and left one of them to die on their way to court, they tried to bridge the gap between the strident rhetoric of territorial jurisdiction and the still evolving tenets of jurisdictional practice. In doing so they showed that jurisdictional practice in Georgia's borderlands had been transformed between 1815 and 1830, but according to a different meter from state sovereignty talk, and even from state legislation.

Farmbrough wrote on behalf of squatters on Cherokee land. His neighbors were squatters on improvements within the Cherokee Nation abandoned by Cherokee emigrés after 1828 but not ceded by the nation to the United States. Chuwoyee and a large band of Cherokees acting on the orders of the Cherokee Council had burned "14 or 15 . . . houses" occupied by squatters in Vann's Valley in the Cherokee Nation within the charted boundaries of Georgia in an attempt to force them off Cherokee land.[57]

Vann's Valley, where Chuwoyee's murder took place, was disputed territory. In a treaty with the Western Cherokee in 1828, the federal government undertook to purchase "the property" of Cherokee Indians willing to immigrate to the west.[58] As the secretary of war pointed out later, the treaty comprehended *"no cession . . . of the soil,"* merely compensation for Cherokee farmhouses, stock, and other personal property.[59] Georgia demanded that the improvements and the land on which they stood be turned over immediately to the benefit of the citizens of the state.

Farmbrough and his neighbors used this controversy to argue that Chuwoyee's death was not punishable by law. J. B. Pendleton wrote to Governor Gilmer of Georgia, calling himself a recent emigrant to "what is called the disputed land claimed by Georgia, in the Cherokee Nation" who had paid "dearly" for Cherokee improvements. Pendleton declared his intention to defend his house "to the last extremity" against Cherokee house burners.[60] When he reported Chuwoyee's death the next day, he took pains to stress that twenty-five settler houses had been burned, all "valued and paid for and as such, was in every since of the word, the property of the State of Georgia."[61] There was strategy here. If Pendleton could establish settler title as property owners, common-law courts might read Chuwoyee's death as the unfortunate but excusable upshot of the defense of settler property, even if Georgia's courts refused to read it as a valid act of jurisdiction under Georgia's law.[62]

In early 1830, before Georgia's extension of jurisdiction came into force, however, not even the governor of Georgia had the temerity to assert that Georgia's law governed Cherokees on Cherokee land. When Farmbrough wrote to assert that Chuwoyee's crimes and his death had all occurred in Georgia and under Georgia's sovereignty and jurisdiction,

Governor Gilmer pointed out that by "removal to the territory of Georgia inhabited by the Cherokee tribe of Indians," Farmbrough and his neighbors had "placed themselves without the full protection of our laws."[63] The Carroll County inferior court agreed, freeing the only Cherokee whom Farmbrough's neighbors had managed to transport to prison unharmed.[64] The settlers' act of "law" exceeded the real boundaries of Georgia's jurisdiction. The state may have claimed the right to survey Indian Country, to divide and to sell Indian lands, but it did not claim jurisdiction over everyday Indian-settler violence in February 1830.

The very manner of Chuwoyee's murder bespeaks a much more subtle transformation of local jurisdictional practice between 1815 and 1830. When Farmbrough's neighbors arrested Chuwoyee, Rattling Gourd, The Waggon, and Daniel Mills for burning the houses of squatters on Cherokee land and proceeded to take all four men back to the Carroll County court, they showed a new sensibility about the nature and limits of state law, however misguided.

Since Georgia's settlement, militiamen had chased Indians across Georgia's jurisdictional boundaries quite frequently. However, before 1812, raiding parties rarely brought indigenous people within the borders of the state for trial. Usually they sought much rougher justice—death, violent retribution, or restitution. In Indian Country in the early years of the century, settlers effected syncretic rules of violent reciprocity and exchange, and were usually forgiven for it by Georgia's constables, magistrates, and juries.

The juridical economy of this incident in 1830 was different, however. In 1830, Chuwoyee received his mortal injuries not as an end in themselves, but in the brutal process of transporting him to court. The squatters sought specifically to exploit new claims of jurisdiction made by Georgia and Georgian settlers in Indian Country. This incident, then, represents a drive to exercise state jurisdiction in Indian Country—albeit in defiance of state jurisdictional boundaries, of treaties, and of federal law.

Constables and magistrates had started issuing (chiefly civil) warrants for arrest and seizure in Indian Country before 1812 as Georgian creditors began to target debtor Indians and their property (rather than the Indian nations as corporate units). However, before 1812, the state had had very little luck exercising criminal jurisdiction over Creek and Cherokee crime, even when it was committed within the ordinary jurisdiction of the state. This is not to say that Indian Country lay entirely outside the purview of the courts. Citizen-settlers over the Indian boundary appeared at least once in a Franklin County civil case before 1812.[65]

State intervention in indigenous crime and contract after 1814 is some-what of a puzzle.[66] As noted above, in 1814 Georgia passed radical legis-lation attaching all Indian territory within its boundaries to Jasper County in order to punish the myriad "crimes of the most aggravating nature" that occurred there. Though this act was amended in 1818 to make clear that only settler crimes fell within its scope, the act neverthe-less contained broad and unprecedented claims to territorial jurisdiction over citizens and sojourners in Indian Country—claims that, at least in part, were put into practice.

Anecdotal evidence suggests that the Cherokee, at least, were more frequently involved in court cases in surrounding states after 1815. Lawyers' claims and agency records document an explosion of litigation involving Cherokees from 1817, though almost all of this pertained to Cherokees who had taken U.S. citizenship and land reserves under the controversial treaty of 1817.[67] In addition, John Ross refers to the arrest and escape of some Cherokees accused of cow theft in Tennessee in 1826.[68]

Very little comprehensive data survive from frontier county courts in Georgia where most interracial crime and commerce was litigated be-tween 1789 and 1830. Franklin County's records are the best preserved, and though it bordered the Cherokee Nation until at least 1820, indige-nous people seem to appear in only one Franklin County criminal case between 1815 and 1831. This case hints at deep changes in jurisdictional practice in and around Indian Country, however. Half a dozen Cherokees came before the Franklin County superior court in 1818 when Samuel Commander accused them of stealing two slave children. Walter and Ed-ward Adair, Charles and Samuel Ward, James Helton and William En-gland were all charged with a simple larceny by the court—a wonder-fully mild charge given the value of the property taken. John Martin, a prominent Cherokee, gave bond to appear on the charge of assisting in the theft and concealment of the slaves. He had allegedly assisted in the disposal of Commander's human property.[69]

The case makes clear that the crime occurred in the "unlocated terri-tory" in the Cherokee Nation "attached by a late act of the Legislature of Georgia to Jasper County," referring to the act of 1818.[70] As such, it con-stitutes a singular exercise of jurisdiction over prominent Cherokee men in the Cherokee Nation. There were two Walter Adairs in the Cherokee Nation, and both were important men. The Wards were related to the Cherokee's most prominent eighteenth-century woman, Nancy Ward. John Martin was a judge in the nation. At least Walter Adair and John Martin were arrested by the sheriff, and both gave bond before the court.

Adair and his codefendants were later discharged for want of prosecution, whereas Martin was excused altogether from appearance.

This case also represents a remarkable acquiescence in jurisdiction by the Cherokee. The very status of these men may have induced them to appear before Franklin County court to give bond. They were, most of them, mixed-race leaders in the nation, with interests on both sides of the Indian boundary. More importantly, John Martin had taken out citizenship under the treaty of 1817. This treaty ceded a portion of territory to the United States and stipulated Cherokee residents therein could immigrate to Arkansas or could stay on and take citizenship and a 640-acre allotment.[71] Many prominent Cherokee residents took the allotment, sold it at a profit, and moved back into the reduced borders of the Cherokee Nation. As a "citizen"-Indian, Martin may well have fallen within a narrow reading of the 1814 act.

Finally, however, the case was both abortive and unique. Neither Martin nor Walter Adair and his cohorts stood trial in Franklin County—a fact which suggests that, when push came to shove, neither the state prosecutor nor the court itself was willing to exercise jurisdiction. Just months after this case, the 1814 law was amended to ensure that no more Cherokee were hauled into court.

Accordingly, it seems that no indigenous people came before Franklin County's superior court between 1818 and 1831. The Franklin County superior court took cognizance of cases involving citizens in Cherokee Country only after the Adair case failed to go to trial. Nathan Thompson stole a horse from Donald Davis in 1819 in "that part of the Cherokee unlocated Territory which is by law attached to the County of Franklin" and was sent to the Milledgeville Penitentiary as a result.[72] None other than William Reed (Georgia citizen, longtime resident and sometime killer of a white man in the Cherokee Nation) accused William, John, and Phillip Chambers, William Moore, and Enoch Nelson of stealing his horse in 1821. The grand jury refused to find a bill against the accused and ordered Reed to pay all costs.[73]

However, the fact that the state even entertained the complaints of settler residents like Reed who resided in the Cherokee Nation, and the fact that it brought charges against settlers for crimes committed outside the "ordinary jurisdiction" of the state mark a watershed in state claims and in settler practice in and around Indian Country. Before 1814, neither the state nor the federal government purported to have any jurisdiction over settler crime against settlers in Indian Country. The narrow terms of the Trade and Intercourse Acts exhausted the responsibility of settlers in Indian Country to law. From 1814, however, the state of Georgia made expansive claims to have jurisdiction over its citizens within its charted boundaries. This was not an unfettered claim—Georgia balked at trying indigenous citizens for crimes against settlers. Nevertheless, they show that changes were afoot in Georgia's Indian Country.

Federal Practice in Transition

Meanwhile, the federal government had other ideas, reflecting early post-war transformations in its own jurisdictional aspirations in Indian Country. From 1815, federal prosecutors in Tennessee began to lay indictments against settlers and Indians for crimes on the Federal Road in Cherokee Country. Federal courts in Tennessee were more ambivalent. A Tennessee federal court declared in October 1815 that federal jurisdiction did not govern a settler-settler murder on the Federal Road in the Cherokee Nation. In October 1816 the same court found that an Indian who killed a settler on the Federal Road had committed no crime against federal law.[74] The newly assertive federal Congress responded with the General Crimes Act in 1817 (also known as the Enclaves Act, and the Indian Country Crimes Act), providing

> that if any Indian, or other person or persons, shall, within the United States, and within any town, district or territory, belonging to any nation or nations, tribe or tribes, of Indians, commit any crime, offence, or misdemeanor, which if committed in any place or district of country under the sole and exclusive jurisdiction of the United States, would, by the laws of the United States, be punished with death, or any other punishment, every such offender, on being thereof convicted, shall suffer the like punishment.[75]

This statute is often invoked to show the tenuous nature of Indian jurisdiction before 1820,[76] and it certainly suggests that the federal Congress had new jurisdictional aspirations over what it deemed to be enclaves "under the sole and exclusive jurisdiction of the United States." However, the act itself is equivocal. Section 1 stipulated only that offenders suffer "like punishment," not legislated penalties for their wrongs. Section 2 made federal jurisdiction subject to the operation of "treaties in force between the United States and any Indian nation" and explicitly excluded "any offence committed by one Indian against another within any Indian boundary." The act gave no authority to federal officials to seize Indian offenders for trial.[77]

The scanty records of the federal court in Georgia tell an even more equivocal story. It seems that no indigenous people were tried in this court, even after the General Crimes Act of 1817 asserted federal jurisdiction over Indian crime there.[78] Indeed, federal jurisdiction over settler crimes in Indian Country was even more restrained than it was before 1812. After 1815, only two indictments for murder, not clearly marked as piracy, were issued by the circuit court.[79] Three indictments, all in 1824, charged citizens for settling on Indian land (probably under the Trade and Intercourse Act). Two were tried to conviction, but recommended for mercy.[80] Eight other men were charged with misdemeanors unrelated to piracy in the circuit court in this period. Again, only two were found guilty.[81] Finally, William Reed and George Stinson were indicted by the district court for misdemeanors in 1820 and 1824. Though both men lived in Indian Country, only William Reed was clearly charged for breaching the Trade and Intercourse Acts.[82]

The real limits of federal jurisdiction became apparent in 1834, when Bailey, a Tennessee settler accused of murdering another settler in Cherokee Country, challenged the federal government's right to try him under the General Crimes Act. The federal court in Tennessee argued that the federal government could not exercise this jurisdiction. Its decision, however, was not grounded in the strength of Indian rights, but in constitutional limitations on federal power. Even as it preserved Bailey from federal prosecution, then, the court implicitly endorsed state rights to exercise jurisdiction over settler crimes in Indian Country within the state's chartered boundaries.[83]

Despite Georgia's extravagant claims to territorial jurisdiction, indigenous-settler crime remained largely outside the purview of state and federal courts before 1830. Indeed federal and state courts occasionally acted as ambivalent defenders of Indian rights. Even the local court of Carroll County refused to exercise jurisdiction over Cherokee crime against the Farmbrough's neighbors in the Cherokee Nation in 1830. After June 1830, when Georgia's new and radical jurisdiction act came into force, state and federal courts acted occasionally to defend Cherokee rights against the most egregious acts of legislative and extralegal expropriation endorsed by the state.[84] Farmbrough, himself a Carroll County magistrate, went into what he termed "the Cherokee Nation" in July 1830 to do justice for the Cherokees. He gathered evidence against settlers who had forged notes of credit against Cherokees and set about bringing them to trial in Georgia's inferior courts.[85]

Local Practice in Transition

In Georgia, then, the transformation of local jurisdictional practice was located largely outside the courts. Sometimes the charge toward jurisdiction was led by the state's executive, eager to implement its new rhetoric of territoriality. When a Creek Indian in the service of Major Joseph Woodruff was killed in the ordinary jurisdiction of Georgia in 1826, the state itself negotiated with the Creeks to exercise an unprecedented (yet still tentative) degree of jurisdiction over intratribal violence in the ordinary jurisdiction of the state. George, a Creek Indian, was killed in a settled county of Georgia. According to the logic of jurisdiction set up in United States–Creek treaties, his killers should therefore be tried in Georgia's courts. However, never before had the state tried to interfere in the killings of an Indian by an Indian, wherever it was committed. Law and practice combined to ensure that it had no authority to arrest George's killers in Creek Country, or even to negotiate with the Creeks for the right to do so. Not even the government of New South Wales arrogated to exercise jurisdiction over indigenous inter-se killings before 1830, even when they were committed in the heart of British settlements.[86] This was a radical departure indeed.

On July 17, 1826, the *Savannah Georgian* reported that George had nursed some drunken Creeks visiting Woodruff's plantations, and was killed after one of his patients died as a result of his ministrations. This could be construed as an instance of revenge killing, still widely practiced in the Creek Nation. Local judges and militiamen "informed" Creek chiefs that "the civil power of the Territory should be brought into action, that the disorderly and refractory should be brought in and punished; and that for this purpose, it was determined to send the marshal into the country, protected by a small body of troops to apprehend them." The Creeks were told "with great distinctness the friendly and necessary character of the proceeding." When they agreed to the proposition, a judge of a superior court issued a warrant "for the apprehension of Long John, accused as one of the murderers of George."[87]

This novel attempt to exercise jurisdiction seems not to have ended in the trial of George's killers. Most likely it ended as all like efforts before it—in frustration.[88] The *Savannah Georgian*, and no doubt the officials involved, had no illusions about the meaning of the incident: it was no more or less than a tentative but revolutionary step toward territorial jurisdictional practice. The editors of the *Savannah Georgian* declared, "[W]e hope the execution of these processes will be effectual, and that the Indians will be taught to respect the sovereignty of our laws."[89]

George's case was an anomaly. It was chiefly ordinary settlers, not the executive of Georgia, who transformed jurisdictional practice in and around Georgia's Indian Country before 1830. The fact that a settler and longtime resident in the Cherokee Nation like William Reed would dream of inciting a criminal action against Georgia citizens in Franklin County's court for stealing his horse in Indian Country in 1821 attests to a new expectation that the state could or should intervene there. Illegal local exercises of jurisdiction also indicate that Georgia settlers of all ranks— from squatters on Cherokee land to local sheriffs and constables— increasingly expected Indians to be subject to Georgia's law. When Cherokee chief Path Killer complained in 1821 that when "any axdent happens of that kind they meattately apprehend us wether it is just or not," he referred to illegal and informal proceedings in and out of local settler courthouses.[90] The attempt by Farmbrough's neighbors to take Chuwoyee, Rattling Gourd, The Waggon, and Daniel Mills to court—itself illegal and attended by brutality—constituted a real attempt to bring Cherokee offenders against Georgian property in the Cherokee Nation to trial.

These sorts of quasi-legal encounters were supplemented by other, even more informal pageants of law. Oilia Baldridge, a Cherokee, claimed before the Second Spoilation Committee that, in 1830 or 1831, white men from Georgia took her family and her slave and held them to ransom for $185.[91] Witnesses claimed that the Georgia settlers had taken the slave as compensation after Cherokee Indians robbed a store in Cass County. They arrested Baldridge's husband, her son, and the slave "and marched them off to Hightower river, & then had a mock trial, & found the negro subject to be sold." Baldridge had to buy her slave back from the Georgians for $185, though no evidence linked her family to the crime of robbing the Georgian store.[92] This too marks a qualitative change in the parameters of law-like lawlessness. Settlers robbed Indians in the 1820s and 1830s perhaps more than ever, but they paused more often to assert the legality of their actions. Acts like the trial of Baldridge's slave were little more than glorified theft, but they gesture to a new notion of legal rights in Georgia's periphery. In this brave new world, justice as jurisdiction— even as a parody of jurisdiction—indicates the rise of a popular discourse of sovereignty that challenged older notions that Indians in Georgia should be objects of violence and diplomacy but never of law.

It was a popular discourse, moreover, that had tremendous geographical and social reach. The arrest and fatal beating of Chuwoyee was performed with the aid of the Poney Club—a band of notorious thieves and brigands who counted magistrates, sheriffs, and constables among them. Indian accounts of the incident suggested that a bandit called Old Philpot, stabbed The Waggon. Old Philpot was no stranger to theft and violence, but in this instance he stabbed The Waggon in order to ensure that the latter came to court. Unlike the coalition of farmers, workers, and brigands who staged the murder of a Creek Indian at Blackshear's Mill in 1802 to look like a botched arrest, this band of thieves in 1830 seem actually to have sought to exercise Georgia's jurisdiction. Old Philpot and his neighbors, after all, took their one remaining Cherokee prisoner to a Carroll County jail. Like many other Georgians, the Poney Club used law and lawlessness together to hasten Creek and Cherokee Removal.[93]

Law and lawlessness were intimately intertwined in the jurisdictional machinations of the Carroll County squatters in 1830 from the outset. When they set out under the leadership of the Carroll County sheriff to arrest The Ridge and other senior Cherokees involved in the house burning, they were clearly bent more on retribution than on law. While "Swearing and yelling in the most savage manner," they fired on a number of Cherokees.[94] Brigands and officers of the state worked together to conflate law and lawlessness in Georgia's periphery.

In the process, however, their activities show us that something changed in the State of Georgia after the War of 1812. Even though they were themselves squatters and thieves operating outside the juridical boundaries of the state, in self-conscious defiance of federal (if not state) law, this band of squatter-brigands, more than any of their forebears, pursued and defended their own logic of territorial jurisdiction.

Change in Cherokee Country

When Farmbrough's neighbors arrested Chuwoyee and his colleagues in the Cherokee Nation in 1830, they did more than synthesize and controvert Georgia's claims to territorial sovereignty in Indian Country. They protested the legitimacy of another act of territorial jurisdiction: the Cherokee Nation's attempt to evict squatters from Cherokee land. Even before Jeremiah Evarts translated Cherokee national rights into a comprehensive theory of sovereignty and jurisdiction in the William Penn essays in 1832, Cherokee discourse and Cherokee practice had staked claims to jurisdiction that were predicated increasingly on territorial boundaries rather than on personal relationships of kinship, trade, or violence.[95] By 1830, a Congressional Committee would declare that "The Cherokees have decreed the integrity of their territory, and claimed to be as sovereign within their limits, as the States are in theirs."[96]

From the late eighteenth century, the Cherokee Nation, itself a modern coalition of Indian survivors and trader adoptees, developed legal institutions that were increasingly legible to their settler counterparts. The national council—a body created in the eighteenth century to wage war—turned its attention in the nineteenth century to internal rule. It established a mounted militia in 1798 to suppress horse theft. It "regularized the force," exempted its officers from blood revenge, and attempted to curtail blood revenge in 1808.[97] It forgave all debts of blood in 1810, and between 1817 and 1827, published "over one hundred complex laws" and distributed them throughout the nation.[98] Among these was a law in 1820 establishing four circuit courts, eight district courts, and a superior court.[99]

Cherokee institutional reform reflected their growing economic and political self-sufficiency, even as it followed the practices and sensibilities of a syncretic mixed-race elite.[100] Cherokee institutions looked like and were modeled on their settler equivalents, yet they encompassed peculiarly Cherokee approaches to balance, equality, and justice.[101] Indeed, they mask strong continuities in customary legal practice in the nation. Notwithstanding the establishment of courts in 1820, the first Cherokee was executed for homicide only in 1827—a fact that suggests "Either [that] the Cherokees were exceptionally law-abiding or [that] a dual system of jurisprudence existed in which some people, perhaps most, applied customary methods of social regulation to a traditional code of behavior and others followed the laws of the republic."[102] Nor does institutional reform necessarily import the wholesale embrace of a sovereignty premised on territorial jurisdiction. The National Council gathered to itself the accoutrements of modern sovereignty in the early national period, but territoriality was only institutionalized by the Cherokee Constitution of 1827.

The most important practical manifestation of the logic of territoriality in Cherokee Country was the exercise of jurisdiction over settlers in the nation. Although the hybrid committees presided over by Return J. Meigs in the Cherokee Nation to adjust disputes between settlers and Indians dwindled after 1812, independent Cherokee assertions of jurisdiction over settler crime became somewhat more self-assured. The nation seldom punished settler-thieves before the Cherokee Constitution of 1827. However, the nation's light horsemen arrested a number of settler-brigands and delivered them to the agent for arrest, removal, and possibly trial by federal authorities.[103] The nation also kept a log of claims for property stolen by settlers, for which it sought compensation, in the manner long practiced in the agency.[104]

On the few occasions that the Cherokee did assert jurisdiction over settler crime, they did not always adhere to modern notions of territorial jurisdiction. In 1819, the chiefs of the nation wrote to tell Return J. Meigs that the murder of a Cherokee named Sawney by a U.S. soldier in 1815 in the nation would be "pardoned" by the relations of the deceased if the state paid them modest compensation.[105] Under Cherokee law, when he committed murder on Cherokee land, the soldier had created a personal relationship with Sawney's kin independent of the location of Sawney's demise. So, while the nation asserted that the soldier's crime fell under Cherokee jurisdiction, that jurisdiction lay with Sawney's kin according to a syncretic logic of blood feud, not with the national council.[106]

Territoriality in Cherokee reasoning is much more evident in Cherokee evictions of squatters, like Farmbrough, from their land between 1820 and 1830.[107] Chuwoyee's house-burning party acted under the authority of the Cherokee National Council to protect Cherokee territorial rights. Of course, Cherokee actions against Georgian squatters occurred only because federal troops were withdrawn from the Cherokee Nation in 1818 to pressure the Cherokee to leave.[108] When the Cherokee Nation demanded that the federal government honor its treaties with the nations by removing squatters from Cherokee lands, John C. Calhoun argued that the Cherokee should remove squatters "by their own force with little or no aid from the Government, as they *assume* to be an *independent people*, they ought to act up to its spirit."[109] The chiefs of the Cherokee Nation were quick to point out the legal and moral failings of Calhoun's reasoning, but Cherokee actions against squatters show that they took Calhoun's sarcasm to heart.[110]

Cherokee tax policy also pursued a logic of territoriality that was heavily contested in the center and periphery of the state. From 1823 the nation taxed settlers trading within the boundaries of the nation. Taxation pertained intimately to contests over territorial sovereignty between indigenous people, the state, and the federal government because the 1787 United States Constitution gave the federal government the exclusive power to govern trade and intercourse between citizens and Indians. A number of Indian treaties also contained ambiguous clauses to this end. The Treaty of Hopewell in 1785, for example, gave the federal government the right to legislate for the Cherokee on the matter of Indian trade. The question then became: Did the federal government's constitutional rights (or its rights under treaty) extinguish Cherokee rights to impose taxes on settler-traders operating within Cherokee national boundaries?[111]

The Cherokee consulted Judge Hugh Lawson White of Tennessee (former superior court judge and congressman) to support their claim. White argued that

the Nation have the right to impose this tax—By treaty, the United States have the power to regulate *trade* and *intercourse* with the Cherokee Indians. In pursuance of the treaty stipulations congress have vested a power in certain officers to issue licenses to individuals to enter the nation. . . . The license is an evidence that the United States think the individual may safely be trusted in the nation . . . but was not intended to take from the Nation the right of judging, whether their people should trade with them or not.[112]

With White's opinion in hand, the Cherokee seized and sold the property of traders refusing to pay the tax.[113] However, the nation subsequently deferred to the adjudication of Congress on the matter. In 1825, Congress demanded that the Cherokee make restitution for the seizures on the grounds that they had no right to tax traders.[114]

The Removal controversy itself prompted the clearest articulations of Cherokee territoriality. When Joseph McMinn claimed in 1818 that, by the Treaty of Hopewell, the federal government could pass laws for the Cherokee Nation, forcing them to take individual reservations or to migrate, they declared:

> We consider ourselves as a free and distinct nation, and that the government of the United States have no police over us, further than a friendly intercourse in trade.[115]

Cherokee separateness was grounded in their rights to territory, sovereignty, and jurisdiction. In 1822, John Ross protested to John C. Calhoun against the avarice of Georgia, which sought "the whole . . . of our chartered limits":

> We have been told that the State of Georgia have got the Genl. Government bound to her in strong terms to extinguish Indian titles to land within her chartered limits. But we hope that the United States will never forget her obligation to our nation of an older date. . . . By the Treaty of Tellico 1798 the United States have solemnly guaranteed forever to our nation this country which have been bestowed upon our ancestors by the Great Creator of this world.[116]

When Georgian commissioners met with the Cherokee Council to press Georgia's claims at the height of the Removal controversy in 1823, the Cherokee challenged the very basis of Georgia's claims to sovereignty, jurisdiction, and territory. The council rejected Campbell and Meriwether's claims that the Cherokee Nation had no rights to property or sovereignty within Georgia's territorial boundaries by asserting that neither "nations" nor "individuals" of civilized or uncivilized communities had ever practiced perfect territorial sovereignty on their colonial peripheries.[117] They rejected arguments that their rights to territory and independence had been abrogated by discovery, by conquest, and by treaty.[118] They argued instead that their title derived from a "supreme source" and was confirmed by centuries of settler-indigenous treaties.[119]

When in 1824, the secretary of war himself declared that Cherokee independence could not withstand federal or state law in the east, and that their independence was incompatible with the system of government in the United States,[120] the Cherokee responded with an explicit declaration of the territoriality of sovereignty:

> ... the Cherokees are not foreigners, but original inhabitants of America; and that they now inhabit and stand on the soil of their own territory, and that the limits of their territory are defined by the treaties which they have made with the Government of the United States; and that the states, by which they are now surrounded, have been created out of lands which were once theirs; and that they cannot recognize the sovereignty of any state, within the limits of their territory. . . . It rests with the . . . free consent of the nation, to remain as a separate community, or to enter into a treaty with the United States, for admission as citizens, under the form of a territorial or state government.[121]

Escalating Cherokee claims to property, to territorial sovereignty, and to jurisdiction culminated in the Cherokee Constitution of 1827. Article 1, Section 2, of the Cherokee Constitution provided, "The sovereignty & jurisdiction of this government shall extend over the country within the boundaries above described."[122] Indigenous people in the southeast had asserted and exercised almost all of the powers of independent jurisdiction within their territorial boundaries before 1827. However, Article 1, Section 2, contained the nation's first unqualified assertion of modern, territorial sovereignty. More than any other document, the Cherokee Constitution shows the extent to which the Cherokee participated in, and to important degrees spurred on, the discourse of territoriality in Georgia and the United States. Its practical import, meantime, is evident in the fact that settler horse thieves were tried in the nation, even as Georgia extended its laws over Cherokee land and Cherokee people.[123]

When Chuwoyee and a posse of Cherokees burned improvements occupied by Georgia squatters in Vann's Valley in 1830, they did so to achieve two objects: the physical defense of their territory against encroachment and the defense of their territorial jurisdiction as an abstraction. Before 1812, Indian Country and indigenous jurisdiction had negated Georgia's aspirations to territorial jurisdiction. After 1815, increasingly, the Cherokee Nation mirrored Georgia's territoriality. In doing so, they transformed the sovereignty debate of the 1820s into the policy of Removal in the 1830s.

In his letter to the governor of Georgia, Farmbrough did more than report an incident of desultory violence in Indian Country. He described a tripartite struggle over who held territorial power in the Cherokee Nation fought among Georgia, the federal government, and the Cherokee Nation itself. More importantly, perhaps, he showed the investment of Georgia's peripheries in the outcome. He sought, unsuccessfully, to defend a territorial jurisdiction to which Georgia only aspired in the beginnings of 1830. He and his neighbors showed that the logic of territoriality that underpinned the controversies of the 1820s drove, reflected, then outgrew changes in federal, state, and indigenous jurisdictional practice in Georgia's peripheries.

This story of contest and transformation—of the rise of territoriality in Georgia's peripheries—grew out of the unique and unstable legal pluralism of the southeastern United States. Yet it has a larger context. Territoriality was not a logic grown, sui generis, in the United States of America. From 1815, it gripped the world. Post-Napoleonic Europe, British India, South Africa, South America, New South Wales—the whole world began to tidy its peripheries by parceling them into neat and recognizable systems of jurisdiction. The debate over sovereignty, jurisdiction, and property that gripped Georgia in the 1820s, moreover, is itself a global settler story—the North American version of a series of fundamental settler questions about the appropriation of territory from indigenous people and the production of cash crops on it for nineteenth-century global consumption. It is a story that has another unique but related iteration in the colony of New South Wales between 1824 and 1835.

CHAPTER SEVEN

Lego'me and Territoriality in New South Wales

M EANWHILE, BETWEEN 1824 AND 1835, the officers of the Crown and the new Supreme Court together invented jurisdiction over Aboriginal Australians in New South
Wales. The first Aborigine was tried for rape in 1816 and the first for
murder in 1822, but no fewer than twenty-one Aborigines were brought
before the court for theft, rape, or murder in 1835.[1] The court wrought a
revolution in the theory and practice of jurisdiction in New South Wales
in between—a revolution grounded in the logic of territoriality. This
revolution was never as bitter, as complete, or as sensational as the Indian Removal debates in Georgia, but it was every bit as erosive of legal
pluralism. New South Wales, with Georgia, strove to articulate a new settler sovereignty.

The significance of this jurisdictional revolution has been uniformly
downplayed by scholars of indigenous legal history, who focus on the
gradual shift toward exercising jurisdiction over violence between Aborigines in this period. Most discuss the latter as if it were the resolution
of a legal anomaly—the disjuncture between the legal doctrines of settlement and the very American attitudes toward indigenous legal status
harbored by Caribbean-born and American-trained Chief Justice Forbes
after 1824.[2] Others argue that the extension of British law over indigenous people reflected the intense religiosity of British policy makers in
the second quarter of the nineteenth century. In this frame, increased
legal scrutiny of Aboriginal communities was a strategy of "protection
and civilization"—the new mantra of metropolitan elites.[3] I argue here

that the revolution in jurisdictional practice wrought in the lead-up to R. v. Murrell in 1836 forms part of the global settler story of territorial sovereignty. It is part of a settler story that has important local and global origins.

The local and international settler context of legal reform in New South Wales between 1824 and 1835 is nowhere more apparent than in the transformation of New South Wales's judicial system. This momentous administrative transformation, more than any other single factor, portended the drive to end legal pluralism in the colony.[4] Judicial reform in New South Wales was the product both of administrative reform throughout the British Empire, and of rapid economic development in New South Wales.[5]

From the arrival of Saxe Bannister in 1823, a new class of attorney-general sought to tease out the nature and limits of government power over settlers, convicts, and Aborigines alike in New South Wales. The first Supreme Court of New South Wales was constituted in 1823 to meet the growing backlog of legal controversies in the colony. The rapid growth of wool exports (fed by free settlers and maintained by convict labor) fueled civil and criminal litigation that overwhelmed a hybrid court system established to police convicts. Like Georgia, New South Wales transformed itself into a settler enterprise in this period, an enterprise grounded in the production of export commodities using unfree, nonindigenous labor. Accordingly, the erstwhile penal colony needed a new legal system that could deal with fundamental questions about the governance, expansion, and ultimately, about the nature and legality of settlement itself on the vast peripheries of New South Wales.[6]

The new Supreme Court's part in solving these dilemmas centered, of necessity, on the logic of territoriality—the assertion that British sovereignty gave certain inalienable rights and responsibilities to everyone living within the territorial boundaries of the colony of New South Wales. In New South Wales, as in Georgia, indigenous legal status posed fundamental questions about the theory and practice of the settler project.

In practice, the uncontrollable growth of the colony between 1824 and 1835,[7] the rise in frontier indigenous resistance and bushranging,[8] and the fact that more and more of Australia fell within the reach of the colonial administration, all conspired to keep Aboriginal legal status before the court and the colony between 1824 and 1835.[9] While few indigenous people or settlers were tried for interracial violence in the period, state intervention in border violence was increasing. As a matter of practice, then, indigenous people came within the purview of the colonial governments and the colonial courts, as they had never done before.

In theory, Aboriginal legal status threatened all exercises of colonial authority—for on it rested the legitimacy of the project of settlement itself. Lowe's case had shown that Aboriginal crime on the fringes of the colony begged the question: whose law, if any, governed the frontier? The legal status of the colony lay in the balance.[10] Aboriginal crime on the highways and byways of settlement, meanwhile, reanimated questions first addressed by Lachlan Macquarie in 1816: Did British law govern settled territory or British people? By what right did Britain rule the land? Indigenous legal status lay at the heart of these questions. It became a touchstone for colonial concerns about how to govern people and space within and without the geographical reach of the government. It was in this context that the new Supreme Court of New South Wales effected a revolution in jurisdictional practice, by turning its sustained attention for the first time to the legal problem of indigenous-settler crime.

This jurisdictional revolution, however, was never unidirectional, inevitable, or uncontested.[11] Even as the new Supreme Court extended its jurisdiction over indigenous-settler crime, legal officers and administrators in Sydney quibbled over the status of indigenous people in the center of the colony. Settlers and local officials on the New South Wales frontiers pursued the goal of expansion through their own plural vision of indigenous status on the peripheries. However, a simple center-periphery binary cannot capture the significance of this period of change. In New South Wales, as in Georgia, settlers and magistrates had to participate in exercising jurisdiction over border violence—something that they did haltingly and bitterly between 1824 and 1835. The result was a decade of judicial prevarications—and the growing power and the limits of territoriality in New South Wales underpinned them all.

The New Supreme Court

On February 12, 1835, an Aboriginal man named Lego'me (or Leggamy) came before the Supreme Court of New South Wales, accused of robbing settler Patrick Sheridan on the King's Highway and putting him in deadly fear. Sheridan had met the accused on the road in the vicinity of Brisbane Water in the northern reaches of the colony. Walkeloa Aborigines had been resisting settlement in the region steadily for several years through campaigns of theft, murder, cattle killing, and even rape. Sheridan testified that Lego'me and a group of armed companions had approached him to ask for tobacco (which Sheridan gave them). Afterward, Lego'me drove his spear into the ground at Sheridan's feet. Sheridan had heard that local Aborigines were looking for him, knew full well that Aborigines had long since "commenced robbing the settlers" in the area, and expected that this well-armed group of indigenous people meant him some harm. He was mistaken. Lego'me merely reached into Sheridan's pockets and extracted a pipe and a knife. Sheridan lived to tell the tale, but for his paltry takings, Lego'me was transported from the colony for seven years.

Lego'me did not go quietly, however. Despite the fact that Aborigines had appeared before the Supreme Court of the colony sporadically from 1823 to 1835, Lego'me's counsel, Mr. Therry, ensured that the shaky foundations of British Empire in Australia intruded on the court. He did not plead to the court's jurisdiction, though others had done so before him. Instead, during his cross-examination, Therry asked Sheridan "if he was not aware that he had been a squatter for some time on Lego'me's ground, and had frequently committed great depredations on his kangaroos." Sheridan responded with the logic of territoriality: "The prosecutor . . . said, that he believed the ground belonged to Government, and, as for kangaroos, he had something else to do than look for them."[12]

Lego'me's trial marks both the culmination and the anxieties of the quiet judicial revolution between 1824 and 1835. The fact that Therry questioned the legal status of British settlement in Australia only in cross-examination shows his sense that pleading against the jurisdiction of the court was futile by 1835. Instead, he gestured to the rising tide of territoriality by claiming that Lego'me himself was entitled to hold and to defend some territory of his own against the intrusions of British settlers. Like many Georgia squatters before him, Sheridan's response shows the power and the reach of territoriality among settlers by 1835. As far as Sheridan was concerned, Lego'me had no rights to land, to game, or even to the smallest degree of reciprocity from the settlers who had stolen both. Sheridan cared for sheep and cattle, not for kangaroos, and he squatted on land belonging to the settler government, not to Aborigines. This case, one of nearly two dozen involving Aboriginal defendants before the court in 1835, bespeaks the triumph of British jurisdiction over Aboriginal crime against settlers.

In some respects, the new court extended jurisdiction over indigenous crime with breathtaking temerity. This judicial revolution, for example, was accompanied by the rewriting of history. Even as he refused to exercise jurisdiction over Aboriginal crimes inter se in 1829, Chief Justice Francis Forbes declared that, as a matter of history, in New South Wales and beyond:

In all transactions between the British Settlers & the natives, the laws of the mother country have been carried into execution. Aggressions by British subjects, upon the natives, as well as those committed by the latter upon the former, have been punished by the laws of England where the execution of those laws have been found practicable.[13]

In 1832, Justice James Dowling, in the first criminal trial ever of Aborigines for theft, asserted:

> The general principle acted upon, I believe, with respect to these people since the foundation of this as a British Colony, is to regard them as being entirely under the protection of the law of England for offences committed against them by the white settlers & subjects of the Crown, & on the other hand to render them liable for any infraction of the British Law which may be injurious to the persons or properties of His Majesty's white subjects.[14]

The court did not always engage in such bold feats of fiction, however. What we know of the argument and disposition of cases involving Aborigines suggests that Aboriginal legal status troubled the court's notions of British territorial jurisdiction deeply. So much is apparent from the court's consistent refusal to endorse the jurisdiction claimed for it by the colony's attorneys-general. First, the court persistently refused to hear any but the clearest cases against Aborigines who had no access to interpreters or no understanding of their crime. In 1825, the court refused to sentence Devil Devil, the first Aborigine convicted of a capital crime, on the grounds that he had not fully understood his trial.[15] In 1828, Justice Dowling refused to hear the case against Binge Mhulto for willful murder despite the assurances of Attorney-General Saxe Bannister that the evidence against him was so clear that no interpreter was necessary to explain the proceedings. Dowling declared that Binge Mhulto stood "before the Court in the same light as a dumb man—as void of all intellect. . . . The man knows nothing of what is being said against him. He is incapable of making any defence."[16]

Cases like these prompted the defenders of Jackey Jackey's executioner Lieutenant Lowe to declare in 1827 that "many [Aborigines], who have been known, and proved to have committed murders, have been turned out of the gaols."[17] Such was the pattern of nonprosecution by the attorney-general and the courts before 1827 that when Tommy was tried for murder before the court, the *Monitor* declared:

> Up to the present date of the trial of *Jackey Jackey* [Tommy], we had always concluded, that our Chief Justice and Mr. Bannister, had mutually agreed on the unconstitutionality of the position, that the Heathen tribes of New Holland were in respect of murder subject to English law.[18]

The *Monitor* had been particularly unhappy about the release of Devil Devil (who was reputed to have eaten his victim). It declared, on the occasion of his release that, if the colony would not discipline Aborigines, settlers should pursue rougher justice.[19]

Second, the court seemed to prevaricate about whether Aborigines could be tried without a mixed jury of Aborigines and British subjects, or whether they could be tried at all as British subjects when they were denied access to many of the benefits of British law. In practice, the court resolved the issue by trying Aborigines anyway, but in law these issues had a long afterlife. In law, the question rested on a determination that Aborigines were not aliens under the protection of the colony. In common law, aliens under the protection of the Crown were entitled to be tried by a mixed jury comprised of an equal number of Englishmen and their countrymen.[20] The attorney-general himself conceded in Binge Mhulto's case (1828) that failing to constitute a mixed jury was a departure from the letter of the British Constitution, even though he went on to argue that it should not deter the court from trying the case.[21] In Lowe's case, the chief justice prevaricated over whether Lowe's victim, Jackey Jackey, was a British subject or an *alien ami*. In the end he avoided the question by declaring that, in either case, Jackey Jackey was protected by British territorial jurisdiction or, at very least, by British jurisdiction to try a British citizen (Lowe) for his crimes.[22] Justice Dowling had apparently overcome these qualms by 1832, when he declared that Aborigines could be tried "as British Subjects."

Third, before 1836, the court tempered its implicit claims that Aborigines were always British subjects under British jurisdiction with appeals to the principles of natural law. Chief Justice Forbes uniformly justified the exercise of jurisdiction over Aboriginal murderers on the grounds *both* of their probable status as British subjects *and* on the basis of natural law. When instructing a jury that it could convict Tommy guilty of murder in 1827, the chief justice stated:

> With regard to the liability of the Aboriginal Natives to English law, (continued His Honor) they certainly were amenable in every essential point to be controlled by it: —but how much more so in the case of murder which was an offence against the law of nature and of nations; and which required that whosoever shed man's blood, should pay his own in forfeit.[23]

In this light, it is also significant that indigenous thieves did not come before the court until 1832, despite at least two major Aboriginal campaigns of killing and theft in the interim.[24] Notwithstanding that natural law valued property almost as much as it did life, the rarity of theft cases before 1835 shows persistent uncertainty on the part of the infrastructures of the state (here, magistrates and the attorney-general) about the limits of British jurisdiction over Aborigines for all but the clearest of crimes against nature.[25]

In the first theft case, the court and jury tempered their claims to jurisdiction over Aboriginal theft by deferring to syncretic local practice. In R. v. Boatman or Jackass and Bulleye in 1832, two of three defendants charged with sheep stealing were acquitted on the grounds that they did not understand that sheep were valuable property. Local settlers had been in the habit of releasing diseased sheep into the bush and not inquiring after their fate at the hands of Wonnarua Aborigines. The court heard evidence to the effect that Aboriginal custom (hunting game in their territory) and local settler practice combined here to convince Aborigines that they were entitled to hunt sheep in the neighborhood. By acquitting two of three Aboriginal defendants, the court recognized the capacity of indigenous and syncretic customs to displace British law.[26]

Thus, if in moments of hyperbole key members of the Supreme Court of New South Wales claimed that Aborigines, by virtue of their residence in the colony of New South Wales, were and always had been British subjects under British law, the reality of Supreme Court reasoning was quite different. Even on the issue of Aboriginal crime against settlers, the first Supreme Court of New South Wales did not resort consistently to the logic of territorial jurisdiction before 1835.

The court debated the territoriality of British sovereignty directly in only three forums: cases involving settler civil rights and the applicability of the laws of England; cases involving settler violence against Aborigines; and cases involving Aboriginal crimes against Aborigines.

Cases involving settler civil rights declared Britain's extension of territorial sovereignty and jurisdiction over New South Wales with increasing certainty from the late 1810s onward. The first argument that New South Wales was empty of law at the moment of settlement came early, in Lord v. Palmer (1803). George Crossley used William Blackstone's distinction between conquest, cession, and settlement to argue that the law of England (not the law of Pennsylvania) applied in New South Wales. He did so to justify his client's claim against the assets of an insolvent deceased estate. The case went to the Privy Council, which was altogether more demure in its pronouncements about the applicable laws. The Privy Council based its application of British law to civil disputes in law and in equity on "His Majesty's Letters Patent," which required the governor to "administer Justice according to the Laws of England, no other Laws having been ever given or enacted for such Colony."[27]

The most important judicial pronouncement on the territorial rights of Britain in New South Wales arose when settlers Fork, Brennan, and Riley killed wild cattle on the western boundaries of settlement in 1817. The governor had proclaimed that the cattle were government property and that hunting or purloining them was a capital offense. Fork, Brennan, and Riley claimed that the government could not establish property in the beasts, as they were strays or ferae naturae, so settlers could hunt them at will. The judge advocate argued in response that the Crown had a special property in the beasts because they wandered on Crown lands:

> The law gives [property in the cattle] to the *King, as the general owner and lord paramount of the soil,* in re-compence for the damage they have done therein. But in respect of occupation, absolute possession *ratione soli,* and as *bona vacantia,* an indefeasible right and property were clearly vested in the Crown; for possession of the land carries with it to the owner all of valuable property to be found on it.[28]

Even as Governor Lachlan Macquarie tried to draw rudimentary lines of territorial jurisdiction around British towns by forbidding Aborigines from holding trials on the streets of Sydney, his law officers produced one of the first—and most complete—articulations of Crown sovereignty, property, and jurisdiction over the unsettled regions of New South Wales.

At the same time, law officers in the metropolis produced remarkably similar readings of British sovereignty and jurisdiction in New South Wales, unconstrained by the exigencies of practice on this far-flung periphery. In 1819, Colonial Office lawyers reported to the Earl of Bathurst that New South Wales was not conquered or ceded but "desart and uninhabited" and therefore Parliament must legislate taxes in the colony.[29]

By the early 1820s, settlers were asking much harder questions about the legal status of New South Wales. In 1822 or 1823, a settler brought suit against a New South Wales magistrate and constable for seizing his property to settle a debt for wages. He argued that the governor needed the consent of a local legislature to make a law authorizing his officers to seize debtors' property. According to the law officers, the crux of the petitioner's claim was that the colony was neither conquered nor ceded, but settled:

> It is denied . . . that New South Wales falls within either of these exceptions, since that colony was acquired neither by conquest nor cession, but by the mere occupation of a desert or uninhabited land. . . . His Majesty's subjects settling in a Country thus acquired carry with them the law of England so far as it is adapted to their peculiar circumstances—that the invariable usage in all such cases has been to require the Governor to convene an assem-

bly elected by the freeholders within the Colony—that thus the Colonists have lived under the constitution of England, varied only so as to meet the new circumstances in which they have been placed.

The law officers agreed with this proposition, but argued that constituting a magistracy was an exercise of prerogative (i.e., Crown) power rather than legislative power. Accordingly it could be delegated by the governor. In this case, however, it had not been included in his instructions.[30]

The Supreme Court of New South Wales also construed British jurisdiction very broadly in its adjudication of settler civil rights. When the court turned its attention to whether courts of Quarter Sessions could try free settlers without juries in 1824, it embraced the notion that New South Wales was "uninhabited" and therefore British law was completely and immediately in force from 1788 onward:

> Besides this statutable recognition of its English character, the nature of the original settlement of the colony brings it within that class to which I have assigned it; namely, a colony in which the English law prevails, as the birthright of the subject, and the bond of allegiance between the colonists and their sovereign. The Chief Justice then mentioned the authorities from the books . . . to shew, that if an uninhabited country be discovered and planted by English subjects, all the English laws then in being are immediately there in force.[31]

This meant, in effect, that free settlers in New South Wales must be tried by jury unless a statute expressly abrogated that right. The New South Wales Act of 1823, which allowed the governor to constitute Quarter Sessions courts, expressly allowed the trial of convicts without juries. In a bold defense of civil rights in the colony, the court declared that to try free settlers without a jury would violate their rights under the Magna Carta and the British Constitution. It was a defense that rested on the juridical emptiness of New South Wales.

Disputes over title to land provided another forum for the logic of territoriality in New South Wales. Many settlers facing ejectment from Crown lands argued either that they had been promised title by a government official, or that the Crown had acquiesced in their improvement, or that they held the land in adverse possession against the true grantee or the Crown. Possessors had the sympathy of colonial juries,[32] but the court itself invariably asserted the rights of the Crown to hold absolute sovereignty and title over the territory of New South Wales:

> By the laws of England, the King, in virtue of his crown, is the possessor of all the unappropriated lands of the kingdom; and all his subjects are presumed to hold their lands, by original grant from the crown. The same law

applies to this colony. It is a matter of history that New South Wales was taken possession of, in the name of the King of Great Britain, about fifty-five years ago.... The right of the soil, and of all lands in the colony, became vested immediately upon its settlement, in his Majesty, in right of his crown, and as the representative of the British nation. His Majesty by his prerogatives is enabled to dispose of the lands so vested in the Crown.[33]

All of these cases and queries posited a perfect, territorial British sovereignty in New South Wales on the basis that no property, sovereignty, or jurisdiction subsisted. They imagined a juridical world without Aborigines—but this world became much more complicated when colonial legal institutions confronted the messy business of Aboriginal dispossession.

Cases involving settler-indigenous violence show the court's uncertainty about whether British jurisdiction was determined by territory or tempered by personal status. R. v. Lowe constitutes the most dramatic and important example of the second category. As we saw in Chapter 5 when Lieutenant Lowe executed an Aborigine suspected of murder, his counsel argued that he simply acted in accordance with natural law. They argued that, as Jackey Jackey was not bound by treaty or consent into British law, he was a creature of nature and his crimes could and should be punished by summary execution. The court met this plea with decided ambivalence that nevertheless resorted to the logic of territoriality. It declared that, "If the Act of Parliament has recognised a sovereignty over this country, and recognised the application of English law here, we must look to the British law as established here *de facto*."[34] As a commissioned officer of the 40th Regiment, Lieutenant Lowe, in any case, was "personally within the jurisdiction of this Court." The location of his crime also fell within the court's territorial jurisdiction:

> The next thing to consider is whether the place, where the offence for which the prisoner stands charged is said to have been committed, is within the jurisdiction of the Court. It is stated to be at Wallis's Plains, in the district of Newcastle, in the Territory of New South Wales.... The question then resolves itself into this, whether this case comes under the New South Wales Act. Now, this Act of Parliament gives this Court jurisdiction to try all offences as in England; and *prima facie,* this comes properly before this Court. The Court then has jurisdiction.[35]

Thus, whether Jackey Jackey was "a British subject" or "an alien friend . . . he is entitled to *lex loci*, and it is only under peculiar circumstances he can be excluded from that right."[36] Forbes relied primarily on the logic of territoriality, though he stopped short of embracing it fully.

Indigenous legal status, here as elsewhere, blurred the edges of British jurisdiction in the colony of New South Wales.

The degree to which the court shied away from asserting uncomplicated territorial jurisdiction over New South Wales is most apparent in R. v. Ballard in 1829.[37] In this case, an Aboriginal man called Ballard was arrested for murdering Dirty Dick (another Aborigine) in an intertribal battle fought "under the Domain" in the center of Sydney. The attorney-general asked the chief justice whether such a crime could come within the purview of the court. It is highly likely that the attorney-general took interest in the case only because it occurred in the colony's largest town. Twelve years after Lachlan Macquarie had tried to preserve the spatial sanctity of British towns by warning indigenous people not to hold tribal punishments there, Dirty Dick's murderers showed the persistent plurality of the colony's most intimate spaces.

Chief Justice Forbes's initial reaction to the query made a very North American distinction between personal submission to British law and tribal exemption from it:

> If, for instance, a dispute arose amongst a tribe, and that they dedided [sic] it according to their own customs, and what was, in fact the ancient law of England—namely, by battle, and that one or more of the combatants were slain, such a case would, clearly not be cognizable by our law. If, on the other hand, a native, living in the town, and who, by such residence, had placed himself within the protection of the municipal law, was attacked and slain by any other native, then he conceived the native by whom he was slain would be rendered amenable to our law.[38]

A few days later in open court, American practice prompted Forbes categorically to excuse indigenous-indigenous violence from British jurisdiction, wherever and by whomever they might be committed. The chief justice declared Ballard and his victim to be "wild savage[s] . . . wandering about the country, and living in the uncontrolled freedom of nature." The colony of New South Wales, like the North American colonies before it, had never "interfere[ed] with or enter[ed] into the quarrels that have taken place between or amongst the natives themselves." This was a principle of "natural justice":

> The savages decide their differences upon a principle of retaliation. They give up no natural rights. This is not merely matter of theory but practice. . . . In the absence of a magistracy which is an institution peculiar to an advanced state of refinement, the savage is governed by the laws of his tribe—& with these he is content. . . . They make laws for themselves, which are preserved inviolate, & are rigidly acted upon. . . . There is reason & good sense in the principle that in all transactions between the natives &

British subjects, the laws of the latter shall prevail, because they afford equal protection to all men whether actually or by fiction of law brought within their cognizance. But I know no principle of municipal or national law, which shall subject the inhabitants of a newly found country, to the operation of the laws of the finders, in matters of dispute, injury, or aggression between themselves. If part of our system is to be introduced amongst them, why not the whole? Where will you draw the line: the intervention of our courts of justice, even if practicable, must lead to other interferences, as incompatible as impolitic, in the affairs of harmless inoffensive savages.[39]

Forbes suggests that British jurisdiction over indigenous-settler violence is a creature of "good sense" and legal "fiction," rather than grounded legal principle. Natural law and common law reasoning, however, required that Aborigines should for all other purposes be free of British law—notwithstanding the terms of the Judiciary Act of 1787, or any other territorial measure of British jurisdiction.

Justice Dowling was even more adamant regarding the personal nature of British jurisdiction in the settler state:

It is an undoubted principle that a Colony of Englishmen settled in a new found country shall be governed by the laws of the parent state so far as those laws are applicable to the condition of the Colony. This principle is carried a step farther, where the new found country is inhabited by aborigines. If the inhabitants hold intercourse with the new settlers then the laws of the settlers shall be appealed to in case of dispute injury or aggression, arising from the one side or the other. . . . Amongst civilized nations this is the universal principle, that the lex loci shall determine the disputes arising between the native & the foreigner. But all analogy fails when it is attempted to enforce the laws of a foreign country amongst a race of people, who owe no fealty to us, and over whom we have no natural claim of acknowledgment or supremacy.[40]

Territoriality might belong to European nations, but settler polities had more palpable limits. Their territorial jurisdiction was tempered by indigenous people, "who owe no fealty to us, and over whom we have no natural claim of acknowledgment or supremacy."[41]

Finally, Aborigines and their lawyers ensured that the court's prevarications about the details of its jurisdiction over Aboriginal theft and violence never strayed far from the fundamental question of whether Aborigines were entitled in theory or in practice to maintain their own laws in defiance of British sovereignty. In 1827, a huge crowd of local Aborigines gathered to watch the execution of Tommy, the first indigenous person to be sentenced and hanged for murdering a settler.[42] It is not clear whether they came to sanction or protest the hanging, but it is clear that all were sensible of the novelty of the act. They gathered again in 1834 to storm a jail holding two visiting Aborigines accused of killing another Aborigine at the Governor's Domain.[43] In 1834, when Jackey was tried for spearing a stockman who had come to his camp with an armed posse, he declared that he wanted to be tried by "black-fellows," according to the requirements of British common law. His request was ignored, and did not become an issue before the court, but Jackey was allowed to choose a civilian rather than a military jury.[44] In the same case, Jackey's counsel, Mr. Nichols, repeatedly questioned the legality of trying an Aborigine who was arrested without a warrant, who was unable to defend himself intelligibly before the jury, and who had merely defended his campsite against an armed party in "open warfare."[45] The chief justice would not dismiss the case, but deferred these circumstances to the jury, which found Jackey guilty, but commended him for mercy. As late as 1834, then, arguments about jurisdiction over Aboriginal-settler crime had power before the court.

Between 1824 and 1835, the new Supreme Court of New South Wales pursued a revolutionary course by extending jurisdiction over Australian Aborigines. They built on, without resolving, the tensions between territoriality and plurality that beset the colony before 1824. Though at least three Aborigines had been tried by the court before 1824, the new Supreme Court strove to articulate a coherent notion of British sovereignty in New South Wales—a notion that relied increasingly, but inconsistently, on the presumption that British jurisdiction governed everyone in the territory. By the time that Lego'me and his twenty countrymen came before the court in 1835, indigenous people had largely been absorbed into British jurisdiction, despite the persistent dissents of Aborigines and their lawyers. This absorption however had palpable practical and discursive constraints.

The Transformation of Practice

The Supreme Court's prevarications over the nature and reach of British jurisdiction form only one of many stories about jurisdiction to be told between 1824 and 1835. In some respects they obscured extensive uncertainty about Aboriginal status even as they occasioned subtle shifts in jurisdictional practice in the centers and peripheries of the colony.

Administrative and local responses to Aboriginal theft and violence were a fraught and uncertain business between 1824 and 1835. Local jurisdictional practice shows both change and persistent plurality on the peripheries of New South Wales. In the first place, the few cases involving

Aborigines that did come to court in this period could only do so with the cooperation of local magistrates and constables. In this period, the professionalization of government in the colony meant that many more stipendary officers filled the ranks of the local magistracy and constabulary.[46] Ex-soldiers, whose loyalties were at least divided between center and periphery, also tended to become local officeholders on far-flung peripheries.[47] Having said that, the 1830s marked the beginning of uncontrolled squatting and the establishment of clear and close administrative boundaries that had nothing to do with the expanse of settlement.[48] The Sydney administration tried to come to terms with the problem of governing squatting runs only in the 1840s when Aboriginal resistance reached an unprecedented level.[49] In the meantime, however, more and more Aborigines and settlers made it into court for their transgressions on the colony's peripheries, reflecting halting change in the local administration of New South Wales.

At the same time, the Supreme Court's extension of jurisdiction over violence between nonconvict settlers and Aborigines after 1826 subtly changed the ways that local communities responded to Aboriginal crime. Before 1824, a steady stream of settlers freely acknowledged the use of local reprisals to prevent crime in the peripheries. To be sure, they used the language of personal peril to avoid prosecution: the colonial state had always insisted that settlers would be tried for unauthorized retaliation against Aborigines, though it had exercised that jurisdiction rarely. As late as 1828, Darling preached the virtues of self-defense against Wonnarua depredations against the Hunter Valley community.[50] However, the growing tide of territorial jurisdiction marked a change in the ways that settlers thought and talked about frontier violence.

After 1824, settlers tended to ask how rather than whether to arrest Aborigines who committed depredations.[51] In addition, after 1824, settler discourses of self-defense became more detailed, and focused increasingly on the inability of British law to restrain indigenous crime.[52] Anecdotal reports from various peripheries also suggest that settlers hesitated to "defend" their property against Aboriginal thieves for fear that they would be charged with murder. In 1826, Robert Scott of the Hunter Region noted, "The dislike, indeed absolute unwillingness of people to go after them principally arises from the high responsibility attached to any violence committed on them."[53]

Then, in 1827, the trial of free men of status in the colony laid bare the new limits of self-defense in colonial legal practice. In the cases of R. v. Jameison and R. v. Lowe, both defendants had more or less confessed to killing Aborigines early in the investigations. Lieutenant Lowe's troops reported the shooting of three Aborigines in the Hunter who were "endeavouring to escape."[54] Jameison actually wrote to Governor Darling to inform him that "Hole-in-the-book" had killed and eaten his convict servant, then detailed the circumstances of the Aborigine's arrest, attempted escape, and execution. He wrote later to tell the governor that the missing servant had been found alive, but still defended arresting and killing the Aboriginal suspect. In 1827, such narratives did not stop colonial officials from bringing these men to trial. Yet they did stop juries from finding them guilty: both Lowe and Jameison were acquitted.[55]

These prosecutions warned settlers of a new approach to frontier violence. Settlers met the challenge with a two-pronged strategy: by bringing more Aborigines in for trial and by keeping silent about their own violence. The importance of silence as a community strategy is apparent in a mysterious incident in 1833. John Berryman, a free man and overseer on Sidney Stephen's farm near Wollongong led a group of men in one of two activities: the brutal and deliberate massacre of Tharawal Aborigines living and working on Sidney Stephen's farm, or the "accidental" killing of a few Aborigines in the bush nearby. Hugh Thompson, whom a local magistrate described as a free and "intelligent man," accused Berryman of ordering convict servants to massacre all of the Aborigines working or camping at the farm (including a pregnant woman). Thompson alleged that Berryman had threatened Thompson with violence when he protested the slaughter. The local community, aided by Sidney Stephen himself, however, cast Thompson as an unstable man whose word could not be trusted—they relegated him to silence.

Berryman responded to Thompson's accusations by telling a different story. He said that after Aborigines had speared cattle on Stephen's farm, he led an armed posse out to confront the tribe (which had lately removed itself from the property—a clear sign of guilt). While he was there, he fired a gun in the air out of sight of his men, to scare the Aborigines into confession. His men then opened fire against orders, thinking that Berryman had fired in distress. Preferring Berryman's narrative of error, the local magistrate wondered whether "for the needs of justice" Berryman should "be put on trial" at all, given that the incident seemed to amount to no more than a lamentable accident in which Berryman was only tangentially involved.[56]

The fact was that these Aborigines were suspected of killing cattle—and therein lay the real dilemma. Because Aborigines were perceived to be beyond the everyday reach of jurisdiction, many in the colony thought settler violence just; in their view it was the only viable form of justice. As one commentator put it (probably the colonial secretary, judging by the hand):

> If Thompson is to be believed, there can be no doubt of Berryman & others having been guilty of murder. But as Natives undoubted *did* slaughter cattle, this may be a case showing the necessity of enacting a law which, by providing a remedy for such acts, deprives Europeans of all excuse for inflicting punishment with their own hands.[57]

"Excuse," here, had legal as well as moral connotations. Excuses like these in 1827 led to the acquittal of settler murderers by colonial juries. In 1833, Berryman's excuses prevented his trial. So law still had its limits on the frontiers of the colony, but by the 1830s, frontier settlers were increasingly mindful of the advance of colonial jurisdiction.

The Administration of Territory

The most important debate about the nature and extent of colonial jurisdiction over Aboriginal crime did not occur on the peripheries or in court, however. It occurred within the cloisters of government in Sydney, and in a series of remarkable dialogues between the executive and the judiciary. In 1824, 1832, and 1834, key members of the colonial administration betrayed persistent uncertainty about indigenous legal status—uncertainty that they argued could and should be resolved by legislation, not by the courts. Significantly, all three moments stemmed from widespread Aboriginal resistance to the rapid expansion of settlement. Aborigines themselves, by protesting British presence and, with it, the extension of British law, ensured that their legal status was a persistent problem for the colonial state.

One year after the arrival of Saxe Bannister as attorney-general to the colony, Governor Brisbane declared martial law to quell Aboriginal (Wiradjuri) resistance to the rapidly expanding settlement at Bathurst. Bannister convinced the new governor that British territorial sovereignty in New South Wales required state retaliation against Aborigines to be grounded in an act of law, not of war. Martial law suspends civil law in times of civil disturbance: "in time of rebellion the Crown might, for the restoration of peace, declare war, and exercise its severities, against rebels." Brisbane's declaration of martial law in 1824 declared war on Aborigines *as British subjects* in rebellion against their rightful government.[58] As such, it contained within it a new assertion of governmental jurisdiction over Aborigines.[59]

Brisbane's declaration of martial law did not answer the question of Aboriginal subjecthood definitively, however. It seemed instead to have reflected the peculiar bent of his new attorney-general.[60] Metropole and colony remained deeply ambivalent about the status of indigenous people. Just one year later, Lord Bathurst advised Brisbane's successor, Governor Darling, to treat Aboriginal depredations "as if they proceeded from subjects of any accredited State."[61] Darling, acting on this recommendation, refused to declare martial law against Aborigines in the Hunter Region in 1826. He did so despite Bannister's insistence that "indiscriminate slaughter of offenders, except in the heat of immediate pursuit of other similar circumstances, requires preliminary solemn acts; and that to order soldiers to punish any outrage in this way, is against the law."[62] Darling saw no need to observe such niceties in the case of "a few naked Savages, who, however treacherous, would not face a Corporal's Guard."[63]

Six years later, Aboriginal legal status was still openly debated in the ranks of the New South Wales executive—with respect both to Aboriginal depredations against settlers and to Aboriginal violence inter se. In December of 1832, Major Sullivan, the resident magistrate at Port Macquarie, wrote to the colonial secretary to ask what legal measures he could take against local Biripi Aborigines who were spearing cattle. Cases like R. v. Lowe in 1827 had taught soldiers and mounted policemen that violence against Aborigines could result in prosecution. Major Sullivan wrote in 1832 to request plausible alternatives to violence. He noted that it was utterly untenable to send Aborigines to the Supreme Court in Sydney for trial. It was almost impossible to gather compelling evidence against them because they were difficult to identify and their evidence could not be sworn on oath. This exposed "the property of His Majesty's Subjects to be molested by them with impunity from the inability of procuring legal conviction." Local trial, he thought, could be the only plausible alternative to violence.[64]

The exchange that followed among Crown law officers, the governor, and the colonial secretary reveals that Major Sullivan was not alone in his confusion and concern. The colonial secretary agreed that Aboriginal crime could not be controlled adequately by British jurisdiction; a high-level legal and political response was required. He noted that query must "of course be referred to the Law Officers," and that

> the principal difficulty in all such cases is rightly stated by Mr Sullivan to be that of procuring Evidence such as the existing Law requires—the difficulty of identifying them prevents their being punished and their inadmissibility as Witnesses prevents them from obtaining redress when injured by Europeans.

He advocated a political rather than judicial solution to the problem. He proposed "Enactments," legislating first, that any Aborigine in company with others spearing cattle could be tried as a principal in the crime, and second, that Aboriginal evidence could be admitted in court despite Aboriginal ignorance of religious oaths.[65] He was even less certain of indigenous legal status when Jackey killed a settler attacking his camp in 1834, declaring there that "it has long appeared that the only light in which aggressions between Natives & Europeans can be judicially considered is that of *Warfare*—as such I know not whether Individuals can be put on trial without some new law."[66]

The attorney-general, John Kinchela, responded to Sullivan's query with the line of reasoning he and his predecessors had argued before the Supreme Courts since 1824:

> As the aborigines are free people living under the protection of H.M. Government, they are as of right entitled to the benefits & protection of the English laws, & liable to the Penalties of those laws for any violation thereof.

He noted also that, since an act of Parliament had recently declared that many offenses against cattle were no longer capital in nature, Aborigines could be tried summarily in local courts.[67] To the colonial secretary, however, this response was wholly insufficient. He recommended grumpily that, despite Kinchela's lawyerly response, the governor ought to consult the chief justice "on the subject—or perhaps the residence of Judge Burton in the Cape may have given him some practical Experience of the modifications necessary when exercising the Laws of a Civilized on an uncivilized Community." The governor agreed to consult the chief justice, but thought the attorney-general had stated the law correctly.[68]

This exchange is significant for a number of reasons. First and foremost, it reveals the tension between judicial law and politics over the juridical status of indigenous people. The insufficiency of criminal law as it stood to govern indigenous-settler violence was felt at the highest levels of government. Not for the last time, the governors, law officers, and judges conferred over the political ramifications of indigenous legal status, and over the need to bend and mold rules of law. More significantly still, the colonial secretary suggested that Justice Burton (recently arrived from the Cape) might constitute a better politico-legal adjudicator of indigenous legal status than Chief Justice Forbes. In short, he advocated that the colony turn away from North American precedent toward a new conception of settler sovereignty. In 1836, Justice Burton would write the Murrell decision, declaring Australian Aborigines had no sovereignty, no jurisdiction, and no law.

This exchange shows, finally, that administrators considered frontier violence to be a problem of administration and a deficit in legal process, if not legal authority. After Lowe's case in 1827, Major Sullivan was reticent to act against Aboriginal violence and theft without a clear mandate from the central government. As John Berryman's massacre showed, magistrates, even judges, demonstrated a deep unwillingness to investigate settlers, servants, and overseers for killing Aborigines, especially when the latter had been involved in the real or imagined theft of cattle. The colonial secretary articulated persistent uneasiness over the capacity of colonial courts to try Aborigines for crime against settlers or to treat their aggressions as acts of war. He felt that indigenous crime fell through the cracks in the legal edifice of settler sovereignty.

Jurisdiction over crimes between Aborigines troubled the legal officers of the colonial state more deeply. In late 1833, two Aborigines, Quart Pot and Numbo, were arrested for killing an Aborigine in the Governor's Domain.[69] Attorney General John Kinchela consulted the chief justice about what to do; only four years before, after all, Chief Justice Forbes and Justice Dowling had told the attorney-general not to prosecute Ballard or Barrett for murdering Dirty Dick in Sydney. It seems that times had changed in the colony, even in the brief interim between 1829 and 1834.

By 1834, the chief justice himself agreed that indigenous legal status was a problem for the executive and not the courts. He told the solicitor-general to consult the governor:

> In the last week I had applied to the Chief Justice on the Subject for his Opinion whether these people were subject to the Laws of England for such a Crime and his Honor recommended me to lay the law before the Executive for directions on the Subject and as I understand his Excellency will be in town tomorrow I will thank you to let me know His Excellencies wishes and directions, whether I shall bring the case again before the Court for their Solemn decision or have the prisoners discharged."[70]

Just a few days later, Kinchela wrote back stating that he would "bring the men to trial." He noted that

> the only hesitation I had on the Subject arose from the previous decision of the Chief Justice in which Judge Dowling concurred—The Solicitor General thinks the Case ought to be tried and if the parties are found Guilty, that the Executive may decide what shall ultimately be done respecting those men.[71]

However, this was not the end of the matter. The judges again pressed the attorney-general not to bring the case to trial as "the decision of the court must be against me." He noted, regardless of the Court's position, the executive must decide "the question as to the policy of bringing the case before the court."[72] According to the colonial secretary's annotations, Governor Bourke equivocated:

If the Superior Court has given any *formal judgment* in the matter I do not desire to bring it forward again nor in that case should an indictment have been laid against the native—but if the matter has *not* been *formally decided* by the Court, the Governor is interested in obtaining their judgment as the foundation upon which to [unclear] such other measures as it may be necessary to adopt for the prosecution of such Murders as this under consideration, if the Judges declare that there is no legal course to be taken before them for the punishment of these crimes.[73]

The case, however, did not go to trial.[74] Instead, the incarceration of Quart Pot and Numbo wrought a minor sensation in Sydney. The *Australian* declared it to be "unreasonable, oppressive and impolitic" to try Aborigines for crimes inter se, when they received none of the benefits of subjecthood.[75] Local Aborigines seemed to agree. Though Quart Pot and Numbo were not from Sydney, local Aborigines crowded around the jail during their incarceration, whether to demand their release or to impose customary punishment for their misdeeds.[76] They were released, and returned to their home district.[77] Indigenous people, the public, and possibly the chief justice himself combined to defeat the extension of jurisdiction over Aboriginal-Aboriginal crime in 1834.

Aboriginal-settler violence on New South Wales peripheries and crimes between Aborigines in the center of Sydney raised more than the legal status of indigenous people in the British law between 1824 and 1835. In this period of rapid economic and geographical expansion, both Aboriginal and settler violence begged the question of British authority over people and places throughout New South Wales. Aboriginal combatants in Sydney reminded the colony that it did not have a juridical monopoly in the heart of settlement, even in the Governor's Domain. Those few settlers tried for murdering Aborigines reminded officials of the many squatters busy negotiating with and killing indigenous people hundreds of miles away. The administrative problem of bringing Aborigines to trial for their crimes against people and property in New South Wales taught administrators that court rules and procedures could not cope with cultural plurality on the fringes of New South Wales, let alone the plural legal practice fostered by center and periphery between 1788 and 1824. In the early 1830s, in short, judges and administrators in New South Wales confronted the impossibility of territorial sovereignty in New South Wales, and quaked. From 1835, however, they began to confront plurality head on.

The Revolution of 1835

When Lego'me came before the court in 1835, courts in the colony of New South Wales had tried Aborigines for twelve years. Yet the court had refused to try Aborigines for crimes against Aborigines, and had been called upon to adjudicate only nine cases of settler violence against Aborigines, most of which dealt with poor or convict settler-murderers. In Sydney, as late as 1834, high-ranking members of the colonial administration contended over whether or to what degree Aborigines and their crimes fell within the purview of British law.

In 1835, however, local magistrates, law officers, and the courts reached a temporary accord. From February, 1835, twenty-one Aboriginal men were tried before the court for a variety of crimes ranging from theft to rape. Meanwhile, in June 1835, a group of adventurers led by John Batman signed a treaty with the Kulin people on the southeastern tip of the continent, recognizing their rights to land and to self-determination in the process. Both marked the beginning of a new drive in the center and periphery of New South Wales to puzzle out the meaning of British colonization—a process that would culminate in 1836, when Murrell and Bungaree were tried for killing their countrymen on the public road near Windsor.

Lego'me's trial and incarceration for stealing a pipe from Patrick Sheridan on a country road is significant for a number of reasons. It was part of a mass incarceration and, more importantly, of the mass trial and conviction of Aborigines in the colony of New South Wales. Only Lachlan Macquarie had incarcerated more Aborigines for any period of time in 1816. But as we saw in Chapter 2, Macquarie tried no Aborigines for frontier violence.

All but one of the men tried in 1835 were tried for crimes other than murder. Charley Myrtle and Mickey Muscle were tried for raping a white woman—a crime for which the *Sydney Herald* thought they should be absolved. Rape, they thought, was customary in Aboriginal society.[78] Another Charley was tried for murder. Everyone else was tried for some species of theft. Only one Aboriginal man had been tried to conviction for theft in the history of the court.[79]

Fifteen of these men were sentenced to death, though only Charley (convicted of murder) and Mickey Muscle (convicted of rape) were executed. Thirteen were transported instead to Goat Island. Between 1824 and 1835, only two Aboriginal men had been executed by the colonial state in Sydney, both for murdering settlers. Tim Castle argues that the disjuncture between conviction and execution reflects public ambivalence about execution—especially of groups under some legal disability (like women or Aborigines). This was an ambivalence shared, albeit only briefly, by Governor Bourke.[80]

Finally, despite the novelty of this mass incarceration and trial, according to the surviving newspaper accounts of the cases, counsel in these cases rarely demurred against the court's jurisdiction.[81] Occasionally, however, the court still asked its favorite expert on the subject of Aborigines, missionary Lawrence Threlkeld, if Aborigines coming before the court understood the criminality or wrongfulness of their transgressions.[82]

Of all the trials that came before the court in 1835, Lego'me's was the most absurd and therefore the most significant. It represented a paltry theft, perhaps a mere miscommunication—the taking of a pipe. Yet a constable, a magistrate, a solicitor-general, a court, and a jury all decided that Lego'me had committed a capital crime. Of course, Lego'me took Sheridan's pipe in the midst of persistent uprisings on the newest frontiers of the colony. Sheridan was alone on the road, had heard that he would be a target of Aboriginal reprisals, and feared (perhaps irrationally) for his life when approached by Lego'me. The legal system of New South Wales here mobilized itself to recognize and validate settlers' fears of Aboriginal violence to show that it could and would act to make settlers safe.

Moreover, by mobilizing its considerable resources against such a minor act of theft, the court and the colony signaled their determination to exercise intimate legal control over Aboriginal crime. They declared, after years of prevarication, that, at least in their interactions with settlers, Aborigines were bound by British law anywhere in the colony of New South Wales, but particularly near the symbols of civilization: towns, farms, and in this case, on a country road. It was an incomplete assertion of territorial jurisdiction, but it was new, insistent, and portentous. It signaled the arrival of the logic of territoriality in the colony of New South Wales.

Meanwhile, John Batman shook the foundations of the British Empire in Australia by exchanging some cheap trinkets with the Kulin people of Port Phillip for 600,000 acres of land. This shamefully unequal exchange constituted the first and possibly the only written treaty in the history of the colony.[83]

Batman's treaty forced Governor Bourke to formalize, once and for all, the relationship of British sovereignty to territory in the continent of Australia—without fundamentally resolving the problem of indigenous legal status or indigenous rights. He did so by applying the North American doctrine of preemption to Australia, declaring that "every . . . treaty, bargain and contract with the Aboriginal Natives . . . for the possession, title or claim to any Lands . . . is void and of no effect against the rights of the Crown."[84] If Bourke preferred to revert to North American practices, Governor Arthur of Van Diemen's Land wondered whether "in contemplation of law that a migratory savage tribe, consisting of from perhaps 30 to 40 Individuals roaming over an almost unlimited extent of country could acquire such a property in the soil."[85]

The episode also serves to highlight the ambivalence of the Colonial Office in London about Aboriginal rights. In the mid-1830s, the paradox of settlement without consent in New South Wales prompted humanitarian Parliamentarians to defend, qualifiedly, Aboriginal rights, though with no palpable effect outside the metropolis.[86] Colonial Office officials, George Grey among them, at times explicitly endorsed the "proprietary rights" of indigenous tribes.[87] Soon afterward, they reached some manner of consensus. They agreed that British Law applied to Aboriginal peoples in every settler periphery from Canada to New South Wales, but that zones of exception might be tolerated in the interests of justice, humanity, or civilization.[88]

The legal controversy over the status of Batman's treaty drew together the strands of territorial sovereignty in local and metropolitan thought about New South Wales. As Reynolds has pointed out, the Colonial Office did not respond to Batman's treaty with a plain rejection of indigenous rights; rather, it clung to a decidedly North American doctrine of preemption. From the very early years of settlement, North American colonies had declared that only the Crown or the colony could purchase Indian land in North America. No settler could take good title from a private contract or treaty. This principle lay at the center of the Proclamation of 1763, which purported to limit settlement to the land east of the Appalachian Mountains in North America and to preserve Indian title to all lands beyond. Finally, it formed a core of American policy under the Constitution and at common law under Johnson v. McIntosh (1823). In Australia, it became the basis of Colonial Office dissent against Batman's treaty with the Port Phillip Aborigines.

However, even in this humanitarian opposition to Batman's treaty lay subtle negations of Aboriginal jurisdiction. Like Johnson v. McIntosh, and unlike the Proclamation of 1763, the Colonial Office read preemption as a limitation on Aboriginal as well as settler rights. Dr. Stephen Lushington, an eminent jurist hired to comment on the dispute, argued that the Crown could prevent the Port Phillip association as British subjects from establishing a colony on Kulin land. However, he did "not think that the right to this Territory is [was] . . . vested in the Crown" as it had engaged in "no [consistent] act of ownership."[89] The Colonial Office rejected Lushington's argument, because it would upset British claims to all wasteland in Australia and overturn the basis on which settlements were being undertaken in the south and west of the continent, and prevented elsewhere:

> Glenelg is not aware of any fact of principle which can be alleged in support of such a conclusion, which would not apply with equal force to all the waste Lands in any other part of the Colony of New South Wales, his Lordship must decline to acquiesce in the doctrine.[90]

Crown rights to limit settlement throughout the continent, in short, rested on a rejection of the treaty. More importantly, however, the Crown rejected the Port Phillip adventurer's proposal to set up an independent proprietary colony as an *imperium in imperio*—an unallowable derogation from the constitutional authority of New South Wales over the eastern half of the continent:

> To place a territory so extensive under any other management than that of the responsible Officers of the Crown would in Lord Glenelg's opinion be to create an unconstitutional power which if not subvert the authority of the local Government would unavoidably fetter its movements.[91]

Sidestepping direct engagement with the issue of indigenous rights to land and sovereignty, Colonial Secretary Glenelg nevertheless endorsed the sovereignty and jurisdiction of the colony of New South Wales over the full extent of its territory.

In both the metropolis and the periphery, the Batman treaty operated to foreground the problem of sovereignty and jurisdiction over New South Wales's peripheries. The result of long if sporadic debate on the issue was to endorse the territoriality of sovereignty—a sovereignty that would not tolerate indigenous jurisdiction, except perhaps as a temporary expedient or exception to the rule of British common law.[92]

In the 1820s and early 1830s, Georgia and New South Wales struggled to define and practice perfect territorial sovereignty by incorporating indigenous people and indigenous land into their jurisdictions. Strident words in Georgia, Washington, and New Echota (the most important town in the Cherokee Nation) were belied by ambivalent jurisdictional deeds in Georgia's borderlands. In New South Wales, a drive in London and Sydney to rationalize settler legal order in the expanding colony foundered again and again on the theoretical and practical problem of Aboriginal and settler violence. The new Supreme Court of New South Wales invented jurisdiction over Aboriginal crime against settlers, though it showed persistent uncertainty about the details of the project. Settlers and magistrates used jurisdiction and concealed violence in equal measure, prompting and responding to the court's territoriality. By 1835, the administration, itself deeply divided over the extent of its power on New South Wales's peripheries, led the drive toward bringing the pettiest Aboriginal crimes within the purview of the colonial state.

The ambivalent efforts echoing from the centers and peripheries of these two very different settler polities illustrate a fundamental change in the articulation of settler sovereignty and the exercise of settler jurisdiction after 1820. They attest, finally, to the rise of the logic of territoriality—the conviction that sovereignty imported perfect territorial jurisdiction over space, not subjects. In both places, indigenous people and their land lay at the center of this project as its primary objects and its insistent bane.

CHAPTER EIGHT

Perfect Settler Sovereignty

B Y 1830 A N D 1835, Georgia and New South Wales had both reached a precipice. Decades of plural practice stood in tension with rapidly evolving local discourses of perfect settler sovereignty. Economically, juridically, and figuratively, Georgia and New South Wales sought to redefine themselves as modern states by erasing indigenous rights. The State of Georgia proclaimed to the world that its sovereign integrity was premised, as never before, on the full legislative and juridical control of its territory, even as its rhetorical excesses were spurred on by indigenous and federal participation in the logic of territoriality. In New South Wales, a crisis of jurisdiction was brought on by rapid and uncontrolled settler expansion, indigenous resistance, and the ongoing problem of urban indigenous violence. All three worked together to create a new but incomplete logic of territoriality that enveloped more and more of Australia within the imagination of the court.

Between 1830 and 1836, courts in Georgia, Washington, and Sydney completed what they had started a decade before: they perfected settler sovereignty by subordinating indigenous jurisdiction.[1] In doing so they joined other settler jurisdictions who, at the same time, cobbled together a new definition of sovereignty from the imperfections of the law of nations, of settler discourse, and of practice. A convention of judges in Georgia added judicial logic to Georgia's extension of jurisdiction over the Cherokee territory in 1830 by declaring that Cherokee law could not exist on Georgia's soil. The Supreme Court equivocated in Cherokee Nation v. Georgia and Worcester v. Georgia. It gave indigenous people legal relief against the state of Georgia, but could not protect them from the

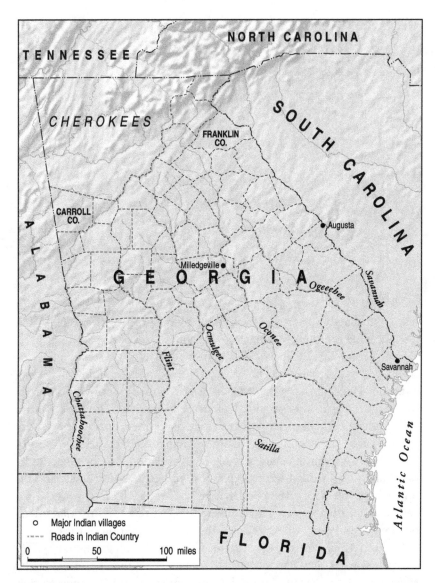

Georgia, 1831

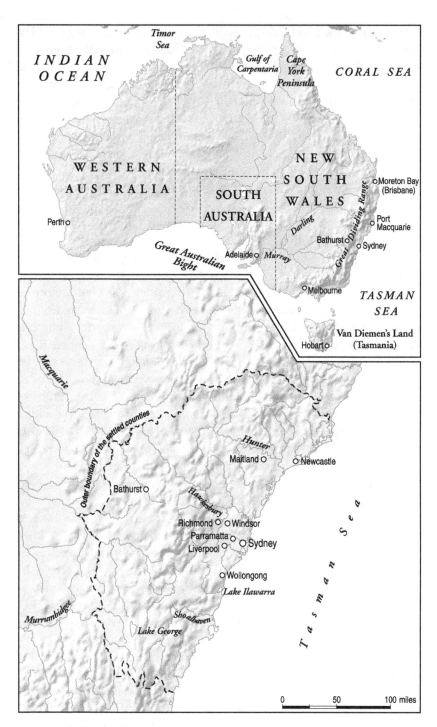

New South Wales, 1838

complicity of state and federal policy, nor could it shield indigenous law from the territorial sovereignty of Congress—a territorial sovereignty that the Marshall court had fought for decades to create and defend against the states.[2] In New South Wales, the new Supreme Court responded to a much less sensational crisis of territoriality. Using the same logic as Georgia's judges, it declared that Aboriginal Australians had no rights—to land or to self-governance—that could withstand British territorial sovereignty. In their way, all of these cases cleared the path for settlement by unsettling indigenous jurisdiction.[3]

In doing so, Georgia and New South Wales followed and set an Anglophone settler pattern. In 1822, the court of Oyer and Terminer, Western District Assize, in Upper Canada convicted an Ottawa Indian named Shawanakiskie for killing an indigenous woman on the streets of a strategically important British town called Amherstburg. The court argued that indigenous blood feud fell within the purview of the court, at least in British towns and probably on Indian reservations. The court ignored a treaty between the British and the Ottawa after the French and Indian Wars that had specifically left local indigenous people to adjudicate crime among themselves. Instead it argued that indigenous people living on the good graces of the colonial state could no longer disorder settler towns with reminders of their prior occupation, their jurisdiction, or their sovereignty. This case was confirmed by an appellate court, then by the Colonial Office. Shawanakiskie's case marked London's first and last intrusion into the definition of settler sovereignty between 1822 and 1850.[4]

In April 1840, Richard Hobson convinced Māori chiefs to sign the first Treaties of Waitangi so that (he claimed) the British could control British settlers there. Just weeks later, the first British act of sovereignty in New Zealand was the trial of a Māori man named Towranga (Tauranga) for murder. Though local Māori chiefs protested the trial, Hobson ordered eighty men and a ship to Kororarika to ensure both that the accused had his day in court and that local chiefs understood fully that British jurisdiction was but the softest touch of British sovereignty.[5] Only seven years later, Ranitapiripiri, alias Kopitipita, was indicted for murdering another Māori by "drowning him . . . in the river Manawatu." Justice Chapman, tentatively applying the principles of the Tanistry case, noted that "the laws of the ceded country were in force among the natives of that country, unless they were contrary to humanity or the Christian religion," yet he asserted perfect territorial jurisdiction over cases of indigenous murder. In this case no one protested British jurisdiction. The Māori concerned explicitly "confessed the superiority of our laws."[6] In 1849, Ratea or Kai Karoro was tried for murdering Parata-Wanga for seducing his wife (a killing sanctioned by customary law). Again, Chapman asserted British jurisdiction to try all murders in British territory—a tempered territoriality to be sure, but one that made clear that indigenous law could be curtailed on the basis of local legal reasoning by settler courts.[7]

This new judicial discourse of perfect settler sovereignty left precious little space for first peoples. Even as settler communities in North America and the Antipodes started to romanticize the slow disappearance of their noble savages,[8] common-law courts condemned them to juridical death—though, in the United States, Canada, and New Zealand, the sentence was somewhat ambiguous or temporarily deferred.[9]

What happened? In the United States, Canada, and Australia, the local administration of law, combined with British jurisdictional chaos and flexible early modern notions of sovereignty, had created and maintained space for legal pluralism. Fostered in the peripheries and spilling over into the centers of government, indigenous jurisdiction challenged settler order, even as indigenous people strove to stem the expansion of settlement. Indigenous jurisdiction and indigenous land rights together held the potential to shatter the legal foundations of settler society because both indicated prior, better, and unjustly subordinated claims to the cotton farms and sheep runs that animated settler economies. Anglophone institutions of local government and the flexibility of the common law, meanwhile, meant that settlers themselves could easily subvert law in the interests of pluralism. They did this unevenly before the 1820s, to serve their own interests in frontier exchange or disorderly expansion. These conditions sprang from the juridical and administrative fluidity of the early British Empire. By 1830, they ill-suited the pretensions of modern settler polities.

This is not merely a story about Anglophone settler polities, however. European states themselves embarked on a remarkable drive to conflate sovereignty and jurisdiction after the Napoleonic Wars—to render the sovereign states imagined by Bodin and Hobbes into the nation-states that dominated nineteenth-century Europe and much of the globe.[10] At the same time, the British Empire and its trading partners formalized and/or eroded legal pluralism everywhere, from Uruguay to the trading ports of China.[11]

I suspect that, in settler polities, indigenous jurisdiction was in some respects a casualty of British globalization and industrialization in the nineteenth century. Legal opinions about the relationship between jurisdiction and sovereignty on the fringes of the British Empire appear frequently in Colonial Office records from the turn of the nineteenth century.[12] However, from the 1830s, the legal officers of the Colonial Office turned their attention as never before to the status of people in territory occupied, claimed, or controlled by the British Empire.[13] As the Empire fretted endlessly about its rights to punish crime on the streets of Gibraltar villages, on the frontiers of the Cape, or in the manufacturing villages surrounding Bombay, indigenous legal status in settler colonies presented a logical anomaly not only to common-law order in North America and the Antipodes, but also to the global system of exchange presided over by the British Empire. As rising producers of cotton and wool for the factories of Britain—endeavors supported by unfree, nonindigenous labor—Georgia and New South Wales had little space for indigenous orders or for indigenous peoples. Settler polities met the British call for raw materials to support a new global order with a new juridical scheme for orderly settlement and orderly exchange.[14] In the process, they styled themselves modern states with perfect territorial sovereignty.

Material conditions, however, do not alone explain the transformation of jurisdictional practice in Georgia and New South Wales: the transformation of settler sovereignty has a semi-autonomous legal and intellectual history. Courts redefined settler sovereignty not merely for economic convenience; nor did they do so because they finally had the capacity to subordinate indigenous people. Settler governments had long had enough constables to arrest at least some indigenous malefactors. They did it instead because they could no longer imagine plural sovereignty in their local contexts. Though in the 1830s both Georgia and New South Wales were deeply enmeshed in processes of colonization, they defined themselves in many respects as nation-states. Perfect territorial sovereignty was an idea fit for the times in Anglophone settler polities, where it took on a unique and uniquely destructive meaning. Settler sovereignty was defined against indigenous people and indigenous customary law.

So it was that the transformation of settler sovereignty between 1822 and 1847 lodged indigenous people in the heart of settler polities. In the 1830s, Georgia and New South Wales, in particular, founded settler sovereignty precariously, anxiously, and in some ways incompletely on the subordination of indigenous jurisdiction.

Georgia's Resolutions

In June 1830, three parties contended for territorial authority in Georgia's borderlands. Though Andrew Jackson's federal administration had little interest in defending its claim to territorial jurisdiction in the Cherokee Nation, various factions of Congress and the Supreme Court continued to urge the supremacy of federal over state rights, invoking the logic of territoriality.[15] The leaders and defenders of the Cherokee Nation advocated Cherokee rights to land and self-governance in Cherokee territory. While everyone else talked, Georgia acted. In June 1830, Georgia extended its jurisdiction into Indian Country, carving the Cherokee Nation into a number of counties to be administered by local governments and presided over by various state courts.[16] From this moment onward, hundreds of Cherokee Indians found their way into Georgia's courts. Georgia attorney William Underwood alone claimed to have defended 315 Cherokees between June 1830 and 1838.[17]

Georgian and Cherokee sovereignty both came before the courts of the state mere months after the extension of Georgia's jurisdiction, when Cherokee George Tassel killed a man in the Cherokee Nation. The details of George Tassel's arrest, trial, and execution by the state of Georgia are lost to history. Tim Garrison's exhaustive research has barely managed to identify George Tassel, let alone the name, race, or status of his victim. Despite some evidence to the contrary, however, it is fairly certain that George Tassel, and most likely his victim, were Cherokee Indians and that his crime was committed on Cherokee land.[18] Under Georgia's 1827 law extending state jurisdiction over the Cherokee Nation (which became effective in June 1830), Tassel was arrested and scheduled for trial in Hall County. When Tassel challenged the jurisdiction of the court, Judge Clay referred the case to a convention "of all the Judges of the different [superior] circuits of the State."[19]

Tassel's attorney, William Underwood, argued that Georgia's act extending jurisdiction was unconstitutional and void. He argued that "by various treaties" signed with the United States, "the Cherokee nation had been treated with, and considered an independent sovereign State, and, therefore, could not be subjected to the laws of a State." In those treaties, Cherokee "self-government had been expressly recognized and distinctly maintained by the Cherokee tribe of nation," including the right to declare war.

The convention responded with the new mythology of settler sovereignty. As all great myth-makers must, the convention of Georgia judges began their tale of perfect settler sovereignty with history and legend. They promised to tell the history of European relations with "aboriginal tribes" as an unbroken series of British claims and indigenous incapacities. The convention declared, "Whatever right Great Britain possessed over the Indian tribes is vested in the State of Georgia." However, it recovered these rights, not from the history of practice—the myriad negotiations and compromises of the colony and state of Georgia—but from Johnson v. McIntosh. Therein, Marshall had declared that Indians were mere occupants of land and that the state or federal governments held "ultimate dominion in themselves." Though Marshall had doubted the normativity of such a system, he declared that, as "an Act of State" it lay without the scrutiny of the court.

Leaving Marshall's uncertainty behind them, the Georgia convention declared that history, religion, and the law of nations all denied Cherokee rights to land and to sovereignty. It declared that the United States had never formally declared war against Indians, though many de facto wars had been waged. The Constitution gave power to the federal government to treat with Indians, but it also gave the federal government power to govern Indian trade (and with it, Indians). This, the convention argued, indicated that indigenous people "are members of communities that are not sovereign states."

The convention then stressed the Cherokees' status as pupils of a civilized state and invoked Emer de Vattel's Lockean presumption that the indigenous people of North America could, by natural law, be confined "within narrower limits." The convention noted that Vattel himself had suggested that the New Englanders, out of moderation and not legal obligation, acknowledged indigenous rights to the land granted them by charter.[20] Finally, it revived Calvin's Case, long abandoned by the courts of the United Kingdom.[21] The convention argued that the Cherokee were a savage, conquered people, and as such they were incapable of accepting the benefits secured to conquered people by the law of nations.

The convention then turned to the newer mythologies of the early republic. Again, Marshall's jurisprudence provided rich pickings. It cited Marshall's contention in Johnson v. McIntosh that the rights of any settler state included within them any powers "indispensable to that system under which the country has been settled." The convention projected this theory of property rights into a theory of states' rights, arguing that the system of government established and maintained by the United States left no space for independent indigenous communities. Federation preserved the sovereignty of the states, but state sovereignty could not tolerate indigenous jurisdiction.

In short, indigenous people were a logical anomaly in settler polities—an embarrassment to the sovereign settler state. Georgia's settler sovereignty was inviolable. It could not be abrogated by default, whether or not Georgia had claimed or exercised it in the past. Nor could it be subordinated to the claims of indigenous peoples:

> Indeed it is difficult to conceive how any person who has a definite idea of what constitutes a sovereign state, can have come to the conclusion that the Cherokee Nation is a sovereign and independent state. . . . That a Government should be seized in fee of a territory and yet have no jurisdiction over that country is an anomaly in the science of jurisprudence; but it may be

contended that altho' the state of Georgia may have the jurisdiction over Cherokee Territory, yet it has no right to exercise jurisdiction over the persons of the Cherokee Indians who reside upon the territory of which the State of Georgia is seized in fee. Such a distinction would present a more strange anomaly than that of a government having no jurisdiction over a territory of which it is seized in fee.

The logic of territoriality underpinning this new science of jurisprudence pitted settler sovereignty against indigenous juridical independence. In June 1830, the Georgia legislature asserted its sovereignty by extending jurisdiction over the Cherokee Nation within its charted bounds, and only a few months later, its convention of judges perfected Georgia's claims.

The pageant of sovereignty constructed around George Tassel was marred before completion, however. The Supreme Court and Chief Justice Marshall issued a writ of injunction staying Tassel's execution until his case came before the court.[22] The state replied to Marshall's injunction with words of sovereignty and jurisdiction. Georgia's legislature passed a series of resolutions declaring that

the right to punish crimes, against the peace and good order of this State, in accordance with existing laws, is an original and necessary part of sovereignty which the state of Georgia has never parted with.[23]

They enjoined the governor to rebuff any federal interference with state criminal law and declared "that the State of Georgia will never so far compromit the sovereignty [sic] . . . as to become a party to" such a cause. The governor of Georgia responded in form. He ordered Tassel's immediate execution, and Tassel was hanged with little ceremony on December 24, 1830—hardly a triumphant beginning for Georgia's newly perfected sovereignty.[24]

The Cherokee Nation responded by asserting its own inviolability. In 1830, the famous lawyer William Wirt filed a writ of injunction "to restrain . . . the Governor, Attorney General, Judges, justices of the peace, sheriffs, deputy sheriffs, constables and others, officers, agents, and servants of that State, from executing process, or doing anything toward the execution or enforcement of those laws within the Cherokee Nation." Trying to avoid the political minefield of indigenous rights, the Supreme Court in Cherokee Nation v. Georgia reduced the case to "a single question": whether the nation was a foreign state, and therefore able to bring suit within the original jurisdiction of the court.[25] Marshall found that it was not. Indian tribes were, instead, "domestic dependent nations . . . in a state of pupilage" to the United States. Adopting some of the reasoning of the Tassel court, he declared that the Constitution made Indians a special case—the subject of treaties and the object of the regulation of commerce. He argued that this status had never given them rights to appeal to American courts, notwithstanding the long history of colonial and early national litigation on behalf of Indian nations and Indian people.[26]

This, however, was not a simple endorsement of Georgia's jurisprudence. Marshall emphasized the capacities of the Cherokee for self-government, war-making, and peacemaking and suggested that they had legitimate claims to function as a corporate and distinct polity.[27] The Cherokee were within the territorial sovereignty and dominion of the United States—they were domestic—but only insofar as they could not treat or trade with foreign nations.[28] Yet, whatever these rights might entail, they were not for the court to defend against a government.

His fellows in the majority were less equivocal. Henry Baldwin refused the injunction on the grounds that it would open the court to many frivolous indigenous claims. William Johnson declared that Indians might have property in land, but they were so low on the scale of civilization that they could be considered as nothing more than "an anomaly . . . which the law of nations would regard as nothing more than wandering hordes, held together by ties of blood and habit, and having neither laws or government beyond what is required in a savage state."[29] Meanwhile Smith Thompson and Joseph Story—the latter among the most able jurists and constitutional scholars on the court—voted in favor of the injunction, declaring that the Cherokee were a "foreign state" for the purposes of the Constitution.[30]

Cherokee Nation v. Georgia left the Cherokee with a bundle of rights and no capacity to defend them—at least until Samuel Worcester provided them with an indirect route to the Supreme Court in 1832. As one of its many draconian acts of legislative jurisdiction over the Cherokee, Georgia's legislature required all white people to leave the nation or to sign an oath of allegiance to the State of Georgia.[31] Samuel Worcester, with many other missionaries in the nation, refused. The state arrested a number and tried and convicted two citizen-missionaries. Worcester proceeded to contest his conviction under Georgia's statutes by arguing that they were unconstitutional, and that they impinged on Cherokee sovereignty.[32]

This time, the Supreme Court could not deny its jurisdiction to hear the matter. Worcester was a citizen, so he had standing to contest his criminal conviction before the court.[33] Instead, Marshall and a majority acted to end their role in the oppression of indigenous people. They did so by vindicating both federal and indigenous sovereignty at the expense of Georgia's jurisdiction.

The court first bolstered indigenous rights to land in Georgia. It rejected its own reasoning in Johnson v. McIntosh by declaring that British

Empire in America claimed no more sovereignty and dominion in North America than a superior right (over other Europeans) to purchase lands from indigenous people.[34] Under the law of nations, according to the court, Britain claimed "the exclusive right to purchase, but did not found that right on a denial of the right of the possessor to sell."[35]

The majority argued that indigenous rights to land carried rights to self-government as a matter of principle and practice. In practice, Britain and the United States had never asserted the right to govern the Cherokee or to interfere with their internal affairs. By treaty, the Cherokee had submitted to British and American protection, but always as a sovereign, corporate body. As such they retained rights as sovereign polities, though those rights were constrained by the United States:

> The Indian nations had always been considered as distinct, independent political communities, retaining their original natural rights, as the undisputed possessors of the soil, from time immemorial, with the single exception of that imposed by irresistible power, which excluded them from intercourse with any other European potentate than the first discoverer . . . : and this was a restriction which those European potentates imposed on themselves, as well as on the Indians.[36]

Here, the court drew a legal distinction between "protection" of sovereign entities and protection of individuals. Citing Vattel, the court claimed that, by submitting by treaty to the protection of a strong state, "Tributary or feudatory states . . . do not thereby cease to be sovereign and independent states, so long as self government and sovereign and independent authority are left in the administration of the state."[37] Only an individual, protected by a state, would be subject to its jurisdiction. In doing so, they resuscitated a distinction falling into abeyance in other settler jurisdictions.[38]

Where did this leave the logic of territoriality, nursed so long by federal, state, and indigenous governments and fostered by the court itself? Georgia's territorial sovereignty was rejected by the court. In his narrow concurring judgment, John McLean pointed out that territoriality itself was a recent invention of the state. To Georgia's arguments "against the existence of an independent power within a sovereign state," he answered that history had shown that indigenous independence could and should be tolerated by settler sovereignty. "The residence of Indians, governed by their own laws, within the limits of a state, has never been deemed incompatible with state sovereignty, until recently."[39]

However, Marshall's decision flirted with the logic of territoriality in unstable ways. Federal territorial sovereignty, for example, remained an open question. The Supreme Court's jurisdiction to nullify Georgia's laws rested only partly on Cherokee rights to self-governance; it also rested on Georgia's violation of the federal Constitution.[40] Georgia's laws extending jurisdiction violated both federal treaties and the Trade and Intercourse Law (1802). As such they were null and void. Had the U.S. Congress acted to abrogate Indian rights, the decision may have been different. As Marshall himself put it:

> The Cherokee Nation, then, is a distinct community occupying its own territory . . . in which the laws of Georgia can have no force, and which the citizens of Georgia have no right to enter, but with the assent of the Cherokees themselves, or in conformity with treaties, and with the acts of congress.[41]

John McLean's concurring judgment put it differently. He declared that Georgia's acts were unconstitutional, yet the state and federal governments acting together could, as a matter of policy in the interests of indigenous welfare, abrogate Indian treaties and either relocate the Cherokee from or incorporate them into the State of Georgia.[42]

Cherokee sovereignty, so vindicated, was a delicate thing. Its delicacy only became apparent in 1883, when in *Crow Dog*, the Supreme Court held that Sioux tribal law governed intratribal murder. In 1884, Congress extended jurisdiction over selected intratribal crimes. As a matter of common-law principle, Worcester v. Georgia ensured that indigenous people might be free from the interference of United States' courts, but no court would save them from Congress.[43]

Marshall's unstable territoriality opened Cherokee rights to attack from another direction. He argued that indigenous independence stemmed from the Cherokee's status as first inhabitants of the region. Theirs were "original right[s] possessed by the undisputed occupants of every country." They "had always been considered as distinct, independent political communities, retaining their original natural rights, as the undisputed possessors of the soil, from time immemorial."[44] The court rejected Georgia's claims that Indian rights were hunting rights only. Marshall declared that indigenous people were entitled to the full benefit of their proprietorship in land. However, he did not try to articulate what might remain of indigenous "original rights" after Removal.[45]

Marshall thereby left a gap that southern jurists were eager to fill. As early as 1830, U.S. Attorney General John Macpherson Berrien, a Georgia lawyer who held the office from 1829 to 1831, had argued that Cherokee independence could not survive Removal. In 1830, General Samuel Houston, a white man, Cherokee adoptee, and resident trader in the Cherokee Nation west of the Mississippi, claimed that, as a member of the nation, he was exempt from United States Trade and Intercourse Laws governing citizen-traders in Indian Country.[46] Berrien disagreed. He argued that, even though the Treaty of 1828 granted the Cherokee absolute title in land west of the Mississippi, and guaranteed their continued exemption from state, territorial, and even federal jurisdiction, the treaty granted "soil, not . . . sovereignty." New Cherokee lands fell within the "sovereignty and jurisdiction" of the United States. Berrien based his opinion on the Treaty of Hopewell (1785) and two provisions in the Treaty of 1828: one allowing Congress to pass laws for the Cherokee, and the other recognizing the continuation of all treaties signed before 1828. Berrien declared that the Cherokees'

> stipulation that the jurisdiction of a State or territory should never be placed over the lands which they occupied left their relations with the United States precisely as it found them. The United States by that treaty agree "to preserve the Cherokees, and to guarantee to them forever," of seven millions of acres of land but there is no *grant of dominion or sovereignty*, no *relinquishment of jurisdiction*.[47]

Even in the juridical wilderness beyond the Mississippi, the Cherokee were in the thrall of Congress.[48] After the Worcester case, Berrien's opinions were reinforced by the new attorney general, Roger Taney, who declared in 1833 that an Indian could be prosecuted under federal legislation regulating the unauthorized sale of liquor in western Indian Country.[49] Worcester v. Georgia defended Cherokee independence in the state of Georgia on tribal lands, but did little to preserve their rights over the Mississippi.

Finally, the Cherokee cases had little bearing on the articulation of sovereignty in the early United States.[50] The juridical solution to Georgia's sovereignty problems lay not in the Supreme Court's pallid defense of Indian sovereignty and jurisdiction in Cherokee Nation v. Georgia or Worcester v. Georgia, but in the legislatures and the courts of the South. Throughout the southeast, and in Congress and the White House, State v. Tassel sealed the fate of indigenous people east of the Mississippi River. Long after Georgia's law extending jurisdiction was struck down by the Supreme Court, congressmen, statesmen, and most importantly, southern courts used the logic perfected in Tassel's case to justify the exercise of state jurisdiction over indigenous people in the southeast. This was more than a "legal ideology of removal"; it was a powerful, efficacious and new practice of sovereignty that harried the Cherokee over the Mississippi and followed close behind—all with a degree of aid and comfort from the United States Supreme Court.[51]

The legal contests over settler jurisdiction in the Cherokee Nation produced the most precocious and complete articulations of territoriality in the Anglophone settler world. In 1802, Georgia, not New South Wales, was the first settler polity to declare its intention to create a jurisdictional world without Indians. Between 1830 and 1838, Georgia, not New South Wales, articulated then effected perfect settler sovereignty by dissolving indigenous polities and forcing indigenous people from its borders.

The Trial of Murrell

Far removed from the volatile politics of Jacksonian America, a very different but equally important contest was waged over the relationship between sovereignty and jurisdiction in New South Wales. Twelve years of considered legal opinion, fifty years of partial or total jurisdictional exemption, and the persistence of Aboriginal custom and practice left the colony of New South Wales with a dilemma. Colonial claims to power and authority over the far reaches of a largely unsettled continent rang hollow as Aborigines exercised tribal law, drank and brawled on the streets of major British settlements—all outside the purview of settler law. In 1836, the Supreme Court of New South Wales filled this gaping crack in settler sovereignty by incorporating Aborigines formally within the British jurisdiction.

In December 1835, Jack Congo Murrell and George Bummaree, both Aborigines, killed two of their countrymen on the road between Richmond and Windsor in the colony of New South Wales.[52] Local constables arrested Murrell and Bummaree, and a local coronial inquiry proclaimed their guilt. Then, for the first time since 1829, the attorney-general resolved to bring an intratribal dispute before the Supreme Court. And for the first time since 1829, the court reluctantly agreed to hear it. In February 1836, Jack Congo Murrell stood before the Supreme Court of New South Wales, tried with the murder of an Aborigine. The attorney-general, the court, and the colony all saw the case as a final contest over the nature and extent of British sovereignty in New South Wales.

Murrell's counsel, John Stephen, argued by way of demurrer that Aborigines were not subjects of the Crown or aliens bound by British law because they were *ante nati*, first peoples, with their own rules and society. Great Britain had neither conquered nor treated with Murrell's tribe; it had simply ignored it. British authority in New South Wales meanwhile was premised on the subjecthood and allegiance of British settlers, rather than the absolute territorial sovereignty of the British Crown. Murrell and his victim, therefore, were not protected by British law and could not be tried for killing their countrymen. Aboriginal tribes, like the Cherokee, were distinct political communities exempt from the operation of settler sovereignty and jurisdiction.

There was nothing revolutionary about this pleading in 1836. It echoed the key arguments of Nathaniel Lowe's counsel, Wentworth and Wardell, in 1827. In 1829, Chief Justice Forbes himself had used very similar reasoning to prevent the solicitor-general from bringing Ballard to trial for the murder of Dirty Dick in Sydney. Forbes had argued, indeed, that New South Wales, like North America, had always acknowledged the juridical independence of indigenous people. Finally, Stephen's demurrer echoed persistent if ever less fervent objections raised by counsel to cases involving indigenous-settler crime between 1824 and 1835.

However, in 1836, the executive and judicial negotiations of the 1830s combined with the changing nature of imperial legal orthodoxy to alter the position of the court. The greater British Empire had always overshadowed the jurisprudence of the New South Wales Supreme Court. 1836 was the final year of Francis Forbes's tenure as chief justice of the court. Trained by an exiled loyalist, and accused frequently of holding republican sentiments learned from his American relatives, Forbes had cobbled together a new territorial sovereignty in New South Wales in the shadow of North American pluralism.[53]

From 1832, however, new imperial orthodoxies crept into the court with the arrival of William Burton. Burton was an Englishman trained at the Temple Bar. Like so many officers of the New South Wales establishment before him, Burton arrived in New South Wales as a man of the world: having served for several years as a puisne judge in the Cape Colony.[54] Burton's brief tenure at the Cape had coincided with momentous legal reform, including the establishment of the first Supreme Court of the Cape and fierce local debate about the status of African labor in the colony. Liberal metropolitan reformers sought to liberate enslaved and indentured Africans and to protect them against Dutch settlers. Local settler-conservatives crafted counternarratives about African incapacity, their nomadic habits, and their consequent absence of legal rights.[55] Burton played a central role in the legal articulation of indigenous status in the Cape. In 1828, he drafted "Ordinance 50 for the improvement of 'the Conditions of Hottentots and other Free Persons of Colour' and giving them civil and political equality with the settlers." Indigenous rights, in his frame of reference, were best protected by colonial jurisdiction.[56]

In 1832, the colonial secretary had enjoined the governor to let Burton bring his knowledge of savage subordination to bear on the legal policy of New South Wales. In 1836, he had his way. Chief Justice Forbes indicated in initial hearings that Aboriginal legal status was a matter for the legislature, not for the courts. But Burton, not the new colonial legislature, defined sovereignty in New South Wales. Burton used a new logic of territoriality, based in newly refined distinctions between various levels of savagery and race, to sweep aside the Ballard case. Again, applying Vattel's *Law of Nations*, he declared that the British were entitled to settle New South Wales because indigenous people were not using the land and they did not have rules and customs worthy of European notice. Thus it was that two murders on a highway ended in the juridical death of Aboriginal people in Australia.[57]

However, a complicated jurisdictional story unfolded between these two performances—two murders on a highway and Justice Burton's 1836 decision. This story began with the murders themselves. Jack Congo Murrell killed Jabingee in a fit of drunken violence. He told the coroner that "he could not help killing Jabinguy he was Drunk." George Bummaree told the coroner that he'd killed Pat Cleary as an act of vengeance "because Captain killed his brother."[58] If these killings were not legitimized by tribal law, then both were liable to tribal punishment. Therefore, as Stephen pointed out to the Supreme Court, these crimes (if they were crimes at all) were not without remedy.[59]

Nor was the attorney-general's decision to prosecute a simple decision to assert the jurisdiction of the colony over Aboriginal violence inter se. Like Tuskegee Tustunnagau before them, Murrell and Bummaree made it into court only because their people abdicated jurisdiction. Under the influence of the controversial missionary Lancelot Threlkeld, they asked the King's courts to try these two intratribal crimes, at least one of which had roots in ongoing conflict.[60] It seems unlikely that the tribe intended to abdicate its right to deal with all future intratribal disputes in the process. Perhaps the killings were contentious or contested within the group, and British courts provided an independent arbiter of social conflict. Whatever the reason, it is a great irony that this small act of sovereign independence (requesting the trial of two men) should end in the denial of indigenous jurisdiction throughout in the colony of New South Wales.

Despite Burton's decision and, indeed, despite counsel's remarkable demurrer against the territorial authority of the British Empire, the case itself trod a fine line between customary and common law. Both men pleaded indigenous customary law in their defense (though they could not testify on oath before the court). At their arraignment they asserted "that they had assaulted the deceased men in consequence of injuries they had received from them, which was entered by the Court as a plea of 'Not Guilty.'"[61] The accused asked for a "Jury of Blackfellows," which they were refused. Murrell's counsel later sought to bring evidence of

Aboriginal custom before the court, which the court also refused.[62] Aboriginal jurisdiction on the one hand and Aboriginal legal disabilities on the other harried the case from every standpoint.

Meanwhile, the attorney-general's pleadings before the court made it clear that he was at least as interested in preventing Aboriginal violence in or near settler towns as he was in regulating Aboriginal crimes against Aborigines. Various records of his pleadings suggest that he placed great emphasis on the location of the crimes. In one rendering, he noted that this was a "Murder committed in a Populous part of the territory of N.S.W. in the neighbourhood of Windsor" and asked, "Can the Court say that Murders & Outrages can be permitted to be committed in such a situation?"[63] His arguments for perfect settler sovereignty came second, but were familiar by 1836. Like the convention of Georgia judges in Tassel, he argued that "the laws of Great Britain did not recognise any independent power to exist in a British territory, but what was recognized by law."[64]

His ambivalence paled before the ambivalence of the jury. After "a few minutes" deliberation, the jury acquitted Murrell of murder, despite Murrell's inadmissible confession and the fact that two settler-witnesses attested to the murder and identified Murrell as its perpetrator.[65] Murrell's jury accepted, it seems, that indigenous people were, to some degree, independent of British law. The jury's deliberations are lost to history, but a letter to the *Sydney Herald* may well echo their thinking about the case. Therein, a correspondent argued that race and law negated British jurisdiction over Murrell's crime. Murrell was too ignorant and savage to testify, to be tried by his peers, or even to understand British law. His very inferiority rendered him exempt from settler law:

> Now our laws must be almost invisible to the unenlightened Natives, and certainly far beyond their reach; and yet here is a poor wretch taken by surprise and made answerable to an authority of which he was not aware. The operation of such a law upon him will have almost the cruelty and injustice of an *ex-post facto* law. . . .
>
> What then shall we call this act of ours—we who are an enlightened people, upon a poor benighted black whose country we have invaded? Is it not a violation of the law of nations? For it is not demanding satisfaction of a foreign people for a wrong done to one of our own nation, but usurping the power of judging in an affair of their own—judging, too, on a law which will take away life.[66]

Meanwhile, the jury's decision in Murrell's case also determined Bummaree's fate. His counsel Mr. Therry told the *Sydney Gazette* that "he did not suppose the Attorney-General would proceed against the other Black, as the cases were similar, and both depended on the same evidence."[67] In

1836, at least, Aboriginal law, not British law, determined the exercise of colonial power in this case.

However, Burton's decision, not Murrell's acquittal, made it into the canons of law. R. v. Murrell was the only judgment of its kind from New South Wales to be reported in a nineteenth-century law report. To this day, his judgment determines the common-law status of indigenous jurisdiction and sovereignty in Australia. Yet even his judgment had its peculiarities. Like Marshall and the convention of judges in the State of Georgia, Burton had to weave a new definition of sovereignty from the loose strands of law, lore, and practice that constituted the colonial project in New South Wales. Like them, he made myth and law by ignoring the plurality of history.

Burton's decision exists in a number of forms. The version recorded in the Legge Reports was drawn from the *Sydney Gazette*. However, a number of longer versions of the judgment in Burton's hand are collected together in a body of documents gathered under the auspices of the court. The briefest archival version grants "1st that the aboriginal natives of New Holland [Australia] are entitled to be regarded by Civilized nations as a free and independent people," but that "the various tribes had not attained at the first settlement of the English people amongst them to such a position in point of numbers and civilization, and to such a form of Government and laws, as to be entitled to be recognized as so many sovereign states governed by laws of their own."[68] Here Burton mixed Enlightenment stadial logic with law. If savagery came in many stages, Burton reasoned that indigenous Australians occupied too low a stage to profit by legal recognition of their customs and institutions.[69]

Then Burton indulged in and expanded the fictions propagated by the New South Wales Supreme Court since 1824. He argued "2ndly," that the British state had taken into "actual possession" half of the continent, between Cape York and the South Coast, between 10°27'S to 39°12'S "and embracing all the country inland to the Westward as far as 129° East longitude"—this despite the fact that a large portion of the colony remained uncharted, and government itself was limited to a number of officially settled counties within a few hundred miles of the east coast. "3rdly," Burton contended "[t]hat the English nation has obtained and exercised for many years the rights of Domain and Empire over the country"—this despite the fact that it seems the first Aborigine was tried by a settler court in 1816 and the second and third were tried (and acquitted) in 1822. "4thly," Burton argued that the crime fell within the territorial jurisdiction of the court as laid down by statute—a jurisdiction that, he argues elsewhere, the court could not dispute. Finally, he noted, "This Court has repeatedly tried and even executed aboriginal natives of this Colony, for offences committed by them upon subjects of the King"; accordingly, "there is no distinction in law in respect to the protection due to his person between a subject living in this Colony under the Kings Peace and an alien living therein under the Kings . . . Peace."[70]

A heavily annotated draft of the decision in Burton's hand gives much more insight into basic tenets underpinning the judgment. It appears from Burton's draft that he was convinced that Aboriginal custom was so debased by 1836 that it did not amount to a viable, alternative system of justice. His chief source of evidence here was Lancelot Threlkeld, whom he considered "as authority on the point."[71] Threlkeld informed the court by letter that tribal punishments were inconsistent, often did not punish murderers with death, and seemed increasingly unable to regulate a range of brutal murders of women and children near his missionary establishment. After presenting the inconsistency and degradation of local Aboriginal custom, Threlkeld concluded that, "although they do punish crime in a certain sense, yet it would be mercy perhaps to them, were they placed under the *protection* as well as the *power* of the British laws, & much more safe for the Country Resident & his family."[72]

On this basis, Burton's draft noted that Aborigines were "only just removed from the most simple state of nature," and as such their "loose & vague practices" were not "entitled to be respected as . . . 'in the nature of laws by a Christian Community.' " Burton denied that Aborigines had a "settled form of Government": "the several tribes have never owned any common superiority or any common bond of union, but have ever lived in a state of enmity with one another—their practices are only such as are consistent with a state of the grossest darkness & irrational superstition." Their rituals of tribal punishment, "a show of justice," are merely "vindication for personal wrongs" grounded "upon the wildest most indiscriminatory notions of revenge."[73]

Nineteenth-century notions of race and savagery did not determine the outcome of the case. They merely provided "scientific" bases for a new judicial science of perfect settler sovereignty. Rather, like the state and federal courts of the United States, Burton used European law to define the nature and extent of settler sovereignty. Using Vattel as his main source, Burton argued that Aborigines had no property or dominion in land because they had not appropriated it to themselves through cultivation.[74] He acknowledged, in his draft judgment, that Aborigines were a category of persons sui generis living under the King's protection within the King's Peace. Yet, unlike Marshall, he assumed, as Forbes had done before him, that Aboriginal Australians were protected as individuals, not as corporate groups, by the British sovereign. As such, under the law of nations, they fell within the jurisdiction of colonial courts and governance.[75]

Burton also resolved a decade of uncertainty about whether indigenous people were aliens or subjects of Great Britain. He argued that they were neither. He categorized them instead (again using Vattel) as "perpetual inhabitants . . . who have received the rights of perpetual residence. These are certain of citizens of an inferior order, & are united & subject to the Society without participating in all its advantages."[76] As such they could be denied fundamental rights as subjects and defendants, yet still fall within the purview of British sovereignty and common law.

At the foundation of these fine distinctions lay a fundamental endorsement of territoriality. John Stephen had argued that British law was determined by subjecthood and allegiance rather than territory. Burton argued instead that in New South Wales, as in Britain, the King's Peace could not coexist geographically with distinct Aboriginal social and legal orders. Burton argued, citing a range of sources, that "[the] King's Majesty . . . is by his office & dignity royal then principal conservator of the peace within all his dominions; & may give authority to any other to see it kept & to punish such as break it." Thus, "all offences committed within his realm are & must be laid to be committed against the king." The magistracy itself in Great Britain was enjoined to

> inquire of all felonies &c and of all & singular other crimes & offences of which the Justices of our peace may or might lawfully to inquire by whomsoever & after what manner sown . . . in the said County done or perpetrated. . . .
>
> From this it is evident that not only all those who are subjects but all who live within any country of the realm are under the King's peace or protection, & that any offence committed against any local person is committed against the King's Peace—all offences are local & triable at common law.[77]

Burton premised this discussion on ancient sources of British law, but the novelty of his argument lay in his application of British national law without qualification to a settler periphery. British sovereignty, he argued, necessitated the exercise of jurisdiction over every person on British land. Unlike Chief Justice Forbes, Chief Justice Marshall, and many other judges and magistrates on settler peripheries before the 1830s, Burton expunged the exigencies of imperial practice from the principles of British law. By announcing the territoriality of sovereignty, he declared that the colony of New South Wales was more than a periphery of empire, it was part and parcel of a modern territorial state—a state in which indigenous jurisdiction was an unacceptable anomaly.

Burton conceived of the juridical death of indigenous people as a way to preserve and improve indigenous life. *Murrell* achieved neither. After *Murrell*, more and more Aborigines came before settler courts. In the Port Phillip settlement, established in 1838, law was used both as a method of Aboriginal civilization and an instrument of terror. Attorney-General John Plunkett recommended "if it be seen expedient by the police Magistrates for the purpose of example or of striking terror into the Aborigines of Port Phillip to prosecute them" for their depredations against the new British settlement.[78] Settler jurisdiction, meanwhile, displaced neither Aboriginal customary law nor frontier settler violence. Despite *Murrell*, Aboriginal communities on New South Wales peripheries continued to regulate themselves for generations to come.[79] *Murrell* also sought Aboriginal protection by finally rejecting natural law justifications for settler violence championed in R. v. Lowe and applied by almost every settler-jury to try settler-indigenous crime. Yet, the colonial executive continued to have great difficulty procuring sentences against settler-murderers—even in the most horrifying cases.[80] The real significance of *Murrell*, then, was not what it changed about jurisdictional practice, but the way that it defined settler sovereignty by subordinating indigenous people and their law.

Like Georgia before it, in 1836 New South Wales premised its legal integrity as a settler polity on the regulation of indigenous crime. The *Tassell* case and R. v. Murrell both declared the advent of a new settler sovereignty that could not tolerate indigenous law. From the 1830s onward, settler sovereignty in Georgia and New South Wales was predicated on the exercise of territorial jurisdiction. The difference was that in New South Wales, *Murrell* changed little about the gradual but brutal displacement of Australian Aborigines. Despite the Supreme Court's disapproval, Georgia effected indigenous annihilation with guns, rounding up unwilling Cherokee Indians in 1838 and marching them westward.

Conclusion

B Y ENDING THIS STORY with the great cases of the 1830s, I create historiographical closure where there was none historically. Indigenous people went on to govern themselves in Indian territory beyond the Mississippi—as the Supreme Court reminded Congress in *Crow Dog's Case* (1883).[1] A Colonial Office directive issued just two years after R. v. Murrell stipulated that indigenous Australians were free to govern themselves so long as their law did not impinge in any way on settlers.[2] Pluralism persisted despite judicial efforts to expunge it. In some form it exists to this day. Although in Australia indigenous customary law exists only as a legislative exception, in the United States, indigenous customary law is one of very few judicially contained but inherent indigenous rights.[3]

The myths of settler sovereignty created in Georgia and New South Wales between 1830 and 1836 followed decades of legal and ideological change, and they changed the world incompletely. But change the world they did. After the Supreme Court declared that the Dakota territory had no jurisdiction to try Crow Dog for murdering Spotted Tail on a Sioux reservation, the federal Congress used the "guardianship" secured to it by the Cherokee cases to bring indigenous people within federal criminal jurisdiction for crimes of "murder, manslaughter, rape, assault with intent to kill, arson, burglary and larceny."[4]

The Creek and Cherokee fought on the wrong side in the Civil War, and all Indians suffered from the peace.[5] The postwar Congress abandoned the treaty system altogether in 1871. Thus began an era of Indian "protection," in which Congress altered existing federal-indigenous treaties at whim in the interests of Indian welfare. In 1887, through the Dawes Severalty Act, Congress ensured the rapid erosion of tribal lands by destroying the institution of communal property in many parts of western Indian Country. In a series of acts thereafter, Congress abolished not only Creek and Cherokee communal property, but also tribal governance and, by 1898, tribal courts. In 1952, Congress went further, unilaterally dissolving dozens of indigenous tribes throughout the United States.[6]

After 1836, colonial Australian judiciaries declared in case after case that British sovereignty was an absolute measure of jurisdictional and territorial right.[7] In Attorney-General v. Brown (1847), Chief Justice Stephen declared:

> The territory of New South Wales, and eventually the whole of the vast island of which it forms a part . . . belong . . . to the British Crown. . . . In a newly-discovered country, settled by British subjects, the occupancy of the Crown with respect to the waste lands of that country, is no fiction. . . . Here is a property, depending for its support on no feudal notions or principle.[8]

Though Britain had long entertained the notion that it had no legal obligation to honor Aboriginal property rights, it was only after 1830 that the Privy Council and other benches distinguished systematically between legally empty and legally full peripheries of empire. The former, they argued, had no law—whether or not they had indigenous populations. In these figuratively empty places, British law governed from the moment of British settlement.[9]

By the early twentieth century, Aborigines' rights as individuals and collectives were so decimated by settler sovereignty that the states of the new Australian Commonwealth took it upon themselves to attack Aboriginal families as a matter of policy. State "welfare" boards took thousands of Aboriginal children from their parents and put them into foster families or institutions to craft them into unequal, but more familiar, citizens.[10] Even after the civil rights movement crossed the Pacific and indigenous activists forced Australian states to remove voting restrictions on Aboriginal people, the High Court of Australia declared that Aborigines had not even the limited rights of self-governance secured to American Indians by the Cherokee cases.[11] In Coe v. Commonwealth (1979), Justice Gibbs stated:

> The history of the relationship between the white settlers and the Aboriginal peoples has not been the same in Australia and in the United States, and it is not possible to say, as was said by [Chief Justice] Marshall . . . of the Cherokee Nation, that the Aboriginal people of Australia are organized as a

"distinct political society separated from others," or that they have uniformly been treated as a state.[12]

In this frame, the watershed cases of the 1830s were not unimportant: they were central. They redefined settler sovereignty as a territorial measure of authority that left little or no space for indigenous rights to property, to sovereignty, or to jurisdiction. They recrafted plural settler polities into modern nation-states whose legitimacy was predicated on the subordination of indigenous rights. The many acts of dissolution, oppression, and marginalization that followed were all performances of sovereignty. State legislation displaced Aborigines from their country to missions—a systematic attempt to erase indigeneity through spatial, social, and legal domination. In the United States, Removal itself was the ultimate act of territoriality for Georgia. Congress shored up its sovereignty through more sanctimonious and qualified acts of territorial domination, by dissolving tribes, destroying property regimes, and banning lawmaking bodies that could compete with Congress in Indian Country.

Indigenous people in the United States enjoyed a brief and incomplete respite from settler sovereignty in the civil rights era. The Indian Civil Rights Act (1968) revived the status of indigenous peoples as communities rather than individuals in the eyes of the law.[13] This law recognized a circumscribed and supervised tribal jurisdiction. Since then, courts and Congress have recognized indigenous rights to conduct tax-free gaming, to hunt and fish endangered species, to adjudicate membership disputes and custody issues, and most importantly, to hold tribal courts with fairly broad jurisdiction over indigenous crime, contract, and tort—all free from state law.[14]

However, the post-Reagan judiciary has reasserted federal and state jurisdiction over Indian Country. In a series of striking endorsements of state over indigenous sovereignty, the Supreme Court of the United States has stripped Indian Nations of the right to sue settler-businesses in tribal courts; denied tribal jurisdiction over settler-sojourners; declared federal or state jurisdiction over highways; and allowed state troopers to enter Indian homes to deliver warrants and to make arrests.[15] These cases all remove indigenous rights to govern territorially—they cast Indian jurisdiction as a partial, personal exception to the territorial rule of settler sovereignty.[16] Meantime, the Major Crimes Act still operates in Indian Country, ensuring that defendants charged with serious crimes can be tried and sentenced consecutively by tribal and federal courts for a single crime.[17] In the twenty-first century, the logic of territoriality that underpinned both Georgia v. Tassel and, to a lesser degree, Cherokee Nation v. Georgia is being reasserted by settler courts to bring modified territorial order to Indian Country.

In 1992, the High Court of Australia declared to the world that it would right the wrongs wrought by two centuries of settlement. This could all be done, the judges thought, by recognizing indigenous rights to land. They called these rights "native title," a title to land defined by native "laws and customs" but subject to extinguishment, without compensation, by the sovereign.[18] Native title comprised a bundle of traditional rights over lands used by indigenous people continuously since settlement. According to the court, these were fragile rights indeed. Crown grants or state or federal legislation could extinguish native title by granting a superior right—freehold or unqualified leasehold property.[19] Indigenous people could lose their connection with their land merely by ceasing to be sufficiently connected to it. Forcible displacement, assimilation, even modernization could destroy the fragile bond of indigenous people to their land.[20]

Moreover, the court refused to inquire into the fiction of settler sovereignty—though the Mabo case, from the outset, had been mired in uncertainty about the relationship of territory, jurisdiction, and sovereignty in the Mer Islands in the Torres Strait. The Torres Strait Islands, unlike the rest of Australia, had originally been annexed to Queensland on terms that explicitly recognized some indigenous rights to sovereignty. Moreover, they'd not been overrun by settlers in any meaningful way. The State of Queensland tried to prevent the litigation in 1985 by passing legislation explicitly asserting jurisdiction over the islands.[21] However, the court found as a matter of law and practice that the islands fell within perfect settler sovereignty.[22]

Territoriality is and was always the measure of settler sovereignty according to Australia's most radical High Court.[23] In 1994, an Aborigine named Walker argued on the strength of Mabo v. Queensland that New South Wales had no authority to arrest him on what he alleged was tribal land. The court responded by making its logic of territoriality explicit:

> The proposition that [state] laws could not apply to particular inhabitants or particular conduct occurring within the State must be rejected. . . . There is nothing in the recent decision in *Mabo v. Queensland* . . . to support the notion that the Parliaments of the Commonwealth and New South Wales lack legislative competence to regulate or affect the rights of Aboriginal people, or the notion that the application of Commonwealth or State laws to Aboriginal people is in any way subject to their acceptance, adoption, request or consent.[24]

In both places then, indigenous crime remains the central site of settler sovereignty. In Australia and the United States, indigenous people are among the most incarcerated of any ethnic minority.[25] These statistics reflect unemployment, alcohol abuse, and other grave ramifications of continuing colonization.[26] However, at another level, incarceration reflects the peculiar centrality of indigenous people to settler sovereignty. The exercise of jurisdiction over indigenous crime performs the myth of settler sovereignty over and over. Sovereignty as territorial jurisdiction defines the parameters of indigenous rights to this day.

This book has told the story of settler sovereignty, tracking its emergence in disputes about the parameters of legal pluralism in early nineteenth-century Anglophone peripheries. In it, I have argued that the model of British Empire established in North America was premised on a legal pluralism that produced and negated different discourses of sovereignty in a number of sites. As all the world—metropolis and periphery—engaged in the legal and practical redefinition of sovereignty, fixing its relationship to territorial boundaries and to jurisdiction, settler polities stood apart as unique and uniquely fraught endeavors.

In early North American Anglophone peripheries, a peculiarly decentralized mode of governance, European competition, cash crops, indigenous trade, and a flexible regime of law combined with ever-shifting legal arguments for empire to make the project of settlement juridically contingent. Georgia and the new United States inherited this mess after 1783. Despite Georgia's concerted efforts to craft a perfect settler state in which jurisdiction was coextensive with territory, plural practice continued there for forty years after the revolution. Practice, in both federal and state spheres, was locked in the discursive frame of mutual violence and reciprocity. These, in turn, were syncretic notions adapted from European, natural, and indigenous law. Indigenous jurisdiction—robust, if ill-defined—was explicitly preserved and nurtured by the early national treaty system. It was a necessary supplement to the populist bent of the common law. Settlers in Georgia, deeply enmeshed in the culture of the common law, used its wide margins to exercise their own skewed version of "Indian justice," or simply to bring their rank lawlessness into the fold of legality. Finally, Anglophone institutions of local government inherited from empire gave frontier settlers a monopoly on jurisdiction—a jurisdiction they used as often to defend as to erode pluralism. Pluralism, then, could not be contained by borders or treaties. It inhered in state and local practice and, accordingly, spilled over the boundaries of Indian Country into the jurisdictional havens of the states.

New South Wales, a settler exception in the great British imperial project of the nineteenth century, was beset by legal pluralism in startlingly similar ways. Because imperial officials hoped that the great southern continent would prove practically free of indigenous people, they commenced settlement with almost as little constitutional planning as they had in the first North American colonies. Their miscalculation enmeshed the new settler regime in familiar, makeshift jurisdictional practices. Though they signed no treaties with Australian Aborigines, early governors used laws of war, and what they imagined were indigenous principles of retaliation, to structure state-indigenous relations; and these practices, at times, received explicit endorsement from the Colonial Office. As in Georgia, indigenous jurisdiction was an acknowledged, alternative legal order in the early colony, though it was never institutionalized like its Cherokee and Creek equivalents. As in Georgia, settlers mobilized anti-pagan testimony laws to tell legal stories about their lawless behavior on New South Wales frontiers. They too went to extraordinary lengths to cast their violence as self-defense, justifiable homicide or, at least, mere retaliation. Finally, as in Georgia, Anglophone structures of local governance in New South Wales turned frontier communities into effective guardians of colonial jurisdiction. Only divisions of class and race and, very occasionally, community disagreements over the treatment of Aborigines opened frontier violence to the gaze of the colonial state.

These two very different settler polities, then, stand at two ends of the spectrum of Anglophone settler experience. Both show that before the 1820s, settler sovereignty was a flexible thing indeed. Though imperial statutes and charters all claimed sovereignty and jurisdiction over land, settler practice did not equate sovereignty to territorial jurisdiction. Instead, for settlers, sovereignty defined the allegiance of settlers and sojourners and adjudicated settler crimes committed within the practical limits of governance. Settler sovereignty seldom, if ever, required the exercise of jurisdiction over indigenous people, whether or not settlers acknowledged indigenous rights to land.

Most importantly, however, settler sovereignty before the 1820s and 1830s was an unstable and contentious notion. Tracing contests over jurisdiction among executives, courts, local government, settlers, and indigenous people shows how, in the early nineteenth century, plural jurisdictional practice began to chafe hardening notions of sovereignty. Again and again, troubled executives and their law officers tried to perfect settler sovereignty by bringing indigenous-settler conflict within the bounds of settler law. Again and again, they tried at the very least to preserve order in their towns and on the roads that connected them. Again and again, they were thwarted by indigenous people, by frontier settlers or by local magistrates. Occasionally, they participated, albeit bitterly, in their own juridical subordination. The period described here, then, is one of plurality in transition, when a new vision of perfect sovereignty emerged from long-practiced and institutionally entrenched pluralism.

From the 1820s onward, settler polities in North America and Australia struggled, at the same time, to juridically erase their indigenous people in order to craft a perfect settler sovereignty. In doing so, they participated in a global transformation of sovereignty, likely flowing from Europe, through London, to the farthest corners of the globe. In this period, many have argued, the moment of territoriality arrived in nation-states, colonies, everywhere.[27] This transformation, no doubt, was largely discursive. The international market in law books—especially Vattel's *Law of Nations* and, in common-law jurisdictions, Blackstone's *Commentaries*—may not have unified legal practice, but it placed new constraints on sovereignty talk.

In a more practical sense, however, the British Empire was the agent of the new sovereignty on many colonial peripheries. From the early nineteenth century, the Empire puzzled endlessly about its jurisdictional rights in territories from St. Vincent to Gibraltar. It established the "extra-territoriality" system in the port towns of China, and pressured its Latin American trading partners to rein in pluralism to facilitate orderly trade. Perhaps in the southern United States and in New South Wales, large-scale production of cotton and wool for British factories prompted settler courts to put a judicial end to pluralism in their peripheries. This story, then, is a global story, but it is also a particularly Anglophone one. On Anglophone settler peripheries, new notions of sovereignty had a uniquely destructive impact on indigenous communal rights.

Settler sovereignty has a history—a history that is more recent, more local, and more contingent than many have supposed. It is one of the most brutal iterations of nineteenth-century territoriality. It was made and challenged on the farthest peripheries of empire, in the context of global discourse and global networks of trade. Finally, however, it was defined as the exercise of jurisdiction over indigenous crime. The most powerful legal myth in common-law settler polities, then, cannot be purged of its plural origins. Settler sovereignty starts and ends with indigenous people.

NOTES / ACKNOWLEDGMENTS / INDEX

Notes

Introduction

1. For a comparative analysis of these cases, see P. G. McHugh, *Aboriginal Societies and the Common Law: A History of Sovereignty, Status, and Self-Determination* (Oxford and New York: Oxford University Press, 2004), 61–116.

2. M. D. Walters, "The Extension of Colonial Criminal Jurisdiction over the Aboriginal Peoples of Upper Canada: Reconsidering the Shawanakiskie Case (1822–1826)," *University of Toronto Law Journal* 46, no. 2 (1996): 273–310.

3. D. A. Rosen, *American Indians and State Law: Sovereignty, Race, and Citizenship, 1790–1880* (Lincoln: University of Nebraska Press, 2007), 23–33; A. Taylor, *The Divided Ground: Indians, Settlers and the Northern Borderland of the American Revolution* (New York: Alfred A. Knopf, 2006), 317–322; A. Mt. Pleasant, "Reconsidering the Case of Tommy-Jemmy: Contexts for Criminal Prosecution in the Early Republic," in *29th Annual Meeting of the Society for Historians of the Early American Republic* (Worcester, MA, 2007).

4. State of Georgia v. Tassel, 1 Dud. 229–235; and *Virginia Enquirer* (Richmond), 9 December 1830, 4; T. A. Garrison, *The Legal Ideology of Removal: The Southern Judiciary and the Sovereignty of Native American Nations.* Studies in the Legal History of the South (London and Athens: University of Georgia Press, 2002), 103–124. Note that this reasoning was rejected by the Supreme Court in Cherokee Nation v. Georgia, 30 U.S. 1 (1831), and Worcester v. Georgia, 31 U.S. 515 (1832).

5. R. (Rex or Regina, the Crown) v. Murrell and Bummaree, February 5 or 8, 1836, Decisions of the Superior Courts of New South Wales, 1788–1899, published by the Division of Law, Macquarie University, http://www.law.mq .edu.au/scnsw/. The incompatibility of settler and indigenous jurisdiction was confirmed in Mabo v. Queensland (No. 2) (1992) 175 CLR 1, 129 (Dawson J).

6. See William Hobson to Major Bunbury Kitt, 25 May 1840, The National Archives, Public Records Office, Colonial Office 209/6, f 245–247, Kew (TNA: PRO CO 209/6).
7. *New Zealand Spectator and Cook's Strait Guardian* (Wellington), 4 December 1847, 2, 3–4, 3, 1–2. Shaunnagh Dorsett, "'Sworn on the Dirt of Graves': Sovereignty, Jurisdiction and the Judicial Abrogation of Barbarous Customs in New Zealand in the 1840s," *Journal of Legal History* 30, no. 2 (2009): forthcoming. In 1877, the New Zealand Supreme Court achieved what these early trials portended: declaring that British courts could neither countenance nor adjudicate Māori rights: P. G. McHugh, "From Sovereignty Talk to Settlement Time: The Constitutional Setting of Māori Claims in the 1990s," in *Indigenous Peoples' Rights in Australia, Canada and New Zealand,* ed. P. Havemann (Auckland, NZ: Oxford University Press, 1999), 447.
8. F. H. Hinsley, *Sovereignty* (Cambridge and New York: Cambridge University Press, 1986), 26.
9. See N. G. Onuf, "Sovereignty: Outline of a Conceptual History," *Alternatives* 16, no. 4 (1991): 425–446. Benton describes early sovereignty— particularly in the imperial setting—as an uncertain blend of *dominium,* "the control over territory or the right to its possession," of which "jurisdiction . . . was one especially important marker," with imperium, "the rule of a sovereign over extensive or aggregate territories and peoples." L. Benton, "Spatial Histories of Empire," *Itinerario: Geographies of Empire* 30, no. 3 (2006): 24–27. For an account of the instability of sovereignty as a concept to this day, see M. R. Fowler and J. M. Bunck, *Law, Power, and the Sovereign State: The Evolution and Application of the Concept of Sovereignty* (University Park: Pennsylvania State University Press, 1995), 8–9. For a succinct discussion of the problem of sovereignty in the context of indigenous rights, see Garrison, *The Legal Ideology of Removal,* 34–102.
10. For a nuanced definition and history of the term, see S. Dorsett, "Thinking Jurisdictionally: A Genealogy of Native Title" (Sydney: University of New South Wales, 2005), 11–32, 47–94. See also S. Dorsett and S. McVeigh, "Introduction," in *Jurisprudence of Jurisdiction,* ed. S. McVeigh (Abingdon, UK: Routledge-Cavendish, 2007), 3–6.
11. State of Georgia v. Tassel, 1 Dud. 229–235; and *Virginia Enquirer* (Richmond), 9 December 1830, 4.
12. "Judgment of Justice Burton in the Case of Jack Congo Murrell," February 1836, *Original Documents on Aborigines and the Law, 1790–1840,* Document no. 47, 211, Macquarie University, http://www.law.mq.edu.au/scnsw/Correspondence/index.htm.
13. I understand legal pluralism as "a situation in which two or more legal systems coexist in the same social field." S. E. Merry, "Legal Pluralism," *Law and Society Review* 22, no. 5 (1988): 870; J. Griffiths, "What Is Legal Pluralism," *Journal of Legal Pluralism and Unofficial Law* 24 (1986): 1–55; Benton, "Spatial Histories of Empire," 7–12.

14. Contrast M. F. Borch, *Conciliation, Compulsion, Conversion: British Attitudes towards Indigenous Peoples, 1763–1814* (Amsterdam: Rodopi, 2004), 29–72, with P. Wolfe, "*Corpus Nullius:* The Exception of Indians and Other Aliens in U.S. Constitutional Discourse," *Postcolonial Studies* 10, no. 2 (2007): 130–135; and P. Wolfe, *Settler Colonialism and the Transformation of Anthropology: The Politics and Poetics of an Ethnographic Event,* Writing Past Colonialism Series (London and New York: Cassell, 1999), 25–27.

15. McHugh, "From Sovereignty Talk to Settlement Time," 447.

16. L. A. Benton, *Law and Colonial Cultures: Legal Regimes in World History, 1400–1900* (Cambridge: Cambridge University Press, 2002), 206–209. See also W. J. Mommsen and J. Moor, eds., *European Expansion and Law: The Encounter of European and Indigenous Law in 19th- and 20th-Century Africa and Asia* (Oxford and New York: Berg, 1992); and R. Travers, *Ideology and Empire in Eighteenth-Century India: The British in Bengal* (Cambridge: Cambridge University Press, 2007)

17. See, for example, "Reports from Protectors of Slaves in Colonies of Demerara, Berbice, Trinidad, St Lucia, Cape of Good Hope and Mauritius," British House of Commons, Sessional Papers, 1829, vol. 335; J. E. Mason, *Social Death and Resurrection: Slavery and Emancipation in South Africa* (Charlottesville: University of Virginia Press, 2003); R. Smandych, "To Soften the Extreme Rigor of Their Bondage: James Stephen's Attempt to Reform the Criminal Slave Laws of the West Indies, 1813–1833," *Law and History Review* 23, no. 3 (2005): 537–588.

18. Z. Laidlaw, *Colonial Connections, 1815–1845: Patronage, the Information Revolution and Colonial Government* (Manchester, UK: Manchester University Press, 2005); D. Lambert and A. Lester, *Colonial Lives across the British Empire: Imperial Careering in the Long Nineteenth Century* (Cambridge: Cambridge University Press, 2006), 1–31. For specific biographical studies, see, for example, M. H. Ellis, *Lachlan Macquarie: His Life, Adventures and Times,* 4th ed. (Sydney: Angus & Robertson, 1965), 1–144; and see Lachlan and Elizabeth Macquarie Project published by Macquarie University, http://www.library.mq.edu.au/digital/lema/projects.html (accessed August 9, 2008). Francis Forbes came via Bermuda, Newfoundland, and London: H. Curry, *Sir Francis Forbes: The First Chief Justice of the Supreme Court of New South Wales* (Sydney: Angus & Robertson, 1968); J. M. Bennett, *Sir Francis Forbes: First Chief Justice of New South Wales, 1823–1837,* Lives of the Australian Chief Justices (Annandale, NSW: Federation Press, 2001); Governor Ralph Darling came to NSW via the Caribbean, Europe, and Mauritius: in Brian H. Fletcher, *Ralph Darling: A Governor Maligned* (Melbourne: Oxford University Press, 1984), 1–69. See also: J. Evans, *Edward Eyre: Race and Colonial Governance* (Dunedin, NZ: University of Otago Press, 2005); C. Hall, *Civilising Subjects: Metropole and Colony in the English Imagination, 1830–1867* (Cambridge: Polity, 1992). For the importance and contestation of Vattel in American federation, see P. S. Onuf, *The Origins of the Federal Republic: Jurisdictional Controversies in the United States, 1775–1787* (Philadelphia: University of Pennsylvania Press, 1983).

19. See, for example: J. Sheehan, "The Problem of Sovereignty in European History," *American Historical Review* 111, no. 1 (2006): 1–15; P. Sahlins, "The Nation in the Village: State Building and Communal Struggles in the Catalan Borderland during the 18th and 19th Centuries," *Journal of Modern History* 60 (1988): 234–263; P. Sahlins, *Boundaries: The Making of France and Spain in the Pyrenees* (Berkeley: University of California Press, 1989); Clive Emsley, "The Changes in Policing and Penal Policy in Nineteenth-Century Europe," in *Crime and Empire, 1840–1940: Criminal Justice in Local and Global Context,* ed. Barry S. Godfrey and Graeme Dunstall (Cullompton, UK: Willan, 2005), 8–24.

20. C. S. Maier, "Consigning the Twentieth Century to History: Alternative Narratives for the Modern Era," *American Historical Review* 105, no. 3 (2000): 807–831. Also see Sahlins on territoriality as a post–seventeenth-century process culminating in the nineteenth century: P. Sahlins, "The Nation in the Village: State Building and Communal Struggles in the Catalan Borderland during the 18th and 19th Centuries," *Journal of Modern History* 60, no. 2 (1988): 236–237.

21. D. Armitage, *Declarations of Independence: A Global History* (Cambridge, MA: Harvard University Press, 2008), 103–104.

22. For the importance of local histories to break down simple binaries between metropole and periphery, see: Sahlins, "The Nation in the Village," 7–8; K. McKenzie, *Scandal in the Colonies: Sydney and Cape Town, 1820–1850* (Carlton, VIC: Melbourne University Press, 2004), 7–8; Lambert and Lester, *Colonial Lives across the British Empire,* 8–13.

23. On the importance of state-level analysis, see Rosen, *American Indians and State Law.*

24. For the assertion that the British Empire, like the new American Federation, was inherently federal, see E. H. Gould, "A Virtual Nation: Greater Britain and the Imperial Legacy of the American Revolution," *American Historical Review* 104, no. 2 (1999): 476–489. See also: J. P. Greene, *Peripheries and Center: Constitutional Development in the Extended Polities of the British Empire and the United States, 1607–1788* (London and Athens: University of Georgia Press, 1986); D. C. Hendrickson, *Peace Pact: The Lost World of the American Founding* (Lawrence: University Press of Kansas, 2003).

25. For a recent discussion of the value of studying continuity as well as difference in imperial history, see E. Gould, "Entangled Histories, Entangled Worlds: The English-Speaking Atlantic as a Spanish Periphery," *American Historical Review* 112, no. 3 (2003): 764–786.

26. On customs and common law, see P. Karsten, *Between Law and Custom: "High" and "Low" Legal Cultures in the Lands of the British Diaspora— The United States, Canada, Australia, and New Zealand, 1600–1900* (Cambridge: Cambridge University Press, 2002), 2–5. For the interface between statute law, common law, and custom generally, see E. P. Thompson, *Whigs and Hunters: The Origin of the Black Art* (London: Pantheon, 1976). The phrase "customs in common" is taken from E. P. Thompson, *Customs in Common* (London: Merlin Press, 1991). Regarding "culture of legality," see

J. C. Weaver, *The Great Land Rush and the Making of the Modern World, 1650–1900* (Montreal: McGill Queens University Press, 2003), 351, quoting J. L. Comaroff, "Foreword," in *Contested States: Law, Hegemony, and Resistance,* ed. M. Lazarus-Black and S. Hirsch (New York: Routledge, 1994), xi. McHugh rejects the value of the approach taken here of reading government pronouncements, legislation, and court rulings as an important part of a continuum of legal behaviors: McHugh, *Aboriginal Societies,* 1–58.

27. Dorsett and McVeigh, "Introduction," 4. On the links between English pluralism and colonial practice, see Dorsett, "Thinking Jurisdictionally: A Genealogy of Native Title," 45–94.

28. D. K. Fieldhouse, *Colonialism 1870–1945: An Introduction* (London: Weidenfeld & Nicolson, 1981), 181–192.

29. M. Adas, "From Settler Colony to Global Hegemon: Integrating the Exceptionalist Narrative of the American Experience into World History," *American Historical Review* 106, no. 5 (2001): 1706–1708.

30. Notable exceptions here include South Carolina's attempt to enslave and trade in Indians and the centrality of Aboriginal labor to the cattle industry in Australia after mid-century: A. Gallay, *The Indian Slave Trade: The Rise of the English Empire in the American South, 1670–1717* (London and New Haven, CT: Yale University Press, 2002); A. McGrath, *Born in the Cattle: Aborigines in Cattle Country* (Sydney: Allen & Unwin, 1987).

31. Wolfe, *Settler Colonialism,* 1–3. For other continuities not canvassed here, see Weaver, *The Great Land Rush,* 11–13.

32. I argue for the importance of violence and of criminal jurisdiction here. Regarding the primacy of land, see: Weaver, *The Great Land Rush,* 3–132; S. Banner, *How the Indians Lost Their Land: Law and Power on the Frontier* (Cambridge, MA: Harvard University Press, 2007).

33. For a recent account of Cherokee modernization and slavery, see F. A. Yarbrough, *Race and the Cherokee Nation: Sovereignty in the Nineteenth Century* (Philadelphia: University of Pennsylvania Press, 2008).

34. Borch, *Conciliation, Compulsion, Conversion,* 73–96; compare S. Banner, "Why Terra Nullius? Anthropology and Property Law in Early Australia," *Law and History Review* 23, no. 1 (2005): 95–132.

35. For an account of early indigenous-settler relations, see I. Clendinnen, *Dancing with Strangers: Europeans and Australians at First Contact* (Cambridge and New York: Cambridge University Press, 2005).

36. Regarding the Canadian–New York borderlands, see Alan Taylor, *The Divided Ground,* 295–407. Regarding the proximity of Amherstburg to Detroit, see "Detroit (Gazette) Aug. 8," *American Sentinel* (Middletown, CT), 3 September 1823, 3, 3; and "June; Canada; Nothing; Should," *Salem Gazette* (Salem, MA), 14 May 1824, 1, 2–3.

37. For Georgia's use of New York as a precedent for the extension of jurisdiction, see "Legislative Acts or Legal Proceedings," *Augusta Chronicle and Georgia Advertiser,* 14 March 1827, 2, 2. For coverage of the Tommy Jemmy case in South Carolina, see "Aboriginal Severity," *City Gazette* (Charleston), 6 November 1821, 2, 1–2.

38. News about U.S.-Indian conflict was comparatively rare and seldom detailed, though the launching of the *Cherokee Phoenix* prompted an unusually long story: *Sydney Gazette*, 23 July 1829, 3, 2. For other American Indian news, *Sydney Gazette*, 3 August 1816, 3, 2; *Sydney Gazette*, 6 February 1819, 3, 2; *Sydney Gazette*, 8 April 1820, 3, 2; *Sydney Gazette*, 16 June 1831, 4, 2; *Sydney Gazette*, 21 August 1832, 2, 5; *Sydney Gazette*, 12 September 1833, 2, 5. Contrast South African–Australian news networks and Indian-Australian news networks, sustained directly by the path of ships from the United Kingdom to Australia: A. Lester, "British Settler Discourse and the Circuits of Empire," *History Workshop Journal* 54, no. 1 (2002): 24–48.
39. Bennett, *Sir Francis Forbes*, 57–100; Curry, *Sir Francis Forbes*, 237–280.
40. K. G. Allars, "Sir William Westbrooke Burton," *Journal and Proceedings (Royal Australian Historical Society)* 37, no. 5 (1951): 257–294.
41. J. Adelman and S. Aron, "From Borderlands to Borders: Empires, Nations, and the Peoples in between in North American History," *American Historical Review* 104, no. 3 (1999): 814–841. Regarding French and Russian exploration, see: C. Dyer, *The French Explorers and the Aboriginal Australians, 1772–1839* (St. Lucia: University of Queensland Press, 2005); V. Fitzhardinge, "Russian Ships in Australian Waters, 1807–1835," *Journal of the Royal Historical Society* 51, no. 2 (1965): 113–147.
42. J. Belich, *Replenishing the Earth: The Settler Revolution and the Rise of the Angloworld* (London and New York: Oxford University Press, 2009).
43. A. Rothman, *Slave Country: American Expansion and the Origins of the Deep South* (Cambridge, MA: Harvard University Press, 2005); J. Weaver, "Beyond the Fatal Shore: Pastoral Squatting and the Occupation of Australia, 1826–1852," *American Historical Review* 101, no. 4 (1996): 981–1007; J. Ker, "The Wool Industry in New South Wales, 1803–1830," *Business Archives & History* 2, no. 1 (1962): 18–54.
44. D. Williams, *The Georgia Gold Rush: Twenty-Niners, Cherokees, and Gold Fever* (Columbia: University of South Carolina Press, 1993).
45. M. Hickford, "'Decidedly the Most Interesting Savages on the Globe': An Approach to the Intellectual History of Māori Property Rights, 1837–53," *History of Political Thought* 27, No. 1 (2006): 131–167.
46. For comparative studies of settler colonialism, see, for example: D. Denoon, *Settler Capitalism: The Dynamics of Dependent Development in the Southern Hemisphere* (Oxford, UK: Clarendon Press, 1983); T. R. Dunlap, *Nature and the English Diaspora: Environment and History in the United States, Canada, Australia, and New Zealand* (Oxford, UK: Clarendon Press, 1999); Karsten, *Between Law and Custom*; Weaver, *The Great Land Rush*. Andrew Buck and others have edited an impressive series of articles about property law in various settler polities, for example, J. McLaren, A. R. Buck, and N. E. Wright, *Despotic Dominion: Property Rights in British Settler Societies* (Vancouver: University of British Columbia Press, 2005). For comparative studies of the United States and Australia, see, for example: H. C. Allen, *Bush and Backwoods: A Comparison of the Frontier in Australia and the*

United States (East Lansing: Michigan State University Press, 1959); G. Cross, "Comparative Exceptionalism: Rethinking the Hartz Thesis in the Settler Societies of Nineteenth-Century United States and Australia," *Australasian Journal of American Studies* 14, no. 1 (1995): 15–41; R. E. Lonsdale and J. H. Homes, eds., *Settlement in Sparsely Populated Regions: The United States and Australia* (New York: Pergamon Press, 1981); J. McQuilton, "Comparative Frontiers: Australia and the United States," *Australasian Journal of American Studies* 12, no. 1 (1993).

47. Contrast a small but growing number of works focused on indigenous people, for example, McHugh, *Aboriginal Societies;* K. Ellinghaus, *Taking Assimilation to Heart: Marriages of White Women and Indigenous Men in the United States and Australia, 1887–1937* (Lincoln: University of Nebraska Press, 2006); G. Smithers, *Science, Sexuality, and Race in the United States and Australia, 1780s–1890s* (New York: Routledge, 2008).

48. For example: G. R. Lamplugh, *Politics on the Periphery: Factions and Parties in Georgia, 1783–1806* (London: Associated University Press, 1986); D. C. Crass, *The Southern Colonial Backcountry: Interdisciplinary Perspectives on Frontier Communities* (Knoxville: University of Tennessee Press, 1998); S. Hahn, *The Roots of Southern Populism: Yeoman Farmers and the Transformation of the Georgia Upcountry, 1850–1890* (New York: Oxford University Press, 1983).

49. For example, Rothman, *Slave Country.*

50. A short list of the many works tracing cultural change in the southeast includes J. F. Brooks, *Confounding the Color Line: The Indian-Black Experience in North America* (Lincoln: University of Nebraska Press, 2002); G. E. Dowd, *A Spirited Resistance: The North American Indian Struggle for Unity, 1745–1815* (Baltimore, MD: Johns Hopkins University Press, 1992); R. F. Ethridge, *Creek Country: The Creek Indians and Their World* (Chapel Hill: University of North Carolina Press, 2003); K. E. Holland, *Deerskins and Duffels: The Creek Indian Trade with Anglo-America, 1685–1815* (Lincoln: University of Nebraska Press, 1993); W. G. McLoughlin, *Cherokees and Missionaries, 1789–1839* (London and New Haven, CT: Yale University Press, 1984); J. H. Merrell, *The Indians' New World: Catawbas and Their Neighbors from European Contact through the Era of Removal* (Chapel Hill: University of North Carolina Press, 1989); T. Miles, *Ties That Bind: The Story of an Afro-Cherokee Family in Slavery and Freedom* (Berkeley: University of California Press, 2005); T. Perdue, *Cherokee Women: Gender and Culture Change, 1700–1835* (Lincoln: University of Nebraska Press, 1998); T. Perdue, *Slavery and the Evolution of Cherokee Society, 1540–1866* (Knoxville: University of Tennessee Press, 1979); Yarbrough, *Race and the Cherokee Nation;* T. Perdue and M. D. Green, *The Columbia Guide to American Indians of the Southeast* (New York: Columbia University Press, 2001); C. Saunt, *A New Order of Things: Property, Power, and the Transformation of the Creek Indians, 1733–1816* (Cambridge: Cambridge University Press, 1999); M. Young, "The Cherokee Nation: Mirror of the Republic," *American Quarterly* 33, no. 5 (1981): 502–524.

51. For example: D. K. Richter, *Facing East from Indian Country: A Native History of Early America* (Cambridge, MA: Harvard University Press, 2001); R. White, *The Middle Ground: Indians, Empires, and Republics in the Great Lakes Region, 1650–1815* (Cambridge and New York: Cambridge University Press, 1991); C. G. Calloway, *The American Revolution in Indian Country: Crisis and Diversity in Native American Communities* (Cambridge and New York: Cambridge University Press, 1995).

52. Compare M. Daniel, "From Blood Feud to Jury System: The Metamorphosis of Cherokee Law from 1750 to 1840," *American Indian Quarterly* 11, no. 2 (1987): 97–125; and T. Perdue, "Clan and Court: Another Look at the Early Cherokee Republic," *American Indian Quarterly* 24, no. 4 (2000): 562–569.

53. For example: S. P. McSloy, "Revisiting the Courts of the Conqueror: American Indian Claims against the United States," *American University Law Review* 44 (1994): 537–644; J. Norgren, *The Cherokee Cases: The Confrontation of Law and Politics* (New York: McGraw-Hill, 1996); H. W. Wilson, "'An Anomaly Unknown': Supreme Court Application of International Law Norms on Indigenous Rights in the Cherokee Cases (1831–1832)," *Tulsa Journal of Comparative and International Law* 1 (1994): 339–358; D. G. Bell, "Was Amerindian Dispossession Lawful? The Response of 19th-Century Maritime Intellectuals," *Dalhousie Law Journal* 23 (2000): 168–182; P. P. Frickey, "Marshalling Past and Present: Colonialism, Constitutionalism, and Interpretation in Federal Indian Law," *Harvard Law Review* 107, no. 2 (1993): 381–440; E. Kades, "History and Interpretation of the Great Case of Johnson v. M'Intosh," *Law and History Review* 19, no. 1 (2001): 67–116; L. G. Robertson, *Conquest by Law: How the Discovery of America Dispossessed Indigenous Peoples of Their Lands* (Oxford and New York: Oxford University Press, 2005). This imbalance has been somewhat corrected by two important recent works: Garrison, *The Legal Ideology of Removal;* and Rosen, *American Indians and State Law.*

54. Rothman, *Slave Country.*

55. D. J. Hulsebosch, *Constituting Empire: New York and the Transformation of Constitutionalism in the Atlantic World, 1664–1830* (Chapel Hill: University of North Carolina Press, 2005); C. Cumfer, *Separate Peoples, One Land: The Minds of Cherokees, Blacks, and Whites on the Tennessee Frontier* (Chapel Hill: University of North Carolina Press, 2007); R. Harper, "Looking the Other Way: The Gnadenhutten Massacre and the Contextual Interpretation of Violence," *William and Mary Quarterly* 64, no. 3 (2007): 621–644.

56. For example, see A. C. Castles, *An Australian Legal History* (Sydney: Law Book Company, 1982); Banner, "Why Terra Nullius," 95–132; B. Kercher, *An Unruly Child: A History of Law in Australia* (St. Leonards, NSW: Allen & Unwin, 1995), 3–21; H. Reynolds, *Aboriginal Sovereignty: Reflections on Race, State and Nation* (St. Leonards, NSW: Allen & Unwin, 1996); H. Reynolds, *The Law of the Land,* 2nd ed. (Ringwood, VIC: Penguin, 1992). For a defense of this narrow, legalistic source-base, see McHugh, *Aboriginal Societies,* 1–58.

57. H. Reynolds, *Dispossession: Black Australians and White Invaders,* Australian Experience (St. Leonards, NSW: Allen & Unwin, 1989); H. Reyn-

olds, *Fate of a Free People* (Ringwood, VIC: Penguin, 1995); R. Broome, "The Struggle for Australia: Aboriginal-European Warfare, 1770–1930," in *Australia: Two Centuries of War and Peace*, ed. M. McKernan and M. Browne (Canberra: Australian War Memorial, 1988), 92–120; J. Connor, *The Australian Frontier Wars, 1788–1838* (Randwick, NSW: University of New South Wales Press, 2002); R. Evans, K. Saunders, and K. Cronin, *Race Relations in Colonial Queensland: A History of Exclusion, Exploitation and Extermination*, 3rd ed. (St. Lucia: University of Queensland Press, 1993).

58. K. Windschuttle, *The Fabrication of Aboriginal History* (Sydney: Macleay Press, 2002), 1–10. See Patricia P. Grimshaw, "The Fabrication of a Benign Colonisation? Keith Windschuttle on History," *Australian Historical Studies* 35, no. 123 (2004): 11–17; R. Manne, *Whitewash: On Keith Windschuttle's Fabrication of Australian History* (Melbourne: Black Inc., 2003); B. Attwood and S. G. Foster, *Frontier Conflict: The Australian Experience* (Canberra: National Museum of Australia, 2003); B. Attwood, *Telling the Truth about Aboriginal History* (St. Leonards, NSW: Allen & Unwin, 2005), 124–135. For nuanced work on frontier legal history and customary law, see A. Nettelbeck and R. Foster, *In the Name of the Law: William Willshire and the Policing of the Australian Frontier* (Kent Town, SA: Wakefield Press, 2007); H. Douglas, *Aboriginal Australians and the Criminal Law: History, Policy, Culture* (Saarbrücken: VDM Verlag, 2009).

59. B. Buchan, "The Empire of Political Thought: Civilization, Savagery and Perceptions of Indigenous Government," *History of the Human Sciences* 18, no. 2 (2005): 1–22; and B. Buchan, *Empire of Political Thought: Indigenous Australians and the Language of Colonial Government* (London: Pickering and Chatto, 2008). Damen Ward makes the more complicated argument that, by the 1830s, pluralism was deemed to be an exception to settler jurisdiction: D. Ward, *"Savage Customs" and "Civilised Laws": British Attitudes to Legal Pluralism in Australasia, c. 1830–1848*, London Papers in Australian Studies 10 (London: Menzies Centre for Australian Studies, 2003).

60. In doing so it joins a small but growing body of work, for example: Evans, *Edward Eyre*; Nettelbeck and Foster, *In the Name of the Law*; Douglas, *Aboriginal Australians and the Criminal Law*; M. Finnane and J. Richards, "'You'll get nothing out of it'? The Inquest, Police and Aboriginal Deaths in Colonial Queensland," *Australian Historical Studies* 35, no. 123 (2004): 84–105.

61. Kercher, *An Unruly Child*, 3–21; L. Ford, "Empire and Order on the Colonial Frontiers of Georgia and New South Wales," *Itinerario: Geographies of Empire* 30 (2006): 95–113; L. Ford and B. Salter, "From Pluralism to Territorial Sovereignty: The 1816 Trial of Mow-watty in the Superior Court of New South Wales," *Indigenous Law Journal* 7 (2008): 67–86.

62. For example, see W. Tench, *Sydney's First Four Years: Being a Reprint of a Narrative of the Expedition to Botany Bay and a Complete Account of the Settlement at Port Jackson*, ed. L. F. Fitzhardinge (Sydney: Angus & Robertson in Association with the Royal Australian Historical Society, 1961), 35.

1. Jurisdiction, Territory, and Sovereignty in Empire

1. A. Anghie, *Imperialism, Sovereignty and the Making of International Law* (Cambridge and New York: Cambridge University Press, 2005), 150–180.
2. R. D. Sack, *Human Territoriality: Its Theory and History* (Cambridge and New York: Cambridge University Press, 1986), 1–4, 127–168.
3. J. T. Juricek, "English Claims in North America to 1660: A Study in Legal and Constitutional History" (Ph.D. diss., University of Chicago, 1970), 37; J. T. Juricek, "English Territorial Claims in North America under Elizabeth and the Early Stuarts," *Terrae Incognitae* 7 (1975): 7–22.
4. D. Armitage, *The Ideological Origins of the British Empire* (Cambridge: Cambridge University Press, 2000), 14–23; J. Tully, "Aboriginal Property and Western Theory: Recovering a Middle Ground," *Social Philosophy and Policy* 11, no. 2 (1994): 154; Anghie, *Imperialism, Sovereignty,*
5. Eliga Gould has described eighteenth-century North America as "a continent of disputed and ambiguous jurisdictions" deemed by European states to be outside the ordinary laws of war and peace: E. H. Gould, "Zones of Law, Zones of Violence: The Legal Geography of the British Atlantic, circa 1772," *William and Mary Quarterly* 60, no. 3 (2003): 475–510.
6. A. Fitzmaurice, *Humanism and America: An Intellectual History of English Colonisation, 1500–1625,* Ideas in Context (Cambridge and New York: Cambridge University Press, 2003), 137–166; K. MacMillan, *Sovereignty and Possession in the English New World: The Legal Foundations of Empire, 1576–1640* (Cambridge: Cambridge University Press, 2006).
7. See A. Pagden, "Dispossessing the Barbarian: The Language of Spanish Thomism and the Debate over the Property Rights of the American Indians," in *Theories of Empire,* ed. D. Armitage (Aldershot, UK: Ashgate, 1998), 159–178.
8. P. Seed, *Ceremonies of Possession in Europe's Conquest of the New World, 1492–1640* (Cambridge and New York: Cambridge University Press, 1995), 69–99; R. A. Williams, *The American Indian in Western Legal Thought: The Discourses of Conquest* (Oxford and New York: Oxford University Press, 1990), 88–92.
9. For a discussion of their legal novelty, see G. Loughton, "Calvin's Case and the Origins of the Rule Governing 'Conquest' in English Law," *Australian Journal of Legal History* 8, no. 2 (2004): 150–180.
10. Calvin's Case (1608) 7 Coke reports 1a, 77 *English Reports* at 398.
11. See C. Yirush, "Conquest Theory and Imperial Governance in the Early Modern Anglo-American World" (paper presented at the Clark Library Conference on Imperial Models in the Early Modern World, Los Angeles, California, November 3–4, 2006). Note, however, Loughton's argument that Coke's formula had an afterlife in Blackstone: Loughton, "Calvin's Case," 150–180.
12. See, for example: J. Muldoon, *Popes, Lawyers, and Infidels: The Church and the Non-Christian World, 1250–1550* (Philadelphia: University of Pennsylvania Press, 1979); J. Muldoon, *Canon Law, the Expansion of Europe, and World Order* (Aldershot, UK: Ashgate, 1998).

13. And he was not the only one who came "perilously close" to challenging Spanish rights to dominium in the New World; see Pagden, "Dispossessing the Barbarian," 160–178.
14. L. C. Green and O. P. Dickason, *The Law of Nations and the New World* (Edmonton: University of Alberta Press, 1989), 4–63. For the focus of early theorists on the vindication rather than the destruction of indigenous rights to land and to political community, see A. Fitzmaurice, "Genealogy of *Terra Nullius*," *Australian Historical Studies* 38, no. 129 (2007): 1–15.
15. Early modern English law had a multitude of competing legal systems: see S. Dorsett, "Thinking Jurisdictionally: A Genealogy of Native Title" (Ph.D. diss., University of New South Wales, 2005), 47–94.
16. K. MacMillan, "Sovereignty 'More Plainly Described': Early English Maps of North America, 1580–1625," *Journal of British Studies* 42, no. 4 (2003): 427–428; MacMillan, *Sovereignty and Possession in the English New World.*
17. MacMillan, "Sovereignty 'More Plainly Described,' " 429–431.
18. D. Armitage, "John Locke, Carolina, and the Two Treatises of Government," *Political Theory* 32, no. 5 (2004): 602–627.
19. This, of course, was gravely inaccurate. Indigenous societies, particularly those of the southeast, engaged in fixed agriculture and lived in semipermanent towns.
20. For the use of "improvement" to curtail communal property in England, see L. Brace, "Husbanding the Earth and Hedging Out the Poor," in *Land and Freedom: Law, Property Rights and the British Diaspora,* ed. J. McLaren, A. R. Buck, and N. E. Wright (Aldershot, UK: Ashgate, 2001), 5–17.
21. See Tully, "Aboriginal Property," 159–160; Williams, *The American Indian in Western Legal Thought,* 246–250; B. Arneil, *John Locke and America: The Defence of English Colonialism* (Oxford and New York: Oxford University Press, 1996).
22. L. Benton, "Passages to Imperial Sovereignty: The Geography of Treason in the European Atlantic World" (paper presented at the Columbia Legal History Seminar, New York City, January 25, 2007). See also: L. Benton, *A Search for Sovereignty: Law and Geography in European Empires, 1400–1900* (Cambridge and New York: Cambridge University Press, forthcoming); A. S. Keller, O. J. Lissitzyn, and F. J. Mann, *Creation of Rights of Sovereignty through Symbolic Acts, 1400–1800* (New York: Columbia University Press, 1938); MacMillan, *Sovereignty and Possession in the English New World;* Seed, *Ceremonies of Possession.*
23. C. L. Tomlins, "The Legal Cartography of Colonization, the Legal Polyphony of Settlement: English Intrusions on the American Mainland in the Seventeenth Century," *Law and Social Inquiry* 26, no. 2 (2001): 338.
24. Charter of Virginia, in *America's Founding Charters,* vol. 1, 28–32, 30.
25. Charter of Massachusetts Bay, in *America's Founding Charters,* vol. 1, 82–93, 86. The same document, however, vested jurisdiction only over "subjects." For a discussion of the limits of early charters, see P. G. McHugh, *Aboriginal Societies and the Common Law: A History of Sovereignty, Status, and Self-Determination* (Oxford and New York: Oxford University Press, 2004), 91–98.

26. Charter of Georgia, in *America's Founding Charters*, vol. 2, 511–520, 518.

27. See Tully's notion of "empire of uniformity" in J. Tully, *Strange Multiplicity: Constitutionalism in an Age of Diversity* (Cambridge: Cambridge University Press, 1995), 58–98. Compare C. Helliwell and B. Hindess, "The Empire of Uniformity and the Government of Subject Peoples," *Journal for Cultural Research* 6, no. 1 (2002): 139–152. Helliwell and Hindess argue that Tully projects back a modern moment of political liberalism onto settler projects, masking the older, hierarchical models of governance in place there.

28. P. Wolfe, "*Corpus Nullius:* The Exception of Indians and Other Aliens in US Constitutional Discourse," *Postcolonial Studies* 10, no. 2 (2007): 134.

29. B. Slattery, "Paper Empires: The Legal Dimension of French and English Ventures in North America," in *Despotic Dominion: Property Rights in British Settler Societies,* ed. J. McLaren, A. R. Buck, and N. E. Wright (Vancouver: University of British Columbia Press, 2005), 50–78.

30. Spain's claim was acknowledged by England in a treaty signed in 1670 as well as in the treaties of Utrecht and Madrid (1713 and 1721). The first Florida governor to acknowledge the fact but not the legitimacy of Georgia, in the Sanchez treaty of 1736, was recalled and hanged for his efforts: see H. E. Bolton and M. Ross, *The Debatable Land: A Sketch of the Anglo-Spanish Contest for the Georgia Country* (New York: Russel & Russel, 1968), 74; H. E. Bolton, *Arredondo's Historical Proof of Spain's Title to Georgia: A Contribution to the History of One of the Spanish Borderlands* (Berkeley: University of California Press, 1925).

31. Regarding Scotland and Ireland, see: Armitage, *Ideological Origins;* N. P. Canny, *Kingdom and Colony: Ireland in the Atlantic World, 1560–1800* (Baltimore, MD: Johns Hopkins University Press, 1988), 24–60; J. Robertson, *A Union for Empire: Political Thought and the British Union of 1707* (Cambridge and New York: Cambridge University Press, 1995).

32. For a detailed discussion of these categories, see Juricek, "English Claims in North America to 1660," 258–323; and J. Goebel Jr., "The Matrix of Empire," in J. H. Smith, *Appeals to the Privy Council from the American Plantations* (New York: Columbia University Press, 1950), xii–lxi.

33. Compare the legal foundations of empire discussed by MacMillan, *Sovereignty and Possession in the English New World,* with discussions of early economic development, for example: J. P. Greene, *Pursuits of Happiness: The Social Development of Early Modern British Colonies and the Formation of American Culture* (London and Chapel Hill: University of North Carolina Press, 1998), 8–18; J. C. Appleby, "War, Politics, and Colonization, 1558–1625," in *The Oxford History of the British Empire: The Origins of Empire,* ed. N. Canny (Oxford and New York: Oxford University Press, 2001), 55–78.

34. A. Gallay, *The Indian Slave Trade: The Rise of the English Empire in the American South, 1670–1717* (London and New Haven, CT: Yale University Press, 2002); Charter of Georgia, in *America's Founding Charters: Primary Documents of Colonial and Revolutionary Era Governance,* vol. 2, ed. Jon L. Wakelyn (Westport, CT: Greenwood Press, 2006), 511–520.

35. Compare A. Balachandran, "Of Corporations and Caste Heads: Urban Rule in Company Madras, 1640–1720," *Journal of Colonialism and Colonial History* 9, no. 2 (2008). See Appleby, "War, Politics, and Colonization," 68–77.

36. See for example, R. Price, ed., *Maroon Societies: Rebel Slave Communities in the Americas,* 3rd ed. (Baltimore, MD: Johns Hopkins University Press, 1996).

37. Note that jurisdiction was exercised sporadically in some other eighteenth-century colonies. On Pennsylvania, see L. M. Waddell, "Justice, Retribution, and the Case of John Toby," in *Friends and Enemies in Penn's Woods: Indians, Colonists, and the Racial Construction of Pennsylvania,* ed. W. A. Pencak and D. K. Richter (University Park: Pennsylvania State University Press, 2004), 129–143. On the incorporation of remnant tribes in Virginia and Maryland, see T. E. Davidson, "Indian Identity in Eighteenth Century Maryland," *Oklahoma City University Law Review* 23 (1998): 133–140. On religious origins of the northeast and their transformation, see R. L. Bushman, *From Puritan to Yankee: Character and the Social Order in Connecticut, 1690–1765* (New York: Norton, 1970), 3–106.

38. Y. Kawashima, *Puritan Justice and the Indian: White Man's Law in Massachusetts, 1630–1763* (Middletown, CT: Wesleyan University Press, 1986); Y. Kawashima, "The Pilgrims and the Wampanoag Indians, 1620–1691: Legal Encounter," *Oklahoma City University Law Review* 23 (1998): 115–131; W. B. St. Jean, "Inventing Guardianship: The Mohegan Indians and Their 'Protectors,'" *New England Quarterly* 72, no. 3 (1999): 362–387; D. J. Silverman, *Faith and Boundaries: Colonists, Christianity, and Community among the Wampanoag Indians of Martha's Vineyard, 1600–1871* (Cambridge and New York: Cambridge University Press, 2005), 78–120.

39. K. A. Hermes, "Jurisdiction in the Colonial Northeast: Algonquian, English and French Governance," *American Journal of Legal History* 43, no. 1 (1999): 52–73; J. A. Strong, "The Imposition of Colonial Jurisdiction over the Montauk Indians of Long Island," *Ethnohistory* 41, no. 4 (1994): 561–590; A. M. Plane, "Legitimacies, Indian Identities and the Law: The Politics of Sex and the Creation of History in Colonial New England," in *Empire and Others: British Encounters with Indigenous Peoples, 1600–1850,* ed. M. J. Daunton and R. Halpern (London: University College of London Press, 1999), 217–237.

40. For another example, see the appeals of the Stockbridge Indians in New York: Henry Moore to Secretary of State, 22 December 1766, the National Archives: Public Records Office, Colonial Office 5/1137 (TNA: PRO CO 5/1137), which encloses the report of the Council in New York on the claims of the Stockbridge Indians, and protests the intervention of the Colonial Office in the case.

41. "Proceedings of the Court of Enquiry & Determination of the Complaint of the Mohegan Indians" (3 November 1705), quoted in Walters, "Mohegan Indians v. Connecticut," 812.

42. "Report of the Committee for hearing of Appeals from the Plantations touching ye Mohegan Indians Lands" (21 May 1709), quoted in Walters, "Mohegan Indians v. Connecticut," 814.

43. L. E. Ivers, *British Drums on the Southern Frontier: The Military Coloniza-tion of Georgia, 1733–1749* (Chapel Hill: University of North Carolina Press, 1974); J. R. Snapp, *John Stuart and the Struggle for Empire on the Southern Frontier* (Baton Rouge: Louisiana State University Press, 1996); J. P. Corry, "Indian Affairs in Georgia, 1732–1756" (Ph.D. diss., University of Pennsylvania, 1936).

44. Regarding the strength of the Creeks, see J. A. Sweet, *Negotiating for Geor-gia: British-Creek Relations in the Trustee Era, 1733–1752* (London and Athens: University of Georgia Press, 2005).

45. Williams, *The American Indian in Western Legal Thought,* 255–307.

46. See, for example, W. A. Pencak and D. K. Richter, *Friends and Enemies in Penn's Woods: Indians, Colonists, and the Racial Construction of Pennsylva-nia* (University Park: Pennsylvania State University Press, 2004); L. Ford, "Empire and Order on the Colonial Frontiers of Georgia and New South Wales," *Itinerario: Geographies of Empire* 30 (2006): 95–113.

47. G. E. Dowd, *War under Heaven: Pontiac, the Indian Nations, and the British Empire* (Baltimore, MD: Johns Hopkins University Press, 2002), 174–212.

48. J. P. Greene, *Peripheries and Center: Constitutional Development in the Ex-tended Polities of the British Empire and the United States, 1607–1788* (London and Athens: University of Georgia Press, 1986); J. G. A. Pocock, *The Discovery of Islands: Essays in British History* (Cambridge and New York: Cambridge University Press, 2005), 134–163.

49. P. S. Onuf, *The Origins of the Federal Republic: Jurisdictional Controversies in the United States, 1775–1787* (Philadelphia: University of Pennsylvania Press, 1983).

50. See W. S. Coker and T. D. Watson, *Indian Traders of the Southeastern Span-ish Borderlands: Panton, Leslie & Company and John Forbes & Company, 1783–1847* (Gainesville and Pensacola, FL: University Presses of Florida and University of West Florida Press, 1986).

51. W. B. Phillips, *Georgia and State Rights: A Study of the Political History of Georgia from the Revolution to the Civil War, with Particular Regard to Federal Relations* (Washington, DC: Government Printing Office, 1902). For the importance of authority in Indian Affairs to all states, see F. P. Prucha, *The Great Father: The United States Government and the American Indians* (London and Lincoln: University of Nebraska Press, 1984), 36–38.

52. In the 1787 Constitution, this clause was replaced by another vesting Indian trade and diplomacy exclusively in the federal government.

53. R. N. Clinton, "There Is No Federal Supremacy Clause for Indian Tribes," *Arizona State Law Journal* 34 (2002): 113–260.

54. Quoted in Clinton, "There Is No Federal Supremacy Clause," 115.

55. Treaty of Galphinton, Article 1 in *Indian Treaties, Cessions of Land in Geor-gia, 1705–1837,* bound transcripts, Works Progress Administration (hereaf-ter cited as WPA) Project No. 7158, ed. L. F. Hays (Atlanta: Georgia Ar-chives, 1941), 171–173. Interestingly, this treaty contained weaker cessions of jurisdiction than the Treaties of Hopewell and New York (but much greater land cessions). Article 5 provided that "[if] any Indian shall commit a

robbery or murder or other capital crime on any white person, such offenders shall receive a punishment adequate to such offence, and due notice of such intended punishment shall be given to his honor the Governor." This sort of jurisdictional concession is dangerously ambiguous. Indian offenders may not have to be handed over to Georgia's judicial system, but the article does not specify whether Indians or settlers should inflict summary "adequate" punishment. Only retaliatory "punishment of the innocent" was expressly forbidden.

56. Alexander McGillivray to William Clark, 24 April 1785, in *Creek Indian Letters, Talks and Treaties, 1705–1839*, vol. 1, bound transcripts, WPA Project No. 665-34-3-224, ed. L. F. Hays (Atlanta: Georgia Archives, 1939), 32–33; J. L. Wright, "Creek-American Treaty of 1790: Alexander McGillivray and the Diplomacy of the Old Southwest," *Georgia Historical Quarterly* 51 (1967): 380–400.

57. "An Act to ratify and confirm certain articles of agreement and cession entered into on the 24th day of April 1802, between the Commissioners of the State of Georgia on the one part, and the Commissioners of the United States on the other part, ratified 16 June 1802, 1, Acts of the General Assembly of the State of Georgia Passed in June and November 1802, vol. 1, 3, *Georgia's Legislative Documents*, University of Georgia Libraries, http://www.galileo .usg.edu/express?link=zlgl.

58. T. H. Parsons, *The British Imperial Century, 1815–1914: A World History Perspective* (Lanham, MD: Rowman & Littlefield, 1999); M. Chanock, "The Law Market: The Legal Encounter in British East and Central Africa," in *European Expansion and Law: The Encounter of European and Indigenous Law in 19th- and 20th-Century Africa and Asia*, ed. W. J. Mommsen and J. Moor (Oxford and New York: Berg, 1992), 279–306; P. H. Ch'en, "The Treaty System and European Law in China: A Study in the Exercise of British Jurisdiction in Late Imperial China," in *European Expansion and Law*, ed. Mommsen and Moor, 83–109; F. von Benda-Beckmann, "Symbiosis of Indigenous and Western Law in Africa and Asia: An Essay in Legal Pluralism," in Mommsen and Moor, *European Expansion and Law*, 307–321.

59. L. A. Benton, *Law and Colonial Cultures: Legal Regimes in World History, 1400–1900* (Cambridge: Cambridge University Press, 2002), 127–282. Compare E. H. Gould, "A Virtual Nation: Greater Britain and the Imperial Legacy of the American Revolution," *American Historical Review* 104, no. 2 (1999): 476–489.

60. Parsons, *The British Imperial Century*.

61. D. J. Murray, *The West Indies and the Development of Colonial Government, 1801–1834*, vol. 1965 (Oxford, UK: Clarendon Press, 1965).

62. Chanock, "The Law Market"; H. B. Giliomee, "The Eastern Frontier, 1770–1812," in *The Shaping of South African Society, 1652–1840*, ed. R. Elphick, H. B. Giliomee, and J. C. Armstrong (Middletown, CT: Wesleyan University Press, 1988), 421–471.

63. Parsons, *The British Imperial Century*.

64. Pocock, *The Discovery of Islands*, 181–198.

65. For a brief account of the complications of European contact and trade in New Zealand, see J. Evans, *Edward Eyre: Race and Colonial Governance* (Dunedin, NZ: University of Otago Press, 2005), 53–66; E. Tapp, *Early New Zealand; a Dependency of New South Wales, 1788–1841* (Carlton, VIC: Melbourne University Press, 1958).

66. See M. Gillen, "Convicts Not Empire," in *Uncertain Beginnings: Debates in Australian Studies*, ed. G. Whitlock and G. Reekie (St. Lucia: University of Queensland Press, 1993), 25–36. Compare G. Martin, "The Founding of Australia: The Argument about Australia's Origins," in *Uncertain Beginnings*, ed. Whitlock and Reekie, 7–13; A. Frost, "Convicts and Empire: A Naval Question, 1776–1811," in *Uncertain Beginnings*, ed. Whitlock and Reekie, 19.

67. A. Atkinson, *The Europeans in Australia: A History: The Beginning*, vol. 1 (Melbourne: Oxford University Press, 1997), 37–58. J. Gascoigne and P. Curthoys, *The Enlightenment and the Origins of European Australia* (Cambridge: Cambridge University Press, 2005).

68. S. Banner, "Why Terra Nullius? Anthropology and Property Law in Early Australia," *Law and History Review* 23, no. 1 (2005): 95–132.

69. Second Commission, 2 April 1787, 12 October 1786, *Historical Records of Australia, Series 1, Governors' Despatches to and from England*, vol. 1 (Sydney: The Library Committee of the Commonwealth Parliament, 1914–1925), 13–14, contrast 9; Charter of Justice, *Historical Records of Australia: Series 4, Legal Papers*, vol. 1 (Sydney: The Library Committee of the Commonwealth Parliament, 1922), 6–12.

70. For a recent discussion linking metropolitan ideologies of empire in Australia, North America, and South Africa, see M. F. Borch, *Conciliation, Compulsion, Conversion: British Attitudes towards Indigenous Peoples, 1763–1814* (Amsterdam: Rodopi, 2004).

71. B. A. Buchan, "Aboriginal Welfare and the Denial of Indigenous Sovereignty," *Arena Journal* 20 (2002–2003): 97–121; Anghie, *Imperialism, Sovereignty*, 32–114. See also P. H. Russell, *Recognizing Aboriginal Title: The Mabo Case and Indigenous Resistance to English Settler Colonialism* (Toronto: University of Toronto Press, 2005), 30–50, 69–80.

72. E. Vattel, *The Law of Nations, or, Principles of the Law of Nature Applied to the Conduct and Affairs of Nations and Sovereigns* (London: G. G. and J. Robinson, 1797), vol. 1, 98–101. I used a British edition contemporaneous with settlement.

73. Yirush, "Conquest Theory and Imperial Governance"; D. J. Hulsebosch, "The Ancient Constitution and the Expanding Empire: Sir Edward Coke's British Jurisprudence," *Law and History Review* 21, no. 3 (2003): 439–482. See also, for example, William Blackstone, *Commentaries on the Laws of England in Four Books*, 11th ed. (Dublin: H. Chamberlaine, 1788), vol. 1, 107–110.

74. This point has been made most forcefully in the substantive sections of M. Connor, *The Invention of Terra Nullius: Historical and Legal Fictions on the Foundation of Australia* (Sydney: Macleay Press, 2005), 258–269.

75. Fitzmaurice, "Genealogy of *Terra Nullius*"; Connor, *The Invention of Terra Nullius*.
76. B. Attwood, *Possession: Batman's Treaty and the Matter of History* (Carlton, Vic.: Miegunyah Press, 2009).
77. L. Benton, "Spatial Histories of Empire," *Itinerario: Geographies of Empire* 30, no. 3 (2006): 19–34; L. Benton, *A Search for Sovereignty.*

2. Pluralism as Policy

1. Before the eighteenth century, many acts of violence, including rape, were considered private wrongs rather than crimes: see J. M. Carter, *Rape in Medieval England: An Historical and Sociological Study* (Lanham, MD: University Press of America, 1985); and J. Horder, *Provocation and Responsibility* (Oxford, UK: Clarendon Press, 1992), 6. Note Hermes's timely reminder that reciprocity was not "the" but "one" principle of indigenous law: K. Hermes, "'Justice Will Be Done by Us': Algonquian Demands for Reciprocity in the Courts of European Settlers," in *The Many Legalities of Early America,* ed. C. L. Tomlins and B. H. Mann (London and Chapel Hill: University of North Carolina Press, 2001), 130.
2. Return J. Meigs, "Some Reflections on Cherokee Concerns, Manners and State," 19 March 1812, Records of the Cherokee Indian Agency in Tennessee 1801–1835, National Archives and Records Administration, Microfilm Publication M208, Reel 5 (hereafter cited as Cherokee Agency, NARA, M208, Reel 5). They were described as "quarteroons" by James Blair and H. Montgomery to Meigs, 18 March 1812, *Cherokee Indian Letters, Talks and Treaties, 1786–1838,* vol. 1, bound transcripts, Works Progress Administration (WPA) Project No. 4341, ed. L. F. Hays (Atlanta: Georgia Archives, 1939), (hereafter cited as *Cherokee Letters* 1, 117); Meigs to H. Montgomery and James Blair, 19 March 1812, Cherokee Agency, NARA, M208, Reel 5.
3. See, for example, Ka'la'was'kee and Charles Hicks to Meigs, 25 October 1811, Cherokee Agency, NARA, M208, Reel 5; Meigs to Judges of the Courts in Jackson County, 30 October 1811, Cherokee Agency, NARA, M208, Reel 5; Meigs to Eustis, 19 March 1812, in *Cherokee Letters* 1, 129.
4. Meigs had written to Jackson County Judges protesting Daniel's imprisonment in 1811: Meigs to Judge of the Courts in Jackson County, 30 October 1811, Cherokee Agency, NARA, M208, Reel 5. Buffington and Daniel were still at large in 1813: Hicks to Meigs, 17 March 1813, Cherokee Agency, NARA, M208, Reel 6.
5. For the term "ordinary jurisdiction," see: James Jackson to James McHenry, 15 February 1798 in *Governor's Letter Books of George Matthews, 20 August 1795–17 January 1796 and James Jackson, 24 January 1798–3 January 1799,* Georgia Archives, Record Group: 001–01–001, bound transcripts, WPA Project No. 5993, ed. L. F. Hays (Atlanta: Georgia Archives, 1939), 105 (hereafter cited as *Governor's Letter Books: Matthews and Jackson,* 105). See also E. Surrency, *The Creation of a Judicial System: The History of Georgia Courts, 1733 to Present* (Holmes Beach, FL: Gaunt, 2001), 83.

6. Richard Stites (a lawyer) advised Elijah Clarke in 1807 of the problem of serving process in Indian Country: "[I]f Amistead resides over the Oakmulgee he must be induced to come on this side and there let the [obscured] serve him with a copy." Richard Stites to Elijah Clarke, 28 September 1807, Wayne-Stites-Anderson Collection, Letterbook, 1805–1808, 004:1046, Georgia Historical Society, Savannah.

7. See P. S. Onuf, *The Origins of the Federal Republic: Jurisdictional Controversies in the United States, 1775–1787* (Philadelphia: University of Pennsylvania Press, 1983); D. C. Hendrickson, *Peace Pact: The Lost World of the American Founding* (Lawrence: University Press of Kansas, 2003).

8. For Georgia's protests against the exercise of federal jurisdiction over Georgia settlers, see Jackson to McHenry, 1 June 1798, *Governor's Letter Books: Matthews and Jackson,* 172.

9. Meigs, "Some Reflections," 19 March 1812, Cherokee Agency, NARA, M208, Reel 5.

10. For one of the first recorded uses of this term by Georgia's legislature, see "In the House of Representatives," 35/35, 2 December 1801, Acts of the General Assembly of the State of Georgia, passed in November and December, 1801, vol. 1, 116, *Georgia Legislative Documents,* University of Georgia Libraries, http://www.galileo.usg.edu/express?link=zlgl.

11. C. J. Kappler, *Indian Affairs: Laws and Treaties,* vol. 2 (Washington, DC: Government Printing Office, 1904), 27, 31.

12. Note, however, that that agent seemed to have followed a very similar investigation and reporting procedure for wrongs in Indian Country (further discussed in Chapter 3).

13. F. P. Prucha, ed., *Documents of United States Indian Policy,* 2nd ed. (Lincoln: University of Nebraska Press, 1990), 17–20.

14. Meigs was a stickler for protocol; see, for example, his refusal to pursue a request for compensation without a letter from the Secretary of War: Meigs to Buckner Harris, 7 July 1808, *Cherokee Letters* 1, 94.

15. James Blair and H. Montgomery to Meigs, 18 March 1812, *Cherokee Letters* 1, 117; Meigs to H. Montgomery and James Blair, 19 March 1812, Cherokee Agency, NARA, M208, Reel 5. Note the careful but conflicting codification of race: Meigs describes them as "Half blood" in his "Reflections" 19 March 1811, Cherokee Agency, NARA, M208, Reel 5.

16. No one who can clearly be identified as an Indian appeared as a defendant before the federal circuit and district courts in Georgia according to my survey of Minutes of the U.S. Circuit Court for the District of Georgia, 1790–1842, and Index to Plaintiffs and Defendants in the Circuit Courts, 1790–1860, National Archives Microfilm Publication M1184, Reels 1–2; and Index Books, 1789–1928, and Minutes and Bench Dockets, 1789–1870, for the United States District Court for the Southern District of Georgia, 1789–1928, NARA, M1172, Reels 1–2. I found no instances in which Indians were tried before the superior court of Franklin County between 1806 and 1815. The WPA volumes in the Georgia State Archives, the Cherokee Agency Records (NARA), and the correspondence of Benjamin Hawkins revealed, inter

alia, the following cases: Arrest of Tuskeegee Tustunnagau: James Jackson to William Bailey, Sheriff of Oglethorpe, 19 February 1798, *Governor's Letter Books: Matthews and Jackson,* 99. Arrest and murder of Creek at Black-shear's Mill: Deposition of James Bush Jnr, 23 December 1802, and Deposition of Abraham Blackshear, 28 December 1802, in *Creek Indian Letters, Talks and Treaties, 1705–1839,* vol. 1, bound transcripts, WPA Project No. 665-34-3-224, ed. L. F. Hays, (Atlanta: Georgia Archives, 1939), 652, 654 (hereafter cited as *Creek Letters* 2, 652, 654). On the pursuit and drowning of an unnamed Cherokee horse thief by "regulator" John Rogers Jr: Meigs to Black Fox, 9 April 1808, Cherokee Agency, NARA, M208, Reel 4. Reference to the sentencing of Tites: Deposition of Thompson Bailey and James Arnett, undated, *Cherokee Letters* 1, 87. On the arrest of James Vann: Meigs to Governor Lowry, 23 October 1808, Cherokee Agency, NARA, M208, Reel 4. Reference to Tobler (Creek Indian) in custody in Clarke County: John McAllister, 12 August 1804, *Creek Letters* 2, 698. Reference to Daniel (Cherokee) in custody: Ka'la'was'kee and Charles Hicks to Meigs, 25 October 1811, Cherokee Agency, NARA, M208, Reel 5. Some indigenous people were arrested and likely tried in Mississippi Territory courts in this period also, see: Benjamin Hawkins to Henry Dearborn, 25 September 1808, in *Letters, Journals and Writings of Benjamin Hawkins,* vol. 2, 1802–1816, ed. C. L. Grant, (Savannah, GA: Beehive, 1980), 539; arrest and escape of a burglar named Spinse in Madison County, Mississippi, in Judge Campbell to Meigs, 8 October 1811, Cherokee Agency, NARA, M208, Reel 5. More cases seem to have occurred in Tennessee. See Cumfer's discussion and citations on the arrest of Stone (Cherokee) in 1801: C. D. Cumfer, "'The Idea of Mankind is so Various': An Intellectual History of Tennessee, 1768–1810" (Ph.D. diss., University of California, 2001), 195; and on the acquittal of a Cherokee in Tennessee in 1809: Meigs to Eustis, 22 February 1810, Cherokee Agency, NARA, M208, Reel 5.

17. Deposition of Thompson Bailey and James Arnett, undated, *Cherokee Letters* 1, 87. The deposition records that the killer "went to take" Tites to court, it is unclear whether this occurred at the penitentiary or in Indian Country.

18. See Chapters 5 and 6 for changes in jurisdictional practice before and after 1812.

19. On Creeks: R. F. Ethridge, *Creek Country: The Creek Indians and their World* (Chapel Hill: University of North Carolina Press, 2003), 92–119. On Cherokees: T. Perdue, *Cherokee Women: Gender and Culture Change, 1700–1835* (Lincoln: University of Nebraska Press, 1998), 17–61.

20. See for example, J. A. Piker, *Okfuskee: A Creek Indian Town in Colonial America* (Cambridge, MA: Harvard University Press, 2005), 111–195. Perdue, *Cherokee Women,* 65–114.

21. For a rich rendering of treaty making as the establishment of mythical and kin-based obligations of reciprocity across North American indigenous cultures, see Robert A. Williams, *Linking Arms Together: American Indian Treaty Visions of Law and Peace, 1600–1800* (Oxford and New York: Ox-

ford University Press, 1997), 40–82. For a discussion of the meaning of diplomacy for the Cherokee, see C. Cumfer, *Separate Peoples, One Land: The Minds of Cherokees, Blacks, and Whites on the Tennessee Frontier* (Chapel Hill: University of North Carolina Press, 2007), 23–41, 53–64, 77–90.

22. For discussions of Cherokee law, see R. Strickland, *Fire and the Spirits: Cherokee Law from Clan to Court* (Norman: University of Oklahoma Press, 1975). See Cumfer's description of balance as the prevailing logic of Cherokee diplomacy before 1810: Cumfer, *Separate Peoples, One Land*, 23–41, 53–64. For the survival of retribution in 1820s Cherokee legal culture, see T. Perdue, "Clan and Court: Another Look at the Early Cherokee Republic," *American Indian Quarterly* 24, no. 4 (2000): 562–569. For Creek law, see: Ethridge, *Creek Country*, 92–119; Hawkins, "A Sketch of the Creek Country in the Years 1798 and 1799," in *Letters, Journals and Writings of Benjamin Hawkins* (unpaginated).

23. For a discussion of the persistence of retaliation and compensation in eighteenth- and nineteenth-century England, see M. J. Wiener, "Judges v. Jurors: Courtroom Tensions in Murder Trials and the Law of Criminal Responsibility in Nineteenth-Century England," *Law and History Review* 17, no. 3 (1999): 467–506; and N. Landau, "Indictment for Fun and Profit: A Prosecutor's Reward at Eighteenth-Century Quarter Sessions," *Law and History Review* 17, no. 3 (1999): 507–536.

24. This statement is based on a survey of criminal court records in Franklin County between 1800 and 1830. For one of many examples, see State v. John Temples, March Term 1821, Franklin Superior Court Records, Miscellaneous, 159-1-41, Box 5, Georgia Archives.

25. On the rationale for private revenge: H. Grotius, *The Rights of War and Peace*, 3 vols. (London: Brown, D., Ward, T., Meares, W., 1715), vol. 2, 457–459. On the justifiable nature of exemplary punishment of savages: E. Vattel, *The Law of Nations, or, Principles of the Law of Nature Applied to the Conduct and Affairs of Nations and Sovereigns* (London: G. G. and J. Robinson, 1797), vol. 3, 348.

26. R. White, *The Middle Ground: Indians, Empires, and Republics in the Great Lakes Region, 1650–1815* (Cambridge and New York: Cambridge University Press, 1991), x.

27. P. Spruhan, "A Legal History of Blood Quantum in Federal Indian Law to 1935," *South Dakota Law Review* 51, no. 1 (2006): 4–9.

28. Perdue, *Cherokee Women*, 41–44.

29. Passing was not the only way to stay in the east, however: see J. R. Finger, "The Abortive Second Cherokee Removal, 1841–1844," *Journal of Southern History* 47, no. 2 (1981): 207–226.

30. F. A. Yarbrough, *Race and the Cherokee Nation: Sovereignty in the Nineteenth Century* (Philadelphia: University of Pennsylvania Press, 2008), 1–55.

31. See Chapter 5; James Vann to Meigs, 28 December 1801; Journal of Occurrences &c Relating to the Cherokee Nation, 1801 (filed end of 1801); Meigs to Judge John McNary, 1 January 1802; William Stothart to Meigs, 10 Janu-

ary 1802; McNary to Meigs, 17 January 1802; Meigs to Vann, 28 January 1802; Vann to Meigs, 5 February 1802; McNary to Meigs, 21 February 1802; Vann to Meigs, 10 April 1802; Passport for Stone, 23 April 1802; Colonel Overton to Meigs, 5 May 1802; Meigs to Overton, 10 June 1802; all in Cherokee Agency, NARA, M208, Reel 1. For fuller discussion, see Cumfer, "'The Idea of Mankind Is So Various,'" 195.

32. Meigs to Dearborn, 23 October 1808, Cherokee Agency, NARA, M208, Reel 4. Meigs applied to Governor Sevier of Tennessee not very hopeful that Vann could be tried in federal court for the crime, but hoping he could be forced by the state court to pay compensation to his victims: Meigs to Governor Sevier, 23 October 1808, Cherokee Agency, NARA, M208, Reel 4.

33. Meigs to Dearborn, 30 September 1808, Cherokee Agency, NARA, M208, Reel 4.

34. Annotation on Meigs to Vann, 28 October 1808, NARA, M208, Reel 4. Note however that in 1809, James Tremble argued for a client that slave property could be seized by the federal troops in the Cherokee nation: Tremble to Meigs, 23 April 1809, Cherokee Agency, NARA, M208, Reel 4.

35. Meigs doubted the sincerity of Vann's attempt to buy off his victim, Samuel Moore: Meigs to Dearborn, 30 September 1808, Cherokee Agency, NARA, M208, Reel 4. Moore complained in 1810 that he had yet to be paid: Deposition of Samuel Moore, 29 October 1810, Cherokee Agency, NARA, M208, Reel 5.

36. The Glass, Richard Justice, Turkirague, Big Bear, War'Hach'ee to Mitchell, 12 December 1812, *Cherokee Letters* 1, 114.

37. See Cumfer's discussion of like instances in Tennessee: C. Cumfer, "Local Origins of National Indian Policy: Cherokee and Tennessean Ideas about Sovereignty and Nationhood, 1790–1811," *Journal of the Early Republic* 23, no. 1 (2003): 21–46.

38. The Glass, Richard Justice, Turkirague, Big Bear, War'Hach'ee to Mitchell, 12 December 1812, *Cherokee Letters* 1, 114.

39. Meigs, Some Reflections, 19 March 1812, Cherokee Agency, NARA, M208, Reel 5. Note that admissibility of Cherokee evidence was not mentioned in the letter sent by Meigs to Eustis the same day: Meigs to Eustis, 19 March 1812, *Cherokee Letters* 1, 129. Meigs did demand their surrender, using words of justice and fairness, not of law: Meigs to the Cherokee Nation, 12 July 1812, *Cherokee Letters* 1, 135.

40. Meigs, Some Reflections, 19 March 1812, Cherokee Agency, NARA, M208, Reel 5. The phrase "varied materially" was included in Meigs to Eustis, 19 March 1812, *Cherokee Letters* 1, 129. For an instance of varying testimony in Creek Country, see Barnard to Hawkins, Recorded in Journal of the Treaty of Fort Wilkinson, 15 April 1802, *Letters, Journals and Writings of Benjamin Hawkins*, 421–422. For Meigs on the injustice of laws of evidence, see Meigs to Jenkins Whiteside, 22 February 1810, Cherokee Agency, NARA, M208, Reel 5. Meigs was aware of exceptions made in the British Empire; for example, for Moors in Gibraltar, see Meigs to Colonel Overton, 10 June 1802, Cherokee Agency, NARA, M208, Reel 1.

41. Meigs, Some Reflections, 19 March 1812, Cherokee Agency, NARA, M208, Reel 5. However, Meigs did demand the surrender of Buffington and Daniel from the nation: Meigs to Chiefs of the Cherokee Nation, 12 July 1812, *Cherokee Letters* 1, 135. For the benefits of using compensation and diplomacy to remedy settler violence against indigenous people, see Meigs's calls for compensation to Longbeard: Meigs to Eustis, 1 January 1810, Cherokee Agency, NARA, M208, Reel 5.

42. For example, see Meigs to Eustis, 5 April 1811, Cherokee Agency, NARA, M208, Reel 5; Meigs to Eustis, 30 May 1811, Cherokee Agency, NARA, M208, Reel 5. Contrast his apprehension of their independence on the eve of the 1812 war: Meigs to Eustis, 8 May 1812, Cherokee Agency, NARA, M208, Reel 5.

43. See, for example, James Jackson to James McHenry, 24 January 1798, *Governor's Letter Book: Matthews and Jackson,* 65–67 (protesting Hawkins's claim that a Creek murderer had been tried in the Nation); and John Cooke to Enoch Parsons, 25 December 1812, *Creek Letters* 2, 764 (protesting Hawkins's failure to demand the surrender of a Creek accused of murder for trial in the state in 1812).

44. For examples of tribal punishment as fulfillment of the treaty, see: Hawkins to Constant Freeman, 2 August 1798, in *Letters, Journals and Writings of Benjamin Hawkins,* vol. 1, ed. C. L. Grant, (Savannah, GA: Beehive, 1980), 214; Hawkins to Georgia Wells Foster, 22 December 1798, *Letters, Journals and Writings of Benjamin Hawkins,* vol. 1, 227; Hawkins to Alexander Cornells, 5 November 1799, *Letters, Journals and Writings of Benjamin Hawkins,* vol. 1, 267–268; Hawkins to James McHenry, 6 November 1799, *Letters, Journals and Writings of Benjamin Hawkins,* vol. 1, 269; Hawkins to Vicente Folch, 8 December 1799, *Letters, Journals and Writings of Benjamin Hawkins,* vol. 1, 277.

45. For an overview, see Wallace, *Jefferson and the Indians.*

46. Ethridge, *Creek Country,* 235.

47. Jackson to Jared Irwin, 22 March 1798, *Governor's Letter Books: Matthews and Jackson,* 149–150. The same standards applied in the agency: see Hawkins to Henry Dearborn, 15 July 1802, *Letters, Journals and Writings of Benjamin Hawkins,* vol. 2, 450.

48. J. P. Reid, "A Perilous Rule: The Law of International Homicide," in *The Cherokee Indian Nation: A Troubled History,* ed. D. H. King (Knoxville: University of Tennessee Press, 1979), 33.

49. Jackson to Hawkins, 23 March 1798, *Governor's Letter Books: Matthews and Jackson,* 158. John Sevier of Tennessee did something similar in 1804 when he made clear that a settler murderer was not from Tennessee and enjoined the Cherokee therefore not to take revenge on citizens of that state: Sevier to Cherokee Nation, 9 February 1804, Governor Sevier Collection, 1:1:1054, tl054, Tennessee State Library and Archives.

50. James Jackson to Irwin, 3 March 1798, *Governor's Letter Books: Matthews and Jackson,* 135; Jackson to Irwin, 23 March 1798, *Governor's Letter Books: Matthews and Jackson,* 149–150; Jackson to Hawkins, 23 March

1798, *Governor's Letter Books: Matthews and Jackson,* 158. For another example in which jurisdiction is offered to restore balance and facilitate diplomacy, see Jackson to Creek Nation, 5 March 1799, *Creek Letters* 2, 551.

51. Creek Nation to Edward Telfair, 13 November 1790, *Creek Letters* 1, 236; Capt. Joseph Savage to Telfair, 13 January 1791, *Creek Letters* 1, 234; and James Durouzeaux to Savage, 13 and 29 January 1791, *Creek Letters* 2, 235. On the logic of retaliation in another murder in 1791, see Richard Call to Telfair, 5 June 1791, *Creek Letters* 1, 239.

52. Buckner Harris to Cherokee Nation, 4 June 1808, Cherokee Agency, NARA, M208, Reel 4.

53. Hugh Montgomery to Meigs, 8 January 1813, Cherokee Agency, NARA, M208, Reel 6.

54. Mitchell to Floyd, 12 September 1812, Governor's Letter Books, D. B. Mitchell, 14 December 1809 to 26 October 1813, and Peter Early, 9 November 1813 to 17 May 1814, Record Group 001-01-001, Georgia Archives, 71.

55. For example, historians who read Washington's and Jefferson's assimilation policies as a (flawed) means to expropriation; see: A. Wallace, *Jefferson and the Indians: The Tragic Fate of the First Americans* (Cambridge, MA: Belknap Press of Harvard University Press, 1999), 206–240; B. W. Sheehan, *Seeds of Extinction: Jeffersonian Philanthropy and the American Indian* (Chapel Hill: University of North Carolina Press, 1973); R. Horsman, *Expansion and American Indian Policy, 1783–1812* (Ann Arbor: Michigan State University Press, 1967), 53–65. Regarding diplomacy as expedience generally, see F. P. Prucha, *The Great Father: The United States Government and the American Indians* (London and Lincoln: University of Nebraska Press, 1984), 35–60. Regarding expropriation as policy generally, see R. N. Satz, "Rhetoric versus Reality: The Indian Policy of Andrew Jackson," in *Cherokee Removal: Before and After,* ed. W. L. Anderson (London and Athens: University of Georgia Press, 1991), 29–54. For a very recent and forceful articulation of this view, see P. Wolfe, "*Corpus Nullius:* The Exception of Indians and Other Aliens in US Constitutional Discourse," *Postcolonial Studies* 10, no. 2 (2007): 127–151. Contrast the more complex view presented in D. A. Rosen, *American Indians and State Law: Sovereignty, Race, and Citizenship, 1790–1880* (Lincoln: University of Nebraska Press, 2007).

56. Duall was arrested in Gundungurra Country occupied by the Muringong tribe. Note that Kristyn Harman identifies Duall himself as a Tharawal speaker, which is a coastal region. This may be a confusion with Durelle: K. Harman, "Aboriginal Convicts: Race, Law, and Transportation in Colonial New South Wales" (Ph.D. thesis, University of Tasmania, 2008), 18–37; J. Connor, *The Australian Frontier Wars, 1788–1838* (Randwick, NSW: University of New South Wales Press, 2002), 36, 51; G. Karskens, *The Colony: A History of Early Sydney* (St. Leonards, NSW: Allen & Unwin, 2009), 511; David Horton, *Aboriginal Australia* (Acton, ACT: AIATSIS, 2000).

57. See State Records New South Wales: Colonial Secretary's Papers, 1788–1825, Government and General Orders, 20 July 1816 [SZ1044], Reel 6038, 226–231 (hereafter cited as SR NSW: CSP, 1788–1825). See also SR NSW:

CSP, 1788–1825, Macquarie, Instructions to John Warby and John Jackson, 22 July 1814 [4/1730], Reel 6044, 218–223.

58. For example: K. Windschuttle, *The Fabrication of Aboriginal History* (Sydney: Macleay Press, 2002), 186; S. Banner, "Why *Terra Nullius*: Anthropology and Property Law in Early Australia," *Law and History Review* 23, no. 1 (2005): 95–132; S. Banner, *Possessing the Pacific: Land, Settlers, and Indigenous People from Australia to Alaska* (Cambridge, MA: Harvard University Press, 2007), 13–46; B. Buchan, "The Empire of Political Thought: Civilization, Savagery and Perceptions of Indigenous Government," *History of the Human Sciences* 18, no. 2 (2005): 1–22; P. Wolfe, *Settler Colonialism and the Transformation of Anthropology: The Politics and Poetics of an Ethnographic Event*, Writing Past Colonialism Series (London and New York: Cassell, 1999), 25–27; B. Attwood, *Telling the Truth about Aboriginal History* (St. Leonards, NSW: Allen & Unwin, 2005), 124–135. Compare B. Kercher, *An Unruly Child: A History of Law in Australia* (St. Leonards, NSW: Allen & Unwin, 1995), 3–21; and J. Evans, *Edward Eyre: Race and Colonial Governance* (Dunedin, NZ: University of Otago Press, 2005), 12–13.

59. Wolfe, "*Corpus Nullius*."

60. R. H. W. Reece, "Feasts and Blankets: The History of Some Early Attempts to Establish Relations with the Aborigines of New South Wales, 1814–1846," *Archaeology and Physical Anthropology in Oceania* 2, no. 3 (1967): 190–206.

61. Philip King to Hobart, 30 October 1802, *Historical Records of Australia: Series 1, Governors' Despatches to and from England,* vol. 3 (Sydney: The Library Committee of the Commonwealth Parliament, 1915), 582–583 (hereafter cited as *HRA* 1:3, 582–583).

62. For example, see Samuel Marsden's negotiations with hostile Aborigines: *Sydney Gazette,* 5 May 1805, 3, 2; and negotiations by magistrates, attempting to discover grievances: *Sydney Gazette,* 22 December 1805, 2, 1. For King's negotiations with hostile Aborigines, see: King to Hobart, 20 December 1804, *HRA* 1:5, 166–167; King to Camden, 30 April 1805, *HRA* 1:5, 306.Those termed "branch natives" are likely Darkingung people, but to avoid ambiguity, I use "Branch tribe" here, after Karskens, *The Colony,* 485–486.

63. *Sydney Gazette,* 26 May 1805, 2, 3.

64. See, for example, the mixed purposes of feasts held on 12 January 1817 and 1 January 1818, Macquarie Papers: Diary, 10 April 1816 to 1 July 1818, Mitchell Library A773, CYA773, Reel 301, 313 & 362 (hereafter cited as Macquarie Diary, ML A773).

65. Diary entry, 6 June 1816, Macquarie Diary, ML A773, 259, "Bidjee Bidjee Brought in *Coggie* the late chief of the Cow Pasture Tribe, who made his submission, delivered up his arms, and promised to be friendly in future to all White People." See also Diary entry, 12 January 1817, Macquarie Diary, ML A773, 313: "*Narrang Jack,* one of the Hostile Natives some time outlawed, came in on this occasion and gave himself up—to take the benefit of the last *Proclamation*" offering clemency. Another tribe numbering fifty-one visited the governor on the same day.

66. Thomas Brisbane to Bathurst, 14 February 1824, *HRA* 1:11, 226.

67. SR NSW: Colonial Secretary's Correspondence, Special Bundles, Aboriginal Outrages 1830-1, Golburn Plains, Macalister to Colonial Secretary, 24 January 1831 [4/8020.2].

68. In general, see: Connor, *The Australian Frontier Wars;* Karskens, *The Colony,* 386-447. See also, for example: Government and General Orders, 22 November 1801, *HRA* 1:3, 466; *Sydney Gazette,* 17 June 1804, 2, 3; King to Hobart, 14 August 1804, *HRA* 1:5, 17-18; Government and General Orders, 28 April 1805, *HRA* 1:5, 820.

69. W. F. Finlason, *Commentaries upon Martial Law* (Littleton, CO: F. B. Rothman, 1980), 1; quoted and discussed in Kercher, *An Unruly Child.* On the first declaration of martial law, 14 August 1824, *HRA* 1:11, 410-411. On the refusal of Darling to declare martial law against Aborigines, see Darling to Hay, 11 September 1826, *HRA* 1:12: 574-575; Darling to Bathurst, 6 October 1826, *HRA* 1:12, 608.

70. Extract from Orderly Book, 22 February 1797, *Original Documents on Aborigines and Law, 1797-1840,* Document no. 1, Macquarie University, http://www.law.mq.edu.au/scnsw/Correspondence/index.htm). (hereafter cited as *Original Documents on Aborigines,* doc. 1).

71. Government and General Orders, 1 May 1801, *HRA* 1:3, 250. Again, tribal names are very unclear. This violence likely included a number of different tribes including the Bidjigal, Toongagal, and Burramattagal people living in Dharug Country near Parramatta: Connor, *The Australian Frontier Wars,* 37; and Horton, *Aboriginal Australia.*

72. Government and General Orders, 28 April 1805, *HRA* 1:5, 820.

73. In the 28 April Proclamation, he uses the term "Justice" in reference to Aboriginal and "prosecuted" in reference to settler wrongdoing: 28 April 1805, *HRA* 1:5, 820.

74. SR NSW: CSP, 1788-1825, Government and General Orders, 18 June 1814 [SZ758], Reel 6038, 501-505.

75. SR NSW: CSP, 1788-1825, Instructions to John Warby and John Jackson, 22 July 1814 [4/1730], Reel 6044, 218-223.

76. SR NSW: CSP, 1788-1825, Instructions to Captain Shaw, 9 March 1816 [4/1734], Reel 6045, 164. On Macquarie's "satisfaction" that "the several parts of their Instructions" had been carried out, see Diary entry, Macquarie Diary, ML A773, 247.

77. For original printed version, see Proclamation, 4 May 1816, Wentworth Family Papers: Wentworth, D'Arcy Correspondence, 1809-1816, Mitchell Library A752, CY Reel 699, 205 (52) (Wentworth Correspondence, ML A752). For handwritten copy, see *Original Documents on Aborigines,* doc. 6.

78. SR NSW: CSP, 1788-1825, Government and General Orders, 20 July 1816 [SZ1044], Reel 6038, 226-231.

79. SR NSW: CSP, 1788-1825, Government and General Orders, 20 July 1816 [SZ1044], Reel 6038, 226-231; and see SR NSW: CSP, 1788-1825, Macquarie, Instructions to John Warby and John Jackson, 22 July 1814 [4/1730], Reel 6044, 218-223.

80. *Sydney Gazette,* 30 June 1805, 2, 1. More were liberated later, *Sydney Gazette,* 7 July 1805, 1, 3.

81. *Sydney Gazette,* 4 August 1805, 2, 2.

82. Judge-Advocate Atkins' Opinion on the Treatment of Natives, 8 July 1805, *HRA* 1:5, 502–504.

83. See also the report of an inquiry into the shooting of an Aborigine: *Sydney Gazette,* 10 April 1803, 3, 2.

84. On foreigners: Vattel, *The Law of Nations,* vol. 2, 172. On treaties: Grotius, *The Rights of War and Peace,* vol. 1, 169; Vattel, *The Law of Nations,* vol. 2, 193.

85. Atkins had endorsed this principle partially in 1792: "Blood for Blood is justifiable provided it can be executed upon the proper Object, the person who actually committed the fact But to shed the Blood of an innocent man for the crimes of another shows a savageness of disposition not compatible with civilized state." 26 May 1792, Richard Atkins Journal, 1792–1810, Mitchell Library MSS737, FM3/585, 15–16 (hereafter cited as Atkins Journal, ML MSS737). See also Vattel, *The Law of Nations,* vol. 3, 348.

86. King to Camden, 20 July 1805, *HRA* 1:5, 497.

87. Mosquito and Bulldog tried to escape from prison before their transportation: *Sydney Gazette,* 11 August 1805, 2, 1. On transportation: SR NSW: CSP, 1788–1825 [ML Safe 1/51], Reel 6040, 41. In 1814, Governor Macquarie allowed the "banished" (Macquarie's term) Mosquito to return to the colony on the application of his family: SR NSW: CSP, 1788–1825, Colonial Secretary to Lt. Governor Davey, 17 August 1814 [4/3493], Reel 6004, 251.

88. D. Collins, *An Account of the English Colony in New South Wales, with Remarks on the Dispositions, Customs, Manners, etc. of the Native Inhabitants of that Country,* facsimile ed., vol. 1 (London: T. Cadell and W. Davies, 1798), 583–593; Journal entry, 8 June 1792, Atkins Journal, ML MSS737, 19.

89. M. Finnane, "'Payback,' Customary Law and Criminal Law in Colonised Australia," *International Journal of the Sociology of Law* 29, no. 4 (2001): 293–310; L. R. Hiatt, *Arguments about Aborigines: Australia and the Evolution of Social Anthropology* (Cambridge: Cambridge University Press, 1996), 78–99.

90. Collins, *An Account of the English Colony,* 1: 587–588.

91. Connor, *The Australian Frontier Wars,* 1–21. R. Broome, "The Struggle for Australia: Aboriginal-European Warfare, 1770–1930," in *Australia: Two Centuries of War and Peace,* ed. M. McKernan and M. Browne (Canberra: Australian War Memorial, 1988), 92–120; R. Broome, *Aboriginal Australians: Black Responses to White Dominance, 1788–2001* (St. Leonards, NSW: Allen & Unwin, 2002).

92. 26 May 1792, Atkins Journal, ML MSS737, 16.

93. The work of Victoria Gollan on Magistrates' and other court records, and the ongoing work of Brent Salter and Bruce Kercher on Superior Court cases from 1788 to 1824, support this contention. The New South Wales magistracy, however, had very broad and poorly supervised power to hear

criminal matters before 1824, and it is impossible to say definitively that no indigenous people appeared before them.

94. "Trial for the Murder of Two Natives," 2 January 1800, *HRA* 1:2, 409–410.

95. For a discussion of Aboriginal appropriations of the governor's house in this period, see Karskens, *The Colony,* 389–390. Randall was probably Eora, but, as Karskens points out, Sydney very early became a meeting point for many Aboriginal peoples in the region: 351–353; 517–539.

96. R. v. Randall, SR NSW: Bench of Magistrates, 1788–1820, 7 June 1799 [SZ767], Reel 655, 83. I am indebted for this reference to Victoria Gollan: Aboriginal Colonial Court Cases, 1788–1838, SR NSW, http://srwww.re cords.nsw.gov.au/indexes/searchform.aspx?id=1.

97. *Sydney Gazette,* 3 June 1815, 2, 1; *Sydney Gazette,* 17 June 1815, 2, 2.

98. Karskens, 490–491. These are Dharug peoples located near modern-day Penrith: Connor, *The Australian Frontier Wars,* 37.

99. *Sydney Gazette,* 16 November 1811, 2, 2.

100. SR NSW: CSP, 1788–1825, Coroner's Judgment, 3 January 1813 [4/1819], Reel 6021, 193–197; *Sydney Gazette,* 8 January 1813, 2, 2.

101. For example, see: D. J. Neal, *The Rule of Law in a Penal Colony: Law and Power in Early New South Wales* (Cambridge and Melbourne: Cambridge University Press, 1991), 78; P. Muldoon, "The Sovereign Exceptions: Colonization and the Foundation of Society," *Social and Legal Studies* 17, no. 1 (2008); M. Mylonas-Widdall, "The Recognition of Aboriginal Customary Law: Pluralism beyond the Colonial Paradigm—A Review Article," *International and Comparative Law Quarterly* 37, no. 2 (1988): 368–391; R. L. Misner, "Administration of Criminal Justice on Aboriginal Settlements," *Sydney Law Review* 7 (1973): 257–283; R. Cranston, "The Aborigines and the Law: An Overview," *University of Queensland Law Journal* 8 (1972): 60–63; S. Yeo, "Native Criminal Jurisdiction after Mabo," *Current Issues Criminal Justice* 6 (1994): 14–16; Banner, "Why *Terra Nullius*," 95–132. This focus is caused largely by the sources used, which were court cases from 1824 to 1836 recovered by Bruce Kercher: Decisions of the Superior Courts of New South Wales, 1788–1899, published by the Division of Law, Macquarie University, http://www.law.mq.edu.au/scnsw. Yet Kercher's own work highlights the unexpected plurality of early decisions regarding Aborigines: Kercher, *An Unruly Child,* 3–21.

102. For a fuller explanation of the nature and context of this case, see L. Ford and B. Salter, "From Pluralism to Territorial Sovereignty: The 1816 Trial of Mow-watty in the Superior Court of New South Wales," *Indigenous Law Journal* 7.1 (2008): 67–86. Mow-watty was "reared in Parramatta from his infancy" but his precise tribal affiliation is unclear: Marsden's evidence, R. v. Mow-Watty, September 27 or 28, 1816, Decisions of the Superior Courts of New South Wales, 1788–1899, published by the Division of Law, Macquarie University, http://www.law.mq.edu.au/scnsw.

103. R. v. Mow-Watty, September 27 or 28, 1816, Decisions of the Superior Courts of New South Wales, 1788–1899, published by the Division of Law, Macquarie University, http://www.law.mq.edu.au/scnsw.

104. Diary entries, 4 June 1816 and 15 November 1816, Macquarie Diary, ML A773, 258 and 301. On 4 June Macquarie suggested that there were sixteen prisoners in total, of whom he released fifteen. In November he recorded the release of five more men taken "some weeks" before, and the retention in custody of Jabbinguy.

105. SR NSW: CSP, 1788–1825, Instructions to Captain Shaw, 9 March 1816 [4/1734], Reel 6045, 164.

106. Diary entry, 4 June 1816, Macquarie Diary, ML A773, 258. Some of the children were detained and sent to the Native Institution: Diary entry, 6 June 1816, Macquarie Diary, ML A773, 259. Macquarie released five other men held for their "hostile conduct" with "blankets, provisions" and significantly "pardoned [them of] all past crimes": Diary entry, 15 November 1816, Macquarie Diary, ML A773, 301.

107. SR NSW: CSP, 1788–1825, Government and General Orders, 20 July 1816 [SZ1044], Reel 6038, 226–231.

108. Government and General Orders 11 May 1801, *HRA* 1:3, 251–252.

109. SR NSW: CSP, 1788–1825, Government and General Orders, 21 December 1816 [SZ 758], Reel 6038, 299.

110. Compare the use of "pardoned" in Diary entry, 15 November 1816, Macquarie Diary, ML A773, 301: Macquarie "released from Jail Five Black Natives . . . confined for some weeks past on account of their depredations." He "Pardoned all past crimes, and cautioned them against the serious Punishments that would certainly be inflicted on them . . . [for] any further hostility.".

111. SR NSW: Colonial Secretary's Papers, 1788–1825, Government and General Orders, 30 July 1816 [SZ759], Reel 6038, 232–233. Note that Charles Throsby had asserted in April 1816 that Duall was "perfectly innocent of any of the murders that have recently taken place": Charles Throsby to D'Arcy Wentworth, 5 April 1816, Wentworth Correspondence, ML A752, 183.

112. See John Dunmore Lang, *An Historical and Statistical Account of New South Wales* . . . (London, 1836), 16, 180. Note that the statutes do not consistently use the word "banishment": compare 39 Elizabeth, c4, and 4 George 1, c. 11. For a British example, see W. E. Auckland, *Principles of Penal Law,* 2nd ed. (London: B. White and T. Cadell, 1771), 32–37.

113. Hatherly and Jackie were probably Awabakal aborigines: Connor, *The Australian Frontier Wars,* 63. SR NSW: CSP, 1788–1825, Wylde to Colonial Secretary, 28 December 1822 [4/1758], Reel 6054, 145. For correspondence and depositions on this case, see R. v. Hatherly and Jackie, Informations, SR NSW: Court of Criminal Jurisdiction, Depositions and Related Papers [SZ800], Reel 1798, 1–19. For judgment, see R. v. Hatherly and Jackie, 2 January 1823, Decisions of the Superior Courts of New South Wales, 1788–1899, published by the Division of Law, Macquarie University, http://www.law.mq.edu.au/scnsw.

114. For the relevance of pluralism to early French North American colonies, see J. Grabowski, "French Criminal Justice and Indians in Montreal, 1670–1760," *Ethnohistory* 43, no. 3 (1996): 405–429.

3. Indigenous Jurisdiction and Spatial Order

1. The precise value of Wheeler's property was "not proven": see Copy of a Report of a Board of Commissioners: Cormick v. Cherokees, and some notes, 22 December 1812, Records of the Cherokee Indian Agency in Tennessee 1801–1835, National Archives and Records Administration Microfilm Publication M208, Reel 5 (hereafter cited as Cherokee Agency, NARA, M208, Reel 5).
2. For example, Article 5, Treaty with the Cherokee (Holston), 1791, in C. J. Kappler, *Indian Affairs: Laws and Treaties,* vol. 2 (Washington, DC: Government Printing Office, 1904), 30; Article 7, Treaty with the Cherokee, 1798, Kappler, *Indian Affairs,* 53; Article 4, Treaty with the Cherokee, 1805, Kappler, *Indian Affairs,* 83; Article 2, Treaty with the Cherokee, 1805, Kappler, *Indian Affairs,* 84.
3. Cormick's lawyer, Mr. Cobb, suggested to Meigs that Cormick's claim included an array of notes (that is, tradable debts), which he had purchased from Wheeler but had yet to recover, and mortgages over land worth $5,000 at some point, but severely depreciated since: Thomas Cobb to Meigs, 1 July 1812, Cherokee Agency, NARA, M208 Reel 5. Cormick wrote to protest that this advice was both "unauthorized and unnecessary": Cormick to Meigs, 30 November 1812, Cherokee Agency, M208, Reel 5.
4. In early national jurisprudence, there was some question of whether territories, like Mississippi, owed states the obligation of extraditing settler suspects for trial: see D. P. Currie, "The Constitution in the Supreme Court: The Powers of the Federal Courts, 1801–1835," *University of Chicago Law Review* 49 (1982): 673n178.
5. Copy of a Report of a Board of Commissioners: Cormick v. Cherokees, and some notes, 22 December 1812, Cherokee Agency, NARA, M208, Reel 5.
6. James Olive to John Cormick, 28 December 1810, *Cherokee Indian Letters, Talks and Treaties, 1786–1838,* vol. 1, bound transcripts, Works Progress Administration (WPA) Project No. 4341, ed. L. F. Hays (Atlanta: Georgia Archives, 1939), 112 (hereafter cited as *Cherokee Letters* 1, 112).
7. "Customary law" here means a body "of rules . . . to define appropriate reciprocal behaviour of [indigenous] individuals" but also evolving in tension with colonization; C. M. N. White, "African Customary Law: The Problem of Concept and Definition," *Journal of African Law* 9 (1965): 86–89.
8. R. F. Ethridge, *Creek Country: The Creek Indians and Their World* (Chapel Hill: University of North Carolina Press, 2003), 22–31.
9. On this point, see W. G. McLoughlin, *Cherokees and Missionaries, 1789–1839* (London and New Haven, CT: Yale University Press, 1984); T. Perdue, *Cherokee Women: Gender and Culture Change, 1700–1835* (Lincoln: University of Nebraska Press, 1998); F. A. Yarbrough, *Race and the Cherokee Nation: Sovereignty in the Nineteenth Century* (Philadelphia: University of Pennsylvania Press, 2008), 1–55; C. Cumfer, *Separate Peoples, One Land: The Minds of Cherokees, Blacks, and Whites on the Tennessee Frontier* (Chapel Hill: University of North Carolina Press, 2007), 101–123; C. Saunt, "Taking Account of Property: Stratification among the Creek Indians in the Early

Nineteenth Century," *William and Mary Quarterly* 57, no. 4 (2000): 733–760. For a recent comparison on this point with Australia, see G. Smithers, "The 'Pursuits of the Civilized Man': Race and the Meaning of Civilization in the United States and Australia, 1790s–1850s," *Journal of World History* 20, no. 2 (2009): 245–272.

10. J. P. Reid, *A Law of Blood: The Primitive Law of the Cherokee Nation* (New York: New York University Press, 1970), 229–245; R. Strickland, *Fire and the Spirits: Cherokee Law from Clan to Court* (Norman: University of Oklahoma Press, 1975), 30–37, 168.

11. Perdue, *Cherokee Women*, 25–27; M. Daniel, "From Blood Feud to Jury System: The Metamorphosis of Cherokee Law from 1750 to 1840," *American Indian Quarterly* 11, no. 2 (1987): 97–101.

12. For a very nuanced account of this process, see McLoughlin, *Cherokees and Missionaries.*

13. T. Perdue, "Clan and Court: Another Look at the Early Cherokee Republic," *American Indian Quarterly* 24, no. 4 (2000): 562–569.

14. Ethridge, *Creek Country*, 92–119, 108.

15. Ethridge, *Creek Country*, 105.

16. Benjamin Hawkins to James Jackson, 20 December 1799, *Letters of Benjamin Hawkins, 1797–1815*, bound transcripts, WPA Project No. 5993, ed. L. F. Hays (Atlanta: Georgia Archives, 1939), 48–50 (hereafter cited as *Letters of Benjamin Hawkins, 1797–1815*, GA, 48–50). For cultural and legal change in the Creek Nation, see Saunt, "Taking Account of Property," 733–760; J. A. Piker, *Okfuskee: A Creek Indian Town in Colonial America* (Cambridge, MA: Harvard University Press, 2005), 111–195.

17. For a nuanced account of Cherokee understandings of intercultural obligations, see Cumfer, *Separate Peoples, One Land*, 51–98. For shared norms of reciprocity, see K. Hermes, "'Justice Will Be Done by Us': Algonquian Demands for Reciprocity in the Courts of European Settlers," in *The Many Legalities of Early America*, ed. C. L. Tomlins and B. H. Mann (London and Chapel Hill: University of North Carolina Press, 2001), 123–149. For the persistence of satisfaction in intertribal diplomacy, see Articles 7 and 8, Cherokee/Creek Boundary Treaty ratified by the Cherokee 16 March 1822, Cherokee Nation, http://www.cherokee.org/Culture/190/Page/default.aspx (accessed May 25, 2009). Note that this document does not appear in V. Deloria Jr. and R. J. DeMallie, *Documents of American Indian Diplomacy: Treaties, Agreements, and Conventions, 1775–1979*, vol. 2 (Norman: University of Oklahoma Press, 1999); and only part of it is extracted in the *Cherokee Phoenix*, 11 November 1829, vol. 2, no. 31, 1, 1b–5b, 4, 1a–5a.

18. Kappler, *Indian Affairs*, 8–11.

19. Kappler, *Indian Affairs*, 29–33.

20. Kappler, *Indian Affairs*, 25–29.

21. See the difficulties and uncertainties surrounding the arrest of James Vann: Return J. Meigs to Henry Dearborn, 30 September 1808, Cherokee Agency, NARA, M208, Reel 4; Annotation on Meigs to James Vann, 28 October 1808, NARA, M208, Reel 4.

22. Daniel, "From Blood Feud to Jury System," 106–107.

23. Chapter 4 discusses the abortive exercise of this jurisdiction.

24. For jurisdictional claims mounted on the basis of these treaty terms, see Abstract of Charles Hicks and John Ross to Meigs, 11 December 1826, *Papers of Chief John Ross,* vol. 1, ed. Gary E. Mouton (Norman: University of Oklahoma Press, 1983), 126–128.

25. See "Copy of Resolution Adopted by the Committee," 30 November 1836, Cherokee Removal Records, ca. 1820–1854: Cherokee Committee, First Board, 1820–1841, Record Group 75, Records of the Bureau of Indian Affairs, ARC ID 222, folder 1, National Archives and Records Administration, Washington, DC.

26. Benjamin Hawkins to James Jackson, 20 December 1799, *Letters of Benjamin Hawkins, 1797–1815,* GA, 48–50.

27. Hawkins to Thomas Jefferson, 13 September 1806, *Letters, Journals and Writings of Benjamin Hawkins,* vol. 2, 508–509; and see Hawkins to Dearborn, 27 December 1805, *Letters, Journals and Writings of Benjamin Hawkins,* vol. 2, 503–504.

28. Ethridge, *Creek Country,* 74–77, 102.

29. Hawkins to Thomas Jefferson, 11 July 1803, *Letters, Journals and Writings of Benjamin Hawkins,* vol. 2, 455–456.

30. Hawkins to James Jackson, 20 December 1799: *Letters of Benjamin Hawkins, 1797–1815,* GA, 48.

31. Hawkins to Thomas Jefferson, 13 September 1806, *Letters, Journals and Writings of Benjamin Hawkins,* vol. 2, 508. It seems that another slave may have been subjected to Indian jurisdiction. In an 1831 deposition, Thomas Flournoy stated that in 1792 a runaway slave belonging to him was killed in the Creek Nation for "some cause": *Indian Depredations, 1787–1825: Original Claims in Department of Archives & History of Georgia,* vol. 1, part 2, bound transcripts, WPA Project No. 3990-3441, ed. J. E. Hays (Atlanta: Georgia Archives, 1938), 290B.

32. Hawkins to William Eustis, 21 July 1810, *Letters, Journals and Writings of Benjamin Hawkins,* vol. 2, 565.

33. On Meigs's attitude to Cherokee legal status, see Eustis, 5 April 1811, Cherokee Agency, NARA, M208, Reel 5; Meigs to Eustis, 30 May 1811, Cherokee Agency, NARA, M208, Reel 5. Contrast his apprehension of their independence on the eve of the 1812 war: Meigs to Eustis, 8 May 1812, Cherokee Agency, NARA, M208, Reel 5.

34. See, for example, Cherokee request for permission to burn the cabins of squatters: Jacob Moore to Meigs, 3 March 1813, Cherokee Agency, NARA, M208, Reel 6. Other examples not discussed here include: (a) James Vann's desire to "punish a whiteman when he Steals and maiks Plotes with a Negroe to Kill aney man that has property in this Nation": Vann to Meigs, 11 September 1805, Cherokee Agency, NARA, M208, Reel 3; (b) Vann's torture of an Irish servant girl suspected of theft in 1805: "Mr. Wohlfart's narrative of Vann's treatment of a Miss Crawford," undated late 1805, Cherokee Agency, NARA, M208, Reel 3; (c) Vann's determination to punish stolen/escaped

slaves: Nicholas Byers to Meigs, August 28 1805, M208, Reel 3; (d) Vann's punishment of another settler in the nation: Lovely to Meigs, 8 March 1806, Cherokee Agency, NARA, M208, Reel 3; (e) the taking of William Bright's cows as damages for pollution: "Statement of affairs between William Bright of the State of Georgia and Chulech a Headman of the Cherokee Nation," 3 February 1808, Cherokee Agency, NARA, M208, Reel 4; (f) reports of threats of Smiley, a Cherokee, to confiscate or kill trespassing cattle in the nation: Colonel Dirgan to Meigs, 25 March 1808, Cherokee Agency, NARA, M208, Reel 4; and (g) the beating of Bartlett Robbins in 1806: Bartlett Robbins's complaint against James Vann, 25 October 1808, Cherokee Agency, NARA, M208, Reel 4.

35. Meigs to Dearborn, 4 October 1801, Cherokee Agency, NARA, M208, Reel 1. The accused was acquitted by a Knoxville court, and Meigs feared that the Cherokee who "have no proper Idea of the nature of evidence" assumed his guilt and would "punish [him] with Death": Meigs to Dearborn, 13 November 1801, Cherokee Agency, NARA, M208, Reel 1.

36. Lowry to Meigs, 18 May 1808, Cherokee Agency, NARA, M208, Reel 4; errors in original.

37. William Reed to Meigs, 16 January 1810, Cherokee Agency, NARA, M208, Reel 5. On the jurisdictional complexities of the situation, see Meigs to Reid, 20 January 1810, Cherokee Agency, NARA, M208, Reel 5. The state sought jurisdiction over such crimes in 1814: "An Act to add all that part of the unlocated territory of this state which lies without the limits of the present counties, to the county of Jasper, for the purpose of giving the Courts jurisdiction of crimes committed by white persons against white persons in said territory, and for other purposes," 27/50, Assented to 23 November 1814, Acts of the General Assembly of the State of Georgia; Passed in October and November, 1814; volume 1, 41, *Georgia Legislative Documents,* University of Georgia, http://www.galileo.usg.edu/express?link=zlgl. Amended by "An Act to amend an act, entitled an act, to add that part of the unlocated Territory of this state, which lies without the limits of the present counties, to the county of Jasper, passed the 23d day of November, 1814," 19/90, Assented to 18 December 1816, Acts of the General Assembly of the State of Georgia, Passed in November and December 1816, volume 1, 34, *Georgia Legislative Documents,* http://www.galileo.usg.edu/express?link=zlgl.

38. Black Fox and Path Killer to Meigs and Meigs's note on verso, undated, filed at end of 1810, Cherokee Agency, NARA, M208, Reel 5. Note that Meigs had asked the Cherokee to "send to me a Statement of them ... when you have examined into the State of these Cases": Meigs to the Cherokee Nation, Cherokee Agency, 27 March 1810, NARA, M208, Reel 5.

39. Reed to Captain Parrish, 4 April 1811, Cherokee Agency, NARA, M208, Reel 5.

40. Cherokee Nation to John Tally, 15 March 1813, Cherokee Agency, NARA, M208, Reel 6.

41. Enoch Parsons, Attorney at Law, Azariah David, JP, William Lovely, Agent, Nicholas Byars, and Return J. Meigs, "Decision in Matter of *Olive v Cherokee Nation,*" 22 March 1811, *Cherokee Letters* 1, 99–104.

42. Parsons et al., "Decision."
43. See Article 10, Treaty of Holston, 1791, Kappler, *Indian Affairs,* 31.
44. Cormick v. Cherokees, and some notes, 22 December 1812, Cherokee Agency, NARA, M208, Reel 5.
45. Parsons et al., "Decision."
46. Eustis to Cormick, 26 August 1811, Cherokee Agency, NARA, M208, Reel 5. Testimony was collected even after the second commission; see Mr. Colquitt's Testimony, 24 May 1813, Cherokee Agency, NARA, M208, Reel 6.
47. See "Copy of a Report of a Board of Commissioners: Cormick v. Cherokees, and Some Notes," 22 December 1812, Cherokee Agency, NARA, M208, Reel 5. Cobb, Cormick's attorney, had stated repeatedly that Cormick had no claim until property transactions were settled in Georgia, but Cormick disagreed: Cobb to Meigs, 1 July 1812, Cherokee Agency, NARA, M208, Reel 5; Cormick to Meigs, 16 December 1812, Cherokee Agency, NARA, M208, Reel 5.
48. "Copy of a Report of a Board of Commissioners: Cormick v. Cherokees, and Some Notes," 22 December 1812, Cherokee Agency, NARA, M208, Reel 5.
49. Note that Meigs referred to Commissions like the bodies assembled in 1811 and 1812 as a "Mode" of resolution "practiced in this agency in introducing before the Secretary of War such cases for final decision": Meigs to Eustis, 23 March 1811, *Cherokee Letters* 1, 105. The practice of having a body of settlers adjudicate claims started early: see "General Principles of Adjusting Claims," 24 October 1804, Cherokee Agency, NARA, M208, Reel 1. For an early example under Meigs, see 28 October 1801, Cherokee Agency, NARA, M208, Reel 1. For other examples of single arbitrations, see "Award Thomas N. Clark v. Indian Nation," 1 February 1812, Cherokee Agency, NARA, M208, Reel 5; and Secretary of War's suggestion that Meigs seek Cherokee consent to an arbitration regarding Colonel Earle, Eustis to Meigs, 16 December 1812, Cherokee Agency, NARA, M208, Reel 5. On less contentious matters, Meigs and an assistant seem to have examined claims: see "List of Certain claims of Citizens of the United States & of Cherokees examined . . ." 25 August 1811, Cherokee Agency, NARA, M208, Reel 5. On disputes between settlers and indigenous people that came before state courts, see "Re Jack Kinnard's Cattle, Proceedings of the Magistrates," likely 17 August 1803, *Creek Indian Letters, Talks and Treaties, 1705–1839,* vol. 2, ed. L. F. Hays (WPA Project No. 665-34-3-224, 1939), 677 (hereafter cited as *Creek Letters* 2); 17 July 1803, *Creek Letters* 2, 679; "Costs," David Garvin v. Amos Cheek, 20 June 1803, *Creek Letters* 2, 680; Samuel Commander v. Walter Adair et al., October Term 1818, Franklin Superior Court Records, Miscellaneous, Record Group 159–1–59, Georgia Archives.
50. There are too many requests for investigation and compensation to enumerate. This was arguably the primary function of the agent.
51. See ongoing disputes over Georgian property lost or taken into the Creek Nation from the Revolutionary War onward: G. W. Foster to James Jackson, 22 August 1798, *Creek Letters* 2, 529; Abner Hammond to James Jackson,

27 August 1798, *Creek Letters* 2, 531; D. B. Mitchell to Hawkins, 8 October 1810, *Creek Letters* 2, 737; Daniel Stewart to Hawkins, 12 and 16 October 1810, *Creek Letters* 2, 740, 743; Hawkins to D. B. Mitchell, 13 October 1810, *Creek Letters* 2, 747; D. B. Mitchell to Hawkins, 19 October 1810, *Creek Letters* 2, 748. On more recent "continual thefts," see, for example, Sundry Inhabitants of Camden to James Jackson, undated 1798, *Creek Letters* 2, 521.

52. See, for example, the dispute over ownership of Nancy (thought to be a Cherokee), which required investigation of transactions in Tennessee and Virginia: Richard White to Meigs, 10 July 1812, Cherokee Agency, NARA, M208, Reel 5.

53. For an interesting dispute over slaves, see Mr. Tremble's demand for the return of ten slaves claimed by Griffin Minor (either by force or by indigenous consent): Tremble to Meigs, 23 April 1809, Cherokee Agency, NARA, M208, Reel 4; Griffin Minor's Claim, 5 May 1809, Cherokee Agency, NARA, M208, Reel 4. This instance is particularly interesting because Tremble advocates seizing the slaves with troops, and Griffin's claim had allegedly been concluded in Tennessee before this application to the agent.

54. Hawkins to Dearborn, 27 December 1805, *Letters, Journals and Writings of Benjamin Hawkins,* vol. 2, 503–504. This letter notes that Section 4 was intended to give effect to Article 9 of the Treaty of New York and that agents had been instructed to attain "'the best evidence in the power of the agent,'" of whether a settler "applicant is entitled to restitution . . . or Justice." This could not be done without the evidence of "red men."

55. See Chapter 2 for a further discussion. James Watson and James Ball to Meigs, 30 January 1802, Cherokee Agency, NARA, M208, Reel 1; Meigs to Colonel Overton, 10 June 1802, Cherokee Agency, NARA, M208, Reel 1 (regarding the practice in Gibraltar); and Meigs to Jenkins Whiteside, 22 February 1810, Cherokee Agency, NARA, M208, Reel 5.

56. See, for example, Cherokee James McIntosh's quest for compensation from the Creeks: James McIntosh to Meigs, 22 January 1810, Cherokee Agency, NARA, M208, Reel 5. See Perdue, *Cherokee Women,* 135–158.

57. Meigs's Journal of Fort Wilkinson, 19 May 1802, *Letters, Journals and Writings of Benjamin Hawkins,* vol. 2, 428–429.

58. Copy of a Letter of Deposition taken before James Vann, 28 January 1802, Cherokee Agency, NARA, M208, Reel 1.

59. James Vann to Meigs, 5 February 1802, Cherokee Agency, NARA, M208, Reel 1.

60. The Glass, Richard Justice, Turkiragreue, Big Bear and War'hach'ee to Governor Mitchell, 12 December 1812, *Cherokee Letters* 1, 114.

61. "Edward Scott, Wm [William] S. Kelly Counselors acting in behalf [of] the Cherokees case Cormick v Cherokee Nation on a reinvestigation of Cormicks claim before a board of Commissioners," Abstract of disbursements made by Return J. Meigs, 14 November 1812 to 1 December 1812, Penelope Johnson Allen Collection, pa0012, Hoskins Special Collections Library, Knoxville. Regarding the employment of "able attorneys," see Meigs to Eustis, 17 January 1813, Cherokee Agency, NARA, M208, Reel 6.

62. Taylor to Cherokee Nation, 10 March 1811, Cherokee Agency, NARA, M208, Reel 5.

63. Copy of a Report of a Board of Commissioners: Cormick v. Cherokees, and some notes, 22 December 1812, Cherokee Agency, NARA, M208, Reel 5.

64. M. Young, "The Exercise of Sovereignty in Cherokee Georgia," *Journal of the Early Republic* 10, no. 1 (1990): 44.

65. The roads formed part of a drive for national improvement under Jefferson: Henry deLoen Southerland Jr. and Jerry Elijah Brown, *The Federal Road through Georgia, the Creek Nation, and Alabama, 1806–1836* (Tuscaloosa and London: University of Alabama Press, 1989); L. J. Malone, *Opening the West: Federal Internal Improvements before 1860* (Westport, CT: Greenwood Press, 1998).

66. See, for example, "Sixth Compact with the Cherokee," *Cherokee Phoenix,* 21 October 1829, vol. 2, issue 28, 2, 2a. Contrast Tennessee obligations, outlined in Section 19, Trade and Intercourse Acts, F. Prucha, ed., *Documents of United States Indian Policy,* 3rd ed. (Lincoln: University of Nebraska Press, 2000), 20–21.

67. Wade Hampton was instructed to inform the Creeks that "the President can no longer with-hold from the Inhabitants, their right to pass to the waters leading to the Ocean. . . . [and] The United States must have roads for the purpose of transporting their Ordnance and military stores from one military post to another": William Eustis to Wade Hampton, 20 July 1811, in *The Territorial Papers of the United States: The Territory of Mississippi, 1809–1817,* vol. 6, comp. and ed. Clarence Edwin Carter (Washington, DC: Government Printing Office, 1938), 213–214.

68. Southerland and Brown, *Federal Road through Georgia,* 102–122.

69. Though the Creeks agreed to the establishment of a post road in 1806, a functional road was not built until 1811, so these sorts of issues arose during and after the War of 1812: for example, Dennison Darling to James Madison, 1 April 1812, in *The Papers of James Madison, Presidential Series,* vol. 4, ed. J. C. A. Stagg et al. (Charlottesville and London: University of Virginia Press, 1999), 280–281; Statement of Colonel John Lawson and Mr. McDuffir, 15 April 1813, *Creek Letters* 3, 778; Elijah Gordy to D. B. Mitchell, 17 May 1813, 781. On the targeting of "persons disposed to explore this new country" on the road, see Israel Pickens to Josiah Meigs, 4 April 1818, in *Territorial Papers: Alabama, 1817–1819,* vol. 18, 293–294.

70. On Earle's Waggons, see: John Lowry to Meigs, 8 February 1808, Cherokee Agency, NARA, M208, Reel 4; Charles Hicks and Ka'ti'hee to Black Fox, 15 February 1808, Cherokee Agency, NARA, M208, Reel 4; Elias Earle to Meigs, 18 February 1808, Cherokee Agency, NARA, M208, Reel 4; Deposition of William Brown, 15 February 1808, Cherokee Agency, NARA, M208, Reel 4; John Harrison to Meigs, 23 February 1808, Cherokee Agency, NARA, M208, Reel 4; William Shackleford's, Colonel Earle's Case, 14 October 1808, Cherokee Agency, NARA, M208, Reel 4; D. B. Mitchell to Thomas Cobb, 1 April 1811, Governor's Letter Books; D. B. Mitchell, 14 December 1809 to 26 October 1813 and Peter Early, 9 November 1813 to 17 May 1814, Record Group 001-01-001, Georgia Archives, 22.

71. The Postmaster General to Henry Dearborn, 12 March 1801, in *Territorial Papers: Mississippi, 1798–1817,* vol. 5, 118–119; From the Tennessee Congressional Delegation, 1 March 1810, in *Papers of James Madison,* vol. 4, 612–616; Eustis to Hampton, 20 July 1811, in *Territorial Papers: Mississippi,* vol. 6, 213–214; Petition to Congress by Inhabitants of St. Stephens, 29 December 1818, in *Territorial Papers: Alabama,* vol. 18, 504–505.

72. For example, M. Casey to Meigs, 18 November 1812, Cherokee Agency, NARA, M208, Reel 5, expressing his disillusionment with Meigs's summary proceedings, which turned out to be "More dilatory than a Bill in Chancery." For a call for summary means to recover property, see Richard Brown to Meigs, 21 June 1811, Cherokee Agency, NARA, M208 Reel 5; and see William Clark to William Lovely, 21 August 1814, Cherokee Agency, NARA, M208, Reel 6.

73. For example, Talk to the President from John McIntosh, 8 January 1808, Cherokee Agency, NARA, M208, Reel 4. Here Chief John McIntosh sought to demonstrate that the tribe could keep order on the road, reporting that they had a number of men in custody.

74. See, for example, Allan Gallatin's Report on Internal Improvements: "Roads and Canals. Communicated to the Senate, April 6, 1808," *American State Papers 037: Miscellaneous,* vol. 1, pub. no. 250, 724–921. For discussions of the limitations of the federal drive to build and maintain post roads in Indian Country in this period, see Timothy Pickering to Winthrop Sargent, 20 May 1799, *Territorial Papers: Mississippi,* vol. 5, 56–60; Postmaster General to William Piatt, 9 December 1805, *Territorial Papers: Mississippi,* vol. 5, 443–444; Postmaster General to Benjamin Hawkins, 24 April 1806, *Territorial Papers: Mississippi,* vol. 5, 459–461; Postmaster General to Benjamin Hawkins, 10 July 1806, in *Territorial Papers: Mississippi,* vol. 5, 470–471; Postmaster General to Joseph B. Varnum, *Territorial Papers: Mississippi,* vol. 5, 510–511; Postmaster General to Benjamin Hawkins, 21 February 1807, *Territorial Papers: Mississippi,* vol. 5, 516–517; Postmaster General to David Meriwether, *Territorial Papers: Mississippi,* vol. 5, 518–520. On the role of the post roads in the "communications revolution" in the United States from 1790 to 1840, see R. R. John, *Spreading the News: The American Postal System from Franklin to Morse* (Cambridge, MA: Harvard University Press, 1995), 47–63, 109–111. On the increase in funding for the roads under Jackson, see Malone, *Opening the West,* 45; and S. Minicucci, "Internal Improvements and the Union, 1790–1860," *Studies in American Political Development* 18, no. 02 (2005): 166.

75. Minicucci, "Internal Improvements and the Union," 160–185.

76. "Art. IV. Constitutional Interpretation: Roads and Canals," *United States Law Journal* 2 (1826): 257.

77. L. D. White, *The Jeffersonians: A Study in Administrative History, 1801–1829* (New York: Macmillan, 1959), 481.

78. Quoted by G. N. Lieber, "The Use of the Army in Aid of the Civil Power," *American Law Review* 32 (1898): 366–389. Also see Lieber regarding Army regulations authorizing the protection of mail routes (380).

79. Article 9, Treaty with the Cherokee 1791 (Holston), in Kappler, *Indian Affairs,* 30–31; Article 7, Treaty with the Creeks 1790 (New York), in Kappler, *Indian Affairs,* 27.

80. Extract from Articles of Agreement between the United States and the Cherokee Nation, 20 October 1803, Telamon Cuyler Collection, 81:21:05, Hargrett Library, University of Georgia.

81. Section 19, Trade and Intercourse Act 1802, in Prucha, *Documents,* 20–21.

82. United States v. Robert Fluker and James Morgan, December Term, 1810, United States Circuit Court, NARA, M1184, Reel 1, 241 and 246.

83. Parsons et al., "Decision."

84. Olive to Cormick, 28 December 1810, *Cherokee Letters* 1, 111.

85. Cormick to Eustis, 18 April 1811, *Cherokee Letters* 1, 107.

86. For federal correspondence tentatively supporting this conclusion, see Dearborn to Thomas H. Cushing, 18 July 1803, in *Territorial Papers: Mississippi,* vol. 5, 225: deploying soldiers to arrest "any persons who have or shall be guilty of murdering, robbing or in any way annoying the Post Riders."

87. See, for example, Silas Dinsmoor to John Armstrong, 4 August 1813, in *Territorial Papers: Mississippi,* vol. 6, 391.

88. For example, Strate v. A-1 Contractors, 530 U.S. 438 (1997).

89. For original printed version, see Proclamation, 4 May 1816, Wentworth Family Papers: Wentworth, D'Arcy Correspondence, 1809–1816, Mitchell Library A752, CY Reel 699, 205 (52) (hereafter cited as Wentworth Correspondence, ML A752). For handwritten copy, see *Original Documents on Aborigines and the Law,* 1790–1840, Document no. 6, Macquarie University, http://www.law.mq.edu.au/scnsw/Correspondence/index.htm (hereafter cited as *Original Documents on Aborigines,* doc. 6).

90. "Proclamation, May 1816," Wentworth Correspondence, ML A752; and *Original Documents on Aborigines,* doc. 6.

91. J. Connor, *The Australian Frontier Wars, 1788–1838* (Randwick: University of New South Wales Press, 2002), 22–34.

92. *Tanistry Case* (1608) Dav 28; 80 ER 516; *Calvin's Case* (1608) 7 Coke Report 1a, 77 ER 377. On the Irish context of this case, see H. S. Pawlisch, *Sir John Davies and the Conquest of Ireland: A Study in Legal Imperialism* (Cambridge: Cambridge University Press, 1985). On the persistence of this notion of "conquest" versus "settlement" in North America, see: J. P. Greene, *Peripheries and Center: Constitutional Development in the Extended Polities of the British Empire and the United States, 1607–1788* (London and Athens: University of Georgia Press, 1986), 43; G. Loughton, "Calvin's Case and the Origins of the Rule Governing 'Conquest' in English Law," *Australian Journal of Legal History* 8, no. 2 (2004): 150–180; and D. J. Hulsebosch, "The Ancient Constitution and the Expanding Empire: Sir Edward Coke's British Jurisprudence," *Law and History Review* 21, no. 3 (2003): 470–475. On change in legal frame at the end of the eighteenth century, see C. Yirush, "Conquest Theory and Imperial Governance in the Early Modern Anglo-American World" (paper presented at the Clark Library Conference on Imperial Models in the Early Modern World, Los Angeles, California, November

3–4, 2006); M. Connor, *The Invention of Terra Nullius: Historical and Legal Fictions on the Foundation of Australia* (Sydney: Macleay Press, 2005), 272–294. For the continued significance of the case of Tanistry, see S. Dorsett, "Since Time Immemorial: A Story of Common Law Jurisdiction, Native Title and the Case of Tanistry," *Melbourne University Law Review* 26 (2002): 32–59.

93. B. Buchan, "The Empire of Political Thought: Civilization, Savagery and Perceptions of Indigenous Government," *History of the Human Sciences* 18, no. 2 (2005): 1–22.

94. R. v. Murrell, 1 Legge 72, NSW SC.

95. However, note the disruptive effect of disease on local indigenous communities: W. Tench, *Sydney's First Four Years: Being a Reprint of a Narrative of the Expedition to Botany Bay and a Complete Account of the Settlement at Port Jackson,* ed. L. F. Fitzhardinge (Sydney: Angus & Robertson in Association with the Royal Australian Historical Society, 1961), 134–154.

96. L. R. Hiatt, *Arguments about Aborigines: Australia and the Evolution of Social Anthropology* (Cambridge: Cambridge University Press, 1996), 85–99.

97. Hiatt, *Arguments about Aborigines,* 86.

98. H. Reynolds, *Aboriginal Sovereignty: Reflections on Race, State and Nation* (St. Leonards, NSW: Allen & Unwin, 1996), 63; A. W. Howitt, *The Native Tribes of South-East Australia* (Canberra: Aboriginal Studies Press, 1996), 295–296.

99. See Howitt, *Native Tribes of South-East Australia,* 321.

100. Howitt, *Native Tribes of South-East Australia,* 334–347.

101. For example, Tench, *Sydney's First Four Years,* 177.

102. Hiatt, *Arguments about Aborigines,* 84.

103. For example: *Sydney Gazette,* 18 March 1804, 2, 3; 21 October 1804, 3, 3; 13 January 1805, 2, 2; 17 March 1805, 3, 1; 24 March 1805, 3, 1 (may have been a domestic dispute); 31 March 1805, 3, 1; 14 July 1805 2, 1; 10 November 1805, 2, 2; 15 December 1805, 2, 2; 29 December 1805, 2, 2; 12 January 1806, 1, 3; 2 February 1806, 2, 2; 16 March 1806, 2, 2; 23 March 1806, 2, 2; 25 December 1808, 2, 2; 1 January 1808, 2, 2 (may have been a drunken brawl); 15 January 1809, 2, 1; 27 November 1813, 1, 2. For memoir accounts and an excellent description of Aboriginal contests in this period as late as 1824, see G. Karskens, *The Colony: A History of Early Sydney* (St. Leonards, NSW: Allen & Unwin, 2009), 439–446.

104. *Sydney Gazette,* 16 October 1803, 2, 1.

105. *Sydney Gazette,* 29 December 1805, 2, 2.

106. See discussion of Aboriginal jurisdiction in *Sydney Gazette,* 15 January 1809, 2, 1.

107. D. Collins, *An Account of the English Colony in New South Wales, with Remarks on the Dispositions, Customs, Manners, etc. of the Native Inhabitants of That Country,* facsimile ed., vol. 1 (London: T. Cadell and W. Davies, 1798), e.g., 328–329, 408; and see *Sydney Gazette,* 16 October 1803, 2, 1; 17 March 1805, 3, 1; 29 December 1805, 2, 2; and Karskens, *The Colony,* 441.

108. Samuel Smith quoted in Karskens, *The Colony,* 443.

109. *Sydney Gazette,* 21 October 1804, 3, 2.

110. *Sydney Gazette,* 15 January 1809, 2, 1.

111. R. v. Mow-Watty, September 27 or 28, 1816, Decisions of the Superior Courts of New South Wales, 1788–1899, published by the Division of Law, Macquarie University, http://www.law.mq.edu.au/scnsw/.

112. Karskens, *The Colony,* 197.

113. *Sydney Gazette,* 23 August 1817, 3, 1.

114. *Sydney Gazette,* 31 October 1818, 2, 1.

115. R. v. Ballard or Barret, April 21 or 23, 1929, Decisions of the Superior Courts of New South Wales, 1788–1899, published by the Division of Law, Macquarie University, http://www.law.mq.edu.au/scnsw/.

116. Compare Charter of Georgia, *America's Founding Charters: Primary Documents of Colonial and Revolutionary Era Governance,* vol. 2, ed. Jon L. Wakelyn (Westport, CT: Greenwood Press, 2006), 511–521; with *Charter of Justice* 1787, *Historical Records of Australia,* series 4, vol. 1, 6–12 (hereafter cited as *HRA* 4:1).

117. L. Ford and B. Salter, "From Pluralism to Territorial Sovereignty: The 1816 Trial of Mow-watty in the Superior Court of New South Wales," *Indigenous Law Journal* 7 (2008): 67-86.

118. For a discussion of early acts of violence, see Connor, *The Australian Frontier Wars,* 22–34.

119. Tench, *Sydney's First Four Years,* 135.

120. 26 May 1792, Richard Atkins Journal, 1792–1810, Mitchell Library MSS737, FM3/585, 15–16 (hereafter cited as Atkins Journal, ML MSS737).

121. Contrast Atkins's endorsement of wholesale retaliatory violence against Aborigines in 1805: "Atkins Opinion on Treatment to Be Adopted towards the Natives," *HRA* 1:5, 502–504.

122. Tench, *Sydney's First Four Years,* 186–189.

123. Hiatt, *Arguments about Aborigines,* 81–82. On Aboriginal violence as war, see Connor, *The Australian Frontier Wars,* 17–34. On the meaning of violence and the warped gaze of settler observers, I. Clendinnen, *Dancing with Strangers: Europeans and Australians at First Contact* (Cambridge and New York: Cambridge University Press, 2005), 18–36, 57–81, 96.

124. See article protesting this assumption: *Sydney Gazette,* 21 April 1805, 2, 2.

125. Hunter to Portland, 2 January 1800, *HRA* 1:2, 402–403.

126. For example, Marsden's negotiations: *Sydney Gazette,* 5 May 1805, 1, 1; negotiations by magistrates, attempting to discover grievances: *Sydney Gazette,* 22 December 1805, 2, 1. For King's negotiations, see King to Hobart, 20 December 1804, *HRA* 1:5, 166–167; King to Camden, 30 April 1805, *HRA* 1:5, 306.

127. *Sydney Gazette,* 16 November 1811, 2, 1.

128. In his original orders, Darling declared that Aborigines could "seize and deliver up any Men, who shall ill-treat them"—a provision that the Colonial Office disapproved: Bathurst to Ralph Darling, 3 October 1826, *HRA* 1:12,

600. On Darling's injunctions to residents: Darling to the Landholders at Hunter's River, 5 September 1826, *HRA* 1:12: 576–577. Discussed further in Chapters 5 and 7 of this volume. For example, a meaningful relationship with his reputed victim absolved the Aborigine Foley of murder: R. v. Foley, August 16, 1824, Decisions of the Superior Courts of New South Wales, 1788–1899, published by the Division of Law, Macquarie University, http://www.law.mq.edu.au/scnsw/.

129. J. Gascoigne and P. Curthoys, *The Enlightenment and the Origins of European Australia* (Cambridge: Cambridge University Press, 2005). See debates over the convict origins of New South Wales in G. Whitlock and G. Reekie, *Uncertain Beginnings: Debates in Australian Studies* (St. Lucia: University of Queensland Press, 1993).

130. Arthur Phillip to Grenville, 17 June 1790, *HRA* 1:1, 179; General Order, 9 November *HRA* 1:3, 691. And see *Sydney Gazette*, 3 March 1805, 2, 3; 16 November 1806, 1, 3; 8 March 1807, 2, 1; 10 December 1809, 1, 3.

131. SR NSW, Colonial Secretary's Correspondence: Main Series, Commandant of Moreton Bay to Colonial Secretary, 27 February 1833 (and following), [33/1930]; and see SR NSW: Entry 26, 29 January 1933, Schedules of Papers Presented to the Governor for Decision, [4/441].

132. On the murder of stockmen precipitating retaliation, see: Government and General Orders, 1 May 1801, *HRA* 1:3, 250; and *Sydney Gazette*, 28 April 1805, 1, 1 and 5 May 1805, 3, 2. On the murder of families and their servants precipitating retaliation, see: Draft Proclamation, Diary entry, 10 April 1816, Macquarie Papers: Diary, 10 April 1816 to 1 July 1818, Mitchell Library A773, CYA773, Reel 301, 238 (Macquarie Diary, ML A773). See Chapter 2 for more examples.

133. On the use of an Aboriginal tracker to recapture convict escapees, see *Sydney Gazette*, 13 January 1805, 2, 2. On the return of a stolen boat by Philip or Mugalong, Charcoal Will, Jack or Towroa, Jemmy or Manilong, and Jemmy or Bunbungra, see John Andrews to D'Arcy Wentworth and Simeon Lord, Certificate, 24 March 1820, Wentworth Correspondence, ML A753, 393 (295). See SR NSW: Captain Shaw and Wallis' List of Aboriginal Guides, April 1816, [4/1798], Reel 6065, 45; Diary entry, 25 May 1816, Macquarie Diary, ML A773, 252.

134. On the appointment of the Aborigine Jack (alias Nagga) as a constable in the district of Evan, see SR NSW: CSP, 1788–1825, Constable at Evan to Colonial Secretary, 11 July 1822, [4/424], Reel 6039, 84.

135. On later attempts to draw spatial boundaries of governance, see, for example: SR NSW: Colonial Secretary's Correspondence, Commissioner of Crown Lands, 5 March 1844, Special Bundles: Papers Relating to the Regulation of Squatting, Part I, 1839–1844, [5/4774.2]. Much of this file is devoted to ordering squatters. This report in particular stresses the problem of "introducing outside the boundaries improper and troublesome characters."

136. For later attempts, see generally Mitchell Library: Colonial Secretary's Correspondence, Special Bundles: Regarding Aborigines and Native Police, 1835–1844, [4/1135.1].

4. Legality and Lawlessness

1. For a recent discussion of the importance of vengeance in the law of justification, see J. Q. Whitman, "Between Self-Defense and Vengeance/Between Social Contract and Monopoly of Violence," *Tulsa Law Review* 39 (2004): 901–923. For a detailed historical account, see J. Horder, *Provocation and Responsibility* (Oxford, UK: Clarendon Press, 1992).

2. On diversity of settlers in North America, see C. L. Tomlins, "The Legal Cartography of Colonization, the Legal Polyphony of Settlement: English Intrusions on the American Mainland in the Seventeenth Century," *Law and Social Inquiry* 26, no. 2 (2001): 315–372. On the openness of Anglophone institutions, see J. Belich, "Liberty and Cultural Transmission in the British Empire," in *Liberty Fund Symposium* (Cincinnati, Ohio, 2007).

3. P. Karsten, *Between Law and Custom: "High" and "Low" Legal Cultures in the Lands of the British Diaspora—The United States, Canada, Australia, and New Zealand, 1600–1900* (Cambridge: Cambridge University Press, 2002); J. C. Weaver, *The Great Land Rush and the Making of the Modern World, 1650–1900* (Montreal: McGill Queens University Press, 2003). See also B. Kercher, *An Unruly Child: A History of Law in Australia* (St. Leonards, NSW: Allen & Unwin, 1995).

4. G. E. Dowd, *War under Heaven: Pontiac, the Indian Nations, and the British Empire* (Baltimore, MD: Johns Hopkins University Press, 2002), 174–212; C. Cumfer, *Separate Peoples, One Land: The Minds of Cherokees, Blacks, and Whites on the Tennessee Frontier* (Chapel Hill: University of North Carolina Press, 2007), 64–75, 90–98; C. Cumfer, "Local Origins of National Indian Policy: Cherokee and Tennessean Ideas about Sovereignty and Nationhood, 1790–1811," *Journal of the Early Republic* 23, no. 1 (2003): 21–46. See also essays collected in W. A. Pencak and D. K. Richter, *Friends and Enemies in Penn's Woods: Indians, Colonists, and the Racial Construction of Pennsylvania* (University Park: Pennsylvania State University Press, 2004).

5. R. Foster, A. Nettelbeck, and R. Hosking, *Fatal Collisions: The South Australian Frontier and the Violence of Memory* (Kent Town, ZA: Wakefield Press, 2001), 7. Contrast Windschuttle, who argues that the rule of law governed colonial Australian frontiers: K. Windschuttle, *The Fabrication of Aboriginal History* (Sydney: Macleay Press, 2002), 186.

6. Described as a "civil officer" by David Blackshear, JP, who gathered evidence of the crime on his own farm and sent it to Governor John Milledge: David Blackshear to Governor Milledge, 23 December 1802, in *Creek Indian Letters, Talks and Treaties, 1705–1839*, vol. 2, bound transcripts, Works Progress Administration (WPA) Project No. 665-34-3-224, ed. L. F. Hays (Atlanta: Georgia Archives, 1939), 651 (hereafter cited as *Creek Letters* 2, 651). Described as constable by Hawkins: Hawkins to Milledge, 6 September 1803, in *Letters, Journals and Writings of Benjamin Hawkins*, vol. 2, ed. C. L. Grant, (Savannah, GA: Beehive, 1980), 460. The reference to the incident here is somewhat vague: "I am also requested by the town of Cussetuh to inform you that the man shot in Washington by the Constable while under his care, had a gun which would have been of use to his family."

7. Deposition of Abraham Blackshear, 28 February 1802, *Creek Letters* 2, 654.

8. Deposition of James Bush Jr, 23 December 1802, *Creek Letters* 2, 652.

9. Benjamin Hawkins to Milledge, 3 January 1803, in *Letters of Benjamin Hawkins, 1797–1815*, bound transcripts, WPA Project No. 5993, ed. L. F. Hays (Atlanta: Georgia Archives, 1939) (hereafter cited as *Letters of Benjamin Hawkins*, GA).

10. "[Legal opinion in the case of] Benjamin Harrison, 1796 Feb. 23, Louisville, [Georgia]/[signed by] Henry G. Caldwell, D[avid] B. Mitchell, Ben[jamin] Taliaferro, [and] Peter L. Van Alen," 23 February 1796, Telamon Cuyler Collection, 77:32:07, Hargrett Library, University of Georgia (hereafter cited as "Legal Opinion in the Case of Benjamin Harrison," Telamon Cuyler Collec., 77:32:07).

11. Washington County Court records do not survive for this period, but there is no indication in other records that the case went to trial.

12. A. Clayton, *The Office and Duty of a Justice of the Peace, and a Guide to Clerks, Constables, Coroners, Executors, Administrators, Guardians, Sheriffs, Tax-collectors, and Receivers, and Other Civil Officers, according to the Laws of the State of Georgia . . .* (Milledgeville, GA: Grantland, 1819), 18–19, 192–199. See also Section 14, Trade and Intercourse Act 1802, F. P. Prucha, *Documents of United States Indian Policy* (Lincoln: University of Nebraska Press, 1990), 19–20.

13. Compare W. H. Plunkett, *The Australian Magistrate: A Guide to the Duties of a Justice of the Peace for the Colony of New South Wales* (Sydney: Anne Howe, 1835), 235–239. See also B. J. Brown, "The Demise of Chance Medley and the Recognition of Provocation as a Defence to Murder in English Law," *American Journal of Legal History* 7 (1963): 310–318; M. J. Wiener, "Judges v. Jurors: Courtroom Tensions in Murder Trials and the Law of Criminal Responsibility in Nineteenth-Century England," *Law and History Review* 17, no. 3 (1999): 467–506.

14. Brown, "The Demise of Chance Medley," 310–313.

15. On the resistance of jurors in the United Kingdom to murder convictions generally, see Wiener, "Judges v. Jurors," 467–506. On the role of the jury as populist control on the judiciary in the early national United States, see J. P. Reid, *Controlling the Law: Legal Politics in Early National New Hampshire* (DeKalb: Northern Illinois University Press, 2004).

16. Clayton, *Georgia Justice*, 192–199.

17. For eighteenth-century iterations of settler retaliation: Dowd, *War under Heaven*, 174–212; Cumfer, "Local Origins of National Indian Policy," 21–46; J. Smolenski, "The Death of Sawantaeny and the Problem of Justice on the Frontier," in Pencak and Richter, *Friends and Enemies in Penn's Woods*, 104–128; L. M. Waddell, "Justice, Retribution, and the Case of John Toby," in Pencak and Richter, *Friends and Enemies in Penn's Woods*, 129–143; K. Camenzind, "Violence, Patriarchy, and the Paxton Boys," in Pencak and Richter, *Friends and Enemies in Penn's Woods*, 201–220.

18. Section 10, Trade and Intercourse Law, 1802, requires settlers to obtain a special license to buy a horse from an Indian. This breach was pointed out in

Hawkins to John Milledge, 3 January 1803, *Letters, Journals and Writings of Benjamin Hawkins*, vol. 2, 453.

19. Hawkins to Milledge, 18 August 1803, *Letters of Benjamin Hawkins*, GA. See also R. F. Ethridge, *Creek Country: The Creek Indians and Their World* (Chapel Hill: University of North Carolina Press, 2003), 175–194.

20. "[Petition on behalf of William Hodge] Apr. 1799, Jackson County, [Georgia to] Governor [of Georgia] James Jackson," Telamon Cuyler Collec., 44:05:02, Hargrett Library, University of Georgia (hereafter cited as "Petition on Behalf of William Hodge," Telamon Cuyler Collec., 44:05:02).

21. William Melton to John Milledge, 3 September 1804, *Creek Letters 2*, 704. See also John McAllister to Milledge, 12 August 1804, *Creek Letters 2*, 698; Deposition of Joseph White, 9 August 1804, *Creek Letters 2*, 697; William Melton and G. W. Foster to Milledge, 15 August 1804, *Creek Letters 2*, 701; Statement of Henry Walker, 20 August 1804, *Creek Letters 2*, 702; Warrant for arrest of Milligan Patrick or Kilpatrick, 21 August 1804, *Creek Letters 2*, 702; Statement of Thomas Townson, 23 August 1804, *Creek Letters 2*, 703.

22. Meigs to Black Fox, 9 April 1808, Records of the Cherokee Indian Agency in Tennessee 1801–1835, National Archives and Records Administration (NARA) Microfilm Publication M208, Reel 4 (hereafter cited as Records of the Cherokee Agency, NARA, M208, Reel 4).

23. Jackson to McHenry, 24 January 1798, *Governor's Letter Books George Matthews, 20 August 1795 to 17 January 1796 and James Jackson, 24 January 1798 to 3 January 1799* (WPA Project No. 5993, 1939), 65 (hereafter cited as *Governor's Letter Books: Matthews and Jackson*). See also: D. B. Mitchell to the Judges of the Inferior Court of Randolph County, 3 May 1811, Governor's Letter Books, D. B. Mitchell, 14 December 1809 to 26 October 1813, and Peter Early, 9 November 1813 to 17 May 1814, Record Group 001-01-001, Georgia Archives, 30 (hereafter cited as *Governor's Letter Books: Mitchell and Early*). Here Mitchell urges judges to have settlers make restitution of stolen articles, rather than be tried under federal jurisdiction for theft.

24. See, for example, Meigs's list of crimes not tried or acquitted in Tennessee and Georgia: Verso of Some Reflections, 19 March 1812, Records of the Cherokee Agency, NARA, M208, Reel 5.

25. See, for example: Section 27, "An Act To revise, amend and consolidate the several Militia laws of this state, and to adapt the same to the act of the Congress of the United States," 45/48, Assented to December 1807, Acts of the General Assembly of the State of Georgia; Passed in November and December, 1807, vol. 1, 136, *Georgia Legislative Documents*, University of Georgia Libraries, http://www.galileo.usg.edu/express?link=zlgl (hereafter cited as *Georgia Legislative Documents*).

26. Jackson to James Ford, 21 February 1798, *Governor's Letter Books: Matthews and Jackson,* 130.

27. Section 15, Trade and Intercourse Act, 1802, F. Prucha, ed., *Documents of United States Indian Policy*, 3rd ed. (Lincoln: University of Nebraska Press, 2000), 19–20.

28. Survey of Minutes of the U.S. Circuit Court for the District of Georgia, 1790–1842, and Index to Plaintiffs and Defendants in the Circuit Courts, 1790–1860, NARA Microfilm Publication M1184, Reels 1–2 (hereafter cited as U.S. Circuit Court, NARA, M1184, Reels 1–2). This survey includes two writs of habeas corpus and excluding recognizances, ship libels, and rescue prosecutions.

29. U.S. v. Richard Blackstocks, 15 December 1824; U.S. v. Abraham Leathers, 15 December 1824, U.S. v. John Martin, 15 December 1824, U.S. Circuit Court, NARA, M1184, Reel 2, vol. 6, 87, 94, 100–101. The first two were found guilty but commended for mercy; John Martin failed to turn up for his trial.

30. U.S. v. William Yarborough, Mial Monk, Ephraim Moore and Obadiah Morris, November Term 1797, Index Books, 1789–1928, and Minutes and Bench Dockets, 1789–1870, for the U.S. District Court for the Southern District of Georgia, 1789–1928, NARA, Microform Publication 1172, Reel 1, vol. 1, 178–180 (hereafter cited as U.S. District Court, NARA, M1172, Reel 1, vol. 1, 178–180).

31. Jackson to McHenry, 24 January 1798, *Governor's Letter Books: Matthews and Jackson,* 64.

32. Hawkins to Eustis, 24 December 1810, *Letters, Journals and Writings of Benjamin Hawkins,* vol. 2, 578.

33. U.S. v. William Hammet, U.S. v. Gilbert Gay, U.S. v. John Onton, U.S. v. John Wincher, U.S. v. John Buster, U.S. v. James Easley (also Beasley), U.S. v. Thomas Haynes, U.S. v. John Gothard, U.S. v. Edward West (also Westward), U.S. v. Waller Darry, U.S. v. Pains Thompson, U.S. v. Michael Brouard—all December 1810 Term, U.S. Circuit Court, NARA, M1184, Reel 1, vol. 4, 241–243. Note that Michael Brouard was tried for arming a vessel, and so was not a squatter. There is no record in these minutes of these men pleading before the court, let alone standing trial.

34. U.S. v. Turner Hunt, Isaac Simons, Wm Sherlock Sterling Abernethie & John Tripple, April Term, 1800, U.S. Circuit Court, NARA, M1184, Reel 1, pp&132; they were fined $8.

35. Hawkins to Eustis, 24 December 1810, *Letters, Journals and Writings of Benjamin Hawkins,* vol. 2, 578.

36. Meigs to Eustis, 5 April 1811, Records of the Cherokee Agency, NARA, M208, Reel 5.

37. E. G. Meigs to Brahan, 23 September 1808, Records of the Cherokee Agency, NARA, M208, Reel 4.

38. Meigs to William Blount, 24 January 1812, Records of the Cherokee Agency, NARA, M208, Reel 5. Meigs notes that this is a copy in substance only.

39. Meigs protested the cynicism of squatters in 1805 and 1810: Meigs to Henry Dearborn, 30 July 1806, in *Cherokee Indian Letters, Talks and Treaties, 1786–1838,* vol. 1, ed. L. F. Hays, (WPA Project No. 4341, 1939), 81–82; Meigs to Eustis, 13 April 1810, Records of the Cherokee Agency, NARA, M208, Reel 5.

40. Capt. Jonas Fauche to George Matthews, 19 October 1794, *Creek Letters 2,* 418.

41. Hawkins to John Milledge, 15 July 1802, in *Letters, Journals and Writings of Benjamin Hawkins,* vol. 2, 450. Another two settlers escaped and were being pursued.

42. James Jackson to Andrew Burnett and John Clement, 3 February 1798, *Governor's Letter Books: Matthews and Jackson,* 87.

43. A nolle prosequi was entered on the record in November 1800: U.S. v. John de Priest, William Boyd, John Mucklehanon and Robert Montgomery, November Term 1800, U.S. Circuit Court, NARA, M1184, Reel 1, 167, 172–173.

44. U.S. v. John de Priest, William Boyd, John Mucklehanon and Robert Montgomery, 23 April 1800, 25 April 1800, U.S. Circuit Court, NARA, M1184, Reel 1, vol. 3, 167 and 181.

45. Sarah was "enlarged on her owner" in December 1800. John escaped, December 1802. U.S. v. John Stewart and Sarah, November Term 1800, December Term 1801, December Term 1802, U.S. Circuit Court, NARA, M1184, Reel 1, vol. 3, 211, 327.

46. U.S. v. George Peoples, December Term 1802, U.S. Circuit Court, NARA, M1184, Reel 1, vol. 3, 329, 331.

47. U.S. v. Robert Fluker and James Morgan, December Term 1810, U.S. Circuit Court, NARA, M1184, Reel 1, vol. 4, 241, 246.

48. U.S. v. Prior Crittenden, December Term 1812, U.S. Circuit Court, NARA, M1184, Reel 1, vol. 4, 325, 327.

49. U.S. v. John Hand, May Term 1814, U.S. Circuit Court, NARA, M1184, Reel 1, vol. 4, 400.

50. U.S. v. John Watkins, Writ of Habeas Corpus, May Term 1794, U.S. Circuit Court, NARA, M1184, Reel 1, vol. 2, 91 & 94; U.S. v. George Peoples, December Term, U.S. Circuit Court, NARA, M1184, Reel 1, vol. 3, 318, 329–331. For correspondence protesting federal action against squatters, see Buckner Harris to Meigs, 14 July 1808, Records of the Cherokee Agency, NARA, M208, Reel 4.

51. See Jackson to McHenry, 1 June 1798, *Governor's Letter Books: Matthews and Jackson,* 173, which reports that Gaither had refused to comply with the process executed on him by the sheriff of Hancock. See also F. P. Prucha, *The Great Father: The United States Government and the American Indians* (London and Lincoln: University of Nebraska Press, 1984), 112.

52. U.S. v. Watkins, 1 May 1794, 2 May 1794, U.S. Circuit Court, NARA, M1184, Reel 1, 91–94.

53. John Macpherson Berrien went on to be Andrew Jackson's attorney general, where he penned some opinions highly detrimental to indigenous rights; see Chapter 6.

54. U.S. v. Fluker and James Morgan, 17 December 1810, Circuit Court, NARA, M1184, Reel 1, vol. 4, 241, 246. This finding was reiterated in U.S. v. Bailey, 24 Fed. Case. 937, no. 14,495 C.C. D. Tenn (Circuit Court, District of Tennessee) (1834). For other pleas to jurisdiction, see William Hill v. David Blackshear, December Term 1802, U.S. Circuit Court, NARA, M1184, Reel 1, vol. 3, 329, U.S. v. George Peoples, December Term 1802, U.S. Circuit Court, NARA, M1184, Reel 1, 329, 331.

55. "An Act to add all that part of the unlocated territory of this state which lies without the limits of the present counties, to the county of Jasper, for the purpose of giving the Courts jurisdiction of crimes committed by white persons against white persons in said territory, and for other purposes," 27/50, Assented to 23 November 1814, Acts of the General Assembly of the State of Georgia; Passed in October and November, 1814; vol. 1, 41, *Georgia Legislative Documents;* http://www.galileo.usg.edu/express?link=zlgl. Amended by "An Act to amend an act, entitled an act, to add that part of the unlocated Territory of this state, which lies without the limits of the present counties, to the county of Jasper, passed the 23d day of November, 1814," 19/90, Assented to 18 December 1816, Acts of the General Assembly of the State of Georgia, Passed in November and December 1816, vol. 1, 34, *Georgia Legislative Documents,* http://www.galileo.usg.edu/express?link=zlgl.

56. Statement based on survey of court records in M1184 to 1832: U.S. Circuit Court, NARA, M1184, Reel 1 & 2. General Crimes Act 1817: "An Act to provide for the punishment of crimes and offences committed within Indian boundaries. (a)," Statute II, 3 March 1817, 3 Stat. 1811–1823, 383. See discussion of the act in U.S. v. Bailey 24 Fed. Cas. 937, no. 14,495 C.C. D. Tenn. 1834.

57. E. Surrency, *The Creation of a Judicial System: The History of Georgia Courts, 1733 to Present* (Holmes Beach, FL: Gaunt, 2001), 65–83.

58. *Thomas M. C. Harris vs Benjamin Wofford and Nathaniel Wofford,* October Term, Franklin Superior Court Records, Miscellaneous, Record Group 159-01-059, Georgia Archives (Franklin Superior Court Records, Misc., GA). In 1806, Wafford's settlement in the Cherokee Nation was legally incorporated into the state of Georgia: "An Act to extend the operation of the laws of this State, [illegible text] the persons resident in Wafford's Settlement, and to organize the same," 28/43, Assented to 8 December 1806, Acts of the General Assembly of the State of Georgia; Passed in November and December, 1806, vol. 1, 46, *Georgia Legislative Documents,* http://www.galileo.usg.edu/express?link=zlgl.

59. Elisha Simmonds v. Reuben Daniel, April Term 1814, Franklin Superior Court Records, Misc, Georgia Archives.

60. For other contemporary examples of militia revolt in Georgia's Indian Country, see: R. K. Murdoch, "Elijah Clarke and the Anglo-American Designs on East Florida," *Georgia Historical Quarterly* 35 (1951): 174–190; George Matthews to Henry Knox, 19 August 1794, *American State Papers: Indian Affairs,* vol. 1, pub. no. 52, 495 (and following).

61. Nathan Atkinson and Joshua Morgan and others, 21 September 1793, *Creek Letters* 1, 342.

62. Moses Burnett, Will Dawson, James McLeod, Opinion of the Court of Inquiry Respecting the Death of Cornel, 25 October 1793, *Creek Letters* 1, 348.

63. Matthews to James Seagrove, 20 December 1795, *Governor's Letter Books: Matthews and Jackson,* 57.

64. "Petition on Behalf of William Hodge," Telamon Cuyler Collec., 44:05:02.

65. "Legal Opinion in the Case of Benjamin Harrison," Telamon Cuyler Collec., 77:32:07.

66. Jackson to Judges of the Inferior Court of Montgomery County, 1 February 1798, *Governor's Letter Books: Matthews and Jackson,* 80.

67. Verso of Meigs's Reflections, 19 March 1812, Records of the Cherokee Agency, NARA, M208, Reel 5.

68. D. B. Mitchell to Justices of the Inferior Court of Randolph County, 3 May 1811, *Governor's Letter Books: Mitchell and Early,* 30.

69. On Debtors taking refuge in the Cherokee Nation, see: Samuel Love to Return J. Meigs, 13 July 1808, Cherokee Agency, NARA, M208, Reel 4; King and Montgomery to Meigs, 14 July 1808, Cherokee Agency, NARA, M208, Reel 4; John Nichols to Meigs, 14 July 1808, Cherokee Agency, NARA, M208, Reel 4; James Montgomery to Meigs, 14 July 1808, Cherokee Agency, NARA, M208, Reel 4; and John Thombury to Meigs, 14 July 1808, Cherokee Agency, NARA, M208, Reel 4. On uncertainties over the service of legal process in Indian Country, see Judge Toulmin to William Lattimore, 6 December 1805, in *The Territorial Papers of the United States: The Territory of Mississippi, 1798–1817,* vol. 5, comp. and ed. Clarence Edwin Carter (Washington, DC: Government Printing Office, 1937), 431–438, esp. 436.

70. Reported in James Jackson to Edward Telfair, 9 May 1793, *Creek Letters* 1, 30.

71. Capt. William Melton to Jared Irwin, 27 July 1796, *Creek Letters* 2, 482.

72. W. Coner, Batt Wyche John Hill Bryant to Jared Irwin, 2 July 1807, *Creek Letters* 2, 720.

73. "Letter from a Committee appointed by the Citizens of Hartford in Pulaski County addressed to His Excellency Governor Mitchell on the Subject of public [unclear: Arms?]," 1 September 1812, Telamon Cuyler Collec. 46:06:05, Hargrett Library, University of Georgia. For invocation of natural law rights to self-defense in Tennessee, see C. D. Cumfer, "'The Idea of Mankind is so Various': An Intellectual History of Tennessee, 1768–1810" (Ph.D. diss., University of California, 2001), 156; see, generally, Cumfer, *Separate Peoples, One Land.*

74. Jackson to McHenry, 15 February 1798, *Governor's Letter Books: Matthews and Jackson,* 106.

75. On instructions for procuring warrants, see Matthews to Matthew McAllister, 18 December 1795, *Governor's Letter Books: Matthews and Jackson,* 53–54. On the dearth of evidence, see Matthews to James Seagrove, 20 December 1795, *Governor's Letter Books: Matthews and Jackson,* 56. "[S]omething must be done, or our prospects of a Treaty . . . will be blasted": Matthews to General Irwin, 19 December 1795, *Governor's Letter Books: Matthews and Jackson,* 55.

76. Jackson to Hawkins, 3 February 1798, *Governor's Letter Books: Matthews and Jackson,* 90.

77. Meigs, Reflections, 19 March 1812, Records of the Cherokee Agency, NARA, M208, Reel 5.

78. For example, T. Pickering to Matthews, 12 November 1795, *Creek Letters* 2, 456.

79. Deposition of James Bush Jr., 23 December 1802, *Creek Letters* 2, 652; compare Deposition of Abraham Blackshear, 28 February 1802, *Creek Letters* 2, 654.

80. Collins's account suggests that two settlers were killed: D. Collins, *An Account of the English Colony in New South Wales, with Remarks on the Dispositions, Customs, Manners, etc. of the Native Inhabitants of that Country,* facsimile ed., vol. 2 (London: T. Cadell and W. Davies, 1798), 281–282.

81. John Hunter to Portland, 2 January 1800, *Historical Records of Australia: Series 1, Governors' Despatches to and from England,* vol. 2 (Sydney: The Library Committee of the Commonwealth Parliament, 1914), 405 (hereafter cited as *HRA* 1:2, 422).

82. Extract from Orderly Book, 22 February 1797, *Original Documents on Aborigines and the Law,* 1790–1840, Document no. 1, Macquarie University, http://www.law.mq.edu.au/scnsw/Correspondence/index.htm (hereafter cited as *Original Documents on Aborigines,* doc. 1).

83. Hunter to Portland, 2 Jan 1800, *HRA* 1:2, 422, 401–403.

84. Hobart to Philip King, 30 January 1802, *HRA* 1:3, 366–367.

85. See R. v. Lowe, May 18 or 23, 1827, Decisions of the Superior Courts of New South Wales, 1788–1899, published by the Division of Law, Macquarie University, http://www.law.mq.edu.au/scnsw/.

86. Plunkett, *The Australian Magistrate,* 239. Regarding the emergence of the modern law of excusable homicide in England, see G. Binder, "The Rhetoric of Motive and Intent," *Buffalo Criminal Law Review* 6, no. 1 (2002): 1–96.

87. Plunkett, *The Australian Magistrate,* 236.

88. Plunkett, *The Australian Magistrate,* 234: "Aboriginal Natives of the Colony are within 'the King's Peace,' and the unlawful killing of any of them is as much a murder, as the killing of any other of the King's subjects."

89. Plunkett, *The Australian Magistrate,* 238.

90. S. L. Harring, "The Killing Time: A History of Aboriginal Resistance in Colonial Australia," *Ottawa Law Review* 26 (1994): 414.

91. *Sydney Gazette,* 22 July 1804, 3, 2; and for similar reports of shootings not discussed here, see *Sydney Gazette,* 2 September 1804, 2, 2; 6 October 1805, 2, 2; 30 October 1808, 2, 2; 8 October 1809, 2, 2.

92. *Sydney Gazette,* 8 September 1805, Supplement, 2.

93. Deposition of William Witticomb, 2 February 1806, *Original Documents on Aborigines,* doc. 4a.

94. *Sydney Gazette,* 1 October 1809, 2, 1.

95. Diary entry, 26 September 1794, Richard Atkins Journal, 1792–1810, Mitchell Library MSS737, FM3/585, 180.

96. King to Hobart, 20 December 1804, *HRA* 1:5, 166–167.

97. State Records, New South Wales (SR NSW): Unsigned Court Report, 5 December 1825, Governor: Copies of Letters Received from Officials and Private Persons, July–December 1825, 4/1672, 47. The Burraberongal tribe of the Dharug people lived at Windsor and were likely involved in this incident: J. Connor, *The Australian Frontier Wars, 1788–1838* (Randwick, NSW: University of New South Wales Press, 2002), 37; David Horton, *Aboriginal Australia* (Acton, ACT: AIATSIS, 2000).

98. Enclosed with Hunter to Portland, *HRA* 1:2, 404–405.

99. *HRA* 1:2, 406.

100. *HRA* 1:2, 406.

101. *HRA* 1:2, 406.

102. *HRA* 1:2, 417.

103. *HRA* 1:2, 410.

104. Five Islands or Illawarra Aborigines were of the Tharawal people: Horton, *Aboriginal Australia*.

105. R. v. Seth Hawker, SR NSW: Court of Criminal Jurisdiction, Indictments, Informations and Related Papers, 1816–1824, 1 June 1822, [SZ797], Reel 1977, 299.

106. See Harring, "The Killing Time," 385–423. This incident likely occurred in the region of Irwin in Western Australia, and Burges's victim, therefore, was likely of the Amangu peoples.

107. J. K. McLaughlin, "The Magistracy and the Supreme Court of New South Wales, 1824–1850: A Sesqui-Centenary Study," *Journal of the Royal Australian Historical Society* 62, no. 2 (1976): 91–100; L. Ford and B. Salter, "From Pluralism to Territorial Sovereignty: The 1816 Trial of Mow-watty in the Superior Court of New South Wales," *Indigenous Law Journal* 7 (2008): 67–86.

108. Military juries were authorized by the "Act to provide for the better administration of justice in New South Wales and Van Diemen's Land and for the more effectual government thereof," 4 Geo. IV, Clause 96; discussed in Kercher, *An Unruly Child*, 72–73, 202. See also R. v. Hall (No. 4), June 12, 1829, Decisions of the Superior Courts of New South Wales, 1788–1899, published by the Division of Law, Macquarie University, http://www.law .mq.edu.au/scnsw/. This case allowed civilian juries on the application of both parties and with the approval of the court.

109. For some of these references, I am indebted to Victoria Gollan's work: Aboriginal Colonial Court Cases, 1788–1838, SR NSW, http://srwww.records .nsw.gov.au/indexes/searchform.aspx?id=1. R. v. William Millar and Thomas Bevan, SR NSW: Court of Criminal Jurisdiction, Minutes of Proceedings, 1795–1797, 9–10 October 1797, [5/1147B], Reel 2397, 353; R. v. Thomas Hewitt, SR NSW: Bench of Magistrates, 1788–1820, 26 January 1799, [SZ767], Reel 655, 43: notation here suggests that Hewitt was committed for trial after the inquest; R. v. Edward Powell et al., *HRA* 1:2, 403–422; R. v. Edward Luttrill (or Luttrell), SR NSW: Court of Criminal Jurisdiction, Indictments, Informations and Related Papers, 1796–1812, 13 March 1810, [5/1146], Reel 2393, 65. On Edward Luttril: *Sydney Gazette*, 24 February 1810, 2, 1, and 17 March 1810, 2,1; R. v. John Henshaw and John Spears, SR NSW: Court of Criminal Jurisdiction, Indictments, Informations and Related Papers, 1816–1824, 9 September 1818, [SZ784], COD 444, 301; R. v. John Thompson and John Kirby, SR NSW: Court of Criminal Jurisdiction, Indictments, Informations and Related Papers, 1816–1824, 22 November 1820, [SZ792],COD 452B, 496; R. v. Seth Hawker, SR NSW: Court of Criminal Jurisdiction, Indictments, Informations and Related Papers, 1816–1824, 1 June 1822 (or 10 June), [SZ797], Reel 1977, 299.

110. John Kirby was sentenced to death, Powell et al. were pardoned, and John Henshaw and John Spears were released after public reprimand: R. v. John Thompson and John Kirby, SR NSW: Court of Criminal Jurisdiction, Indictments, Informations and Related Papers, 1816–1824, 22 November 1820, [SZ792],COD 452B, 496; R. v. John Henshaw and John Spears, SR NSW: Court of Criminal Jurisdiction, Indictments, Informations and Related Papers, 1816–1824, 1816–1824, 9 September 1818, [SZ784], COD 444, 301. On pardon of Powell et al.: Hobart to King, 30 January 1802, *HRA* 1:3, 366–367. Compare the circumstances leading to the recommendations of mercy in the cases of Chipp, Colthurst, Ridgway, and Stanly in 1827, see Forbes to Wilmot-Horton, 15 May 1827, R. Wilmot Horton's private letters from Sir Francis Forbes, 1825–1827, Mitchell Library A1819, CY Reel 760, 169–172.

111. Indictment: *Sydney Gazette,* 24 February 1810, 2, 1. Acquittal: *Sydney Gazette,* 17 March 1810, 2, 1. For Tedbury's animosity to the colony: *Sydney Gazette,* 19 May 1805, 1, 3; 3 September 1809, 2, 1; 1 October 1809, 2, 1; 15 October 1809, 2, 2.

112. *Sydney Gazette,* 4 August 1805, 2, 2.

113. R. v. John Thompson and John Kirby, SR NSW: Court of Criminal Jurisdiction, Indictments, Informations and Related Papers, 1816–1824, 22 November 1820, [SZ792], COD 452B, 496.

114. McLaughlin, "The Magistracy and the Supreme Court," 91–100; H. Golder and I. Pike, *High and Responsible Office: A History of the N.S.W. Magistracy* (Sydney: University of Sydney Press, 1991), 1–41.

115. For example: Depositions concerning Humphrey Lynch, SR NSW: Bench of Magistrates, Minutes of Proceedings, 1788–1820, 1 June 1788, [SZ 765], COD 17, 47; Alexander Wilson and Robert Forrester, Examination of witnesses concerning Murder of Native boy at the Hawkesbury, SR NSW: Bench of Magistrates, Minutes and Proceedings, 1788–1820, 17 October 1794, [SZ 765], Reel 654, COD 17, 375; for further commentary on the Wilson and Forrester proceedings, see J. F. Nagle, *Collins the Courts and the Colony: Law and Society in Colonial New South Wales, 1788–1796* (Sydney: University of New South Wales Press, 1996) 243–247; Mr. O'Brien, Mr. McLeish, Mr. Weston, concerning Firing at Aborigines at Illawarra, SR NSW: Bench of Magistrates, Minutes and Proceedings, 1788–1820, 24 October 1818, [SZ775], Reel 659, COD 236, 146; Depositions, "Before D'Arcy Wentworth Esq., Magistrate of the Territory, and others His Fellow Justices assigned to keep the Peace," 24 October 1818, Wentworth Family Papers: Wentworth, D'Arcy Correspondence, 1817–1820, Mitchell Library A753, CY Reel 699, 244–254 (189–199) (Wentworth Correspondence, ML A753). See also SR NSW: Court of Criminal Jurisdiction, Indictments, Informations and Related Papers, 1816–1824, [SZ797], Reel 1977, 299–300, 332–337.

116. H. Reynolds, *Frontier: Aborigines, Settlers and Land* (St. Leonards, NSW: Allen & Unwin, 1996); R. H. W. Reece, *Aborigines and Colonists: Aborigines and Colonial Society in New South Wales in the 1830s and 1840s* (Sydney: University of Sydney Press, 1974), esp. 217–219; L. E. Threlkeld and

N. Gunson, *Australian Reminiscences and Papers of L. E. Threlkeld: Missionary to the Aborigines,* 2 vols. (Canberra: Australian Institute of Aboriginal Studies, 1974). Threlkeld and the scholarship built on his correspondence has been dismissed by K. Windschuttle, "The Myths of Frontier Massacres in Australian History, Part III: Massacre Stories and the Policy of Separatism," *Quadrant* 44, no. 12 (2000): 7–10; K. Windschuttle, "The Myths of Frontier Massacres in Australian History, Part I: The Invention of Massacre Stories," *Quadrant* 44, no. 10 (2000): 13, 4–5, 7. See primary documents gathered in *Original Documents on Aborigines;* and the research of Connor, *The Australian Frontier Wars.* The *HRA* is also replete with reports; see indices to series 1.

117. *HRA* 1:2, 403–422, 411.
118. *HRA* 1:2, 417.
119. *HRA* 1:5, 502–504; A. C. Castles, *An Australian Legal History* (Sydney: Law Book Company, 1982), 515–542. See also Plunkett, *The Australian Magistrate,* 118–119.
120. This is the region north of the Shoalhaven River (see maps 2 and 6).
121. "Deposition of William Richards (alias Charcoal Will), Before D'Arcy Wentworth Esqr Magistrate of the Territory, and others His Fellow Justices assigned to keep the Peace," 24 October 1818, Wentworth Correspondence, ML A753, 252 (197).
122. R. v. Fitzpatrick and Colville, June 21 or 24, 1824, Decisions of the Superior Courts of New South Wales, 1788–1899, published by the Division of Law, Macquarie University, http://www.law.mq.edu.au/scnsw/. On the interview with Bulwaddy: SR NSW: Governor: Despatches to Colonial Secretary, June 1824 to November 1825, Brisbane to Secretary, 24 June 1824, [4/1640]. Bulwaddy was likely one of the Wonnarua people whose country surrounded Patrick's Plains.
123. "Before D'Arcy Wentworth Esqr Magistrate of the Territory, and others His Fellow Justices assigned to keep the Peace," 24 October 1818, Wentworth Correspondence, ML A753, 244–254 (189–199).
124. "Deposition of William Richards (alias Charcoal Will), Before D'Arcy Wentworth Esqr Magistrate of the Territory, and others His Fellow Justices assigned to keep the Peace," 24 October 1818, Wentworth Correspondence, ML A753, 252 (197). Note that Richards (or Charcoal Will) completed other compensated, quasi-policing work for the colony: see John Andrews to D'Arcy Wentworth and Simeon Lord, Certificate, 24 March 1820, Wentworth Correspondence, ML A753, 393 (295); also Wentworth, D'Arcy Correspondence, 1809–1816, Mitchell Library A752 (Wentworth Correspondence, A752).
125. "Deposition of Joseph Wild and Deposition of John McArthy, Before D'Arcy Wentworth Esqr Magistrate of the Territory, and others His Fellow Justices assigned to keep the Peace," 24 October 1818, Wentworth Correspondence, ML A753, 246–250 (191–195).
126. "Deposition of Joseph Wild and Deposition of John McArthy, Before D'Arcy Wentworth Esqr Magistrate of the Territory, and others His Fellow

Justices assigned to keep the Peace," 24 October 1818, Wentworth Correspondence, ML A753, 246 (191).

127. Charles Throsby to D'Arcy Wentworth, 5 April 1816, Wentworth Correspondence, ML A752, 183.

128. Lachlan Macquarie to D'Arcy Wentworth, 1 November 1818, Wentworth Correspondence, ML A753, 265–268 (207–210).

129. "Before D'Arcy Wentworth Esqr Magistrate of the Territory, and others His Fellow Justices assigned to keep the Peace," 24 October 1818, Wentworth Correspondence, ML A753, 254 (199).

5. The Local Limits of Jurisdiction

1. James Jackson to Van Allen, 23 March 1798, in J. E. Hays, comp., *Governor's Letter Books of George Matthews, 20 August 1795–17 January 1796 and James Jackson, 24 January 1798–3 January 1799,* bound transcripts, Works Progress Administration (WPA) Project No. 5993, ed. L. F. Hays (Atlanta: Georgia Archives, 1939), 154 (hereafter cited as *Governor's Letter Books: Matthews and Jackson*); Proclamation, 1 March 1798, File II—Subjects: Creeks, 004–02–046: 76, Georgia Archives (hereafter cited as File II: Creeks, GA). Contrast Tuskeegee Tustunnagau's (also spelled Tustunnuggee) account in Hawkins to John Clements, March 1798, *Letters, Journals and Writings of Benjamin Hawkins,* vol. 1, ed. C. L. Grant, (Savannah, GA: Beehive, 1980), 181–182.

2. Burwell Pope, John Davenport, William Harvie, and Phillip Wary, Justices of the Peace for the Inferior Court of Oglethorpe County, 2 March 1798, File II: Creeks, GA.

3. R. v. Lowe, May 18 or 23, 1827, Decisions of the Superior Courts of New South Wales, 1788–1899, published by the Division of Law, Macquarie University, http://www.law.mq.edu.au/scnsw/ (hereafter cited as R. v. Lowe).

4. James Jackson to James McHenry, 15 Feb 1798, *Governor's Letter Books: Matthews and Jackson,* 105.

5. Jackson recognized the Creek's "sovereignty" in this transaction, "Mr Hawkins and the Creeks who acted as Sovereign of the Creek Nation delivered him up freely": Jackson to Van Allen, 23 March 1798, *Governor's Letter Books: Matthews and Jackson,* 152.

6. G. R. Lamplugh, *Politics on the Periphery: Factions and Parties in Georgia, 1783–1806* (London: Associated University Press, 1986), 144–165.

7. F. P. Prucha, ed., *Documents of United States Indian Policy,* 2nd ed. (Lincoln: University of Nebraska Press, 1990), 17–20.

8. Jackson blamed the rape on the new federal system established by the Trade and Intercourse Acts: Jackson to McHenry, 15 February 1798, *Governor's Letter Books: Matthews and Jackson,* 105–106.

9. Jackson to McHenry, 10 February 1798, *Governor's Letter Books: Matthews and Jackson,* 97–98.

10. Contrast Tuskeegee Tustunnagau's account in Benjamin Hawkins to John Clements, March 1798, *Letters, Journals and Writings of Benjamin Hawkins,*

vol. 1, ed. C. L. Grant (Savannah, GA: Beehive, 1980), 181–182. He said the posse was there to kill him.

11. Colonel Philips was assisted by Ezekial Park and Captain John McAlister: Sheriff Richard Bailey to Jackson, 11 March 1798, in *Creek Indian Letters, Talks and Treaties, 1705–1839*, vol. 2, bound transcripts, WPA Project No. 665-34-3-224, ed. L. F. Hays (Atlanta: Georgia Archives, 1939), 515 (hereafter cited as *Creek Letters 2*, 515).

12. See Jackson's protest against this procedure: Jackson to Hawkins, 23 March 1798, *Governor's Letter Books: Matthews and Jackson*, 156–157.

13. Tuskeegee Haujo to Colonel Philips, 13 February 1798, *Letters of Benjamin Hawkins, 1797–1815*, bound transcripts, WPA Project No. 5993, ed. L. F. Hays (Atlanta: Georgia Archives, 1939), 20–21 (hereafter cited as *Letters of Benjamin Hawkins*, GA).

14. Colonel Philips to Hawkins, 7 March 1798, File II: Creeks, GA.

15. Burwell Pope, John Davenport, William Harvie, and Phillip Wray, Justices of the Inferior Court of Oglethorpe County, 2 March 1798, File II: Creeks, GA.

16. Hawkins to Jackson, 11 July 1798, *Letters, Journals and Writings of Benjamin Hawkins*, 211–212.

17. Colonel Philips to Hawkins, 7 March 1798, File II: Creeks, GA. For state treaties negotiated by local elites, see Chapter 1, 24.

18. For horse prices, see R. F. Ethridge, *Creek Country: The Creek Indians and Their World* (Chapel Hill: University of North Carolina Press, 2003), 184. The price of a slave depended very much on who was claiming it. In 1831, Thomas Flournoy sought $400–600 compensation for the loss of a male slave to the Creeks in 1792, but his quantum probably reflected 1830s rather than 1790s prices: *Indian Depredations, 1787–1825: Original Claims in Department of Archives & History of Georgia*, vol. 1, part 2, bound transcripts, WPA Project No. 3990-3441, ed. J. E. Hays (Atlanta: Georgia Archives, 1938), 290B. In 1803, an emancipated slave named Bob was reportedly abducted and sold for $200 to a settler before being resold to a Cherokee for $400: Meigs to William Riddle, 5 February 1803, Records of the Cherokee Indian Agency in Tennessee 1801–1835, National Archives and Records Administration (NARA), Microfilm Publication M208, Reel 2 (hereafter cited as Cherokee Agency, NARA, M208, Reel 2).

19. W. T. Clinton III and K. V. Hartigan, "Police Authority and Reform in Augustan Rome and Nineteenth-Century England: Localizing and Nationalizing Police Work in Traditional and Modern Societies," *Law and Human Behavior* 6, no. 3/4 (1982): 295–311; citing F. W. Maitland, *Constitutional History of England* (Cambridge: Cambridge University Press, 1920).

20. Indeed, some evidence suggests that officers were elected because of their stand against the Trade and Intercourse laws. See discussion of Ford's election in "Jackson to President and Gentlemen of the Court Martial," 17 March 1798, *Governor's Letter Books: Matthews and Jackson*, 145. In general, see S. E. Hadden, *Slave Patrols: Law and Violence in Virginia and the Carolinas*, Harvard Historical Studies (Cambridge, MA: Harvard University Press, 2001).

21. See, for example, James Jackson, who led Georgian troops against the Creeks in the late 1780s, and D. B. Mitchell, who served as a states' commissioner in the 1790s.

22. Militiamen (or indeed males over age 15), acting under the direction of a constable or magistrate, were called a *posse comitatus:* see A. Clayton, *The Office and Duty of a Justice of the Peace, and a Guide to Clerks, Constables, Coroners, Executors, Administrators, Guardians, Sheriffs, Tax-collectors, and Receivers, and Other Civil Officers, according to the Laws of the State of Georgia* . . . (Milledgeville, GA: Grantland, 1819), 20, 291–292. Note the importance of militiamen as "vigilance groups": J. K. Williams, "Catching the Criminal in Nineteenth Century South Carolina," *Journal of Criminal Law Criminology and Police Science* 46 (1955): 264–272.

23. See Major General James Jackson to Edward Telfair, 9 May 1793, *Creek Letters* 1, 310; Capt. William Melton to Jackson, 27 July 1796, *Creek Letters* 2, 482; James Seagrove to John Kinnard, 1 June 1807, *Creek Letters* 2, 714, W. Connor, Batt Wynch, John Hill Bryant to John Milledge, 2 July 1802, *Creek Letters* 2, 720; "Petition, 1812 Sept. 1, Hartford, Pulaski County, [Georgia to] Governor David B. Mitchell, Milledgeville, Georgia/Solomon A. Hopkins . . . [et al.]," 1 September 1812, Telamon Cuyler Collection, 46:06:05, Hargrett Library, University of Georgia.

24. Deposition of Joseph White, 9 August 1804, *Creek Letters* 2, 697; John McAllister to Mitchell, 12 August 1804, *Creek Letters* 2, 699; William Melton to G. W. Foster, 15 August 1804, *Creek Letters* 2, 701; Statement of Thomas Townsend, 23 August 1804, *Creek Letters* 2, 703; William Melton to Milledge, 3 September 1804, *Creek Letters* 2, 704.

25. See efforts of Elijah Clarke and Benjamin Harrison here. On Clark's war and the secession of Wilkes County: Elijah Clark to David Adams, 17 May 1794, *Creek Letters* 2, 380; Elijah Clark to Jared Irwin, undated 1794, *Creek Letters* 2, 374B; Elijah Clarke to Jared Irwin, 26 September 1794, *Creek Letters* 2, 410; John Twiggs to Jared Irwin, 2 October 1794, *Creek Letters* 2, 441; Jared Irwin to Timothy Barnard, 3 October 1794, Georgia Archives; *Creek Letters* 2, 412. For Harrison's attempts to start war with the Creeks: Deposition of William Scarborough, 9 January 1796, *Creek Letters* 2, 462.

26. See charges against Captain Williamson and Lieutenant Hay, 1793: "R. B. Roberts, Capt 2d Su-Legion United States, 4 February 1793 and 19 February 1793, Georgia Archives," in *Cherokee Indian Letters, Talks and Treaties, 1786–1838,* vol. 1, comp. J. E. Hays, WPA Project No. 4341, 1939, 12–13; Henry Gaither to Edward Telfair, 15 February 1793, *Creek Letters* 1, 267; Eligja Clark to Augustus Elholm, 19 February 1793, *Creek Letters* 1, 268.

27. John Floyd to Mitchell, 8 November 1810, *Creek Letters* 2, 750.

28. For an account of his murder, see Deposition of Archer Norris, 1 August 1794, *Creek Letters* 2, 396.

29. Inquiry on the conduct of Major David Adams, 22 July 1794, *Creek Letters* 2, 392.

30. Deposition of David Blackshear, 11 February 1796, *Creek Letters* 2, 464b.

31. George Sibbald to James Jackson, 30 August 1799, *Creek Letters* 2, 561; Jackson to David Blackshear, 31 August 1799, *Creek Letters* 2, 568; Jackson to John Rutherford, 31 August 1799, *Creek Letters* 2, 569; Talk to Indians, 2 September 1799, *Creek Letters* 2, 571. For another example of illegal pursuit, see William Melton to Jared Irwin, 19 July 1796, *Creek Letters* 2, 481.

32. Jackson to Hawkins, 23 March 1798, *Governor's Letter Books: Matthews and Jackson,* 155.

33. Habeas corpus means "[a] judicial order to someone holding a person to bring that person to court" usually to prevent "unlawful imprisonment by forcing the captor and the person being held to come to court for a decision on the legality of the imprisonment or other holding": David Oran, *Oran's Dictionary of the Law* (Albany, NY: West Legal Studies/Thomson Learning, 2000).

34. Compare J. M. Carter, *Rape in Medieval England: An Historical and Sociological Study* (Lanham, MD: University Press of America, 1985).

35. Peter Van Allen to Jackson, 19 March 1798, *Creek Letters* 2, 518.

36. This term includes justices of the peace, sheriffs, constables, and watchmen: K. S. Murphy, "Judge, Jury, Magistrate and Soldier: Rethinking Law and Authority in Late Eighteenth-Century Ireland," *American Journal of Legal History* 44, no. 3 (2000): 233. The office of Justice of the Peace was created by statute in 1344 (18 Edw. III, stat.2, c.2): S. Webb and B. P. Webb, *English Local Government from the Revolution to the Municipal Corporations Act the Parish and the County* (London and New York: Longmans, Green & Co., 1906), 298–439.

37. J. R. Kent, "The Centre and the Localities: State Formation and Parish Government in England, circa 1640–1740," *Historical Journal* 38, no. 2 (1995): 364–404.

38. Senate Resolution, 17 December 1819, Resolutions which Originated in the Senate, Acts of the General Assembly of the State of Georgia, Passed at Milledgeville, in November and December, 1819, volume 1, 152, *Georgia Legislative Documents,* University of Georgia Libraries, http://www.galileo. usg.edu/express?link=zlgl. See also the list of 1,500 subscribers in back of Clayton, *Georgia Justice,* 453–463.

39. E. Surrency, *The Creation of a Judicial System: The History of Georgia Courts, 1733 to Present* (Holmes Beach, FL: Gaunt, 2001), 65–66, 83.

40. Jackson to Judge Carnes, 7 March 1798, *Governor's Letter Books: Matthews and Jackson,* 137.

41. Jackson to Van Allen, 23 March 1798, *Governor's Letter Books: Matthews and Jackson,* 153–154.

42. For example, requests for the removal of Woods Laskey and John Porter: Samuel Love to Return J. Meigs, 13 July 1808; King and Montgomery to Meigs, 14 July 1808; John Nichols to Meigs, 14 July 1808; James Montgomery to Meigs, 14 July 1808; and John Thombury to Meigs, 14 July 1808, *all* Cherokee Agency, NARA, M208, Reel 4.

43. Hawkins to Eustis, 21 July 1810, *Letters, Journals and Writings of Benjamin Hawkins,* vol. 2, ed. C. L. Grant, (Savannah, GA: Beehive, 1980), 565–566.

44. On the seizure of a slave: Meigs to ?, 1 August 1811, Cherokee Agency, NARA, M208, Reel 5.
45. Buckner Harris to Cherokee Nation, 4 June 1808, Cherokee Agency, NARA, M208, Reel 4.
46. See Stone's case discussed in C. D. Cumfer, "'The Idea of Mankind is so Various': An Intellectual History of Tennessee, 1768–1810" (Ph.D. diss., University of California, 2001), 195.
47. Path Killer to Meigs, 24 June 1821, Cherokee Agency, NARA, M208, Reel 9.
48. T. G. Holt, Solicitor General of Dooly County, to Governor Troup, 12 December 1823, *Creek Letters* 3, 975: "At our late superior Court in Dooly County, the Grand Jury found a true bill against John, Sam, Lapiachee, Tikeohkes & Miokes, indians residing in the Creek nation, for the murder of John Tinsley, a white man & formerly a citizen of Dooly. Your excellency will adopt such measures as will procure this appearance at our next superior Court for said county."
49. Regarding other murders by Lowe, see L. E. Threlkeld and N. Gunson, *Australian Reminiscences and Papers of L. E. Threlkeld: Missionary to the Aborigines,* 2 vols. (Canberra: Australian Institute of Aboriginal Studies, 1974), 92, 5. For discussion of these accounts, see R. H. W. Reece, *Aborigines and Colonists: Aborigines and Colonial Society in New South Wales in the 1830s and 1840s* (Sydney: University of Sydney Press, 1974), 112–114.
50. R. v. Lowe. See also R. v. Jamieson, May 16 or 18, 1827, Decisions of the Superior Courts of New South Wales, 1788–1899, published by the Division of Law, Macquarie University, http://www.law.mq.edu.au/scnsw/. Compare Victoria Gollan: State Records, New South Wales (hereafter cited as SR NSW): Aboriginal Colonial Court Cases, 1788–1838, http://srwww.records .nsw.gov.au/indexes/searchform.aspx?id=47: most of the defendants listed here seem to be convicts or low-ranked freemen. Almost all names appear in convict registries, though some are very common names.
51. R. v. Lowe.
52. On the Lowe case, see: B. Kercher, "Native Title in the Shadows: The Origins of the Myth of *Terra Nullius* in Early New South Wales Courts," in *Colonialism and the Modern World: Selected Studies,* ed. G. Blue, M. Bunton, and R. Crozier (New York: M. E. Sharpe, 2002), 100–119; W. A. Wood, *Dawn in the Valley: The Story of Settlement in the Hunter River Valley to 1833* (Sydney: Wentworth Books, 1972), 32–33, 115–119; and J. Connor, *The Australian Frontier Wars, 1788–1838* (Randwick, NSW: University of New South Wales Press, 2002), 64–67. Contrast Vattel's increasingly hegemonic idea that actual settlement and cultivation were necessary bases for sovereignty and property: E. Vattel, *The Law of Nations, or, Principles of the Law of Nature Applied to the Conduct and Affairs of Nations and Sovereigns* (London: G. G. and J. Robinson, 1797), vol. 1, 100–101; vol. 2, 68–71.
53. For the unique and changing British attitude toward Australia, see H. Reynolds, *The Law of the Land,* 2nd ed. (Ringwood, VIC: Penguin, 1992); contrast J. Fulcher, "The Wik Judgment, Pastoral Leases and Colonial Office Policy and Intention in NSW in the 1840s," *Australian Journal of Legal His-*

tory 4 (1998): 33–56; D. Ward, *"Savage Customs" and "Civilised Laws":* *British Attitudes to Legal Pluralism in Australasia, c. 1830–1848,* London Papers in Australian Studies 10 (London: Menzies Centre for Australian Studies, 2003). On North America, see J. C. Weaver, "Concepts of Economic Improvement and the Social Construction of Property Rights: Highlights from the English-Speaking World," in *Despotic Dominion: Property Rights in British Settler Societies,* ed. J. McLaren, A. R. Buck, and N. E. Wright (Vancouver: University of British Columbia Press, 2005), 79–102.

54. For a good account of Georgia's political system at the turn of the nineteenth century, see Lamplugh, *Politics on the Periphery.*

55. B. Kercher, *An Unruly Child: A History of Law in Australia* (St. Leonards, NSW: Allen & Unwin, 1995), 69–73.

56. T. M. Perry, *Australia's First Frontier: The Spread of Settlement in New South Wales, 1788–1829* (Carlton, VIC: Melbourne University Press in Association with the Australian National University, 1963); D. N. Jeans, *An Historical Geography of New South Wales to 1901* (Sydney: Reed Education, 1972), 79–116.

57. H. Golder and I. Pike, *High and Responsible Office: A History of the N.S.W. Magistracy* (Sydney: University of Sydney Press, 1991), 29; P. Stanley, "'Soldiers and Fellow Countrymen': The Military in Colonial Australia," in *Two Centuries of War and Peace,* ed. M. McKernan and M. Browne (Canberra: Australian War Memorial in Association with Allen & Unwin, 1988), 75–77; P. Stanley and L. C. Cox, *The Remote Garrison: The British Army in Australia, 1788–1870* (Kenthurst, NSW: Kangaroo Press, 1986).

58. See the variety of measures proposed to govern settlement "Beyond the Boundaries of Location" between 1839 and 1844, in SR NSW: Colonial Secretary's Correspondence, Special Bundles: Papers Relating to the Regulation of Squatting Part I, 1839–1844 [5/4774.2].

59. Golder and Pike, *High and Responsible Office,* 28–29; J. C. Weaver, *The Great Land Rush and the Making of the Modern World, 1650–1900* (Montreal: McGill Queens University Press, 2003), 12.

60. Francis Forbes to Ralph Darling, 3 October 1827, *Historical Records of Australia: Series 1, Governors' Despatches to and from England,* vol. 13 (Sydney: The Library Committee of the Commonwealth Parliament, 1920), 607–613 (hereafter cited as *HRA* 1:13, 607–613). Also, for a discussion of the crisis posed to government by the power of colonial courts to question the governor's power, see D. J. Neal, *The Rule of Law in a Penal Colony: Law and Power in Early New South Wales* (Cambridge and Melbourne: Cambridge University Press, 1991), 92.

61. H. Golder, *Politics, Patronage, and Public Works: The Administration of New South Wales, 1842–1900,* vol. 1 (Randwick, NSW: University of New South Wales Press, 2005), 36–38. For a primary account of their importance to frontier governance in Tasmania (Van Diemen's Land), see R. v. Wilson and Others, 22 April 1843, Supreme Court of Van Diemen's Land, Decisions of the Nineteenth-Century Tasmanian Courts, published by Macquarie University and University of Tasmania, http://www.law.mq.edu.au/sctas/.

62. T. Griffiths, "The Frontier Fallen," *Eureka Street* 2003, 24–30.
63. Stanley, "'Soldiers and Fellow Countrymen,'" 61–91.
64. Connor argues that they usually did so with some restraint; Connor, *The Australian Frontier Wars*, 53.
65. Golder and Pike, *High and Responsible Office*, 28.
66. J. K. McLaughlin, "The Magistracy and the Supreme Court of New South Wales, 1824–1850: A Sesqui-Centenary Study," *Journal of the Royal Australian Historical Society* 62, no. 2 (1976): 97–98.
67. McLaughlin, "The Magistracy and the Supreme Court," 94. For accounts of magisterial power and its abuse, see *Sydney Gazette,* 17 November 1825, 2, 5; R. Therry, *Reminiscences of Thirty Years' Residence in New South Wales and Victoria* (London: Sampson Low, Son & Co., 1863), 46–47, 167.
68. Contrast R. McQueen, "Master and Servant Legislation as 'Social Control': The Role of Law in Labour Relations on the Darling Downs, 1860–1870," *Law in Context* 10 (1992): 123–139.
69. Charles Throsby to D'Arcy Wentworth, 5 April 1816, Wentworth Family Papers: Wentworth, D'Arcy Correspondence, 1809–1816, Mitchell Library A752, CY Reel 699, 183–186; "Before D'Arcy Wentworth Esq Magistrate of the Territory, and others His Fellow Justices assigned to keep the Peace," 24 October 1818, Wentworth Family Papers: Wentworth, D'Arcy Correspondence, 1817–1820, Mitchell Library A753, CY Reel 699, 244–254 (189–199); SR NSW: Bench of Magistrates, Minutes and Proceedings, 1788–1820, 24 October 1818, [SZ775], Reel 659, COD 236, 146.
70. Neal, *The Rule of Law in a Penal Colony,* 79, 150.
71. G. Blainey, *The Tyranny of Distance: How Distance Shaped Australia's History* (Sydney: Macmillan, 2001).
72. Darling to Hay, 23 Mar 1827, *HRA* 1:13, 179–180; Acting Attorney-General Moore to Colonial Secretary McLeay (also MacLeay), 22 January 1827, *HRA* 1:13, 400–405. See, generally, Governor Darling to Bathurst, 4 June 1827, *HRA* 1:13, 399–413. Note that reports indicated that soldiers had killed three more Aborigines: Alexander McLeay to Robert Scott Esq., 6 September 1826, *Original Documents on Aborigines and the Law,* 1790–1840, Document no. 15, Macquarie University, http://www.law.mq.edu.au/scnsw/Correspondence/index.htm.
73. Acting Attorney-General Moore to Colonial Secretary McLeay, 22 January 1827, *HRA* 1:13, 400–405.
74. Reference to private communications reporting murders and the sending of mounted policemen to investigate: Lieutenant de la Condamine to Captain Allman, 21 June 1826, *HRA* 1:12, 620; and Allman to Condamine, 27 June 1826, *HRA* 1:12, 621–622. See also Landholders to Governor Darling, 4 September 1826, *HRA* 1:12, 576.
75. On the refusal of Darling to declare martial law against Aborigines, see Darling to Hay, 11 September 1826, *HRA* 1:12, 574–575; Darling to Bathurst, 6 October 1826, *HRA* 1:12, 608. Regarding self-defense, see Darling to the Landholders at Hunter's River, 5 September 1826, *HRA* 1:12: 576–577. See also Neal, *The Rule of Law in a Penal Colony,* 79.

76. For example, Murray to Darling, 5 May 1830, *HRA* 1:15, 466; and Richard Bourke to Aberdeen 6 August 1835, *HRA* 1:18, 64–65.

77. R. v. Lowe.

78. L. A. Benton, *Law and Colonial Cultures: Legal Regimes in World History, 1400–1900* (Cambridge: Cambridge University Press, 2002), 167–209.

79. I. Hunter, "Natural Law, Historiography, and Aboriginal Sovereignty," *Legal History* 11, no. 2 (2007): 137–168.

80. Hunter, "Natural Law, Historiography, and Aboriginal Sovereignty," 164.

81. R. v. Lowe.

82. Moore to Colonial Secretary MacLeay, 22 January 1827, *HRA* 1:13, 403.

83. Darling to Hay, 23 March 1827, *HRA* 1:13, 179.

84. R. v. Lowe.

6. Farmbrough's Fathoming and Transitions in Georgia

1. R. N. Satz, "Rhetoric versus Reality: The Indian Policy of Andrew Jackson," in *Cherokee Removal: Before and After*, ed. W. L. Anderson (London and Athens: University of Georgia Press, 1991), 42.

2. F. P. Prucha, "Andrew Jackson's Indian Policy: A Reassessment," *Journal of American History* 56, no. 3 (1969): 527–539.

3. J. Norgren, *The Cherokee Cases: The Confrontation of Law and Politics* (New York: McGraw Hill, 1996), 40. On racial ideology, see W. G. McLoughlin, *Cherokees and Missionaries, 1789–1839* (London and New Haven, CT: Yale University Press, 1984), xv–xvii. For a discussion of various interpretations of Andrew Jackson's Indian policy in particular, see Satz, "Rhetoric versus Reality," 29–34.

4. W. B. Phillips, *Georgia and State Rights: A Study of the Political History of Georgia from the Revolution to the Civil War, with Particular Regard to Federal Relations* (Washington, DC: Government Printing Office, 1902); T. A. Garrison, *The Legal Ideology of Removal: The Southern Judiciary and the Sovereignty of Native American Nations*, Studies in the Legal History of the South (London and Athens: University of Georgia Press, 2002).

5. D. Williams, *The Georgia Gold Rush: Twenty-Niners, Cherokees, and Gold Fever* (Columbia: University of South Carolina Press, 1993).

6. Extract of report, James. G. Williams to Hugh Montgomery, in *Cherokee Phoenix*, 14 April 1830, vol. 2, no. 52, 3, 1b–5b. The wound was inflicted by Old Philpot, one of the Georgia posse and a reputed member of the band of thieves known as the Poney Club.

7. Allen Farmbrough to Gilmer, 21 February 1830, *Cherokee Indian Letters, Talks and Treaties, 1786–1838*, vol. 1, bound transcripts, Works Progress Administration (WPA) Project No. 4341, ed. L. F. Hays (Atlanta: Georgia Archives, 1939, 205–207 (hereafter cited as *Cherokee Letters* 1, 205–207). The situation was complicated by the fact that many of the squatters had purchased their houses illegally from Cherokee families emigrating west under the treaty of 1828, so some squatters claimed to be rightful purchasers of Cherokee improvements.

8. Farmbrough to Gilmer, 21 February 1830, *Cherokee Letters* 1, 205–207.
9. See Garrison, *The Legal Ideology of Removal*. For a more general, recent account of this phenomenon in a number of states including Georgia, see D. A. Rosen, *American Indians and State Law: Sovereignty, Race, and Citizenship, 1790–1880* (Lincoln: University of Nebraska Press, 2007).
10. K. E. H. Braund, *Deerskins and Duffels: The Creek Indian Trade with Anglo-America, 1685–1815* (Lincoln: University of Nebraska Press, 1993); M. D. Green, *The Politics of Indian Removal: Creek Government and Society in Crisis* (London and Lincoln: University of Nebraska Press, 1982), 17–43.
11. T. Perdue, *Slavery and the Evolution of Cherokee Society, 1540–1866* (Knoxville: University of Tennessee Press, 1979); T. Miles, *Ties That Bind: The Story of an Afro-Cherokee Family in Slavery and Freedom* (Berkeley: University of California Press, 2005).
12. D. North, *Economic Growth of the United States, 1790–1860* (New York: Norton, 1966); A. Rothman, *Slave Country: American Expansion and the Origins of the Deep South* (Cambridge, MA: Harvard University Press, 2005). The final drive for Cherokee Country also had economic factors; gold was discovered in Cherokee Country in 1828.
13. Adams-Onis Treaty of 1819.
14. On Cherokee claims for pension and reparations, see, for example: John Lowry to President, 16 February 1816, Records of the Cherokee Indian Agency in Tennessee 1801–1835, National Archives and Records Administration (NARA) Microfilm Publication M208, Reel 7 (hereafter cited as Cherokee Agency, NARA, M208, Reel 7); and Meigs to John C. Calhoun, April 1818, Cherokee Agency, NARA, M208, Reel 7.
15. Green, *The Politics of Indian Removal*, 45–46.
16. Further Creek land was ceded in 1818 and 1821: see C. J. Kappler, *Indian Affairs: Laws and Treaties*, vol. 2 (Washington, DC: Government Printing Office, 1904), 155–156, 95–97.
17. "An Act to add all that part of the unlocated territory of this state which lies without the limits of the present counties, to the county of Jasper, for the purpose of giving the Courts jurisdiction of crimes committed by white persons against white persons in said territory, and for other purposes," 27/50, Assented to 23 November 1814, Acts of the General Assembly of the State of Georgia; Passed in October and November, 1814; vol. 1, 41, *Georgia Legislative Documents*, University of Georgia Libraries, http://www.galileo.usg .edu/express?link=zlgl. Amended by "An Act to amend an act, entitled an act, to add that part of the unlocated Territory of this state, which lies without the limits of the present counties, to the county of Jasper, passed the 23d day of November, 1814," 19/90, Assented to 18 December 1816, Acts of the General Assembly of the State of Georgia, Passed in November and December 1816, vol. 1, 34, *Georgia Legislative Documents*, http://www.galileo.usg .edu/express?link=zlgl.
18. 4 December 1816, 101, Acts of the General Assembly of the State of Georgia, Passed at Milledgeville at an Annual Session 1816, vol. 1, 206, *Georgia Legislative Documents*, http://www.galileo.usg.edu/express?link=zlgl.

19. 11 December 1819, 139, Acts of the General Assembly of the State of Georgia; Passed in November and December, 1819, vol. 1, 153, *Georgia Legislative Documents*, http://www.galileo.usg.edu/express?link=zlgl.

20. A. Wallace, *Jefferson and the Indians: The Tragic Fate of the First Americans* (Cambridge, MA: Belknap Press of Harvard University Press, 1999), 317.

21. See the Yazoo controversy: R. G. Harper, "The Case of Georgia Sales on the Mississippi Considered: With a Reference to Law Authorities and Public Acts; and as Appendix, Containing Certain Extracts, Records, and Official Papers," *American Law Journal* 5 (1814): 364–402. For a more recent analysis of its impact in Georgia politics, see G. R. Lamplugh, *Politics on the Periphery: Factions and Parties in Georgia, 1783–1806* (London: Associated University Press, 1986). Cumfer has pointed early arguments against Cherokee sovereignty in Tennessee: C. Cumfer, *Separate Peoples, One Land: The Minds of Cherokees, Blacks, and Whites on the Tennessee Frontier* (Chapel Hill: University of North Carolina Press, 2007), 93–96.

22. On Return J. Meigs, see: Return J. Meigs to Henry Dearborn, 5 April 1811, Cherokee Agency, NARA, M208 Reel 5; Meigs to William Eustis, 30 May 1811, Cherokee Agency, NARA, M208 Reel 5. See debates between Joseph McMinn and the Cherokee Nation about U.S. jurisdiction under the treaties: McMinn to Cherokee Council, 15 November 1818; Cherokee Council to McMinn, 17 November 1818; McMinn to Cherokee Council, 23 November 1818; McMinn to Cherokee Council, 24 November 1818; McMinn to Cherokee Council, 25 November 1818; Cherokee Council to McMinn, 25 November 1818; McMinn to Cherokee, 26 November 1818, Cherokee Council to McMinn, 27 November 1818: "Extinguishment of Indian title to lands in Georgia. Communicated to the House of Representatives, 2 April 1824," *American State Papers: Indian Affairs*, vol. 2, pub. no. 204, 483–490. See also: McMinn to Cherokee Council, 28 November 1818; Cherokee Council to McMinn, 28 November 1818; McMinn to Cherokee Council, 28 November 1818, all Cherokee Agency, NARA, M208 Reel 7. For a much later rebuttal of these arguments on behalf of the Cherokee, see J. Evarts, *Cherokee Removal: The 'William Penn' Essays and Other Writings*, ed. F. P. Prucha (Knoxville: University of Tennessee Press, 1981), 59–71.

23. Again, see Meigs to Dearborn, 5 April 1811, Cherokee Agency, NARA, M208 Reel 5; Meigs to Eustis, 30 May 1811, Cherokee Agency, NARA, M208 Reel 5. For the importance of this issue in eighteenth-century debate, see D. J. Hulsebosch, *Constituting Empire: New York and the Transformation of Constitutionalism in the Atlantic World, 1664–1830* (Chapel Hill: University of North Carolina Press, 2005), 75–104. For its promulgation by early Tennessee settlers, see C. Cumfer, "Local Origins of National Indian Policy: Cherokee and Tennessean Ideas about Sovereignty and Nationhood, 1790–1811," *Journal of the Early Republic* 23, no. 1 (2003): 21–46.

24. Andrew Jackson to Monroe, 4 March 1817, *The Papers of Andrew Jackson*, vol. 4, ed. Sam B. Smith and Harriet Chappell Owsley (Knoxville: University of Tennessee Press, 1980–), 95–96.

25. Calhoun to the Cherokee Council, 30 January 1824, "Extinguishment of Indian title to lands in Georgia. Communicated to the House of Representatives, 2 April 1824," *American State Papers: Indian Affairs*, vol. 2, pub. no. 204, 473.

26. 10 U.S. 87 (1810) at 141–143. Compare Justice Johnson's opinion that Indians were seized in fee of their lands, at 146–147. Both findings may have been obiter dictum: Garrison, *The Legal Ideology of Removal*, 73–87. Note also that Johnson draws a clear distinction between rights in jurisdiction and rights in property, at 146.

27. Johnson v. McIntosh 21 U.S., 543 (1823) at 578–578, 591–592.

28. Seventeenth-century sources reflect a range of possible meanings here; some merely forbid the buying of land from Indians without permission, others declare that all land is vested in the King in fee: W. Cronon, *Changes in the Land: Indians, Colonists, and the Ecology of New England*, 1st rev. ed. (New York: Hill and Wang, 2003), 70–71. Contrast P. Wolfe, "*Corpus Nullius*: The Exception of Indians and Other Aliens in US Constitutional Discourse," *Postcolonial Studies* 10, no. 2 (2007): 131–135.

29. See L. G. Robertson, *Conquest by Law: How the Discovery of America Dispossessed Indigenous Peoples of Their Lands* (Oxford and New York: Oxford University Press, 2005), 95–116. For an analysis of Johnson v. McIntosh as a federalist decision, see Garrison, *The Legal Ideology of Removal*, 87–102. Note that the court might have adapted this fiction of discovery as conquest from Calvin's case: see C. Yirush, "Conquest Theory and Imperial Governance in the Early Modern Anglo-American World" (paper presented at the Clark Library Conference on Imperial Models in the Early Modern World, Los Angeles, California, November 3–4, 2006); and G. Loughton, "Calvin's Case and the Origins of the Rule Governing 'Conquest' in English Law," *Australian Journal of Legal History* 8, no. 2 (2004): 150–180.

30. Johnson v. McIntosh, 21 U.S., 543 (1823) at 591.

31. R. v. Lowe, May 18 or 23, 1827, Decisions of the Superior Courts of New South Wales, 1788–1899, published by the Division of Law, Macquarie University, http://www.law.mq.edu.au/scnsw/.

32. Johnson v. McIntosh, 21 U.S., 543 (1823) at 596.

33. Campbell and Meriwether to Cherokee Council, 21 October 1823, "Extinguishment of Indian title to lands in Georgia. Communicated to the House of Representatives, April 2, 1824," *American State Papers: Indian Affairs*, vol. 2, pub. no. 204, 469.

34. Troup to Calhoun, 28 February 1824, "Extinguishment of Indian title to lands in Georgia. Communicated to the House of Representatives, 2 April 1824," *American State Papers: Indian Affairs*, vol. 2, pub. no. 204, 475.

35. Troup to Calhoun, 28 February 1824, "Extinguishment of Indian title to lands in Georgia. Communicated to the House of Representatives, 2 April 1824," *American State Papers: Indian Affairs*, vol. 2, pub. no. 204, 475–476.

36. See also Delegation of Georgia Congressmen to President, 10 March 1824, Letters Received Office of Indian Affairs, NARA M234-271, 135–137. In

this letter the delegation protested the General Government's engagement in diplomacy with the Cherokee, and enjoined them to make clear that Cherokee consent was not required for removal.

37. See, in general, Green, *The Politics of Indian Removal*, 69–124. For original correspondence, see "Proceedings of the Legislature of Georgia in relation to the treaty made with the Creeks at the Indian Springs. Communicated to the House of Representatives, January 23, 1827," *American State Papers: Indian Affairs*, vol. 2, pub. no. 249, 727–862.

38. Joseph Marshall et al. to Troup, 9 July 1825, *Creek Indian Letters, Talks and Treaties, 1705–1839*, vol. 3, bound transcripts, WPA Project No. 665-34-3-224, ed. L. F. Hays (Atlanta: Georgia Archives, 1939), 1040–1042.

39. "Address to Governor Troup, At a General Meeting of the Indians friendly to General McIntosh," "Proceedings of the Legislature of Georgia in relation to the treaty made with the Creeks at the Indian Springs. Communicated to the House of Representatives, January 23, 1827," *American State Papers: Indian Affairs*, vol. 2, pub. no. 249, 773.

40. "Address to Governor Troup, At a General Meeting of the Indians friendly to General McIntosh," "Proceedings of the Legislature of Georgia in relation to the treaty made with the Creeks at the Indian Springs. Communicated to the House of Representatives, January 23, 1827," *American State Papers: Indian Affairs*, vol. 2, pub. no. 249, 772–773.

41. For a nuanced account of Creek governance to 1816, see R. F. Ethridge, *Creek Country: The Creek Indians and Their World* (Chapel Hill: University of North Carolina Press, 2003), 92–119. See also Green, *The Politics of Indian Removal*.

42. Testimony before the House of William Lott, 28 June 1825; Testimony before the House of Reverend Isaac Smith, 6 July 1825; both cited by Green, *The Politics of Indian Removal*, 74–76.

43. Congressional Debate, transcribed in *Savannah Georgian*, 10 June 1826, 2, 4; *Richmond Enquirer*, 9 June 1826, 2, 2.

44. Report of Mr. Bevan, "Proceedings of the Legislature of Georgia in relation to the treaty made with the Creeks at the Indian Springs. Communicated to the House of Representatives, January 23, 1827," *American State Papers: Indian Affairs*, vol. 2, pub. no. 249, 784–794. At 786, Bevan described McIntosh as "little less than a dictator among them. . . . Indeed it may be broadly stated that no chieftain has ever had predominating influence over the nation, except as a demagogue, or else through the favor of his white friends."

45. In the Circuit Court of the United States for the district of Georgia, at Milledgeville, May Term, 1825, "Proceedings of the Legislature of Georgia in relation to the treaty made with the Creeks at the Indian Springs. Communicated to the House of Representatives, January 23, 1827," *American State Papers: Indian Affairs*, vol. 2, pub. no. 249, 771–772.

46. "Governor's Message to the General Assembly of the State of Georgia . . . , 8 November 1825," "Proceedings of the Legislature of Georgia in relation to the treaty made with the Creeks at the Indian Springs. Communicated to the

House of Representatives, January 23, 1827," *American State Papers: Indian Affairs*, vol. 2, pub. no. 249, 779 (hereafter cited as Governor's Message, 8 November 1825, *American State Papers*, 2:249, 779).

47. Troup to Joseph Marshall, 3 May 1825, quoted by Green, *The Politics of Indian Removal*, 98.

48. Governor's Message, 8 November 1825, *American State Papers*, 2:249, 779.

49. Jackson County Resolution, *Savannah Georgian*, 8 August 1826.

50. Protests about the erosion of Georgia's sovereignty by the Trade and Intercourse system were not new; see Governor James Jackson's protests in the 1790s, for example, 24 January 1798, *Governor's Letter Books of George Matthews, 20 August 1795–17 January 1796 and James Jackson, 24 January 1798–3 January 1799*, Georgia Archives, Record Group: 001-01-001, bound transcripts, WPA Project No. 5993, ed. L. F. Hays (Atlanta: Georgia Archives, 1939), 105.

51. Governor's Message, 8 November 1825, *American State Papers*, 2:249, 778–779.

52. For an analysis of Locke's views of aboriginal title in North America and its relationships to political community, see J. Tully, *An Approach to Political Philosophy: Locke in Contexts*, Ideas in Context (Cambridge and New York: Cambridge University Press, 1993), 137–178.

53. See annotations to Vernon Smith, "Missionary Activity in New South Wales," on the reverse of O. Coates (Church Missionary Society) to Lord Russell, 14 February 1840, The National Archives, Public Records Office, Colonial Office 201/303, Kew, f396.

54. 23 December 1825, 166, Acts of the General Assembly of the State of Georgia; Passed in November and December, 1825, vol. 1, 204, *Georgia Legislative Documents*, http://www.galileo.usg.edu/express?link=zlgl.

55. Committee of Indian Affairs, "Removal of Indians. February 24, 1830. Accompanied by a Bill (No. 287) . . ." *U.S. Congressional Serial Set*, Vol. No. 200, Session Vol. No. 2, 21st Congress, 1st Session, Report No. 227, 14.

56. Berrien to Eaton, 10 March 1830, Attorney General's Opinions on Legal Questions, 26 June 1826 to 4 January 1832, RG60/2, vol. C, 179–183, National Archives and Records Administration, College Park (hereafter cited as NARA: RG 60: 2C, 179–183).

57. Farmbrough to Gilmer, 8 February 1830, *Cherokee Letters* 1, 203–204; John Ross to Hugh Montgomery, 6 February 1830, *Papers of Chief John Ross*, vol. 1, ed. Gary E. Mouton (Norman: University of Oklahoma Press, 1983), 182–184; Ross to Elias Boudinot, 13 February 1830, *Papers of John Ross*, vol. 1, 184–187.

58. Article 8, Treaty with the Cherokee, 6 May 1828, Kappler, *Indian Affairs: Laws and Treaties*, 290.

59. McKenny to Eaton, 30 November 1829, *Cherokee Letters* 1, 196, emphasis in original.

60. J. B. Pendleton to Gilmer, 6 February 1830, *Cherokee Letters* 1, 201.

61. J. B. Pendleton to Gilmer, 7 February 1830, *Cherokee Letters* 1, 202.

62. A. Clayton, *The Office and Duty of a Justice of the Peace, and a Guide to Clerks, Constables, Coroners, Executors, Administrators, Guardians, Sheriffs, Tax-collectors, and Receivers, and Other Civil Officers, according to the Laws of the State of Georgia* . . . (Milledgeville, GA: Grantland, 1819), 193.

63. Noted in Farmbrough to Gilmer, 21 February 1830, *Cherokee Letters* 1, 205-207.

64. Farmbrough to Gilmer, *Cherokee Letters* 1, 205-207.

65. Thomas M. C. Harris v. Benjamin Wofford and Nathaniel Wofford, October Term 1805, Franklin Superior Court Records, Miscellaneous, 159-1-59, Georgia Archives. Nathaniel Wafford's name was later dropped from the suit.

66. It seems to have been assumed that federal jurisdiction would apply to Indian crime in and around Indian Country in the rare case that an indigenous person was surrendered for trial: see Hugh Montgomery to Governor Forsyth, 13 November 1827, *Cherokee Letters* 1, 185. Montgomery suggested on another occasion that only settler crime in Indian Country could be prosecuted, and then in federal court: Montgomery to Forsyth, 12 July 1827, *Cherokee Letters* 1, 192.

67. See J. Norgren, "Lawyers and the Legal Business of the Cherokee Republic in Courts of the United States, 1829-1835," *Law and History Review* 10, no. 2 (1992): 253-314; Testimony of Robert Mitchell, undated, Special File 107: Underwood, Records Relating to Indian Removal, 1817-1886, Decisions on Claims of Attorneys against the Cherokee Nation, 1837-1838, RG75/235, National Archives and Records Administration, Washington, DC.

68. Abstract of Charles Hicks and Ross to Meigs, 11 December 1826, *Papers of Chief John Ross*, vol. 1, 127.

69. State v. John Martin, October term 1818, Franklin Superior Court Records, Misc. Georgia Archives.

70. Warrant, State v. Walter Adair et al., October term 1818, Franklin Superior Court Records, Misc. Georgia Archives.

71. Treaty with the Cherokee, 1817, Kappler, *Indian Affairs: Laws and Treaties*, 140-144, 3.

72. State v. Nathan Thompson, August Term, Franklin County Superior Court Case Files, 159-1-41, Georgia State Archives.

73. State v. William Chambers, John Chambers, Phillip Chambers, William Moore and Enoch Nelson, March Term 1821, Franklin Superior Court Case Files, Georgia Archives.

74. Cited in U.S. v. Bailey, 24 Fed. Cas. 937, no. 14,495 C.C. D. Tenn. 1834.

75. General Crimes Act of 1817, "An Act to provide for the punishment of crimes and offences committed within Indian boundaries. (a)," Statute II, 3 March 1817, 3 Stat. 1811-1823, 383 (hereafter cited as General Crimes Act of 1817). See discussion of the act in U.S. v. Bailey, 24 Fed. Cas. 937, no. 14,495 C.C. D. Tenn. 1834.

76. For example by Joseph J. D. Matal, "A Revisionist History of Indian Country," *Alaska Law Review* 14 (1997): 283-352.

77. General Crimes Act 1817. For a discussion of some of these limitations, see R. N. Clinton, "There Is No Federal Supremacy Clause for Indian Tribes," *Arizona State Law Journal* 34 (2002): 135.

78. For indigenous suits brought with the help of settler sojourners in the Nation, see Andrew Cowan to Meigs, 12 August 1816, Cherokee Agency, M208, Reel 7. General Crimes Act 1817: see discussion of the act in U.S. v. Bailey, 24 Fed. Cas. 937, no. 14,495 C.C. D. Tenn. 1834.

79. U.S. v. Thomas Hopkins, Edward (or Eldred) Simkins Jnr and John L Wilson, November Term 1829, Minutes of the U.S. Circuit Court for the District of Georgia, 1790–1842, and Index to Plaintiffs and Defendants in the Circuit Courts, 1790–1860, National Archives Microfilm Publication M1184, Reel 2, vol. 6, 292, 296–297 (hereafter cited as U.S. Circuit Court, NARA, M1184, Reel 2). U.S. v. James Aldrich, May Term 1830, U.S. Circuit Court, NARA, M1184, Reel 2, vol. 6, 301–302, 318–319, 320–322. I presume that if these crimes were not piratical, that they occurred in Indian Country.

80. See U.S. v. Richard Blackstocks, December Term, 1824, U.S. Circuit Court, NARA, M1184, Reel 2, vol. 6, 87, 94, 101; U.S. v. Abraham Leathers, December Term 1824, U.S. Circuit Court, NARA, M1184, Reel 2, vol. 6, 87, 94, 101; U.S. v. John Martin, December Term 1824, U.S. Circuit Court, NARA, M1184, Reel 2, vol. 6, 87, 100.

81. U.S. v. William Ramsay, December Term 1818, U.S. Circuit Court, NARA, M1184, Reel 2, vol. 5, 42; U.S. v. William Taylor, December Term 1818, U.S. Circuit Court, NARA, M1184, Reel 2, vol. 5, 42; U.S. v. Robert Vestals, December Term 1818, U.S. Circuit Court, NARA, M1184, Reel 2, vol. 5, 42; U.S. v. John White, December Term 1818, U.S. Circuit Court, NARA, M1184, Reel 2, vol. 5, 41; U.S. v. Reuben Anderson, 18 December 1820, U.S. Circuit Court, NARA, M1184, Reel 2, vol. 5, 167; U.S. v. John or Thomas Tobin, 18 December 1820, U.S. Circuit Court, NARA, M1184, Reel 2, vol. 5, 163, 167.

82. U.S. v. William Reid (Reed), August Term 1820, U.S. District Court for the Southern District of Georgia, 1789–1928, National Archives and Records Administration, Microform Publication 1172, Reel 1, vol. 4, 113–114, 117 (hereafter cited as District Court, NARA, M1172); U.S. v. George Stinson, June & November Terms 1824, District Court, NARA, M1172, vol. 4, 192, 200–201.

83. U.S. v. Bailey (1834) 24 Fed. Case. 937, no. 14,495 C.C. D. Tenn. 1834.

84. M. Young, "The Exercise of Sovereignty in Cherokee Georgia," *Journal of the Early Republic* 10, no. 1 (1990): 43–63.

85. See Farmbrough to Governor Gilmer, 12 July 1830, *Cherokee Letters* 1, 222.

86. R. v. Ballard or Barret, April 21 or 23, 1929, Decisions of the Superior Courts of New South Wales, 1788–1899, published by the Division of Law, Macquarie University, http://www.law.mq.edu.au/scnsw/.

87. *Savannah Georgian*, 20 July 1826, 2, 6; 3, 1.

88. Though frontier county courts started to issue warrants to demand the arrest and demand the prosecution of Indian offenders, it is clear that most crimes committed in Georgia went unpunished. On warrants, see Thomas Miller to Governor Rabun, 8 April 1817, *Creek Indian Letters, Talks and Treaties, 1705–1839*, vol. 3, comp. L. F. Hays (WPA Project P.P. 665-34-3-224, 1939),

888. On Petition demanding that Cherokee Old Man be brought to justice for his crimes, see Random Thompson and William Stokes to Troup, 12 August 1827, *Cherokee Letters* 1, 181. Regarding Cherokee murderers still at large in the nation after June 1830 (including Ellis Buffington), see Jacob R. Brooks to Gilmer, 12 November 1830, *Cherokee Letters* 2, 242.

89. *Savannah Georgian*, 20 July 1826, 3, 1. Compare *Savannah Georgian*, 10 February 1826, 2, 3, noting the arrest of a "notorious war chief" for murdering a Saginaw Indian.

90. Path Killer to Meigs, 24 June 1821, Records of the Cherokee Agency, NARA, M208, Reel 9.

91. The committee was convened to hear Cherokee claims under the Schermerhorn Treaty of 1835: Treaty with the Cherokee, 1835, Kappler, *Indian Affairs: Laws and Treaties*, 439–499.

92. Records Relating to Indian Removal, 1817–1886, Decisions on Spoilation Claims, RG75/232, National Archives and Records Administration, Washington, Case 503 (hereafter cited as Records Relating to Indian Removal, Decisions on Spoilation Claims, 75/232, NARA).

93. For examples of the lawless activities of Old Philpot and the Poney Club, see Records Relating to Indian Removal, Decisions on Spoilation Claims, 75/232, NARA, Cases 545, 549, 589, 593. See also William Thompson to Gilmer, 27 December 1830, *Cherokee Letters* 2, 263.

94. Ross to Elias Boudinot, 13 February 1830, *Papers of Chief John Ross*, vol. 1, 186.

95. See W. G. McLoughlin, "Thomas Jefferson and the Beginning of Cherokee Nationalism, 1806–1809," *William and Mary Quarterly* 32, no. 4 (1975): 548–580; and J. P. Ronda, "'We Have a Country': Race, Geography, and the Invention of Indian Territory," *Journal of the Early Republic* 19, no. 4 (1999): 739–755; Compare F. A. Yarbrough, *Race and the Cherokee Nation: Sovereignty in the Nineteenth Century* (Philadelphia: University of Pennsylvania Press, 2008).

96. Committee on Indian Affairs, "Removal of Indians," Delivered in the House of Representatives, 21st Congress, 1st Session, 24 February 1830, No. 227 (Washington, DC: Government Printing Office, 1830), 2.

97. R. Strickland, *Fire and the Spirits: Cherokee Law from Clan to Court* (Norman: University of Oklahoma Press, 1975), 3–4.

98. McLoughlin, *Cherokees and Missionaries*, 124.

99. See, generally, *Laws of the Cherokee Nation: Adopted by the Council at Various Periods, 1808–1835* (Tahlequah, OK: Cherokee Advocate Office, 1852); V. Richard Persico Jr., "Early Nineteenth Century Cherokee Political Organization," in *The Cherokee Indian Nation: A Troubled History*, ed. D. H. King (Knoxville: University of Tennessee Press, 1979), 96; M. Daniel, "From Blood Feud to Jury System: The Metamorphosis of Cherokee Law from 1750 to 1840," *American Indian Quarterly* 11, no. 2 (1987): 97–125.

100. McLoughlin, *Cherokees and Missionaries*, 124–149, 80–212.

101. Cumfer, *Separate Peoples, One Land*, 23–98.

102. T. Perdue, "Clan and Court: Another Look at the Early Cherokee Republic," *American Indian Quarterly* 24, no. 4 (2000): 567.

103. For example see Ross et al. to Thomas McKenny, 29 April 1824, *Papers of Chief John Ross*, vol. 1, 80–81.

104. For example, Cherokee Council to Meigs, 16 February 1817, Cherokee Agency, NARA, M208 Reel 7. Postwar agreements between the Creek Nation and the Federal Government facilitated similar claims in the Creek Nation: C. Saunt, "Taking Account of Property: Stratification among the Creek Indians in the Early Nineteenth Century," *William and Mary Quarterly* 57, no. 4 (2000): 733–760.

105. Cherokee Council to Return J. Meigs, 2 November 1819, *Letters of Chief John Ross*, vol. 1, 38.

106. For a discussion of like "exceptions," see Perdue, "Clan and Court," 562–569. On the shift to compensation as a remedy in the eighteenth century, see Daniel, "From Blood Feud to Jury System," 97–125.

107. It is important to note the impact of federal refusals to remove squatters on Cherokee jurisdiction. On increasing Cherokee responsibility for removing squatters, see Ross to Andrew Jackson, 19 June 1820, 40, *Papers of Chief John Ross*, vol. 1, 40–41. On protests against federal inaction, see Ross to Calhoun, 24 October 1822, *Papers of Chief John Ross*, vol. 1, 45; and Path Killer et al. to Joseph McMinn, 11 October 1823, *Papers of Chief John Ross*, vol. 1, 51.

108. For Joseph McMinn's endorsement of lawlessness as a strategy to prompt removal (that is, by removing U.S. protection of the Cherokee), see McMinn to Calhoun, 29 November 1818, "Extinguishment of Indian title to lands in Georgia. Communicated to the House of Representatives, 2 April 1824," *American State Papers: Indian Affairs*, vol. 2, pub. no. 204," 482.

109. McMinn to the Cherokee Council, 8 October 1824, Letters Received by the Office of Indian Affairs, 1824–1881, National Archives and Records Administration Microfilm Publication, Reel 71, 64 (hereafter cited as Letters Received OIA, NARA, Reel 71); emphasis in original.

110. Cherokee Council to McMinn, 11 October 1823, *Papers of Chief John Ross*, vol. 1, 51.

111. This was the claim made by the federal government: see Ross et al. to Calhoun, 25 February 1824, *Papers of Chief John Ross*, vol. 1, 73–74.

112. Judge White, legal opinion, May 27 1823, enclosed with Ross to Meigs, Letters Received Office of Indian Affairs, NARA, Reel 71, 41–51; emphasis in original.

113. McKenny to Ross, George Lowrey, Major Ridge and Elijah Hicks, 7 April 1824, *Papers of Chief John Ross*, vol. 1, 76.

114. See Treasury Department to Hugh Montgomery, 10 June 1825, Cherokee Agency, NARA, M208, Reel 10.

115. Quoted in McMinn to Cherokee Council, 23 November 1818, "Extinguishment of Indian title to lands in Georgia. Communicated to the House of Representatives, 2 April 1824," *American State Papers: Indian Affairs*, vol. 2, pub. no. 204, 488.

116. Path Killer et al. to John C. Calhoun, 24 October 1822, *Papers of Chief John Ross*, vol. 1, 44.

117. 27 October 1823, "Extinguishment of Indian title to lands in Georgia. Communicated to the House of Representatives, 2 April 1824," *American State Papers: Indian Affairs*, vol. 2, pub. no. 204, 472–473.

118. Campbell and Meriwether to Cherokee Council, 21 October 1823, "Extinguishment of Indian title to lands in Georgia. Communicated to the House of Representatives, 2 April 1824," *American State Papers: Indian Affairs*, vol. 2, pub. no. 204, 469–471.

119. Cherokee Council to Campbell and Meriwether, 27 October 1823, "Extinguishment of Indian title to lands in Georgia. Communicated to the House of Representatives, 2 April 1824," *American State Papers: Indian Affairs*, vol. 2, pub. no. 204, 472–473.

120. Calhoun to the Cherokee Council, 30 January 1824, "Extinguishment of Indian title to lands in Georgia. Communicated to the House of Representatives, 2 April 1824," *American State Papers: Indian Affairs*, vol. 2, pub. no. 204, 473.

121. Cherokee Council to Calhoun, 11 February 1824, *American State Papers: Indian Affairs*, vol. 2, pub. no. 204, 41.

122. Cherokee Constitution, July 1827, *Laws of the Cherokee Nation: Adopted by the Council at Various Periods, 1808–1835* (Tahlequah, OK: Cherokee Advocate Office, 1852), 117–130.

123. See reference to the trial and punishment of a "white man under the laws of the nation, for the crime of horse stealing" by Judge John Sanders (who was later arrested for doing so and tried in Georgia): Ross, Annual Message, 11 October 1830, *Papers of Chief John Ross*, vol. 1, 202.

7. Lego'me and Territoriality in New South Wales

1. For the years 1788–1824, see: R. v. Hatherly and Jackie, State Records, New South Wales (hereafter cited as SR NSW): Court of Criminal Jurisdiction, Indictments, Informations and Related Papers, 1816–1824, 18 December 1822 (or 27 December 1822 and adjourned until 1 January 1823), Informations, Depositions and Related Papers, Court of Criminal Jurisdiction, [SZ800], Reel 197798, 1–19; and R. v. Hatherly and Jackie, January 2, 1823, Decisions of the Superior Courts of New South Wales, 1788–1899. Note however R. v. Randall, SR NSW: Bench of Magistrates, 1788–1820, 7 June 1799, [SZ767], Reel 655, 83.1835: see 1835 index of Decisions of the Superior Courts of New South Wales, 1788–1899, published by the Division of Law, Macquarie University, http://www.law.mq.edu.au/scnsw/ (hereafter cited as Decisions of the Superior Courts of New South Wales, 1788–1899); and note that some additional cases seem to have been heard in Maitland: Victoria Gollan, *Aboriginal Colonial Court Cases*, 1788–1838, http://srwww.records.nsw.gov.au/indexes/searchform.aspx?id=1.

2. For example, A. C. Castles, *An Australian Legal History* (Sydney: Law Book Company, 1982), 520–522; G. Nettheim, "'The Consent of the

Natives': Mabo and Indigenous Political Rights," *Sydney Law Review* 15, no. 2 (1993): 224–225; S. Banner, "Why *Terra Nullius?* Anthropology and Property Law in Early Australia," *Law and History Review* 23, no. 1 (2005): 95–132. Contrast more nuanced accounts in B. Kercher, *An Unruly Child: A History of Law in Australia* (St. Leonards, NSW: Allen & Unwin, 1995), 3–21.

3. See D. Ward, *"Savage Customs" and "Civilised Laws": British Attitudes to Legal Pluralism in Australasia, c. 1830–1848*, London Papers in Australian Studies 10 (London: Menzies Centre for Australian Studies, 2003); C. Bayly, *Imperial Meridian: The British Empire and the World, 1730–1830* (Harlow, UK: Longman, 1989), 136–155.

4. For a brief description of administrative reform in this period, see J. J. Eddy, *Britain and the Australian Colonies, 1818–1831: The Technique of Government* (Oxford, UK: Clarendon Press, 1969), 21–37. For the effect of legal reform on colonial law in this period, see Kercher, *An Unruly Child*, 67–81.

5. Kercher, *An Unruly Child*, 69; A. Atkinson, *The Europeans in Australia: A History: Democracy*, vol. 2 (Melbourne: Oxford University Press, 2004).

6. Kercher, *An Unruly Child*, 69–73.

7. On the extraordinary growth of the colony in this period, see: K. S. Inglis, *The Australian Colonists: An Exploration of Social History, 1788–1870* (Carlton, VIC: Melbourne University Press, 1974), 10; R. Harrison, *Shared Landscapes: Archeologies of Attachment and the Pastoral Industry in New South Wales*, Studies in the Cultural Construction of Open Space (Randwick, NSW: University of New South Wales Press, 2004), 25–26; P. McMichael, *Settlers and the Agrarian Question: Foundations of Capitalism in Colonial Australia* (Cambridge and New York: Cambridge University Press, 1984). See discussions of Aboriginal resistance to migration to Bathurst and the Hunter Valley in: J. Connor, *The Australian Frontier Wars, 1788–1838* (Randwick, NSW: University of New South Wales Press, 2002), 53–67; W. A. Wood, *Dawn in the Valley: The Story of Settlement in the Hunter River Valley to 1833* (Sydney: Wentworth Books, 1972). How to govern peripheries remained a fundamental problem; note the stipulation on 9 June 1827 that the surveyor general not alienate Crown lands more than 15 miles from a magistrate: State Records NSW: Colonial Secretary Correspondence, 1826–1877: Colonial Secretary to Surveyor General, 9 June 1827, Special Bundles, Land: Surveyor General—Mainly Policy Matters Governing the Alienation of Crown Lands, 1826–1841, 2/8015.5.

8. Connor, *The Australian Frontier Wars*, 53–83.

9. Note, however, that squatting from the late 1820s placed many farms outside the reach of the colonial government altogether: Special Bundles: Papers Relating to the Regulation of Squatting Part I, 1839–44, 5/4774.2, State Archives of New South Wales.

10. See pleadings in R. v. Lowe, May 18 or 23, 1827, Decisions of the Superior Courts of New South Wales, 1788–1899.

11. B. Bridges, "The Extension of English Law to the Aborigines for Offences Committed Inter-Se, 1829–1842," *Journal of the Royal Australian Historical Society* (1973): 264–269; B. Kercher, "Native Title in the Shadows: The Ori-

gins of the Myth of *Terra Nullius* in Early New South Wales Courts," in *Colonialism and the Modern World: Selected Studies*, ed. G. Blue, M. Bunton, and R. Crozier (New York: M. E. Sharpe, 2002), 100–119; Bruce Kercher, "Recognition of Indigenous Legal Autonomy in Nineteenth Century New South Wales," *Indigenous Law Bulletin* 4 (1998): 7–9; Kercher, *An Unruly Child*, 3–21.

12. R. v. Lego'me, February 12 or 16, 1835, Decisions of the Superior Courts of New South Wales, 1788–1899 (hereafter cited as R. v. Lego'me).

13. R. v. Ballard or Barret, April 21 or 23, 1929, Decisions of the Superior Courts of New South Wales, 1788–1899.

14. R. v. Boatman or Jackass and Bulleye, February 10, 1832, Decisions of the Superior Courts of New South Wales, 1788–1899.

15. R. v. Devil Devil, June 3 or 9, 1825, Decisions of the Superior Courts of New South Wales, 1788–1899. On the fact that he was not sentenced, see Gollan, Aboriginal Court Cases, and R. v. Devil Devil, SR NSW: Supreme Court of New South Wales, Informations and Related Papers, 1824–1947, 3 June 1825, [T20], (Bundle No. Informations, Depositions and Related Papers, Supreme Court of New South Wales, 1824—1947, 25/90).

16. R. v. Binge Mhulto, September 19 or 26, 1828, Decisions of the Superior Courts of New South Wales, 1788–1899. For another example, see annotation regarding "Dickey" (who was not tried for murder): SR NSW: Supreme Court: Charge Book or Court Book Deposition Books, 1825–1826, [4/467.3].

17. R. v. Lowe, Decisions of the Superior Courts of New South Wales, 1788–1899.

18. Note that a number of Aborigines who came to the notice of the court in the 1820s and 1830s were called Jackey or Jackey Jackey. In this case, the Aborigine in question was also known as Tommy. I have used Tommy for clarity. R. v. Tommy, *Sydney Monitor* Report, 29 November 1827, Decisions of the Superior Courts of New South Wales, 1788–1899.

19. For a *Sydney Gazette* discussion of what I think is the *Monitor*'s reaction to Devil Devil's release, see "Aboriginal Defendant," 29 March 1827, Decisions of the Superior Courts of New South Wales, 1788–1899. In the context of Tommy's case, see "*Sydney Monitor* Report," 29 November 1827, Decisions of the Superior Courts of New South Wales.

20. M. Constable, *The Law of the Other: The Mixed Jury and Changing Conceptions of Citizenship, Law, and Knowledge* (London and Chicago: University of Chicago Press, 1994), 96–113.

21. R. v. Binge Mhulto, Decisions of the Superior Courts of New South Wales, 1788–1899.

22. R. v. Lowe, Decisions of the Superior Courts of New South Wales, 1788–1899.

23. R. v. Tommy, November 24 or 26, 1827, Decisions of the Superior Courts of New South Wales, 1788–1899. See the same bifurcated reasoning (British law or the law of nations governed Aboriginal crime) in R. v. Jackey, May 6, 1834, Decisions of the Superior Courts of New South Wales, 1788–1899. The Court noted, "He should put the case of the prisoner at the bar to them in the same

manner [as he would] against any of his Majesty's subjects because he knew of nothing to prevent these people being considered as such. It was necessary to treat them in this manner on many grounds, but on this principally. The enjoyment and protection of life is as much the law of nature as the law of England. If in a newly inhabited country, there be no municipal law, then the law of nature comes into operation; for if it were not so, the law of retaliation or self-defence would be acted upon."

24. See Connor, *The Australian Frontier Wars*, 53–67.
25. Regarding natural law's attitude to property, see, for example, H. Grotius, *The Rights of War and Peace*, 3 vols. (London: Brown, D., Ward, T., Meares, W., 1715), 2:1, 16–22.
26. R. v. Boatman or Jackass and Bulleye, Decisions of the Superior Courts of New South Wales, 1788–1899.
27. Lord v. Palmer, 1803, Decisions of the Superior Courts of New South Wales, 1788–1899; Lord v. Palmer, 1809, Decisions of the Superior Courts of New South Wales, 1788–1899.
28. Reported in *Sydney Gazette*, 10 May 1817, 2, 2.
29. Law Officers to the Earl of Bathurst, 15 February 1819, The National Archives, Public Records Office, Colonial Office 201/97, f98–101, Kew Gardens (hereafter cited as TNA: PRO CO).
30. Law Officers Opinion in Thomas Dowse's Case undated, TNA: PRO CO 201/158, f107–112.
31. R. v. The Magistrates of Sydney, October 14 and 21, 1824, Decisions of the Superior Courts of New South Wales, 1788–1899.
32. See, for example, R. v. West, October 17 or 18, 1832, Decisions of the Superior Courts of New South Wales, 1788–1899. For a comparative analysis, see J. C. Weaver, *The Great Land Rush and the Making of the Modern World, 1650–1900* (Montreal: McGill Queens University Press, 2003), 264–310.
33. R. v. Steele, October 28 or 30, 1834, Decisions of the Superior Courts of New South Wales, 1788–1899 Contrast Brown v. Alexander, September 30, 1828, Decisions of the Superior Courts of New South Wales, 1788–1899.
34. Note that there are some differences in the newspaper accounts of this case: see *Sydney Gazette*, 21 May 1827, 5, 2, which reported Forbes as saying, "The *lex loci* must therefore be our guide." See annotations to R. v. Lowe, Decisions of the Superior Courts of New South Wales, 1788–1899.
35. See text and annotations in R. v. Lowe, Decisions of the Superior Courts of New South Wales, 1788–1899. Regarding the jurisdiction granted the court by the act: "This Court, like the Court of King's Bench, in England, has a territorial jurisdiction" (*Sydney Gazette*, 21 May 1827).
36. R. v. Lowe, Decisions of the Superior Courts of New South Wales, 1788–1899.
37. R. v. Ballard or Barret, Decisions of the Superior Courts of New South Wales, 1788–1899 (hereafter cited as R. v. Ballard or Barret).
38. R. v. Ballard or Barret. Compare debates over the status of different indigenous tribes in the confederal period in North America, discussed in Chapter 1.
39. R. v. Ballard or Barret.

40. R. v. Ballard or Barret.

41. R. v. Ballard or Barret.

42. R. v. Tommy, Decisions of the Superior Courts of New South Wales, 1788–1899.

43. See discussion below, notes 72–76. Regarding release, see SR NSW: John Kinchela to Colonial Secretary, 29 March 1834, and John Kinchela to Harrington Esq., 18 April 1834, SB: Attorney-General, [4/2221.2].

44. R. v. Jackey, Decisions of the Superior Courts of New South Wales, 1788–1899.

45. R. v. Jackey, Decisions of the Superior Courts of New South Wales, 1788–1899. See colonial secretary's notes on this case in SR NSW: Colonial Secretary's Correspondence, Annotations on John Kinchela to Colonial Secretary, 17 April 1834, Special Bundles: Attorney-General, 1826–1877, [4/2221.2] (SB: Attorney-General, [4/2221.2]).

46. H. Golder and I. Pike, *High and Responsible Office: A History of the N.S.W. Magistracy* (Sydney: University of Sydney Press, 1991), 1–50.

47. Weaver, *The Great Land Rush*, 264–310; P. Karsten, *Between Law and Custom: "High" and "Low" Legal Cultures in the Lands of the British Diaspora— The United States, Canada, Australia, and New Zealand, 1600–1900* (Cambridge: Cambridge University Press, 2002), 146–187.

48. SR NSW: Colonial Secretary's Correspondence, Special Bundles: Papers Relating to the Regulation of Squatting, Part I, 1839–44, 5/4774.2.

49. R. H. W. Reece, *Aborigines and Colonists: Aborigines and Colonial Society in New South Wales in the 1830s and 1840s* (Sydney: University of Sydney Press, 1974), 140–215; 7–9.

50. Darling to the Landholders at Hunter's River, 5 September 1826, *Historical Records of Australia: Series 1, Governors' Despatches to and from England*, vol. 12 (Sydney: The Library Committee of the Commonwealth Parliament, 1919), 576–577 (hereafter cited as HRA 1:12, 576–577). See also D. J. Neal, *The Rule of Law in a Penal Colony: Law and Power in Early New South Wales* (Cambridge and Melbourne: Cambridge University Press, 1991), 79; and Reece, *Aborigines and Colonists*, 113. See Chapter 5.

51. For example, SR NSW: Colonial Secretary's Correspondence 1826–1877, Sullivan to Colonial Secretary, 26 December 1832, Colonial Secretary's Correspondence, 1826–1877: Main Series, [33/2862]; and SR NSW: Colonial Secretary's Correspondence: W. J. Morris to Alexander Berry, 2 October 1830, Special Bundles: Aboriginal Outrages 1830–1, Golburn Plains: 4/8020.2: in which Morris stated that he would arrest Aborigines if he had handcuffs (hereafter cited as SB: Aboriginal Outrages). Contrast SR NSW: Francis Flanaghan to Governor Darling, 4 October 1830, SB: Aboriginal Outrages, 4/8020.2: in which Flanaghan enjoined the government to show local Aborigines our "superiority of power."

52. Correspondence in R. v. Jamieson, May 16 or 18, 1827, Decisions of the Superior Courts of New South Wales, 1788–1899.

53. R. Scott Esq. to Alexander McLeay (also MacLeay)—enclosing Wall's depositions, 17 May 1826, *Original Documents on Aborigines and the Law*,

1790–1840, Document no. 12, Macquarie University, http://www.law.mq .edu.au/scnsw/Correspondence/index.htm (hereafter cited as *Original Documents on Aborigines*, doc. 12).

54. See depositions of mounted policemen John Larnach, Lewis Moore, George Castles, John Lee, and James Fielding, 13 September 1826, *HRA* 1:12, 625–628, 626. Lowe himself deposed that he would have "brought them to trial" if they had not done so: Examination of Nathaniel Low, 13 September 1826, *HRA* 1:12, 626.

55. Harring traces the persistence of this logic in newer Australian colonies: S. L. Harring, "The Killing Time: A History of Aboriginal Resistance in Colonial Australia," *Ottawa Law Review* 26 (1994): 385–423.

56. SR NSW: Colonial Secretary's Correspondence, 1826–1877: Main Series: Constable at Wollongong to Colonial Secretary, 2 January 1833, 33/2119.

57. SR NSW: Colonial Secretary's Correspondence, 1826–1877: Main Series: Comments of McLeay[?], 8 January 1833, 33/2119. Emphasis in original.

58. This definition comes from: W. F. Finlason, *Commentaries upon Martial Law* (Littleton, CO: F. B. Rothman, 1980), 1; quoted and discussed in Kercher, *An Unruly Child*, 8–9. First declaration of Martial Law, 14 August 1824, *Historical Records of Australia, Series 1, Governors' Despatches to and from England*, series 1, vol. 11, (Sydney: The Library Committee of the Commonwealth Parliament, 1914), 410.

59. Contrast Connor, who argues that Aborigines were deemed from settlement to have been subjects of the Crown: Connor, *The Australian Frontier Wars*, 58.

60. For a discussion of relations between Bannister and Darling in this context, see Reece, *Aborigines and Colonists*, 112. Significantly, Saxe Bannister went on to be a passionate advocate of Aboriginal rights in Australia: S. Bannister, *Humane Policy or Justice to the Aborigines of New Settlements Essential to a Due Expenditure of British Money, and to the Best Interests of the Settlers with Suggestions how to Civilise the Natives by an Improved Administration of Existing Means* (London: Thomas & George Underwood, 1830); S. Bannister, *British Colonization and Colored Tribes* (London: William Ball, 1838).

61. Bathurst to Darling, 14 July 1825, *HRA* 1:12, 21. See Reece, *Aborigines and Colonists*, 113.

62. Bannister to Darling, 9 September 1826, quoted by Bannister in his *Statements and Documents Relating to Proceedings in NSW in 1824, 1825 and 1826* (Cape Town, ZA: Bridekirk, 1827), 99, quoted in Reece, *Aborigines and Colonists*, 112.

63. Darling to Hay, 11 September 1826, *HRA* 1:12, 575.

64. SR NSW: Colonial Secretary's Correspondence 1826–1877, Sullivan to Colonial Secretary, 26 December 1832, Colonial Secretary's Correspondence, 1826–1877: Main Series, [33/2862].

65. See SR NSW: Major Sullivan and Annotation, 31 January 1833, Matters Scheduled for the Governor for Decision, [4/441], Schedule No. 7.

66. Annotations to SR NSW: Kinchela to Colonial Secretary, 18 April 1834, SB: Attorney-General, [34/2552]. Emphasis in original. Legislation was not a novel settler solution to the problem of indigenous legal status. See "An Act

to add all that part of the unlocated territory of this state which lies without the limits of the present counties, to the county of Jasper, for the purpose of giving the Courts jurisdiction of crimes committed by white persons against white persons in said territory, and for other purposes," 27/50, Assented to 23 November 1814, Acts of the General Assembly of the State of Georgia; Passed in October and November, 1814; vol. 1, 41, *Georgia Legislative Documents*, University of Georgia Libraries, http://www.galileo.usg.edu/express?link=zlgl; "Legal Opinion Regarding the Extension of Jurisdiction in Indian Country in Upper Canada," 18 December 1802, TNA: PRO CO 42/120; and note regarding the passing of legislation to give jurisdiction over trading companies in Canadian "wastelands" in 1803: Secretary of State to Milne, 11 September 1803, TNA: PRO CO 43/22. Regarding other mentions of Aboriginal independence in this period, see SR NSW: Commandant of Moreton Bay to Colonial Secretary, 27 February 1833 (and following), Colonial Secretary's Correspondence: Main Series, [33/1930]; and SR NSW: Commandant of Moreton Bay and Annotation, 29 January 1833, Matters Scheduled for the Governor for Decision, [4/441], Entry 26.

67. SR NSW: Colonial Secretary's Correspondence: Main Series, John Kinchela to Alexander McLeay, 11 January 1833, [33/347].

68. SR NSW: Colonial Secretary's Correspondence: Main Series, John Kinchela to Alexander McLeay, 11 January 1833, [33/347]; SR NSW: Commandant of Moreton Bay and Annotation, 29 January 1833, Matters Scheduled for the Governor for Decision, [4/441], Entry 26. In his own summary of his comments, the colonial secretary expresses evident frustration with the lawyerly nature of Kinchela's response.

69. The coroner's inquest and charge were reported in *Sydney Gazette*, 4 January 1834, 2, 1–2.

70. SR NSW: Kinchela to McLeay, 16 January 1834, SB: Attorney-General, [4/2221.2].

71. SR NSW: Kinchela to McLeay, 20 January 1834, SB: Attorney-General, [4/2221.2].

72. SR NSW: Kinchela to McLeay, 19 February 1834, SB: Attorney-General, [4/2221.2].

73. SR NSW: Annotation, 20 February 1824 on Kinchela to McLeay, 19 February 1834, SB: Attorney-General, [4/2221.2].

74. Note that they are listed in a schedule of Aborigines tried by the Court between 1832 and 1838: SR NSW: Supreme Court: Returns of Aboriginal natives tried before the Supreme Court between 1832 and 1838, [4/2129] (part). Contrast an earlier list prepared for the Supreme Court: "List of Blacks Tried and Convicted and Executed since 1827, February 1836," *Original Documents on Aborigines*, doc. 49. Note that the men were still in jail in April of 1834: SR NSW: Kinchela to McLeay, 29 March 1834; Kinchela to Harrington Esq., 18 April 1834, SB: Attorney-General, [4/2221.2].

75. R. v. Murrell and Bummaree, February 5 or 8, 1836, Decisions of the Superior Courts of New South Wales, 1788–1899, published by the Division of Law, Macquarie University, http://www.law.mq.edu.au/scnsw/.

76. On Aborigines at the jail: *Australian*, 17 February 1834. See annotations about this case in R. v. Murrell and Bummaree, Decisions of the Superior Courts of New South Wales, 1788–1899.

77. On their release, see SR NSW: McLeay to Kinchela, 18 April 1834, SB: Attorney-General, [4/3742]; *Australian*, 28 February 1834 (reproduced in R. v. Murrell and Bummaree, Decisions of the Superior Courts of New South Wales, 1788–1899).

78. R. v. Mickey and Muscle, Comments in *Australian*, 6 March 1835, Decisions of the Superior Courts of New South Wales.

79. Not including R. v. Randall, SR NSW: Bench of Magistrates, 1788–1820, 7 June 1799, [SZ767], Reel 655, 83. (Randall appeared before the Bench of Magistrates in 1799 but was not convicted by the court; discussed in Chapter 2.)

80. T. Castle, "Watching Them Hang: Capital Punishment and Public Support in Colonial New South Wales, 1826–1836," *History Australia* 5.2 (2008): 43.1–15; T. Castle, "The End of the Line: Capital Punishment and Mercy in New South Wales, 1826–1836" (Honors thesis, University of New England, 2007), 44–46.

81. Contrast R. v. Lego'me. Note public discussions of the trials: *Australian*, 17 February 1835, reproduced in Decisions of the Superior Courts of New South Wales.

82. For example, R. v. Long Dick, Jack Jones, Abraham, and Gibber Paddy, May 12 or 14, 1835, Decisions of the Superior Courts of New South Wales, 1788–1899.

83. For an important discussion of the context and commemoration of the treaty, see: B. Attwood, *Possession: Batman's Treaty and the Matter of History* (Carlton, VIC: Miegunyah Press, 2009). For correspondence and other documentation relating to the Geelong & Dutigalla Association, 1835–1859, see State Library of Victoria, MS10258, http://www.slv.vic.gov.au/portphillip/inter/4703.shtml (accessed 3 August 2008). For discussions of the treaty and early Victorian history, see: C. P. Billot, *John Batman: The Story of John Batman and the Founding of Melbourne* (Melbourne: Hyland House, 1979); A. G. L. Shaw, *A History of the Port Phillip District: Victoria before Separation* (Carlton, VIC: Melbourne University Press, 1996); A. H. Campbell, *John Batman and the Aborigines* (Malmsbury: Kibble Books, 1987); M. F. Christie, *Aborigines in Colonial Victoria, 1835–86* (Sydney: University of Sydney Press, 1979).

84. Proclamation of Governor Bourke, 10 October 1835, TNA: PRO CO 201/247.

85. Lieutenant Governor Arthur to Spring Rice, TNA: PRO CO 280/50, f13–14.

86. "Report of the Select Committee on Aborigines (British Settlements)," *British Parliamentary Papers: Anthropology: Aborigines*, vols. 1–3 (Shannon: Irish University Press, 1968–1969); H. Reynolds, *The Law of the Land*, 2nd ed. (Ringwood, VIC: Penguin, 1992), 97–102.

87. Draft of letter, Grey to Torrens, 15 December 1835, TNA: PRO CO 13/3, f130. South Australian colonizers disagreed adamantly with Grey's propensity to respect indigenous rights, pointing to practices in other colonies: Torrens to Grey, December 1835, TNA: PRO CO 13/3, f169.

88. Ward, *"Savage Customs" and "Civilized Laws,"* 14–17.
89. "Case Stated to Dr Lushington with his Response," 18 January 1836, TNA: PRO CO 201/258.
90. Stephen to Mercer, 14 April 1836, TNA: PRO CO 201/258.
91. Stephen to Mercer, 14 April 1836, TNA: PRO CO 201/258.
92. Reynolds, *The Law of the Land*, 128–131; contrast Ward, *"Savage Customs" and "Civilised Laws."*

8. Perfect Settler Sovereignty

1. London remained aloof from New South Wales's articulations of settler sovereignty, chiefly because, as Murrell was acquitted, his case was not appealed. However, the Colonial Office had intervened in Canada's attempts to grapple with indigenous jurisdiction in 1822 and played a more proactive role in jurisdictional practice in New Zealand. See, generally, M. D. Walters, "The Extension of Colonial Criminal Jurisdiction over the Aboriginal Peoples of Upper Canada: Reconsidering the Shawanakiskie Case (1822–1826)," *University of Toronto Law Journal* 46, no. 2 (1996): 273–310; Mark Hickford, "Decidedly the Most Interesting Savages on the Globe": An Approach to the Intellectual History of Māori Property Rights, 1837–53," *History of Political Thought* 27, no. 1 (2006): 122–147; and D. Ward, *"Savage Customs" and "Civilised Laws": British Attitudes to Legal Pluralism in Australasia, c. 1830–1848*, London Papers in Australian Studies 10 (London: Menzies Centre for Australian Studies, 2003).
2. For a discussion of the federalism of the Marshall Supreme Court, see R. K. Newmyer, "John Marshall, McCulloch v. Maryland, and the Southern States' Rights Tradition," *John Marshall Law Review* 33 (1999): 875–934. For a discussion of the importance of Worcester in setting up "normative and institutional components of American law," see P. P. Frickey, "Marshalling Past and Present: Colonialism, Constitutionalism, and Interpretation in Federal Indian Law," *Harvard Law Review* 107, no. 2 (1993): 383.
3. Regarding the "jurispathic" role of judges in their encounters with indigenous rules, see D. Ivison, "Decolonizing the Rule of Law: Mabo's Case and Postcolonial Constitutionalism," *Oxford Journal of Legal Studies* 17, no. 2 (1997): 253–279; R. Cover, "Nomos and Narrative," in *Narrative, Violence, and the Law: The Essays of Robert Cover*, ed. M Minow, M. Ryan, and A. Sarat (Ann Arbor: University of Michigan Press, 1992), 95–172.
4. Walters, "The Extension of Colonial Criminal Jurisdiction," 273–310.
5. Hobson to Major Bunbury Kitt, 26 April 1840, The National Archives, Public Records Office, Colonial Office 209/6, f146–156, Kew (hereafter cited as TNA: PRO CO).
6. *New Zealand Spectator; Cook's Strait Guardian*, 4 December 1847, 2, 3–4, 3, 1–2. This is the earliest inter-se case recovered so far by Shaunnagh Dorsett et al., who are recovering all early New Zealand case law.
7. Shaunnagh Dorsett, trans. and annot., "Notebook Chapman J—Criminal Trials, Monday Sept 3 1849, The Queen v Native" (unpublished transcript,

Faculty of Law, Victoria University, 2008); and see *New Zealand Spectator; Cook's Strait Guardian*, 5 September 1849, 2–3; Shaunnagh Dorsett, "'Sworn on the Dirt of Graves': Sovereignty, Jurisdiction and the Judicial Abrogation of Barbarous Customs in New Zealand in the 1840s," *Journal of Legal History* 30, no. 2 (2009): forthcoming.

8. J. O'Brien, "Vanishing Indians in Nineteenth-Century New England: Local Historians' Erasure of Still-Present Indian People," in *New Perspectives on Native North America: Cultures, Histories and Representations*, ed. S. Kan, P. T. Strong, and R. Fogelson (Lincoln: University of Nebraska Press, 2006), 414–432.

9. See ambiguous Colonial Office attitudes to Māori jurisdiction in Ward, *"Savage Customs" and "Civilised Laws,"* 8–17. On British/Māori interactions in this period, see: M. Hickford, "Making Territorial Rights of the Natives: Britain and New Zealand, 1830–1847" (Ph.D. diss., University of Oxford, 1999).

10. J. Sheehan, "The Problem of Sovereignty in European History," *American Historical Review* 111, no. 1 (2006): 1–15.

11. L. A. Benton, *Law and Colonial Cultures: Legal Regimes in World History, 1400–1900* (Cambridge: Cambridge University Press, 2002).

12. For example, Law Officers to Lord Hobart, 23 October 1801, TNA: PRO CO 260/17: which denied that Caribs have any land rights not dependent on the Crown in St. Vincent. For later agitation of the question, see Governor Bentick to Hobart, 28 April 1804, TNA: PRO CO 260/18, No. 15; Law Officers to Bentick, 9 January, 1804, TNA: PRO CO 260/18, No. 9 (enclosing opinion on the subject in 1801); Hobart to Bentick, 24 November 1803, TNA: PRO CO 260/18; Bentick to J. Sullivan, Esq., 23 October 1803, TNA: PRO CO 260/18, Private (begging for more specific opinion regarding whether the Crown owned Charib land or, indeed, whether the governor and his courts had jurisdiction over Charib lands in St. Vincent); Hobart to Bentick, 4 June 1804, TNA: PRO CO 260/18. For other examples, see Lord Hobart to Law Officers, 18 December 1802, TNA: PRO CO 324/119, 26; Lord Hobart to Law Officers, 24 March 1803, TNA: PRO CO 324/119, 31–32: requesting their opinion on the legality of extending British law over traders in Canada's Indian Country, and transmitting a bill prepared for the purpose of extending the jurisdiction of the courts.

13. For an indication of the number of jurisdictional issues referred to the law office after 1827, see Index to the Law Officers Reports, 1837–1859, TNA: PRO CO 324/176. This index indicates that the Law Officers gave opinions regarding: (1) whether Jamaican Maroons should be compensated for dispossession (15 August 1837); (2) the power of the Crown over waste lands in Antigua (5 March 1838); (3) whether foreigners guilty of treason could be dealt with like natural born subjects (31 April 1838); (4) whether offenses on the streets outside the Gibraltar Garrison fell within British law (23 July 1838); (5) what rights attended British sovereignty in Honduras (25 September 1838); and (6) whether New South Wales's wastelands were indeed vested in the Crown (3 June 1839). See also Law Officers to Glenelg, 28 May 1838, TNA: PRO CO 42/453, f110–114.

14. Belich, *Replenishing the Earth: The Settler Revolution and the Rise of the Angloworld* (London and New York: Oxford University Press, 2009).

15. For example, J. Evarts, *Cherokee Removal: The 'William Penn' Essays and Other Writings*, ed. F. P. Prucha (Knoxville: University of Tennessee Press, 1981); F. P. Prucha, "Introduction," in Prucha, *Cherokee Removal*, 3–4. Regarding women's participation in protest, see: M. Hershberger, "Mobilizing Women, Anticipating Abolition: The Struggle against Indian Removal in the 1830s," *Journal of American History* 86, no. 1 (1999): 15–40; A. T. Portnoy, "'Female Petitioners Can Lawfully Be Heard': Negotiating Female Decorum, United States Politics, and Political Agency, 1829–1831," *Journal of the Early Republic* 23, no. 4 (2003): 573–610. For John Marshall's and Joseph Story's sympathy with opposition to removal, see John Marshall to Joseph Story, 29 October 1828, *The Papers of John Marshall*, vol. 11, ed. Charles F. Hobson (Chapel Hill: University of North Carolina Press, 2000), 178–180.

16. "An Act to divide the counties of Carrol and Coweta into electoral districts, and to add a certain part of the Cherokee Nation to the counties of Carrol and DeKalb, for the purposes of giving criminal jurisdiction to the same," [74], Assented to 26 December 1827, Acts of the General Assembly of the State of Georgia; Passed in November and December, 1827, vol. 1, 99, *Georgia Legislative Documents*, University of Georgia Libraries, http://www.galileo.usg.edu/express?link=zlgl. "An Act to add the Territory lying within the chartered limits of Georgia, and now in the occupancy of the Cherokee Indians, to the counties of Carroll, DeKalb, Gwinnett, Hall and Habersham, and to extend the laws of this State over the same, and to annul all laws and ordinances made by the Cherokee nation of Indians, and to provide for the compensation of officers serving legal process in said Territory, and to regulate the testimony of Indians, and to repeal the ninth section of the act of eighteen hundred and twenty-eight, upon this subject," [93], Assented to 19 December 1829, Acts of the General Assembly of the State of Georgia; Passed in November and December, 1829, vol. 1, 98, *Georgia Legislative Documents*, http://www.galileo.usg.edu/express?link=zlgl.

17. J. Norgren, "Lawyers and the Legal Business of the Cherokee Republic in Courts of the United States, 1829–1835," *Law and History Review* 10, no. 2 (1992): 253–314.

18. T. A. Garrison, *The Legal Ideology of Removal: The Southern Judiciary and the Sovereignty of Native American Nations*, Studies in the Legal History of the South (London and Athens: University of Georgia Press, 2002), 264–266; D. A. Rosen, *American Indians and State Law: Sovereignty, Race, and Citizenship, 1790–1880* (Lincoln: University of Nebraska Press, 2007), 19–50.

19. The following discussion is premised on the report of the case in State v. Tassels, 1 Dud. 229–235; and *Virginia Enquirer*, 9 December 1830, 4.

20. See E. Vattel, *The Law of Nations, or, Principles of the Law of Nature Applied to the Conduct and Affairs of Nations and Sovereigns* (London: G. G. and J. Robinson, 1797), vol. 1, 100–101.

21. C. Yirush, "Conquest Theory and Imperial Governance in the Early Modern Anglo-American World" (paper presented at the Clark Library Conference

on Imperial Models in the Early Modern World, Los Angeles, California, November 3–4, 2006).

22. See "Notification of Injunction," Chief Justice Marshall to State of Georgia, 12 December 1830, File II—Subjects: Indians, Cherokee, 004-02-046, box 84, Georgia State Archives.

23. "Resolutions which Originated in the House of Representatives," [230], Passed in Milledgeville at an Annual Session in October, November and December 1830, 22 December 1830, vol. 1, 282, *Georgia Legislative Documents*, http://www.galileo.usg.edu/express?link=zlgl.

24. J. Norgren, *The Cherokee Cases: The Confrontation of Law and Politics* (New York: McGraw-Hill, 1996), 98; John Ross to William Wirt, 25 November 1830, *Papers of Chief John Ross*, vol. 1, ed. Gary E. Mouton (Norman: University of Oklahoma Press, 1983), 210.

25. Article 3 of the Constitution granted the Court jurisdiction to hear cases brought by "states, their citizens, foreign states, citizens or subjects."

26. Cherokee Nation v. Georgia, 30 U.S. 1. See Norgren, *The Cherokee Cases*, 98–112. For examples of colonial litigation, see M. D. Walters, "Mohegan Indians v. Connecticut (1705–1773) and the Legal Status of Aboriginal Customary Laws and Government in British North America," *Osgoode Hall Law Journal* 33, no. 4 (1995): 785–802. Regarding the status of Stockbridge Indians in New York: Henry Moore to Secretary of State, 22 December 1766, TNA: PRO CO 5/1137, f7–8. For analysis of the myths propagated by Marshall, see Chief Justice Robert Yazzies's opinion in Cherokee Nation of Indians et al. v. Georgia, Appeal from the Supreme Court of the United States to the Supreme Court of the Indian Nations, Case no. 98–2, Argued 10 October 1998, *Kansas Journal of Law and Public Policy* 8 (1998–1999), 159–173.

27. Cherokee Nation v. Georgia, 15–19. On Marshall's role in the dissents, see J. C. Burke, "The Cherokee Cases: A Study in Law, Politics, and Morality," *Stanford Law Review* 21, no. 3 (1969): 518–519.

28. See contemporary analysis and debate over the meaning of Cherokee statehood in relation to territorial sovereignty: R. Peters, "The Case of the Cherokee Nation against the State of Georgia, Argued and Determined at the Supreme Court of the United States, January Term, 1831," *American Jurist and Law Magazine* 6, no. 12 (1831): 313–326.

29. Cherokee Nation v. Georgia, 27.

30. Cherokee Nation v. Georgia, 50–79.

31. "AN ACT to prevent the exercise of assumed and arbitrary power, by all persons under pretext of authority from the Cherokee Indians, and their laws, and to prevent white persons from residing within that part of the chartered limits of Georgia, occupied by the Cherokee Indians, and to provide a guard for the protection of the gold mines, and to enforce the laws of the State within the aforesaid territory," [88], Assented to 22 December 1830, Acts of the General Assembly of the State of Georgia; Passed in November and December, 1830, vol. 1, 114, *Georgia Legislative Documents*, http://www.galileo.usg.edu/express?link=zlgl.

32. See pleadings in Worcester v. Georgia, 31 U.S. 515, at 529–531.
33. Worcester v. Georgia, 536–537.
34. Worcester v. Georgia, 543–549, esp. 543–544.
35. Worcester v. Georgia, 544.
36. Worcester v. Georgia, 559. Marshall cites Vattel on this point at 561.
37. Cited in Worcester v. Georgia, 561.
38. Note the dismissal of this distinction in R. v. Murrell and Bummaree, February 5 or 8, 1836, Decisions of the Superior Courts of New South Wales, 1788–1899, published by the Division of Law, Macquarie University, http://www.law.mq.edu.au/scnsw/ (hereafter cited as R. v. Murrell).
39. Worcester v. Georgia, 591.
40. "If the objection to the system of legislation, lately adopted by the legislature of Georgia, in relation to the Cherokee nation, was confined to its extraterritorial operation, the objection, though complete, so far as respected mere right, would give this court no power over the subject": Worcester v. Georgia, 561. For a detailed analysis of the judgment on this point, see W. Walters, "Review Essay: Preemption, Tribal Sovereignty; and Worcester v. Georgia," *Oregon Law Review* 62 (1983): 130–133. Walters disagrees that Marshall explicitly endorsed federal supremacy, but does note instabilities in the judgment.
41. Worcester v. Georgia, 561.
42. Worcester v. Georgia, 593–594.
43. P. G. McHugh, "From Sovereignty Talk to Settlement Time: The Constitutional Setting of Māori Claims in the 1990s," in *Indigenous Peoples' Rights in Australia, Canada and New Zealand*, ed. P. Havemann (Auckland: Oxford University Press, 1999), 450–451; S. L. Harring, *Crow Dog's Case: American Indian Sovereignty, Tribal Law, and United States Law in the Nineteenth Century* (Cambridge and New York: Cambridge University Press, 1994).
44. Worcester v. Georgia, 560 and 559.
45. Theories of indigenous rights to this day struggle with the issue of how to define and limit the rights of first people without denying them the right to alter their land usage, their culture, or their locality; see B. Kingsbury, "'Indigenous Peoples' in International Law: A Constructivist Approach to the Asian Controversy," *American Journal of International Law* 92, no. 3 (1998): 419–436.
46. See entry on the matter in 21 December 1830, Registers of Letters Received by the Attorney General, vol. 2, Record Group 60–6, National Records Administration, 650. Enclosures include a letter from Samuel Houston to Captain Vashon, 13 December 1830.
47. John Macpherson Berrien to Secretary of War, 21 December 1830, Attorney General's Opinions on Legal Questions, 26 June 1826 to 4 January 1832, Record Group 60–C, National Records Administration, 239–240; emphasis in original.
48. Contrast the more conventional understanding of the Secretary of War to Colonel Arbuckle, NARA: Record Group 60, Georgia (Attorney General), December 13, 1811–1860.

49. R. B. Taney to Secretary of War, 1 May 1833, Attorney General's Opinions on Legal Questions, 26 June 1826 to 4 January 1832, Record Group 60–2D, National Records Administration, 65–66.

50. Garrison, *The Legal Ideology of Removal*, 1–12.

51. Phrase taken from title of Garrison, *The Legal Ideology of Removal*.

52. Their tribal affiliation is unclear. The Burraberrongal and Gomerigal (Dharug) peoples live in this region, but Bowen Bungaree, son of a well-known leader of the Walkeloa tribe (Kuring-gai), requested the intervention of a court: R. v. Murrell; and see the documents gathered at *Original Documents on Aborigines and the Law, 1790–1840,* Document nos. 41–48, Macquarie University, http://www.law.mq.edu.au/scnsw/Correspondence/index.htm (hereafter cited as *Original Documents on Aborigines,* doc. 41–48); J. Connor, *The Australian Frontier Wars, 1788–1838* (Randwick, NSW: University of New South Wales Press, 2002), 37; David Horton, *Aboriginal Australia* (Acton, ACT: AIATSIS, 2000).

53. Forbes was suspected of republicanism: J. M. Bennett, ed., *Some Papers of Sir Frances Forbes: First Chief Justice in Australia* (Sydney: Parliament of New South Wales, 1998), 186; J. M. Bennett, *Sir Francis Forbes: First Chief Justice of New South Wales 1823–1837*, Lives of the Australian Chief Justices (Annandale, NSW: Federation Press, 2001), 3–11.

54. Governor Richard Bourke had also served as acting governor at the Cape: Z. Laidlaw, "Richard Bourke: Irish Liberalism Tempered by Empire," in *Colonial Lives across the British Empire: Imperial Careering in the Long Nineteenth Century,* ed. D. Lambert and A. Lester (Cambridge: Cambridge University Press, 2006), 113–144. He replaced Ralph Darling, who had toured as a soldier in the West Indies, Europe, and India before taking on the role of governor of Mauritius: B. H. Fletcher, *Ralph Darling: A Governor Maligned* (Melbourne: Oxford University Press, 1984), 5–69.

55. A. Bank, "The Great Debate and the Origins of South African Historiography," *Journal of African History* 38, no. 2 (1997): 261–281.

56. S. Girtin, "The Establishment of the Supreme Court of the Cape of Good Hope and Its History under the Chief Justiceship of Sir John Wilde, Part I," *Journal of South African Legal History* 109 (1992): 301–303; S. Girtin, "The Establishment of the Supreme Court of the Cape of Good Hope and Its History under the Chief Justiceship of Sir John Wilde, Part II," *Journal of South African Legal History* 109 (1992): 652–654; Kahn Ellison, "Trimestrial Potpourri, Notes and Comments," *South African Law Journal* 98 (1992): 557–564.

57. Informations, 1 February 1836, *Original Documents on Aborigines,* doc. 42.

58. See "An Inquisition . . . at the Bricklayers Arms," 2 December 1835, *Original Documents on Aborigines,* doc. 46. For scholarly discussions of this case, see: B. Bridges, "The Extension of English Law to the Aborigines for Offences Committed Inter-Se, 1829–1842," *Journal of the Royal Australian Historical Society* (1973): 264–269; B. Kercher, "Native Title in the Shadows: The Origins of the Myth of Terra Nullius in Early New South Wales Courts," in *Colonialism and the Modern World: Selected Studies,* ed. G. Blue,

M. Bunton, and R. Crozier (New York: M. E. Sharpe, 2002), 100–119; Bruce Kercher, "Recognition of Indigenous Legal Autonomy in Nineteenth Century New South Wales," *Indigenous Law Bulletin* 4 (1998): 7–9; B. Kercher, *An Unruly Child: A History of Law in Australia* (St. Leonards, NSW: Allen & Unwin, 1995), 3–21.

59. Copy of Plea to Information and Brief for Argument on Demurrer, *Original Documents on Aborigines*, doc. 43, 45; and regarding customary law, see A. W. Howitt, *The Native Tribes of South-East Australia* (Canberra: Aboriginal Studies Press, 1996), 334–347.

60. Threlkeld to Attorney-General, February 1836, *Original Documents on Aborigines*, doc. 41. See also R. v. Murrell, notes.

61. R. v. Murrell (from *Sydney Herald*, 16 May 1836).

62. R. v. Murrell (from *Sydney Herald*, 16 May 1836).

63. Arguments and Notes for Judgment in the Case of Jack Congo Murrell, February 1836, *Original Documents on Aborigines*, doc. 48, 223; Hearing Notes re Jurisdiction, Murrell, 16 February 1836, *Original Documents on Aborigines*, doc. 45A; R. v. Murrell (from *Sydney Gazette*, 23 February 1836).

64. R. v. Murrell (from *Sydney Gazette*, 23 February 1836).

65. R. v. Murrell (from *Sydney Herald*, 16 May 1836); "An Inquisition . . . at the Bricklayers Arms," 2 December 1835, *Original Documents on Aborigines*, doc. 46: see general evidence and the eyewitness testimony of one convict on a ticket-of-leave, and a free man, though not of independent means.

66. R. v. Murrell (from *Sydney Herald*, 5 May 1836).

67. R. v. Murrell (from *Sydney Herald*, 16 May 1836).

68. Judgment of Justice Burton in the case of Jack Congo Murrell, February 1836, *Original Documents on Aborigines*, doc. 47, 211.

69. On stadial logic and law, see Mark Hickford, "'Decidedly the Most Interesting Savages on the Globe': An Approach to the Intellectual History or Māori Property Rights, 1837–53," *History of Political Thought* 27, no. 1 (2006): 122–167.

70. Judgment of Justice Burton in the case of Jack Congo Murrell, February 1836, *Original Documents on Aborigines*, doc. 47, 211–214. For authority, inter alia, he cites Vattel and Blackstone. For a detailed discussion of the case, see B. Kercher, "The Recognition of Aboriginal Status and Law in the Supreme Court of New South Wales under Forbes CJ, 1824–1836," in *Land and Freedom: Property Rights and the British Diaspora*, ed. A. R. Buck, J. McLaren, and N. E. Wright (Aldershot, UK: Ashgate, 2001), 93–99.

71. Arguments and Notes for Judgment in the Case of Jack Congo Murrell, February 1836, *Original Documents on Aborigines*, doc. 48, 238–240.

72. L. E. Threlkeld to Burton, Memorandum, 2 March 1836, in Arguments and Notes for Judgment in the Case of Jack Congo Murrell, February 1836, *Original Documents on Aborigines*, doc. 48, 234–236.

73. Arguments and Notes for Judgment in the Case of Jack Congo Murrell, February 1836, *Original Documents on Aborigines*, doc. 48, 238–239. Burton had crossed out the words "loose & vague practices" and "entitled to be respected as . . . 'in the nature of laws by a Christian Community.'"

74. Arguments and Notes for Judgment in the Case of Jack Congo Murrell, February 1836, *Original Documents on Aborigines*, doc. 48, 249. On this point, see Vattel, *The Law of Nations*, vol. 1, 98–101; vol. 2, 68–71.
75. See Vattel's discussion of a foreigner as opposed to a state under protection: Vattel, *The Law of Nations*, vol. 2, 172; vol. 2, 93.
76. Vattel, *The Law of Nations*, vol. 1, 101; quoted by Burton, Arguments and Notes for Judgment in the Case of Jack Congo Murrell, February 1836, *Original Documents on Aborigines*, doc. 48, 252. See Kercher, "The Recognition of Aboriginal Status and Law in the Supreme Court of New South Wales under Forbes CJ, 1824–1836," 93–99.
77. Arguments and Notes for Judgment in the Case of Jack Congo Murrell, February 1836, *Original Documents on Aborigines*, doc. 48, 261.
78. State Records NSW: Attorney General, Opinions of the Attorney-General, 1836–1838, John Plunkett regarding the exercise of jurisdiction over Aborigines in Port Phillip, 13 December 1836, [4/473].
79. "Proclamation of the Governor for Protection of the Aborigines," June 1838, *Original Documents on Aborigines*, doc. 73: "In disputes among themselves, they may be governed by their own ancient usages, wherever these do not interfere with the rights or safety of their more civilized fellow subjects." On the persistence of pluralism, see H. Douglas, *Aboriginal Australians and the Criminal Law: History, Policy, Culture* (Saarbrücken: VDM Verlag, 2009).
80. See, for example, R. v. Kilmeister (No. 1), November 15 or 20, 1838, Decisions of the Superior Courts of New South Wales, 1788–1899, published by the Division of Law, Macquarie University, http://www.law.mq.edu.au/scnsw/; R. v. Kilmeister (No. 2), November 26 or 27, 1838, Decisions of the Superior Courts of New South Wales, 1788–1899, published by the Division of Law, Macquarie University, http://www.law.mq.edu.au/scnsw/; R. v. Lamb, Toulouse and Palliser, February 14, 1839, Decisions of the Superior Courts of New South Wales, 1788–1899, published by the Division of Law, Macquarie University, http://www.law.mq.edu.au/scnsw/. These cases all stemmed from the Myall Creek Massacre, which ushered in the era of protection in New South Wales: R. Milliss, *Waterloo Creek: The Australia Day Massacre of 1838, George Gipps and the British Conquest of New South Wales* (Ringwood, VIC: Penguin, 1994).

Conclusion

1. In re: Crow Dog (109 U.S. 556, 1883).
2. Proclamation of the Governor for Protection of the Aborigines, June 1838, Original Documents on Aborigines and Law, 1790–1840, Macquarie University, http://www.law.mq.edu.au/scnsw/Correspondence/index.htm. See Damen Ward's argument that, from the 1830s, this sort of provision was an exception to the rule of sovereignty and jurisdiction: D. Ward, *"Savage Customs" and "Civilised Laws": British Attitudes to Legal Pluralism in Australasia, c. 1830–1848*, London Papers in Australian Studies 10 (London: Menzies Centre for Australian Studies, 2003), 15–22.

3. P. G. McHugh, "From Sovereignty Talk to Settlement Time: The Constitutional Setting of Māori Claims in the 1990s," in *Indigenous Peoples' Rights in Australia, Canada and New Zealand*, ed. P. Havemann (Auckland: Oxford University Press, 1999), 449–452. W. E. Washburn, *Red Man's Land/White Man's Law: A Study of the Past and Present Status of the American Indian* (Norman: University of Oklahoma Press, 1995), 247–277. Note that U.S. courts have recently revivified "inherent" indigenous sovereignty, but Congressional power over indigenous people is only bound by the principles of "trust" and protection. For examples of how Congress and states can impose on indigenous sovereignty, see summary in United States v. Patch (1997) 114 F.3d 131; 97 Cal. Daily Op. Service 3939; 97 Daily Journal DAR 6604. M. Tehan, "A Hope Disillusioned, an Opportunity Lost? Reflections on Common Law Native Title and Ten Years of the Native Title Act," *Melbourne University Law Review* 27, no. 2 (2003): 523–571; H. Douglas, "Customary Law, Sentencing and the Limits of the State," *Canadian Journal of Law and Society* 20, no. 1 (2005): 141–156.

4. "The Seven Major Crimes Act" (a proviso to the Indian Appropriation Act, 23 Stat. 285, 1885). Washburn, *Red Man's Land/White Man's Law*, 170–171. See also S. L. Harring, *Crow Dog's Case: American Indian Sovereignty, Tribal Law, and United States Law in the Nineteenth Century* (Cambridge and New York: Cambridge University Press, 1994).

5. W. G. McLoughlin, *After the Trail of Tears: The Cherokees' Struggle for Sovereignty, 1839–1880* (Chapel Hill: University of North Carolina Press, 1993), 201–221.

6. Washburn, *Red Man's Land/White Man's Law*, 75–76.

7. Compare R. v. Bonjon, September 16, 1841, Decisions of the Superior Courts of New South Wales, 1788–1899, published by the Division of Law, Macquarie University, http://www.law.mq.edu.au/scnsw/.

8. *R. v. Murrell* 1 Legge Reports 312, 316–319.

9. Lyons (Mayor of) v. East India Co. (1836) 1 Moo PC 175, at 272–273 (12 ER 782, at 818); Advocate-General of Bengal v. Ranee Surnomoye Dossee (48) (1863) 2 Moo N S 22, at 59 (15 ER 811, at 824); 9 Moo Ind App 391, at p 428 (19 ER 786, at 800); Cooper v. Stuart (1889) 14 App Cas 286; The Lauderdale Peerage (1885) 10 App Cas 692, at 744–745; Kielley v. Carson (1842) 4 Moo PC 63, at 84–85 (13 ER 225, at 233).

10. Peter Read notes that estimates of children removed range from 1 in 10 to 1 in 3. Removal of children was approved policy throughout the twentieth century but tended to focus on families who appeared to be Aboriginal and lived with Aboriginal communities. These definitions were extremely "rubbery." See P. Read, "How Many Separated Aboriginal Children?" *Australian Journal of Politics and History* 49, no. 2 (2003): 155–163. Note that removal was practiced for various reasons from settlement onward. For heartbreaking testimony about removal, see National Inquiry into Separation of Aboriginal and Torres Strait Islander Children from Their Families (Australia), in *Bringing Them Home: A Guide to the Findings and Recommendations of the National Inquiry into the Separation of Aboriginal and Torres Strait Islander*

Children from Their Families (Sydney: Human Rights and Equal Opportunity Commission, 1997). See also A. D. Moses, ed., *Genocide and Settler Society: Frontier Violence and Stolen Indigenous Children in Australian History* (New York: Berghahn Books, 2004). Shirleene Robinson traces early child removal and slave labor in colonial Queensland: S. R. Robinson, *Something Like Slavery? Queensland's Aboriginal Child Workers, 1842-1945* (North Melbourne, VIC: Australian Scholarly Publishing, 2008).

11. For a catalogue of the legal disabilities of Aborigines from federation onward under state laws, see J. Chesterman and B. Galligan, *Citizens without Rights: Aborigines and Australian Citizenship* (Cambridge and New York: Cambridge University Press, 1997).

12. (1979) 53 ALJR 403.

13. Public Law 90-284 of 1968 (82 Stat. 77).

14. For example, Williams v. Lee 358 U.S. 217 (1958); Santa Clara Pueblo v. Martinez 436 U.S. 49 (1978). See Washburn, *Red Man's Land/White Man's Law*, 247-172; Miller, "Exercising Cultural Rights to Self-Determination: The Makah Indian Tribe Goes Whaling," *American Indian Law Review* (2001): 165-173.

15. Cabazon Band of Mission Indians v. Smith (2005) 388 F.3d 691; Confederated Tribes of the Colville Reservation v. State of Washington (1991) 938 F.2d 146. States are also successfully limiting gaming on Indian lands: J. N. Baucom, "Bringing Down the House: As States Attempt to Curtail Indian Gaming, Have We Forgotten the Foundational Principles of Tribal Sovereignty," *American Indian Law Review* 30 (2005): 423-422; D. J. Bloch, "Colonizing the Last Frontier," *American Indian Law Review* 29 (2004): 1-42; S. P. Mc-Sloy, "Revisiting the Courts of the Conqueror: American Indian Claims against the United States," *American University Law Review* 44 (1994): 537-644.

16. E. A. Long, "The New Frontier of Federal Indian Law: The United States Supreme Court's Active Divestiture of Tribal Sovereignty," *Buffalo Public Interest Law Journal* 23 (2004): 1-50. However, Long casts the court's erosion of Indian territorial authority as a radical departure.

17. United States v. Wheeler 435 U.S. 313 (1978); C. Z. Cruz, "Four Questions on Critical Race Praxis: Lessons from Two Young Lives in Indian Country," *Fordham Law Review* 73 (2004): 2143.

18. Mabo v. Queensland (No. 2) (1992) 175 CLR 1.

19. See Wik v. Queensland (1996) 187 CLR 1.

20. Aside from the Mabo case itself, recent handbacks of some national parks in New South Wales, and the sensational finding of Native Title over parts of Perth, Native Title has proved to be an illusive right: Tehan, "A Hope Disillusioned," 523-571. However, see Bennell v. Western Australia; Bodney v. Western Australia FCA 1243 (19 September 2006).

21. B. A. Keon-Cohen, "The Mabo Litigation: A Personal and Procedural Account," *Melbourne University Law Review* 24 (2000): 893-951.

22. See Mabo v. Queensland (No. 2) (1992) 175 CLR 1, 33-34 (Brennan J); 80 (Deane and Gaudron JJ).

23. For a criticism of the territorial epistemology of the decision, see S. Dorsett and S. McVeigh, "Just So: 'The Law Which Governs Australia Is Australian Law,'" *Law and Critique* 13, no. 3 (2002): 290–292. Contrast S. Yeo, "Native Criminal Jurisdiction after Mabo," *Current Issues Criminal Justice* 6 (1994): 9–26. Yeo argues that a number of the judgments, at the very least, leave space for the continuation of indigenous jurisdiction after settlement, though according to different and contingent measures.

24. Walker v. New South Wales (1994) 182 CLR 45, 48 (Mason CJ). See also Coe v. Commonwealth (1993) 118 ALR 193.

25. Australia: D. McDonald, "Australia's Royal Commission into Aboriginal Deaths in Custody," in *Indigenous Peoples' Rights in Australia, Canada and New Zealand*, ed. P. Havemann (Auckland: Oxford University Press, 1999), 296; L. Behrendt, *Achieving Social Justice: Indigenous Rights and Australia's Future* (Sydney: Federation Press, 2003), 21–30. United States: R. B. Flowers, *Minorities and Criminality* (New York: Greenwood Press, 1990), 111–112; D. Knowles, "From Chicken to Chignik: The Search for Jury Impartiality in Rural Alaska Native Communities," *Columbia Human Rights Law Review* 37 (2005): 262; L. French, "Introduction," in *Indians and Criminal Justice*, ed. L. French (Totowa, NJ: Allanheld, Osmun, 1982), 11; G. D. Smith, "Disparate Impact of the Federal Sentencing Guidelines of Indians in Indian Country: Why Congress Should Run the Erie Railroad into the Major Crimes Act," *Hamline Law Review* 27 (2004): 483–533.

26. K. K. Washburn, "American Indians, Crime, and the Law," *Michigan Law Review* 104 (2006): 713–714.

27. J. Sheehan, "The Problem of Sovereignty in European History," *American Historical Review* 111, no. 1 (2006): 1–15; L. A. Benton, *Law and Colonial Cultures: Legal Regimes in World History, 1400–1900* (Cambridge: Cambridge University Press, 2002); C. S. Maier, "Consigning the Twentieth Century to History: Alternative Narratives for the Modern Era," *American Historical Review* 105, no. 3 (2000): 807–831.

Acknowledgments

After nearly ten years of endeavor, I know that books are the product of the kindness and hard work of others.

This book would not exist without my family. Alan Ford, Mary Ford, Craig Leech, and Margaret Leech gave months of their time to look after my child so I could research and write. Mary, Alan, and Michele Ford also spent countless hours editing my work. Though the errors are all mine, this is, in many respects, a family effort.

For their generous financial support, I thank the Josephine de Kármán Foundation, the Daughters of the American Revolution, the American Historical Association, Harvard University, the Bancroft Dissertation Prize Fund, and Macquarie University. Above all, I thank Columbia University, which supported me for seven happy years as I read American history and wrote the first draft of this book.

I am also indebted to kindly archivists for their help and advice, particularly those from the PRO in London, the State Records of New South Wales, the Mitchell Library, various offices of the National Archives and Records Administration, the Georgia Historical Society, and the Georgia Archives. Thank you also to Kathleen McDermott and her team of editors at Harvard for their help polishing this text.

So many colleagues and mentors have taken time out of their busy lives to read and contribute to this project that I cannot hope to thank them all here. Among them, I am especially indebted to Bain Attwood, Aparna Balachandran, Shaunnagh Dorsett, Mark Finnane, Evan Haefeli, Mark Hickford, Grace Karskens, Peter Karsten, Bruce Kercher, Claudine Leysinger, Paul McHugh, Tim Rowse, Tali Schaefer, Jennifer Spohrer, and Damen Ward.

To three people, however, I owe particular thanks. The extraordinary work and the intellectual generosity of Lauren Benton pervade this book. Herb Sloan's generosity was no less extraordinary. He waded through many draft chapters and sat through hours of my worries with the wry good humor that only he can muster. I thank them both.

Finally, I owe more thanks than I can deliver to David Armitage. With kindness and diligence, he led me to my subject, read every chapter in several drafts, and sped me on my way. He always said his efforts on my behalf were "all part of the job." I know, however, that they illustrate his tireless dedication to his students.

Index